# Stalingrad

## - The Air Battle: 1942 through January 1943

# *Stalingrad*

## - The Air Battle: 1942 through January 1943

*Christer Bergström*

MIDLAND

An imprint of
Ian Allan Publishing

STALINGRAD - The Air Battle: 1942 through February 1943
© 2007

ISBN (10) 1 857802 76 4
ISBN (13) 978 1 857802 76 4

Produced by Chevron Publishing Limited
Project Editors: Robert Forsyth, Chevron Publishing Limited
Cover and book design: Mark Nelson
© Maps and graphics: Tim Brown

Chevron Publishing would like to thank Neil Page for his kind
assistance in the preparation of this work

Published by Midland Publishing
4 Watling Drive, Hinckley, LE10 3EY, England
Tel: 01455 254 490   Fax: 01455 254 495
E-mail: midlandbooks@compuserve.com

MIDLAND
An imprint of
Ian Allan Publishing

Midland Publishing is an imprint of Ian Allan Publishing Ltd
Worldwide distribution (except North America):
Midland Counties Publications
4 Watling Drive, Hinckley, LE10 3EY, England
Telephone: 01455 254 450 Fax: 01455 233 737
E-mail: midlandbooks@compuserve.com
www.midlandcountiessuperstore.com

North American trade distribution:
Specialty Press Publishers & Wholesalers Inc.
39966 Grand Avenue, North Branch, MN 55056, USA
Tel: 651 277 1400   Fax: 651 277 1203
Toll free telephone: 800 895 4585
www.specialtypress.com

Printed in England by Ian Allan Printing Ltd
Riverdene Business Park, Molesey Road,
Hersham, Surrey, KT12 4RG

Visit the Ian Allan Publishing website at:
**www.ianallanpublishing.com**

# Contents

# Acknowledgements

This book could not have been written without the help of Luftwaffe and VVS veterans and a large number of historians, aviation history enthusiasts, and many others. I am deeply grateful for their interest, encouragement and kindness. These people have shown that history and historical facts belong to us all and that it is in our common interest to co-operate in uncovering every part of mankind's history.

First of all I would like to express my particular gratitude to my friend Andrey Mikhailov, my co-author in two previous books. Andrey's help has been most valuable. I also would like to express my particular gratitude to my friends and colleagues Vlad Antipov, Andrey Dikov, Nikita Egorov and Artem Drabkin. Their unselfish assistance and our exchange of material has been absolutely terrific.

In encouraging me to write this book and liaising with the publisher, Robert Forsyth has played a key role in this work. Without his input this book series would never have been written.

Matti Salonen has provided me with crucial help by allowing me to use his extensive work on Luftwaffe aircraft losses.

My friend and colleague Manfred Wägenbaur at Traditionsgemeinschaft JG 52 has been as crucially helpful as always.

And, of course, my dear family, Maria, Martin and Caroline, have showed a great patience, without which I could not have written this book.

I also wish to express my gratitude to Brigadier Captain Christian Allerman, Alfons Altmeier, Ferdinando D'Amico, Aleksey V. Andreev, Vladislav Arkhipov, Andrew Arthy, Michael Balss, Bernd Barbas, Csaba Becze, Holger Benecke, Dénes Bernád, Jan Bobek, Kent Bobits, Andreas Brekken, Pawel Burchard, Mikhail Bykov, Mikael Byström, Don Caldwell, Eddie Creek, Chris Dunning, Santiago A. Flores, Josef Fregosi, Carl-Fredrik Geust, Dr. Rainer Göpfert, Jürgen Grislawski, Pascal Guillerm, Håkan Gustavsson, Damian Hallor, Peter Hallor, Eric Hammel, Lutz Hannig, Tomislav Haramincic, Bert Hartmann, Thomas Hasselberg, Carlos Herrera, Michael Holm, Ivanova Maya Ivanovna, Tomas Jönsson, Polkovnik Vsevolod Kanaev, Dmitriy Karlenko, Peter Kassak, Tony Kirk, Christian Kirsch, General-Leytenant Aleksandr Anatolevich Kudriavtsev, Viktor Kulikov, Vitse-Admiral Yuriy Kvyatkovskiy, Ola Laveson, Sean Leeman, Brigadier General Håkan Linde, Raimo Malkamäki, George Mellinger, Rolf Mewitz, Eric Mombeek, Donald Pearson, Martin Pegg, Jim Perry, Gennadiy Petrov, Rodion Podorozhny, Dr. Jochen Prien, Rune Rautio, Ondrej Repka, Jean-Luis Roba, Günther Rosipal, Yuriy Rybin, Pär Salomonson, Carlo Sansilvestri, Alan Scheckenbach, Andreas Schmidt, Anneluise Schreier, Reinhard Schröder, Hans Dieter Seidl, Hans E. Söder, James Sterrett, Harold E. Stockton, Boris Sudny, Claes Sundin, Lieutenant Commander B. John Szirt, Peter Taghon, Colonel Raymond F. Toliver, Dariusz Tyminski, Hannu Valtonen, Peter Vollmer, Walter Waiss, Bob Wartburg, Pierre Watteeuw, Carl-Johan Westring, Brigadier General Björn Widmark, Dave Williams, Nikita Yegorov, Mike Young, Director Lyudmila P. Zapryagayeva, Vyacheslav M. Zaretsky, Jan Zdiarsky, Admiral Vasil'yevich Zelenin, and Rolf Zydek.

**WW II VVS airmen:**

*Starshina* Petr Andreyevich Shvets, *General-Leytenant* Petr Vasilyevich Bazanov, *Starshiy Leytenant* Mikhail Petrovich Devyatayev, *Polkovnik* Nikolay Ivanovich Gapeyonok, *Starshiy Leytenant* Vasiliy Matveyevich Garanin, *General-Mayor* Semen Vasilyevich Grigorenko, *Kapitan* Viktor Alekseyevich Grubich, *Starshiy Serzhant* Leonid Yakovlevich Klabukov, *General-Mayor* Vitaliy Ivanovich Klimenko, *General-Leytenant* Arkadiy Fyodorovich Kovachevich, *General-Mayor* Sergey Makarovich Kramarenko, *General-Mayor* Viktor Aleksandrovich Kumskov, *Starshina* Vasiliy Vasilyevich Kurayev, *General-Leytenant* Boris Dmitriyevich Melyokhin, *General-Leytenant* Stepan Anastasovich Mikoyan, *Polkovnik* Vladimir Vladimirovich Onishenko, *Polkovnik* Aleksandr Aleksandrovich Pavlichenko, *General-Mayor* Georgiy Vasilyevich Pavlov, *General-Leytenant* Vitaliy Viktorovich Rybalko, *Starshiy Leytenant* Aron Shavelich Shapiro, Petr Andreyevich Shvets, *Kapitan* Vera Tikhomirova and *General-Mayor* Ivan Petrovich Vasenin.

**WW II Luftwaffe airmen:**

*Oberst* Gerhard Baeker, *Generalleutnant* Gerhard Barkhorn, *Oberstleutnant* Hansgeorg Bätcher, *Major* Helmut Berendes, *Major* Hans-Ekkehard Bob, *Oberleutnant* Johannes Broschwitz, *Leutnant* Hans Ellendt, *Generalleutnant* Adolf Galland, *Oberst* Gordon M. Gollob, *Hauptmann* Alfred Grislawski, *Major* Klaus Häberlen, *Oberleutnant* Hermann Heckes, *Oberfeldwebel* Karl-Heinz Höfer, *Leutnant* Werner Hohenberg, *Oberfeldwebel* Hans Hormann, *Leutnant* Udo Hünerfeld, *Leutnant* Berthold K. Jochim, *Oberleutnant* Fritz Klees, Felix Lademann, *Major* Friedrich Lang, *Major* Heinz Lange, *Oberleutnant* Erwin Leykauf, *Unteroffizier* Friedrich Lühring, *Leutnant* Hermann Neuhoff, *Generalleutnant* Günther Rall, *Oberleutnant* Ernst-Wilhelm Reinert, *Leutnant* Edmund Rossmann, *Unteroffizier* Heinrich Scheibe, *General* Johannes Steinhoff, *Generalleutnant* Hannes Trautloft, *Oberfeldwebel* Dieter Woratz.

To any helpers whose names I may have missed, please accept my apologies and my implied gratitude.

Christer Bergström
5 July 2007

# Table of Equivalent Ranks

| VVS | Luftwaffe | USAAF |
|---|---|---|
| *Enlisted* | | |
| Krasnoarmeyets | Flieger | Private |
| Yefreytor | Gefreiter | Private 1st Class |
| | Obergefreiter | Corporal |
| | Hauptgefreiter | |
| | | |
| *NCOs* | | |
| Mladshiy Serzhant | Unteroffizier | |
| Serzhant | Unterfeldwebel | Sergeant |
| Starshiy Serzhant | Feldwebel | Technical Sergeant |
| Starshina | Oberfeldwebel | Master Sergeant |
| | | |
| *Warrant Officers* | | |
| | Oberfähnrich | Senior Officer Candidate |
| | Stabsfeldwebel | Warrant Officer |
| | | |
| *Commissioned Officers* | | |
| Mladshiy Leytenant | | Flight Officer |
| Leytenant | Leutnant | Second Lieutenant |
| Starshiy Leytenant | Oberleutnant | First Lieutenant |
| Kapitan | Hauptmann | Captain |
| Mayor | Major | Major |
| Podpolkovnik | Oberstleutnant | Lieutenant Colonel |
| Polkovnik | Oberst | Colonel |
| General-Mayor | Generalmajor | Brigadier General |
| General-Leytenant | Generalleutnant | Major General |
| General-Polkovnik | General | Lieutenant General |
| General Armii | Generaloberst | General (4 Star) |
| Marshal Sovyetskogo Soyuza | Generalfeldmarschall | General (5 Star) |
| | Reichsmarschall | |

## Soviet political ranks and their equivalents

| *Rank of Political Instructor* | *Equivalent regular Army Rank* |
|---|---|
| Mladshiy Politruk | Leytenant |
| Politruk | Starshiy Leytenant |
| Starshiy Politruk | Kapitan |
| Batalyonnyy Komissar | Mayor |
| Starshiy Batalyonnyy Komissar | Podpolkovnik |
| Polkovoy Komissar | Polkovnik |
| Divizionny Komissar | General-Mayor |
| Korpusnoy Komissar | General-Leytenant |
| Armeyskiy Komissar Vtorogo Ranga | General-Polkovnik |
| Armeyskiy Komissar Pervogo Ranga | General Armii |

## Glossaries and Abbreviations

**AAA** anti-aircraft artillery.

**Abwehr** "Defence", Germany's intelligence service during World War II.

**AD** (*Aviatsionnaya Diviziya*), Aviation Division (Soviet).

**ADD** *(Aviatsiya Dal'nego Deystviya)* Long Range Aviation(Soviet); Independent branch of aviation, subordinated directly to the Stavka.

**Adjutant Aviator** Rumanian Air Force rank, equivalent to Technical Sergeant.

**AE** (*Aviatsionnaya Eskadrilya*), Aviation Squadron (Soviet).

**Aerial victory**, a confirmed shot-down enemy aircraft.

**Airacobra** U.S.-designed Bell single-engined single-seat fighter.

**ANT** (Andrey Nikolayevich Tupolev), Soviet aircraft designer.

**Armeekorps** Army Corps (German).

**ARMIR** (*Armata Italiana in Russia*) Italian Armed Forces in Russia.

**Aufklärung** Reconnaissance (German).

**Aufklärungsgruppe**, Reconnaissance (aviation) Wing (German).

**AufklObdL** (*Aufklärungsgruppe Oberbefehlshaber der Luftwaffe*), Reconnaissance (aviation) Wing, Commander of the Luftwaffe (German).

**Aviaeskadrilya** *or* **Aviatsionnaya Eskadrilya** Aviation Squadron (Soviet).

**Aviadiviziya** *or* **Aviatsionnaya Diviziya** Aviation Division (Soviet).

**Aviakorpus** *or* **Aviatsionnyy Korpus** Aviation Corps (Soviet).

**Aviapolk** *or* **Aviatsionnyy Polk** Aviation Regiment (Soviet).

**Aviatsiya Voyenno-Morskogo Flota**, Navy Air Force, VVS-VMF (Soviet).

**Aviatsionnaya Shkola Pervonachal'nogo Obucheniya**, Primary Flight Training School (Soviet).

**Aviazveno Svyazi** liaison flight (Soviet).

**B-3** Soviet designation of U.S.-designed Douglas DB-7 (A-20 Havoc) - British designation DB-7B Boston III - twin-engined attack bomber.

**BA** *(Bombardirovochnaya Armiya)* Bomber aviation army (Soviet).

**BABr** (*Bombardirovochnaya Aviatsionnaya Brigada*), Bomber Aviation Brigade (Soviet); the equivalent of the Soviet Navy Aviation to the BAD of the Army Aviation.

**BAD** (*Bombardirovochnaya Aviatsionnaya Diviziya*), Bomber Aviation Division (Soviet).

**BAK** (*Bombardirovochnyy Aviatsionyy Korpus*), Bomber Aviation Corps (Soviet).

**BAP** (*Bombardirovochnyy Aviatsionyy Polk*), Bomber Aviation Regiment (Soviet).

**Barbarossa** code-name of the German attack on the Soviet Union in 1941.

**BBAP** (*Blizhnebombardirovochnyy Aviatsionnyy Polk*), Short-Range Bomber Aviation Regiment (Soviet).

**Bell** U.S. aircraft designer.

**Beriyev** Soviet aircraft designer.

**Bf** (Bayerische Flugzeugwerke), German aircraft designer; designation of Messerschmitt 109 and 110.

**Bf 108** German single-engined Messerschmitt liasion and training aircraft.

**Bf 109** German single-engined Messerschmitt single-seat fighter.

**Bf 110** German twin-engined Messerschmitt two-place heavy fighter and fighter-bomber.

**Boston** British designation of U.S.-designed Douglas DB-7 twin-engine light attack bomber.

**Capitan Aviator** Rumanian Air Force rank, equivalent to Captain.

**Capitano Pilota** Italian Air Force rank, equivalent to captain.

**Chayka** 'Seagull', Soviet Polikarpov I-153 single-engined, single-seat biplane fighter.

**Che-2** Soviet twin-engined Chetverikov amphibian reconnaissance aircraft.

**Chetverikov** Soviet aircraft designer.

**ChF** (*Chernomorskiy Flot*), Black Sea Fleet (Soviet).

**Corpul Aerian** Air Corps (Rumanian).

**Curtiss** U.S. aircraft designer.

**"Curtiss"** an incorrect German identification of the Soviet I-153 single-engined, single- seat biplane fighter.

**DB** (Daimler-Benz) German engine designer.

**DB** (*Dal'niy Bombardirovshchik*) Long-Range Bomber (Soviet).

**DB-3** Soviet twin-engined bomber.

**DBA** (*Dal'ne-Bombardirovochnaya Aviatsiya*), Long-Range Bomber Aviation (Soviet), reorganised into the ADD in March 1942.

**DBAP** (*Dal'nebombardirovochnyy Aviatsionnyy Polk*), Long-Range Bomber Regiment (Soviet).

**Deutsche Luftwaffenmission Rumänien**, German Air Force Mission to Rumania.

**Diviziya** Aviation wing (Soviet); composed of four to six regiments.

**Do** (Dornier) German aircraft designer.

**Do 17** German twin-engined bomber and reconnaissance aircraft.

**Douglas** U.S. aircraft designer.

**Edelweiss** "Edelweiss" (the name of KG 51).

**Ergänzungsgruppe** Replacement Aviation Wing (German).

**ErgGr** (*Ergänzungsgruppe*) Reserve Aviation Wing (German).

**Escadrila** Squadron (Rumanian).

**Eskadrilya** Squadron (Soviet).

**Experten** German designation for fighter aces.

**F** (*Fernaufklärung*) Long-Distance (strategic) Reconnaissance Aviation (German).

**FAB** (*Fugasnaya Aviatsionnaya Bomba*) High-explosive Aviation Bomb (Soviet).

**Fernaufklärungsgruppe** Long-Distance (strategic) Reconnaissance Aviation Group (German).

**Fi** (Fieseler) German aircraft designer.

**Fi 156 Storch** German single-engined liaison and reconnaissance aircraft.

**Fiat** (*Fabrica Italiana Automobili Torino*) Italian aircraft and car designer.

**Fiat BR.20** Italian Fiat twin-engined reconnaissance bomber.

**Flak** (*Fliegerabwehrkanone*), anti-aircraft artillery (German).

**Fliegerdivision** Air Division (German).

**Fliegerkorps** Aviation Corps (German).

**Flotiliya** 'Flotilla'; Soviet small regional fleet.

**Flugzeugführerschule** Pilots' training school (German).

**Folgore** Italian Macchi C.202 single-engined fighter.

**Front** Soviet equivalent to Army Group.

**Führerweisung** "Leader's Instructions", Hitler's Orders.

**Fw** (Focke-Wulf) German aircraft designer.

**Fw 189 Uhu** German Focke-Wulf twin-engined, three-seat reconnaissance aircraft.

**Fw 190** German Focke-Wulf single-engined, single-seat fighter.

**Fw 200** German Focke-Wulf four-engined maritime reconnaissance bomber and transport aircraft.

**G or Gv** (*Gvardeyskiy*), Guards (Soviet); see below.

**GAL** (*Gruparea Aeriană de Luptă* ) Air Combat Group (Rumanian).

**Gefechtsverband** Combat unit (German).

**General der Jagdflieger** Fighter Aviation General; the German Inspector of Fighter Aviation.

**Generaloberstabsarzt** German military medical rank, equivalent to *Generalleutnant*.

**General Wever** the name of KG 4 (adopted after the first Chief-of-Staff of the Luftwaffe, *General* Walther Wever).

**Geschwader** Aviation Group (German); three or four *Gruppen*.

**Geschwaderkommodore** Aviation Wing Commander (German).

**GKO** (*Gosudarstvennyy Komitet Oborony*), State Committee for Defence (Soviet).

**Gorbatyy** 'Hunchback', Soviet nickname for the Il-2 ground-attack aircraft.

**Greif** 'Griffin'; the name of KG 55.

**Grupul Bombardament** Bomber Group (Rumanian).

**Gruppe** Aviation Wing (German); usually three *Staffeln*, see below.

**Gruppenkommandeur** Aviation Group Commander (German).

**Gruppo** Aviation Group (Italian).

**Gruppo Autonomo Caccia Terrestre** Independent Fighter Aviation Group (Italian).

**Grupul Vânătoare** Fighter Aviation Group (Rumanian).

**Guards** Honorary Soviet title to specially distinguished units.

**Gv** see 'G'.

**GVF** (*Grazhdanskiy Vozdushnyy Flot*) Civil Air Fleet (Soviet); civilian aviation.

**H** (*Heeresaufklärung*), Army (Tactical) Reconnaissance Aviation (German).

**Hawker** British aircraft designer.

**He** (Heinkel) German aircraft designer.

**He 111** German twin-engined bomber.

**He 177** German four-engined bomber.

**Heeresaufklärungsgruppe** Army (tactical) Reconnaissance Aviation Wing (German).

**Heeresgruppe** Army group (German).

**Heeresgruppe Mitte** Central Army Group (German).

**Heeresgruppe Nord** Northern Army Group (German).

**Heeresgruppe Süd** Southern Army Group (German).

**Heinkel** German aircraft designer.

**Henschel** German aircraft designer.

**Hero of the Soviet Union** (*Geroy Sovyetskogo Soyuza*); the highest Soviet 'appointment' for bravery in combat.

**Hs** (Henschel), German aircraft designer.

**Hs 123** German single-engined Henschel single-seat ground-attack biplane.

**Hs 126** German single-engined Henschel two-place Army co-operation and tactical reconnaissance aircraft.

**Hs 129** German twin-engined Henschel single-seat ground-attack aircraft.

**Hurricane** British single-engined Hawker single-seat fighter.

**I** ('*Istrebitel*') Fighter (Soviet).

**I-15** Soviet single-engined Polikarpov single-seat, fixed-gear biplane fighter.

**I-15bis** Soviet single-engined Polikarpov single-seat, fixed-gear biplane fighter.

**I-16** Soviet single-engined Polikarpov single-seat fighter.

**I-26** alternate designation for Soviet Yak-1 single-engined, single-seat fighter.

**I-61** an incorrect German name for MiG-1 and MiG-3.

**I-152** alternate designation for Polikarpov I-15bis.

**I-153** Soviet single-engined Polikarpov single-seat fighter and ground-attack biplane.

**I-301** an incorrect German designation for Soviet single-engined, single-seat LaGG-3 fighter.

**IA** (*Istrebitel'naya Armiya*) Fighter aviation army (Soviet).

**IA PVO** (*Istrebitel'naya Aviatsiya PVO*) Fighter aviation of the PVO (Soviet), a part of PVO established in January 1942. Previously, fighter units allocated for PVO duties were part of the VVS and were subordinated to PVO only operationally.

**Il-4** designation of Soviet DB-3F twin-engined bomber from March 1942.

**IAD** (*Istrebitel'naya Aviatsionnaya Diviziya*), Fighter Aviation Division (Soviet).

**IAK** (*Istrebitel'nyy Aviatsionnyy Korpus*), Fighter Aviation Corps (Soviet).

**IAP** (*Istrebitel'nyy Aviatsionyy Polk*), Fighter Aviation Regiment (Soviet).

**I.A.R.** (*Industria Aeronautica Română*), Rumanian Aeronautical Industry (Rumanian aircraft designer).

**I.A.R. 37** Rumanian single-engined, three-place light bomber, liaison and reconnaissance biplane.

**I.A.R. 39** Rumanian single-engined, three-place light bomber, liaison and reconnaissance biplane.

**I-A.R. 80** Rumanian single-engined fighter.

**Il** (Ilyushin) Soviet aircraft designer.

**Il-2** Soviet single-engined Ilyushin single-seat (from late 1942 alternatively twin-seat) ground-attack aircraft.

**Ilyusha** Soviet nickname for the Il-2 ground-attack aircraft.

**Immelmann** The name of St.G. 2 (adopted after WWI ace Max Immelmann).

**Ishak** "Jackass", Soviet Polikarpov I-16 single-engined, single-seat fighter.

**J** (*Jagd*) Fighter (German).

**Jagdflieger** Fighter Pilots (German).

**Jagdgeschwader** Fighter Aviation Group (German).

**Jagdstaffel** Fighter Aviation Squadron (German).

**Jagdwaffe** Fighter Air Arm (German).

**JG** (*Jagdgeschwader*) Fighter Group (German).

**Ju** (Junkers) German aircraft designer.

**Ju 52** German three-engined Junkers transport aircraft.

**Ju 86** German twin-engined Junkers bomber and reconnaissance aircraft.

**Ju 87** German single-engined Junkers dive-bomber.

**Ju 88** German twin-engined Junkers bomber/dive-bomber and reconnaissance aircraft.

**Ju 90** German four-engined Junkers transport plane.

**KA** (*Krasnaya Armiya*), Red Army.

**Kaczmarek** Wingman in German fighter pilots' slang.

**Kampfflieger** "Combat Aviators"; bomber aviators (German).

**Kampfgeschwader** German Bomber Aviation Group.

**Katyusha** "Little Katya", Soviet rocket-missile.

**KBF** (*Krasnoznamyonnyy Baltiyskiy Flot*), Red Banner Baltic Fleet (Soviet).

**Kette** 'Chain'; German tactical air formation (three aircraft).

**KG** (*Kampfgeschwader*), Bomber Group (German).

**KGr** (*Kampfgruppe*), Bomber Wing (German).

**KGrzbV** (*Kampfgruppe zu besonderen Verwendung*), Special Purpose (transport) Bomber Wing (German).

**KGzbV** (*Kampfgeschwader zu besonderen Verwendung*), Special Purpose (transport) Bomber Group (German).

**Kittyhawk** British designation of U.S.-designed Curtiss P-40E single-engined, single-seat fighter.

**Knight's Cross** One of the highest German military awards.

**Kommandeur** See *Gruppenkommandeur*.

**Kommodore** See *Geschwaderkommodore*.

**Komsomol** (*Kommunisticheskiy soyuz molodyozhi*), Communist Youth League (Soviet).

**KOSOS** (*Konstruktorskiy Otdel Opytnovo Samolyotostroeniya*), Experimental Aircraft Design Section (Soviet).

**KOVO** (*Kievskiy Osobyy Voyennyy Okrug*), Kiev Special Military District (Soviet).

**Közelfelderitö-század** Hungarian tactical reconnaissance squadron.

**KüFlGr** (*Küstenfliegergruppe*), Coastal Patrol Group (German).

**KV** (Kliment Voroshilov) Soviet heavy tank.

**La** (Lavochkin) Soviet aircraft designer.

**La-5** Soviet single-engined Lavochkin single-seat fighter.

**LaGG** (Lavochkin, Gorbunov, Gudkov), Soviet aircraft designers.

**LaGG-3** Soviet single-engined Lavochkin-Gorbunov-Gudkov single-seat fighter.

**LBAP** (*Legko-Bombardirovochnyy Aviatsionny Polk*) Light bomber aviation regiment (Soviet).

**Legion Condor** Condor Legion; also the name of KG 53.

**LG** (*Lehrgeschwader*), Training Wing (German).

**Li** Lisunov, Soviet chief engineer of Factory No 84, where production of PS-84s took place.

**Li-2** Designation of military transport and bomber variants of Soviet PS-84 twin-engine

transport from 17 September 1942.

**Locotenent Aviator** Rumanian Air Force rank, equivalent to First Lieutenant.

**Locotenent Comandor Aviator** Rumanian Air Force rank, equivalent to Major.

**Luftflotte** Air Fleet (German).

**Lufttransportführer** Air Transport Commander (German).

**Luftwaffe** Air Force (German).

**Luftwaffengruppe Kaukasus** Air Force Groupment Caucasus (German).

**Luftwaffenkommando** "Air Force Command", command of the aviation within a defined geographical area (German).

**Luftwaffenkommando Ost** "Air Force Command East", the command of the Axis aviation which operated in support of *Heeresgruppe Mitte* from the spring of 1942.

**M** (*Motor*), engine (Soviet).

**Macchi** Italian aircraft designer.

**Maggiore Pilota** Italian Air Force rank equivalent to major.

**MAG NOR** (*Morskaya Aviatsionnaya Gruppa Novorossiyskogo Oboronitel'nogo Rayona*) The Naval Aviation Group of the Novorossiysk Defence Zone (Soviet).

**MAGON GVF** (*Moskovskaya Aviatsionnaya Gruppa Osobogo Naznacheniya GVF*) Moscow Aviation Group of Special Purpose of the GVF (Soviet).

**Magyar Királyi Honvéd Légierö** Royal Hungarian Air Force.

**MBR** (*Morskoy Blizhniy Razvedchik*), Naval short-range Reconnaissance Aircraft (Soviet).

**MBR-2** Soviet twin-engined Beriyev amphibian reconnaissance aircraft.

**Mc. 200 Saetta** Italian single-engined Macchi single-seat fighter.

**Mc. 202 Folgore** Italian single-engined Macchi single-seat fighter.

**Me** (Messerschmitt), German aircraft designer.

**Me 108** alternative designation of Bf 108.

**Me 109** alternative designation of Bf 109.

**Me 110** alternative designation of Bf 110.

**MG** (*Maschinengewehr*), machine-gun (German).

**MiG** (Mikoyan, Gurevich), Soviet aircraft designers.

**MiG-3** Soviet single-engined Mikoyan-Gurevich single-seat fighter.

**MK** (*Maschinenkanone*), automatic cannon (German).

**MTAP** (*Minno-Torpednyy Aviatsionyy Polk*) Mine-Torpedo Aviation Regiment (Soviet).

**Nachtaufklärungsstaffel** Night reconnaissance aviation squadron (German).

**NAGr** (*Nahaufklärungsgruppe*) Short-range (tactical) reconnaissance group (German).

**NBAP** (*Nochnoy Bombardirovochnyy Aviatsionnyy Polk*), Night Bomber Aviation Regiment (Soviet).

**Neman** Soviet aircraft designer.

**NKVD** (*Narodnyy Kommissariat Vnutrennikh Del*), People's Commissariat for Internal Affairs (Soviet).

**NLBAP** (*Nochnoy Legko-Bombardirovochnyy Aviatsionnyy Polk*), Night Light Bomber Aviation Regiment (Soviet).

**O. A.** (*Osservazione Aerea*) Aerial reconnaissance (Italian).

**OAG** (*Osobaya Aviatsionnaya Gruppa*), Special Aviation Group (Soviet).

**Oboronitel'nyy krug** Soviet defensive air combat circle.

**OIAE** (*Otdel'naya Istrebitel'naya Aviatsionnaya Eskadrilya*), Independent Fighter Aviation Squadron (Soviet).

**OKH** (*Oberkommando des Heeres*), Army High Command (German).

**OKL** (*Oberkommando der Luftwaffe*), Air Force High Command (German).

**OKW** (*Oberkommando der Wehrmacht*), Armed Forces High Command (German).

**OMRAP** (*Otdel'niy Morskoy Razvetyvatel'nyy Aviatsionnyy Polk*), Independent Naval Reconnaissance Aviation Regiment (Soviet).

**ORAE** (*Otdel'naya Razvedyvatel'naya Aviatsionnaya Eskadrilya*), Independent Reconnaissance Aviation Squadron (Soviet).

**OShAE** (*Otdel'naya Shturmovaya Aviatsionnaya Eskadrilya*), Independent Ground-Attack Aviation Squadron (Soviet).

**OSNAZ** (*Osoboye Naznachenie*), Special Purpose (Soviet).

**P-40** U.S.-designed single-engined, Curtiss single-seat fighter.

**Panzer** Armour (German).

**Panzerarmee** Armoured (Tank) Army (German).

**Panzerdivision** Armoured Division (German).

**Panzerkorps** Armoured Corps (German).

**Para** Soviet tactical air formation (two aircraft).

**PBAP** (*Pikiruyushchiy Bombardirovochnyy Aviatsionnyy Polk*) Dive-bomber aviation regiment (Soviet).

**Pe** (Petlyakov) Soviet aircraft designer.

**Pe-2** Soviet twin-engined Petlyakov dive-bomber.

**Pe-8** Soviet four-engined Tupolev/Petlyakov heavy bomber, designated TB-7 until 1942.

**Pik As** "Ace of Spades" (the name of JG 53).

**Platzschutzstaffel** Airfield protection (fighter) squadron (German).

**Po** (Polikarpov) Soviet aircraft designer.

**Polikarpov** Soviet aircraft designer.

**Polk** Regiment (Soviet).
**PS-84** Soviet licence-built US twin-engine Douglas DC-3 passenger and transport aircraft.
**PVO** (*Protivo-Vozdushnaya Oborona*), Home Air Defence (Soviet).
**R** (*Razvedchik*) Reconnaissance (Soviet).
**R-5** Soviet single-engined Polikarpov light bomber and reconnaissance aircraft.
**RAG** (*Reservnaya Aviatsionnaya Gruppa*), Reserve Aviation Group (of the *Stavka*) (Soviet).
**Rata** "Rat", German and Spanish nickname for Soviet Polikarpov I-16 single-engined, single-seat fighter.
**Red Falcons** Soviet designation of Soviet fighter pilots.
**Regia Aeronautica** Royal Italian Air Force.
**Reich** "Empire" or "Realm" (German); *the Third Reich,* Hitler's designation for Nazi Germany.
**Rotte** German tactical air formation (two aircraft).
**Rottenflieger** wingman (German).
**Rottenführer** leader of a *Rotte* (German).
**RS** (*Reaktivnyy Snaryad*) aircraft-carried rocket-projectile (Soviet).
**RS-82** Soviet rocket-projectile.
**RS-132** Soviet rocket-projectile.
**R/T** radio-telephone.
**R-Z** an upgrade version of Soviet single-engined Polikarpov light bomber and reconnaissance aircraft R-5.
**Saetta** Italian single-engined, single-seat M.C.-200 fighter.
**SAD** (*Smeshannaya Aviatsionnaya Diviziya*), Composite Aviation Division (Soviet).
**SAK** (*Smeshannyy Aviatsionnyy Korpus*), Composite Air Corps (Soviet).
**SAP** (*Smeshannyy Aviatsionnyy Polk*), Composite Aviation Regiment (Soviet).
**SB** (*Skorostnoy Bombardirovshchik*), High-speed Bomber (Soviet); a particular Tupolev twin-engined Soviet bomber.
**SBAP** (*Skorostnoy Bombardirovohchnyy Aviatsionnyy Polk*), High-speed Bomber Aviation Regiment (Soviet).
**Saetta,** Italian MC-200 single-seat, single-engined fighter.
**SAGr** (*Seeaufklärungsgruppe*) sea reconnaissance aviation group (German).
**Savoia-Marchetti** Italian aircraft designer.
**SC** (*Splitterbombe, cylindrisch*), cylindrical fragmentation bomb (German).
**Sch or Schl** (*Schlacht*) Ground-attack (German).
**SchG or SchlG** Assault Group; German Ground-Attack Aviation Group.
**Schlachtflieger** Ground-attack airman (German).
**Schlachtgeschwader** "Assault Group"; German Ground-Attack Aviation Group.
**Schwarm** "Swarm" or "Flight"; German tactical air formation (four aircraft).
**Schwarmführer** *Schwarm* Leader (German).
**Schwerpunkt** see *Schwerpunktbildung* below.
**Schwerpunktbildung** "Creation of Main Focus", German military tactic of creating individual points of maximum strength at certain front sectors.
**SD** (*Splitterbombe Dickwand*), fragmentation bomb, hard-covered (German).
**Sergente** Italian military rank equivalent to sergeant.
**ShAD** (*Shturmovaya Aviatsionnaya Diviziya*), Ground-attack Aviation Division (Soviet).
**ShAP** (*Shturmovoy Aviatsionnyy Polk*), Ground-attack Aviation Regiment (Soviet).
**ShKAS** (*Shpital'nyy-Komaritskiy Aviatsionnyy Skorostrelnyy*), Rapid-Firing Aircraft machine gun; 7.62-mm, by designers Shpital'nyy and Komaritskiy (Soviet).
**Shkola Voyennykh Pilotov** Military Flight Training School (Soviet).
**Shturmovik** Soviet ground-attack aircraft.
**ShVAK** (*Shpital'nyy-Vladimirov Aviatsionnaya Krupnokalibernaya*), Large-calibre aircraft cannon; 20-mm, by designers Shpital'nyy and Vladimirov (Soviet).
**SM** (Savoia-Marchetti) Italian aircraft designer.
**SM-79** Italian designed Savoia-Marchetti three-engined bomber and torpedo bomber.
**SM-81** Italian designed Savoia-Marchetti twin-engined multi-role bomber, transport and utility aircraft.
**Sonderstab Krim** "Special Purpose Staff Crimea", the equivalent of an air corps commanding the Luftwaffe units in the Crimea in early 1942.
**Sonderstaffel** Special Purpose squadron (German).
**SOR** (*Sevastopol'skiy Oboronitel'nyy Rayon*) Sevastopol Defensive District (Soviet).
**SPB** (*Skorostnoy Pikiruyushchiy Bombardirovshchik*), High-Speed Dive-Bomber (Soviet).
**Squadriglia,** Squadron (Italian).
**St** (see *Stuka*).
**Stab** Staff (German).
**Staffel** Aviation Squadron (German); usually 12 aircraft.
**Staffelkapitän** Aviation Squadron Commander (German).
**Stavka** Headquarters of the Soviet Supreme High Command.
**St.G** (*Sturzkampfgeschwader*), Dive-Bomber Group (German).
**Storch** German Fi 156 single-engined liaison and reconnaissance aircraft.
**Stuka** (*Sturzkampfflugzeug*), Dive-Bomber (German).

**Stukageschwader** Dive-Bomber Aviation Group (German).
**Su** (Sukhoy) Soviet aircraft designer.
**Su-2** Soviet single-engined Sukhoy two-place light bomber.
**Sublocotenent Aviator** Rumanian Air Force rank, equivalent to Second Lieutenant.
**T-34** Soviet medium tank.
**Taran** air-ramming (Russian).
**TB** (*Tyazhyolyy Bombardirovshchik*) Heavy Bomber (Soviet).
**TB-3** Soviet four-engined Tupolev heavy bomber.
**TB-7** Soviet four-engined Tupolev/Petlyakov heavy bomber.
**TBAP** (*Tyazhyolyy Bombardirovochnyy Aviatsionnyy Polk*), Heavy Bomber Aviation Regiment (Soviet).
**Tenente Pilota** Italian military rank equivalent to lieutenant.
**Tomahawk** U.S.-designed Curtiss P-40B and P-40C single-engined, single-seat fighter.
**Transportstaffel** German Transport Aviation Squadron.
**TShch** (*tralshchik*) trawler (Soviet).
**Tu** (Tupolev), Soviet aircraft designer.
**Tupolev** Soviet aircraft designer.
**U** (*Uchebnyy*) (Basic) Training (Soviet).
**UAG** (*Udarnaya Aviatsionnaya Gruppa*) Strike Aviation Group, a groupment of aviation regiments (Soviet).
**U-2** Soviet single-engined Polikarpov training and light bomber biplane
**UT** (*Uchebno-Trenirovochnyy*), Basic Training (aircraft) (Soviet).
**UTI** (*Uchebno-Trenirovochnyy Istrebitel'*), Basic Fighter Trainer (Soviet).
**VA** (*Vozdushnaya Armiya*) Air Army (Soviet).
**Victory** see 'aerial victory'.
**Vitse-Admiral** Vice Admiral (Soviet).
**VMF** (*Voyenno-Morskoy Flot SSSR*), Naval Forces of the USSR.
**VO** (*Voyennyy Okrug*), Military District (Soviet).
**VVS** (*Voyenno-Vozdushnye Sily*), Military Air Force (Soviet).
**Wehrmacht** The Armed Forces (German).
**Wehrmachtführungsstab** Armed Forces Staff (German).
**Westa** See *Wetterkundungsstaffel* Weather.
**Wetterkundungsstaffel** Weather Reconnaissance aviation squadron (German).
**Wiking** "Viking" (the name of KGr 100).
**W.Nr.** (*Werknummer*) (aircraft) Construction Number (German).
**Yak** (Yakovlev) Soviet aircraft designer.
**Yak-1** Soviet single-engined, single-seat fighter.
**Yak-7** Soviet single-engined, single-seat fighter.
**Yakovlev** Soviet aircraft designer.
**Yer** (Yermolayev) Soviet aircraft designer.
**Yer-2** Soviet twin-engined Yermolayev long-range bomber.
**Yermolayev** Soviet aircraft designer.
**Z** (*Zerstörer*) Heavy fighter (German).
**ZAB** (*Zazhigatel'naya Aviatsionnaya Bomba*), Incendiary Aviation Bomb (Soviet).
**Zerstörer** 'Destroyer'; German heavy fighter.
**Zerstörerstaffel** Heavy fighter aviation squadron (German).
**Zerstörergeschwader** Heavy Fighter Aviation Group (German).
**ZG** (*Zerstörergeschwader*) Heavy Fighter Aviation Group (German).
**ZOVO** (*Zapadnyy Osoyy Voyennyy Okrug*), Western Special Military District (Soviet).
**Zveno** Soviet tactical air formation (three aircraft).

### Soviet Alternative Aircraft Designations
I-26 = Yak-1.
I-61 = (an incorrect German name for MiG-1 and 3. In reality, the MiG-1 prototype was I-200, while the serial MiG-3 had no other designation.)
I-152 = I-15bis.
I-301 = (an incorrect German designation for LaGG-3. In reality, I-301 was the designation of LaGG-1, the non-serial prototype of LaGG-3.)
Il-4 = Designation of DB-3F from 1942.
Pe-8 = Designation of TB-7 from 1942.
SB = ANT-40 (incorrectly described as SB-2 or SB2bis/SB-3).
SB-RK = ANT-40, dive-bomber version. The most common designation is Ar-2.
TB-3 = ANT-6.
TB-7 = ANT-42.
Po-2 = Designation of U-2 from 1944.

'Curtiss' = An incorrect German identification of the I-153 biplane fighter.
'Martin' = An incorrect German identification for the SB bomber.
V-11 'Vultee' = An incorrect German identification for the Il-2 *Shturmovik* or Su-2.

**Note:**
Soviet airmen frequently misidentified Bf 109 fighters as 'He 113s'. In reality, the Heinkel He 113 single-engined fighter was not mass-produced and never saw first-line service with the *Luftwaffe*.

**Northern sector
Eastern Front
April-December 1941**

**Southern sector
Eastern Front
January-May 1942**

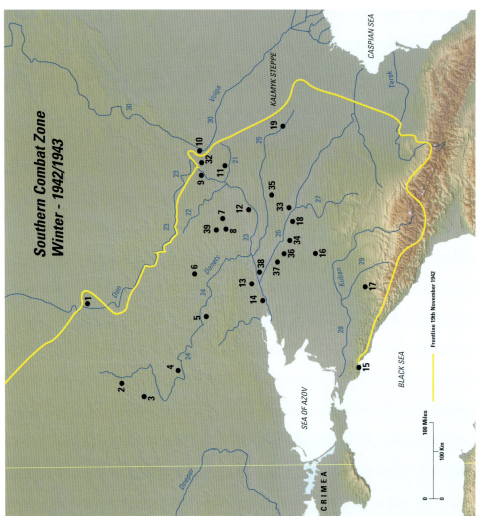

## Southern Combat Zone
### Winter – 1942/1943

| | |
|---|---|
| 1. Voronezh | 29. Laba River |
| 2. Belgorod | 30. Volga River |
| 3. Kharkov | 31. Karpovka |
| 4. Izyum | 32. Pitomnik |
| 5. Voroshilovgrad | 33. Proletarskaya |
| 6. Millerovo | 34. Gigant |
| 7. Morozovsk | 35. Zimovniki |
| 8. Tatsinskaya | 36. Yegorlykskaya |
| 9. Kalach | 37. Mechetinskaya |
| 10. Stalingrad | 38. Manychskaya |
| 11. Kotelnikovo | 39. Skasyrskaya |
| 12. Tsimlyansk | |
| 13. Novocherkassk | |
| 14. Rostov | |
| 15. Novorossiysk | |
| 16. Tikhoretsk | |
| 17. Maykop | |
| 18. Salsk | |
| 19. Elista | |
| 20. Myshkova River | |
| 21. Aksay River | |
| 22. Chir River | |
| 23. Don River | |
| 24. Donets River | |
| 25. Sal River | |
| 26. Manych River | |
| 27. Yegorlyk River | |
| 28. Kuban River | |

Frontline 19th November 1942

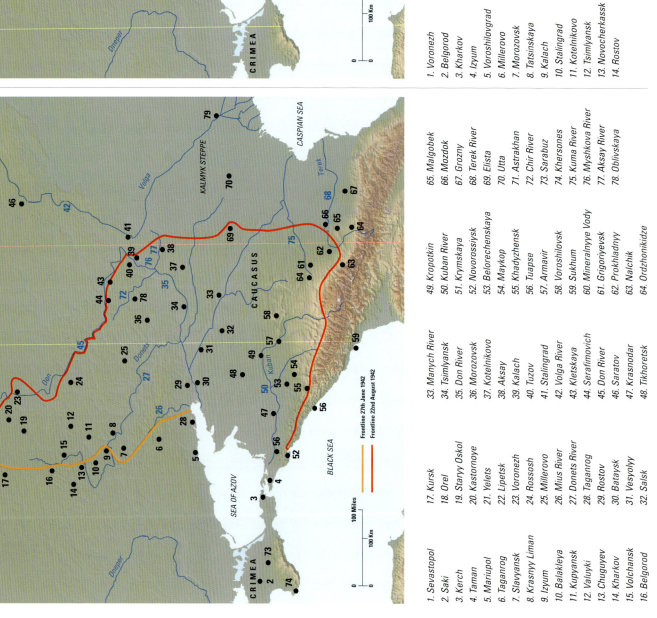

## Southern Combat Zone
### June – November 1942

Frontline 27th June 1942
Frontline 22nd August 1942

| | | |
|---|---|---|
| 1. Sevastopol | 33. Manych River | 65. Malgobek |
| 2. Saki | 34. Tsimlyansk | 66. Mozdok |
| 3. Kerch | 35. Don River | 67. Grozny |
| 4. Taman | 36. Morozovsk | 68. Terek River |
| 5. Mariupol | 37. Kotelnikovo | 69. Elista |
| 6. Taganrog | 38. Aksay | 70. Utta |
| 7. Slavyansk | 39. Kalach | 71. Astrakhan |
| 8. Krasny Liman | 40. Tuzov | 72. Chir River |
| 9. Izyum | 41. Stalingrad | 73. Sarabuz |
| 10. Balakleya | 42. Volga River | 74. Khersones |
| 11. Kupyansk | 43. Kletskaya | 75. Kuma River |
| 12. Valuyki | 44. Serafimovich | 76. Myshkova River |
| 13. Chuguyev | 45. Don River | 77. Aksay River |
| 14. Kharkov | 46. Saratov | 78. Oblivskaya |
| 15. Volchansk | 47. Krasnodar | |
| 16. Belgorod | 48. Tikhoretsk | |
| 17. Kursk | 49. Kropotkin | |
| 18. Orel | 50. Kuban River | |
| 19. Staryy Oskol | 51. Krymskaya | |
| 20. Kastornoye | 52. Novorossiysk | |
| 21. Yelets | 53. Belorechenskaya | |
| 22. Lipetsk | 54. Maykop | |
| 23. Voronezh | 55. Khadyzhensk | |
| 24. Rossosh | 56. Tuapse | |
| 25. Millerovo | 57. Armavir | |
| 26. Mius River | 58. Voroshilovsk | |
| 27. Donets River | 59. Sukhum | |
| 28. Taganrog | 60. Mineralnyye Vody | |
| 29. Rostov | 61. Grigoriyevsk | |
| 30. Bataysk | 62. Prokhladny | |
| 31. Vesyolyy | 63. Nalchik | |
| 32. Salsk | 64. Ordzhonikidze | |

# Chapter One

# The First Air Bridges

uring early 1942 German troops fell back through the snows of the Eastern Front pursued by a vengeful Red Army. Operation 'Barbarossa' – Hitler's invasion of the Soviet Union six months earlier – had proved to be the *Führer's* most decisive miscalculation.

*General Armii* Georgiy Zhukov's brilliantly planned Soviet offensive in the Moscow sector was conducted mainly by infiltration through thinly held German lines. Just as General MacArthur would do in the Pacific area two years later, Zhukov hit the enemy at its weakest points, causing the whole German defence system to crumble. His troops avoided German strong-points and passed over snow-covered fields and through deep forests instead of along roads. This offensive was supplemented by cavalry, ski troops, and partisans operating behind German lines. Soon the demoralised Germans had lost the overall view of the situation.

A huge area to the west of Moscow became the scene of a confused battle with Soviet and German troops fighting without clear front lines. As more Soviet troops poured into the areas where the Red Army's spearheads had made deep inroads, German troops found themselves cut off and isolated. At Sukhinichi, about 150 miles south-west of Moscow, 4,000 troops of the German 216th Infantry Division were enveloped by the Soviet 10th Army in the first week of January 1942.

From the same area, Zhukov sent *General-Mayor* Pavel Belov's 1st Guards Cavalry Corps north-westwards, with the aim of reaching and severing the so-called *Rollbahn* – the vital German supply line which ran eastward from Smolensk. The winter battle

*Lufttransportführer Oberst Fritz Morzik, who commanded the air transport group that had been deployed to the central combat zone in December 1941, received the task of organising the air bridge to Demyansk and Kholm in February 1942. He was born on 10 December 1891 in East Prussia and had flown as a Leutnant during the First World War. After joining the Luftwaffe, he became Kommodore of KGzbV 1, which he led from 26 August 1939 to 1 August 1941. This photograph shows Oberst Morzik wearing the Ritterkreuz he was awarded on 16 April 1942 for his leadership of KGzbV 1 and his role as Lufttransportführer Ost with Luftflotte 1 during the Demyansk airlift.*

would not be able to supply a sufficiently large force to achieve the goal of severing the *Rollbahn* at Vyazma.

In consequence, Hitler ordered the 216th Infantry Division to hold Sukhinichi "under all circumstances" to act as a breakwater against the Soviet offensive tide in this area. To do this, the encircled troops needed to be supplied, and thus an airlift operation was hurriedly organized. The Ju 52-equipped air transport unit KGrzbV 172, commanded by *Major* Walter Hammer, was tasked with flying in supplies to the Sukhinichi garrison, and this it did with success over the following two weeks.

Unable to break German resistance at Sukhinichi, the Soviets also turned to air transportation. On 18 and 19 January, 21 PS-84s (licence-built American Douglas DC-3s) of the Moscow Air Group MAGON GVF, flew 48 sorties to drop 642 elite paratroop soldiers of the 201st Airborne Brigade of 5th Airborne Corps behind the German lines at Ugra, south of Vyazma. During the next five days, these Soviet transport aircraft flew in an additional 1,642 troops to the same area. This took the Germans totally by surprise and before countermeasures could be organised, the air-landed Soviet troops had managed to establish a stronghold which could not be crushed.

On 24 January a German counter-attack managed to restore ground contact with the 216th Infantry Division at Sukhinichi. The airlifted supplies undoubtedly played a vital role in this German defensive success. Three days later the Soviets reinforced their air-landed troops at Vyazma. A total of 39 PS-84s and 25 four-engined TB-3s were used to fly

was also a battle of supply lines. In an area covered by very deep snow, the few main roads were the arteries of the armies on both sides. As long as the Germans held Sukhinichi, blocking the main road in that sector, the Soviets the 4th Airborne Corps to the stronghold behind the German lines in the Vyazma sector. In one week, almost 2,500 Soviet paratroopers were dropped. In February, additional Soviet troops were landed in the same area.

From a strategic point of view, the Demyansk airlift operation was a great success. German troops were able to hold out due to the airlift. Between 19 February and 18 May 1942, a daily average of about 273 tons of supplies comprising material, equipment, ammunition, weapons, spare parts, fuel, clothing, foodstuffs, medical supplies, mail and miscellaneous supplies was flown in to Demyansk. Kholm was at first supplied by Ju 32/3ms which landed under fire to unload, but when Soviet artillery fire increased, supply operations were taken over by the He 111s of KG 4 which air-dropped their cargoes. Freight gliders were also employed at Kholm.

Many Ju 52/3ms were employed on ambulance duties in order to ferry out wounded soldiers from Soviet encirclement. Here, wounded flown from the pocket are being unloaded onto a horse-drawn sledge.

The main landing base in the Demyansk pocket consisted only of a landing strip with small taxiing and unloading areas. During the early stages of the operation, these consisted of hard-packed snow, but in the thaw and muddy period, conditions deteriorated badly. As shown here, however, in the later stages of the operation in April and May 1942, conditions improved once the airfield had dried out. Some of these Ju 52/3ms belonged to I./KGzbV 172, the rudder of the aircraft on the far left showing the Gruppe's star and lucky pig emblem, below which is the Staffel number.

Although the air-landed force south of Vyazma was unable to achieve its goal of severing the *Rollbahn*, it is a remarkable feat that it managed to survive as a fighting force and major menace in the back of German Army Group Centre, *Heeresgruppe Mitte*, well into the summer of 1942. This could not have succeeded without the regular arrival of Soviet airlifted supplies and reinforcements. For several months, this air bridge was successfully upheld, and since the transports flew chiefly at night, the Germans were unable to put an end to it.

At the same time, the Germans themselves were involved in a major air supply operation farther to the north. On 18 January, Soviet North-western Front outflanked the German II *Korps* and the bulk of X *Korps* – 95,000 men – at Demyansk, a forward post and communication hub 50 miles south-east of Lake Ilmen, and advanced westward on both flanks of this garrison. A few days later, 5,500 German troops were enveloped at Kholm on the Lovat River, 50 miles farther to the south-west.

By tearing up the German lines along a 200-mile sector south of Lake Ilmen, the Soviets broke the connection between German Army Groups North and Centre – *Heeresgruppe Nord* and *Heeresgruppe Mitte*. The Germans realized the threat posed by the Red Army advancing another 150 miles westwards, thus reaching Lake Peipus on the border between Estonia and Russia. This would effectively envelop the whole of German Army Group North. But again, control of the main roads was decisive. Thus the Germans placed great importance on holding Demyansk and Kholm, which blocked two of the principal road arteries in the area.

Encouraged by the successful air supply operation at Sukhinichi, the largest air supply operation the world had yet seen was organized. Although no more than 75 Ju 52s were initially available for this task, the operation

One of only two members of KGzbV 172 to receive the Ritterkreuz was Major Erich Zähr, Kommandeur of I. Gruppe in 1942 and 1943. He received the award on 24 December 1942.

enjoyed success from the onset. The first forty Ju 52s landed at Demyansk airfield on 20 January. Over the following days, this small force of Ju 52s managed to make between 60 and 100 landings in Demyansk daily. Although the surrounded area at Kholm was too small to enable multi-engined aircraft to put down, this problem was overcome by the use of DFS 230 and Go 242 gliders which were towed in by He 111s of I./KG 4.

In the meantime, *Oberst* Fritz Morzik was put in charge of the air bridge to Demyansk and Kholm and to meet the assignment he was allocated the bulk of Germany's air transport fleet. By 19 February 1942, the fleet under his command had grown to 220 transports. At the height of the operation, this force attained a strength of 500 transport aircraft – including not only Ju 52s and He 111s used as transports, but also Ju 86s from flight schools and even four-engined Ju 90 and Fw 200 airliners. However, on average no more than 30 per cent of these aircraft were serviceable.[1] Between 19 February and 18 May 1942, Morzik's airmen succeeded in bringing in an average of about 273 tons of supplies per day to the besieged forces at Demyansk. In addition, 15,446 fresh troops were flown in as reinforcements and 22,093 injured were flown out.[2] The air bridge to Kholm was similarly successful. Thus these two German strongholds remained in place, acting as decisive breakwaters against the Soviet offensive, which inevitably stalled in this sector. The price paid by the participating Soviet units was terrible – of 105,000 troops in Soviet North-western Front when the offensive opened on 7 January, 88,908 were killed or reported missing during the period through to 20 May 1942.

# Chapter Two

# The Air War over the Eastern Front in early 1942

The airlift operations described in the previous chapter were carried out against a specific background, the most important part of which was the large gap in quality between the Soviet Air Force and the *Luftwaffe*. When Germany invaded the Soviet Union in the summer of 1941, the defenders' air forces were hampered by a combination of deficiencies. However, the VVS – the Soviet Air Force – did enjoy some advantages. In fact, the Soviet Air Force was not – even early in the war – as inadequately equipped as has often been depicted in the West. The latest combat aircraft models – the MiG-3, LaGG-3 and Yak-1 fighters, the Pe-2 dive-bomber and the Il-2 ground-attack aircraft – were among the best in the world. In particular, Sergey Ilyushin's ingenious creation, the single-engined Il-2 *Shturmovik,* simply had no equivalent when it entered service more or less on the eve of the German attack. Equipped with an armour shell which enabled the pilot to stay in the target area for a prolonged period of time, the Il-2 would eventually form the backbone of Soviet tactical air operations in World War II.

Petlyakov's twin-engined Pe-2 had its origins in a high-speed heavy fighter design and was initially conceived as a dive-bomber, although early in the war, lack of dive-bombing training compelled most VVS units to use the aircraft as a standard horizontal bomber. Even in this role, it was highly successful and was one of the world's fastest bombers in 1941 and 1942. Soviet test flights of front line Pe-2s in September 1941 showed that the aircraft was fast, able to reach a top speed of 329 mph. This was some 60 m/ph faster than the equivalent aircraft being turned out by the German and British aircraft industries, the Ju 88 and the Blenheim Mk. IV – the Pe-2's maximum bomb load of around 2,000lb placed it between the Ju 88's 5,500lb. and the Blenheim's 1,000lb, while its excellent defensive capacity also made it a feared enemy among German fighter pilots. *Ofw.* Alexander Mudin's 18 victories made him I./JG 51's third-ranking fighter ace when he was shot down by Pe-2 gunners on 23 September 1941. Interrogated by a Soviet Air Force officer, Mudin expressed the opinion that the Pe-2 was the best Soviet aircraft: "It is a high-speed aircraft with powerful armament, a combination which makes it most dangerous to any intercepting fighter plane."[3] This subjective impression is confirmed by one interesting fact – among the twelve Knight's Cross recipients lost in action on the Eastern Front between April and August 1942, half fell prey to Pe-2 gunners –

*Ofw.* Rudolf Schmidt, *Lt.* Gerhard Köppen, *Lt.* Hans Strelow, *Hptm.*Carl Sattig, *Lt.* Waldemar Semelka and *Ofw.* Heinz-Wilhelm Ahnert.

The best indicator of the Pe-2's quality was its ability to survive by day, despite the very powerful German fighter force – which in 1941 had forced the two Soviet standard medium bombers, the twin-engined SB and the DB-3/DB-3F, to undertake operations under the cloak of darkness. The SB bomber (often erroneously referred to as 'SB-2' or 'SB-3' in Western publications and German documents) was more or less on a par with the *Luftwaffe's* Do 17 Z-2 and stemmed from the pre-war 'fast bomber concept' – the notion that bombers equipped with powerful engines could outrun intercepting fighters. However, as had already been demonstrated in the case of the *Luftwaffe's* Do 17 during the Battle of Britain, the entry into service of the latest generation of fast monoplane fighters in the second half of the 1930s had effectively killed the fast bomber concept. This truth was painfully brought home to SB crews in 1941. From June to December 1941, the SB was blasted from the skies by German Bf 109 fighters – the number of SBs in front line service dropping from 1,428 to only 97, all of which were relegated to nocturnal service.

A special feature of the air war on the Eastern Front was its predominantly tactical nature. The Soviet Air Force had indeed been one of the pioneers of a strategic air war doctrine, adopting the deterrent strategy which it shared with, for example, Great Britain. According to this strategy – the basis of nuclear deterrence during the Cold War – a mighty force of heavy long-range bombers, capable of dealing terrible blows against targets deep inside enemy territory, would effectively deter any enemy from launching an attack. As early as 1923, Leon Trotsky, the organizer of the Red Army, expressed his strong belief in aviation's capacity to "hack at the root of the enemy army's power of resistance". In line with this idea and its subsequent doctrine of deterrent, Soviet aircraft designers were instructed to produce a strategic bomber. The result was the twin-engined TB-1 in 1929, followed two years later by the four-engined TB-3. Capable of carrying four tons of bombs, it was perhaps the world's most advanced heavy bomber in the mid 1930s. Between 1931 and 1939, a total of 818 of these huge TB-3s were produced. The heavy TB-3 was supplemented during the latter half of the 1930s by the more modern, twin-engined DB-3 medium bomber. On the eve of the German attack, the Soviet long-range (strategic) aviation,

*The Soviet Pe-2 first entered service with the VVS in the summer of 1941 and continued to serve throughout the war as a light bomber, dive-bomber and reconnaissance aircraft. There was also a heavy fighter version which was designated the Pe-3.*

*The aircraft was fast and comparable to the best German aircraft of the day. In this view of a formation of Pe-2s the aircraft nearest the camera still has traces of snow camouflage.*

the DBA, consisted mainly of DB-3s and DB-3Fs, with a number of heavy bomber units equipped with the TB-3.

However, the rapid advance of the German armoured *Blitzkrieg* deep inside Soviet territory in the summer of 1941 – which few on the Soviet side had expected – turned Soviet air strategy upside down. After only a few weeks, German troops had thrust hundreds of miles forward. With the Soviets fighting for the very survival of their country, there was no room for long-term air operations in accordance with a strategic bomber offensive. A relatively successful air offensive was carried out against Rumania in the summer of 1941, but had to be called off when the airfields from which the participating Soviet aircraft operated fell into enemy hands. Soviet air attacks against Berlin in 1941 were merely symbolic in nature – in this sense comparable to RAF Bomber Command's Berlin raids during the Battle of Britain the previous year – and were halted for the same reasons as air operations against Rumania. With the western Soviet Union the scene of a fierce ground war where the upper hand in the battle was often gained by the narrowest of margins, air support was often the last factor helping to tip the scales in favour of one side or the other. Thus there was strong emphasis on tactical air operations, which would endure for the remainder of the war on the Eastern Front.

Under these circumstances, fighter aviation quality assumed utmost importance. When fighter aircraft were able to take control of the air over the front lines, friendly bombers or ground-attack aircraft could strike the enemy's troop positions and supply lines almost at will. Since the 1930s, this has often proved to be the decisive factor on a tactical level.

In early 1941 the standard Soviet fighter was the barrel-nosed Polikarpov I-16 Ishak – known to the Germans as the '*Rata*' (Rat), a name attributed during the Spanish Civil War of 1936-1939. This extremely manoeuvrable fighter has often been underestimated in Western literature, but a comparison seems to place it on a par with the Hawker Hurricane. Nevertheless, while both of these aircraft were capable by world standards, both were considerably inferior to the modern Bf 109 E and Spitfire, which appeared at about the same time as World War II broke out in 1939. By the time the German attack was launched on the USSR, a new generation of Soviet fighters was undergoing development as replacements for the I-16. The first of these was the MiG-3, a small long-nosed aircraft onto which a huge engine had been bolted. Designed as a high-altitude interceptor, the MiG-3 was thrust into air fighting which took place at low or medium altitudes, where the aircraft was relatively cumbersome in comparison with the more agile German Bf 109s. Since the MiG-3's engine was also required

for the Il-2 ground-attack aircraft, of which there was a desperate shortage in 1941, the MiG was phased out of production in late 1941.

Instead, fighter production was concentrated on the two other new generation types – the LaGG-3 and the Yak-1. Both were superior to the Hurricane or the Curtiss P-40 Tomahawk, but inferior to the Spitfire and of course, most importantly, also inferior to the latest German Bf 109 model – the Bf 109 F, '*Friedrich*'. The Yak-1 was undoubtedly the best Soviet fighter in 1941-1942, and was virtually on a par with the German Bf 109 E.

Although Soviet combat aircraft were of comparatively high standards in early 1942, no Soviet aircraft was able to challenge Germany's most recent fighters – the Fw 190 and the Bf 109 F-4. Fortunately for Soviet airmen, the new Focke-Wulf Fw 190 did not see service on the Eastern Front until late in 1942, but the Bf 109 F on its own was more than a handful for a pilot at the controls of any Soviet fighter then in service. Mounting the new 1,180-hp M-105PF engine in the Yak 1 from the early summer of 1942 almost bridged the performance gap with the Bf 109 F-2. However, by that time all German fighter units on the Eastern Front except JG 5 and JG 51 had received the Bf 109 F-4 – which had a 1,350-hp DB 601 N engine instead of the F-2's 1,175-hp E-engine, increasing theoretical top speed from 370 to 390 mph – and were in the process of receiving the further improved Bf 109 G-2.

Soviet arms technology was world-beating in a number of fields. Aviation armament was one of these. The Soviet 7.62mm ShKAS machine gun had a higher rate of fire than any other aircraft gun – 1,800 rounds per minute or, in the case of guns synchronised to the aircraft's propeller, 1,650 rounds per minute, at a muzzle velocity of 825 metres per second (850 for synchronised guns). Moreover, the Soviets were years ahead of all other nations in the development and use of rocket projectiles. Fighters or ground-attack aircraft carried racks of RS-82 rocket projectiles underwing and these could be used either against ground targets or in air-to-air combat (although they were badly hampered by poor accuracy in the latter case). The RS-82 had a 5.55lb warhead with a 1lb explosive charge, capable of penetrating the 15mm - 20mm rear, top, or side armour of any German light tank or half-track vehicle. Il-2s were capable of carrying the heavier RS-132, which became available in greater numbers in early 1942. Its 4.17lb warhead was capable of penetrating the 20mm - 25mm rear, top, or side armour of any German medium tank.

But in many other areas, the Soviets had to fight from a position of disadvantage. Above all, the average quality of airmen was considerably better on the German side – for a number of reasons. Firstly, Stalin's

*A Ju 52 making the flight to Demyansk. During the initial phase of the Demyansk airlift operation, the Ju 52s made the flights in smaller groups or even singly, which made them more vulnerable to Soviet fighter interception.*

German airmen also had the advantage of many months of fresh battle experience. This German advantage was further accentuated throughout the following months – the best German airmen accumulated even more combat experience while the ratio of fledgling aviators in Soviet air units increased proportionately as a result of the heavier losses on the Soviet side. Once again, the Soviets were compelled to shorten their pilot training schemes merely in order to keep pace with combat losses.

Superior German tactics also contributed to this increased qualitative gap. While the German fighter pilots generally were set free to seek the best opportunities to shoot down enemy aircraft, the Soviet fighter pilots were mainly tied to defensive tasks such as regional air defence missions or escort for bombers or ground-attack aircraft – placing them automatically at a disadvantage in terms of speed and flight altitude. During the Battle of Britain, the Germans had learned that fighter cover was best furnished by fighters free to operate as high cover over the intended target area. This was a lesson the *Luftwaffe's* opponents – both in the VVS

emphasis on quantity rather than quality destroyed the previously high average technical abilities of Soviet airmen. Large numbers of inadequately trained airmen were thus sent into combat. These pilots were dubbed 'take-off/landing' by the veterans, to describe what the newcomers primarily were able to do.

In addition, the Soviet Armed Forces still suffered from the consequences of Stalin's purges of the 1930s. The paranoia behind this had deprived the country of a large share of its leading intellectuals, perhaps most of all within the higher echelons of the armed forces. The persecution of leading military thinkers and the system of denunciation fostered a climate of fear which suppressed initiative and resulted in petrification and conservatism.

Their German adversaries had received not only more thorough combat flight training; when Germany invaded the USSR in June 1941, the

and the RAF – had yet to heed. Moreover, the VVS flew in the same inflexible V formations as their RAF counterparts, which as a rule disintegrated into free-for-alls once fighter-vs-fighter combat had started. The German fighter pilots, on the other hand, fought in pairs in excellent team work with the *Rottenführer* serving as the cutting edge, and his wingman, the *Rottenflieger*, acting as shield. Radio communication was a key factor to the success of the *Rotte* tactic, and reliable radio receivers and transmitters were standard equipment in all German fighter aircraft. Although the Soviets had observed this, it would be well into 1944 before radio transmitters became standard equipment in Soviet fighter aircraft – until then many Soviet single-engined aircraft had only receivers.

If the *Luftwaffe* had enjoyed a marked superiority in June 1941, it was even greater by early 1942. In fact, it appears as though the Soviet Air Force went into decline, not only in numbers, but also in the quality of airmen and

## JG 27 in the East and the Mediterranean – a comparison

It is a matter of fact that German fighter units attained very high scores on the Eastern Front in 1941-1942, while their own losses were fairly limited in comparison. To put this into perspective, it is interesting to study the records for a *Luftwaffe Jagdgeschwader* which operated simultaneously against both the RAF and the Soviet Air Force in 1941, in this instance JG 27. While III./JG 27 flew in support of Operation 'Barbarossa', I./JG 27 was stationed in North Africa, confronting the RAF and its allies. Given that Allied air forces in North Africa operated equipment – mainly Hurricanes and P-40 Tomahawks – which was of comparable performance to Soviet Air Force fighters, such a comparison is particularly relevant. From 22 June 1941 until it was withdrawn from the Eastern Front in late October 1941, III./JG 27 filed claims for 223 Soviet aircraft shot down while recording the loss of sixteen Bf 109 Es destroyed in aerial combat. During the same period, I./JG 27 claimed 66 British and Allied aircraft downed while registering no more than a single loss in air combat (a lone Bf 109 E). Among I./JG 27's 66 victories were 12 bombers and 54 Hurricanes or P-40 fighters. III./JG 27 scored 75 per cent of its victories on the Eastern Front against bombers or ground-attack aircraft (168 out of 223), while only 55 were against fighters.

The extent to which these German victory claims tally with their opponent's actual losses is evident through a comparison between the German fighter units' total score of more than 7,300 victories between 22 June and 5 December 1941 on the one hand and the Soviet loss statistics on the other hand – incomplete data on the Soviet side reveals a loss of 10,600 aircraft in combat between 22 June and 31 December 1941. To this figure should be added the 'unaccounted decrease' of 5,240 VVS aircraft between 22 June and 31 July 1941 which has been examined in the author's previous book in this series, *Barbarossa: The Air Battle*.[1]

According to British sources, the RAF and its allies sustained a loss of 198 aircraft in the Middle East between June and mid-October 1941. Although I./JG 27 was not the principal Axis fighter unit in North Africa at that stage, supplementing larger Italian fighter units, I./JG 27 appears to have been responsible for the bulk of Allied aircraft losses in North Africa in 1941. RAF 112 Squadron, one of the principal opponents of the *Gruppe*, reported twenty four P-40 Tomahawks shot down by Bf 109s between September and December 1941, while claiming just ten Bf 109s – of which only half can be identified in German loss records.

[1] Bergström, *Barbarossa: The Air Battle*, p. 116.

*When Ju 52s began to fly in formations, provided with fighter escort, German aircraft losses during the Demyansk airlift operation declined considerably. (Trautloft)*

equipment fielded during the first six months of the war. Indeed, the venerable – if not to say vulnerable – SB bomber disappeared through the cruel natural selection of war. New so-called 'light bomber units' (LBAP) or 'night light bomber units' (NLBAP) were formed, which were equipped with obsolete former reconnaissance R-5 or R-Z biplanes, or former U-2 trainer biplanes. Although these contributed to wearing down German troops and airmen by disturbing their sleep at night, their nocturnal bombings were characterised by atrociously poor accuracy; even though the Germans later copied the Soviet method of these nocturnal harassment air operations, the fact that the Soviets formed such units at all is an indication of the desperate situation in which the VVS found itself. In January 1942, the Soviet army group Volkhov Front – assigned the important task of relieving the surrounded Leningrad – mustered an air force comprising slightly more than 200 aircraft, of which more than fifty per cent were no more than museum specimens. Had there been a choice, the Soviets would naturally have preferred to field Il-2s or Pe-2s instead.

With only 3,600 first-line aircraft available from Murmansk in the Far North to the Crimea in the south, and the enemy still at the gates of Moscow, Leningrad, Moscow and the Caucasus, the importance of the aircraft which Great Britain and the USA delivered to the USSR under Lend Lease terms is self-evident – even though these aircraft were inferior to the home-grown equivalent. Of 740 British and US aircraft delivered to the Soviet Union between September and December 1941, 484 were Hawker Hurricanes and 230 were Curtiss P-40 Tomahawks.

In numerical terms, both sides had already sustained stupendous losses by the time the Soviet counter-offensive turned the tide literally at the gates of Moscow in December 1941. The *Luftwaffe* was unable to field more than 1,500 aircraft on the Eastern Front, compared with 2,700 in June 1941. The blood-letting on the Eastern Front had caused a disastrous decline in the stength of the entire *Luftwaffe*.

Of 4,653 *Luftwaffe* aircraft destroyed or damaged from all causes in front line service from 22 June to 31 December 1941, 3,827 had been lost on the Eastern Front. The result was that by December 1941, the entire German Air Force was down to just 2,300 combat aircraft (night fighters and transport planes not included). The direst consequences had been dealt to the bomber units, where the total number of serviceable aircraft dropped from 900 prior to Operation 'Barbarossa' to 458 on 27 December 1941. This not only bears clear testimony to Hitler's misjudgement in launching a two-front war, but above all is an indictment of the most fateful mistake of all – of invading the Soviet Union in the first place.

What the Soviets lacked in terms of quality, they were able to make up for through an indefatigable will to resist. *Luftwaffe* veterans had been shocked by the tenacious British resistance in the air during the Battle of Britain in the summer of 1940, when all odds had seemed to be against Great Britain. One year later, on the Eastern Front, the Germans encountered at least the same resolve and stamina from Soviet soldiers and airmen. This was displayed in the air not least through the numerous incidents of deliberate Soviet air-to-air rammings, so-called *taran*, or fire *taran* – the latter being suicide attacks by Soviet pilots whose own aircraft had been hit and who dived onto a German target on the ground instead of saving themselves by baling out.

One of the most striking examples of Soviet resistance was delivered during the course of the Red Army amphibious landing on the Kerch Peninsula in December 1941. The Crimean Peninsula was of great strategic importance, dominating the Black Sea and occupying a key position for anyone who wished to control the Ukraine with its vital minerals and fields of corn, or the Caucasus with its oil fields. Following a bitter struggle in which aviation on both sides had played a decisive role, the Germans and their Rumanian allies were able to take control of most of the Crimean Peninsula in November 1941. In the south-western corner of the Crimea, the Soviets still held the main port city of Sevastopol, but in early December 1941 Sevastopol's fate appeared to have been sealed. *Generaloberst* Erich von Manstein, commanding the German XI. *Armee* (which also included Rumanian army units), had massed powerful forces for a final assault on Sevastopol. The Soviet defenders, under command of the Black Sea Fleet's *Vitse-Admiral* Filipp Oktyabrskiy, only barely held out. Four marine brigades had held the enemy at bay, but for a lasting defence, reinforcements were needed. The vessels of the Black Sea Fleet were engaged in an operation to bring in these reinforcements, but when von Manstein launched his offensive on 17 December, there had been time to bring in only one division.

One hundred and fifty miles farther to the east, *Generalleutnant* Graf von Sponeck's German XXXXII. *Armeekorps* and *General-Leytenant* Vladimir Lvov's 51st Soviet Army in the north-western Caucasus were separated by the Straits of Kerch, which is only a few miles wide. But this situation would not last long.

On 26 December 1941, the air forces of the North Caucasus Front and of the Black Sea Fleet (VVS ChF) made an all-out assault against the

*The new Bf 109 G-2 'Gustav' was equipped with a more powerful engine and gave the German fighter pilots an improved advantage in the skies over the Eastern Front in the summer of 1942. The aircraft seen here belongs to I./JG 53, which received G-2s in July 1942. In the huge air battles which would take place over Stalingrad, I./JG 53 claimed*

*230 Soviet aircraft destroyed in the three weeks following the opening of the offensive over the River Don, but in the same period lost 25 per cent of its pilots killed, missing or injured. In September, I. Gruppe was withdrawn to Germany for refitting and then transferred to the Mediterranean theatre.*

German forces besieging Sevastopol. A German Army report reads:

"31 low-level attacks (*Ratas*, Curtiss, ground-attack aircraft, long-range bombers) dropping bombs and machine-gunning our positions. Our own air defence forces are totally insufficient, with the consequence that our troops sustained heavy losses as a result of these attacks."[4]

Meanwhile, a contingent of small sea vessels of the Soviet Azov Sea Flotilla defied raging gale force winds to ferry troops of the 51st Army across the Kerch Peninsula. Historian John Erickson writes: "In temperatures of minus -20 degrees Celsius, Soviet troops waded neck-high through icy water to the shore, where without supplies they clung grimly to bridgeheads in which the immobile wounded inexorably died as stiffened blocks of ice."[5]

A few thousand men, lacking heavy equipment, managed to establish a foothold and thwarted all German efforts to retake the shore.

The 12 to 25-mile wide Kerch Peninsula extends 50 to 60 miles from the west to the east. The Soviet landing on 26 December 1941 took place on the north-eastern tip of the Peninsula, north-west of Kerch. More troops were landed south of Kerch. On 29 December, five thousand men of *General-Mayor* Aleksey Pervushin's 44th Soviet Army were landed at Feodosiya on the south-western end of the Kerch Peninsula.

German *Luftflotte* 4, responsible for covering the entire Ukraine and the Crimea including the Black Sea area, dispatched all available forces in an effort to destroy the invasion fleet. But with only five *Kampfgruppen* from KG 27 and KG 51 and two *Stukagruppen* from St.G 77 available, the forces were inadequate for such a task. Although the comparatively weak Soviet fighter forces in the area were in no position to defend the Soviet ships against *Luftwaffe* air attacks, the anti-aircraft fire from the Black Sea Fleet's warships was sufficient to prevent most German air attacks from being carried out with any accuracy.

Through their skilfully executed operation, the Soviets managed to take control of the Kerch Peninsula within three days of the landing at Feodosiya. But of even greater importance was the stiff-necked do-or-die mentality of the landed Soviet troops. Although half the landed troops were lost in less than ten days, those who survived continued to hold off a numerically superior enemy.

Against this, the Germans were able to field their dominance in the air. A Soviet report from the battle of the Crimea in early January 1942 reads:

"The fact that from the moment of the occupation of Feodosiya, enemy aviation, using the proximity of airfields, attacked the port, the town and approaching transports was of great significance. Four large transports, including the *Tashkent* [a powerful vessel used to transport large numbers of

horses], went to the bottom quickly. Much ammunition and food was sunk with the transports. Enemy aviation operated with impunity since our fighters, operating from inadequate and distant airfields on the Taman Peninsula [on the eastern side of the Straits of Kerch], rarely appeared for longer than 10-15 minutes."[6]

Faced with this onslaught from the air, the Soviet offensive stalled just where the Kerch Peninsula begins. An attempt to land more troops at Yevpatoria, on the Crimean west coast, on 5 January failed mainly due to strong German air attacks – as described in the following account: "Through incessant attacks against the port area, German Stukas forced the Russian forces to keep their heads down. Russian fighters which intervened were involved in combat with German fighters. The Ju 87s of *Stukageschwader* 77 took off from the airfield at Saki [located only 10 miles from Yevpatoria] relentlessly. Their action gave the ground troops time to bring in reinforcements to the threatened area."[7]

*Generaloberst* Erich von Manstein was able to retrieve the situation for the Germans in the Crimea, but at the cost of abandoning his effort to capture Sevastopol. Although the goal of retaking the Crimean Peninsula failed, the momentum which was gained through the cancelled German assault on Sevastopol allowed *Vitse-Admiral* Oktyabrskiy to ship two Rifle divisions to Sevastopol. Here they became part of the Coastal Army, which eventually was able to build up a formidable defence of this vital port.

Hitler was furious, and *Generalleutnant* Graf von Sponeck, commanding XXXXII. *Armeekorps*, was arrested. *Reichsmarschall* Hermann Göring, the *Luftwaffe's* Commander-in-Chief even had him sentenced to death (although this was later commuted to a life sentence). To reinforce the *Luftwaffe's* crucial role, Göring meanwhile summoned *General* Robert Ritter von Greim – one of the *Reichsmarschall's* favourites – to his Karinhall estate and ordered the General to depart for the Crimea, where he was to form a new tactical operations staff, *Sonderstab Krim*, to render air support in the Crimea more effective. *Sonderstab Krim* became subordinated to *Generaloberst* Alexander Löhr's *Luftflotte* 4, which organized all *Luftwaffe* units in the Crimea and the Ukraine.

In general, the air war on the Eastern Front was characterized by marked German superiority – where German air forces were present. It is self-evident that 1500 German aircraft could not cover the entire 1,200-mile front line from Leningrad in the north to the Crimea in the south. Instead, the Germans adopted the method of concentrating forces and would use this with utmost refinement during the remainder of the war in the East – although the airmen themselves came to regard the *Luftwaffe* as merely a fire brigade.

Effectively supported by *General* Ritter von Greim's *Sonderstab Krim*, *Generaloberst* von Manstein launched a counter-offensive against the Kerch Peninsula on 15 January. Three days later, the Soviets were forced to retreat from Feodosiya. Meanwhile, a new crisis at another front sector forced *Generaloberst* Löhr to shift two *Kampfgruppen* and one *Stukagruppe* from the Crimea to this new area. Bearing witness to the key role played by the *Luftwaffe*, this marked the end of the German counter-offensive against the Kerch Peninsula.

The southern combat zone of the Eastern Front had been the scene of the first successful Soviet counter-attack. In late November 1941, Rostov – the key to the Caucasus – was liberated by forces of Soviet Southern Front. *Heeresgruppe Süd* was forced into a humiliating retreat to a position behind the Mius River, and escaped envelopment only as a result of the poor coordination of the attacking Soviet forces.[8] This defeat cost the army group commander, *Generalfeldmarschall* Gerd von Rundstedt, his post. But over the following weeks, the Germans managed to block all further efforts by the Soviets to capitalise on their initial success. As far as aviation is concerned, the southern combat zone became something of a secondary war zone.

In fact, along the 800-mile front line on the southern combat zone in early January 1942, the Soviets had no more than 450 aircraft – divided between VVS Southern and VVS South-western Fronts – while *Luftflotte* 4 with its single air corps, IV. *Fliegerkorps*, fielded less than 350 aircraft.

This actually was quite sound. Both sides – but in particular the Soviets – concentrated the bulk of their resources at the fierce battle in the sector to the west of Moscow. This was a major reason why *General Armii* Georgiy Zhukov's counter-offensive in December 1941 had met with such success. On 5 December 1941, the Soviets were able to muster 1,376 aircraft on the Moscow Front, against fewer than 600 in VIII. *Fliegerkorps* (managing the *Luftwaffe* units in the central combat zone of the Eastern Front).

However, the great success of the counter-offensive caused Stalin to make one of the bigger mistakes of his regime. Instead of continuing to strike as heavy blows as possible against the weakened and shocked *Heeresgruppe Mitte*, Stalin issued a fateful order on 5 January 1942: "Now the moment has come to launch a general offensive along the entire Front!"

Thus he completely disregarded the very heavy losses which the Red Army had sustained during the past months and the production crisis which was the result of the loss of some of the country's most important industrial and mineral regions. Indeed, while the dismantling and transportation of most of these industries to safe areas farther east was little short of miraculous, these factories were only just starting the process of resuming production under the most harsh conditions.

Zhukov and Nikolay Voznesenskiy – the chief of *Gosplan SSSR*, the State Planning Committee – made fruitless attempts to bring Stalin back to reality. As always in such situations, Stalin's obedient sycophants rushed to the dictator's support and lashed out against the critics in their characteristic manner. Georgiy Malenkov, the secretary of the Communist Party Central Committee, and Lavrentiy Beriya, the People's Commissar of Internal Affairs, dismissed Voznesenskiy scornfully and accused him of "being unable to see anything but obstacles."

Over the following days, a series of attacks opened along the entire front line, which would eventually fritter away the Red Army's limited resources.

On 18 January, *Marshal* Semyon Timoshenko, who commanded the South-western Front, opened an attack against the German lines in the Donets River sector some 70 miles south-east of Kharkov. In the initial stage, the Soviet troops surged victoriously forward, but by reinforcing IV. *Fliegerkorps* with elements previously commanded by *Sonderstab Krim*, the *Luftwaffe* soon tipped the scales. "At Balakleya, one Soviet unit did break through to the vital Balakleya-Yakovenkovo road, positions which the men held until blasted away by Stukas and where no one was left alive, burnt to death in the hayrick concealments they had used."[9]

The Soviet airmen made strong efforts to support their hard pressed ground troops, but were faced with the Bf 109s of I./JG 77 which were completely without peer in this area; while most modern aircraft had gone to the Moscow sector, the air forces of the Southern and South-western Fronts had to settle for obsolete aircraft.

Aleksandr Pavlichenko, who flew a Su-2 light bomber as a *St.Lt.* with 210 BBAP during these operations, recounts: "We carried out intensive air operations, each crew never flew less than three sorties per day, sometimes even four or five sorties a day. We suffered losses on almost every mission, mostly through enemy fighters. The Messerschmitt pilots were very self-confident. Early in 1942 I lost several close friends, all of them experienced men and good people."

As VVS losses mounted, even R-5s and R-Zs were used in close-support sorties by day. On 3 and 4 February, I./JG 77's *Oblt.* Friedrich Geisshardt and *Oblt.* Erwin Clausen spotted and shot down three R-5s or R-Zs of 622 LBAP and 672 LBAP. Between 1 and 9 February, these two LBAPs lost nine R-5s and R-Zs.[10]

In the end, Timoshenko's offensive resulted in nothing but a 50 mile-deep wedge into the German lines south-east of Kharkov. This would prove most fateful for his South-western Front a few months later.

Farther north, in the Moscow area, the situation was completely different. On top of its numerical relative weakness, VIII. *Fliegerkorps* was severely hampered by the cold spell which set in at the turn of the year. Temperatures, which had been fairly mild when the Soviet counter-offensive opened on 6 December, suddenly plummeted to minus-30 or even minus-40 degrees Celsius.

"Suddenly there were only small groups of enemy aircraft in the air," recalled Soviet fighter pilot Arkadiy Kovachevich, who served as a *Starshiy Leytenant* with 27 IAP of 6 IAK/Moscow PVO during this time. "This puzzled us, for our air reconnaissance had reported large concentrations of German aircraft at Klin and other German airfields."

"Eighty per cent of the aircraft park of the *Luftwaffe* was paralysed at temperatures below minus-20 degrees Celsius," states a German account.[11] "Due to the sudden cold spell, hardly any aircraft could be made serviceable, since there were was no heating equipment available," reads a report from JG 52: "II./JG 52 lost all its technical equipment, including a large part of its aircraft park at Klin."[12]

According to a report issued by the Air Defence of the Soviet Western Front, German air activity over the Western Front sector in January 1942 dropped to one-third of the activity of the previous month.[13] Testifying to the arrogance of the German high command, the *Luftwaffe* had not been provided with sufficient heating equipment for their aircraft – Hitler and his senior commanders had been so sure that the war in the East would be over before winter set in!

Meanwhile – and owing much to this – the situation on the ground had become so critical for the Germans that the few *Luftwaffe* aircraft which were still able to become airborne, had to be deployed mainly against the advancing Soviet troops. In this situation, Soviet air landings behind the German lines could be carried out relatively successfully.

At first sight, the equally successful simultaneous German airlift operation to the surrounded 216th Division at Sukhinichi may appear contradictory. However, heating equipment was available for the transports' engines, enabling them to operate in temperatures which paralysed many other German aircraft by freezing engine oil.

During the period 9 to 25 January 1942 when the 216th Division was supplied entirely by air, no more than four Ju 52s were shot down.[14] The explanation for this is found not in the quantity of the Soviet air asset, but in its quality. As we have seen previously, for a multitude of reasons the Red Army suffered from a lack of qualified personnel. A report on the operations of VVS Western Front in January 1942 noted: "Insufficient organisation of the air defence of our troops and an incomplete use of available air defence means, together with the impossibility of the few available fighters to fulfil all requests from the armies, resulted in significant losses to our troops."[15]

In fact, Soviet bombers enjoyed more success than Soviet fighters in combating the aircraft of VIII. *Fliegerkorps*. A single bombing raid against the airfield north of Smolensk on 25 January destroyed six Ju 52s on the ground.[16]

By the time Sukhinichi was relieved through a German counter-attack, *Luftwaffe* strength was undergoing a revival. *Generalmajor* Wolfram *Freiherr* von Richthofen, who commanded the German air forces on the Moscow Front, was one of the *Luftwaffe's* most able commanders, a talented tactician and organizer. Under his auspices, the units of VIII. *Fliegerkorps* were getting to grips with the technical problems resulting from the extreme cold. "Warming ovens and all sorts of expedients were devised in an effort to solve this problem. Aircraft designated for standby-alert duty were often pushed nose-first into 'alert boxes,' heated huts which kept the engines warm enough to start at short notice."[17]

Depleted German air units also were replaced with new and rested units from Germany. During the latter half of January 1942, II./KG 54 and I./KG 77 arrived to replace the badly mauled III./KG 53 and 15.(Kroat)/KG 53. From February onwards, it became increasingly obvious that the Soviet offensive had lost its momentum. By the end of February, the Soviet winter offensive had been strategically halted right across its lines of advance.

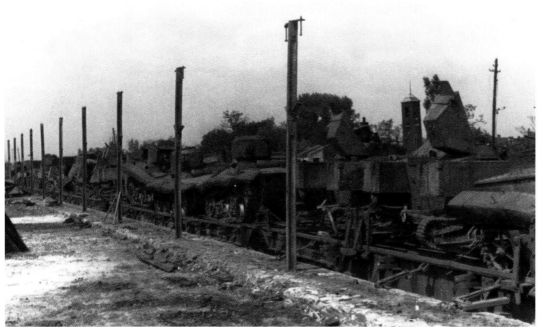

This Soviet train loaded with military equipment was destroyed in a Luftwaffe attack. The Luftwaffe made strenuous attempts to block the flow of reinforcements to the Stalingrad-Don area, but lacked the necessary forces to do so effectively. (Broschwitz)

six aircraft, occasionally even singly.

The first two Ju 52s to arrive on 20 February were shot down. Four other Ju 52s were shot down on 23 February, and six Ju 52s and one He 111 were shot down on 25 February. Others were destroyed on the ground by Soviet bomb attacks.

These achievements were nevertheless brought about at a terribly high cost to the Soviet airmen themselves. Through February 1942, VVS North-western Front lost nearly half of its aircraft in combat – 62 aircraft, of which the bulk were shot down by German fighters.[18] Two *Jagdgruppen*, III./JG 3 and I./JG 51, were assigned to protect the transports. The Bf 109s displayed a huge superiority in encounters with Soviet opponents, and these two *Jagdgruppen* claimed 68 Soviet aircraft shot down for only three combat losses in February 1942.

In spite of this, Soviet fighters continued to take a mounting toll of the German air transport fleet. An average of two transport planes were lost each day during the first week of March, and on 8 March four Ju 52s were destroyed. Between 22 February and 10 March, VVS North-western Front and VVS Kalinin Front claimed the destruction of 60 Ju 52s. Thirty-nine of these claims are verified in German loss lists.[19]

This is explained partly through the significant reinforcements which VVS North-western Front – and particularly its fighter aviation – received, and partly through the increased frequency of German transport flights; but above all the German losses were due to flawed German tactics. The method of dividing the transport planes into numerous small groups facilitated the task of the Soviet fighters but they still suffered more losses than the number of transport planes which they were able to shoot down – on average, two

The successful German air bridges to Demyansk and Kholm also were carried out under these particular circumstances. The *Luftwaffe* was in control of the air over Demyansk and Kholm throughout the airlift operations. In early 1942, the Soviet air forces in the region – VVS North-western Front – had still not recovered from the heavy blows which it had sustained during the first weeks of the German invasion in June 1941. When *Oberst* Morzik arrived to assume command of the 220 transport planes assigned to the airlift operation on 19 February 1942, VVS North-western Front was able to muster no more than 142 serviceable aircraft, of which exactly 32 were fighters.

However, the Soviet fighters scored some initial successes against the lumbering Ju 52s, which made the trip in small formations – two, three or

A Yak-1 takes off, spring 1942. In the Yak-1 the Soviets had a fighter aircraft which could compete with the German Bf 109 E. However, the Bf 109 F was slightly superior to the Soviet fighter, and with the arrival of the new Bf 109 G-2 in June 1942, the Yak-1 was outclassed. (Drabkin)

## Restructuring the Soviet Air Force

Following the double failure of 1941 and the winter offensive in early 1942, it was obvious that a restructuring of the Soviet Air Force was necessary.

The DBA, the long-range bomber aviation – the branch of the Soviet aviation which had sustained the highest losses in 1941 – was first to undergo an organisational overhaul. On 5 March 1942, the GKO – the Soviet State Committee for Defence – ordered the the DBA to be reorganized as the new ADD, *Aviatsiya dal'nego deystviya — long-range aviation. General-Mayor* Aleksandr Golovanov, an experienced DBA unit leader who had commanded the GVF (the civil air fleet) in eastern Siberia in the 1930s, was appointed to command the ADD, and 356 aircraft were transferred to his new command.

Thus the problems of the misuse of the former long-range bomber aviation arm – subordinated to the VVS and frequently employed on tactical missions in daylight – were finally resolved. With the establishment of the ADD, an independent structure was established, including dedicated flight schools and rear echelon units.

Meanwhile, *General-Polkovnik* Pavel Zhigarev, the commander of VVS KA, the Air Force of the Red Army, sent a report to the *Stavka* analysing the organisational shortcomings of the VVS. One of the greatest organisational obstacles was the division of air units into several semi-independent commands: each ground army had its own air force, and this precluded an effective concentration of aviation at critical sectors of the front line. The *Stavka* could provide the air forces of various fronts with additional resources, depending on the priority it gave to certain sectors, and indeed it did so. But the structure of the VVS did not allow for rapid redeployment of air force units to a sector where a sudden crisis developed – as was the case with the more flexible German *Luftwaffe.*

Although it was Zhigarev who had proposed a reformation of the VVS structure, Stalin relieved him from his command on 10 April and sent him to assume command of the Air Force of the Far Eastern Front.

Instead, Stalin proposed that the commander of the new ADD, *General-Mayor* Aleksandr Golovanov, lead the reformation of VVS-KA; he wanted Golovanov to retain his post as head of ADD and at the same time command the entire VVS-KA. When Golovanov baulked at the prospect of shouldering this double responsibility, Stalin turned to *General-Leytenant* Aleksandr Novikov, who had successfully commanded the Soviet aviation establishment in the northern combat zone during the difficult months of 1941. By concentrating aviation units from the VVS Leningrad Front, VVS Volkhov Front, the ADD, and VVS KBF under a single command in March 1942, Novikov – for the first time during the war – was prepared to employ the various Soviet military air arms in a more efficient, coordinated and centralised manner in the interest of two separate fronts.

Novikov's experience formed the benchmark upon which the military council of VVS KA laid down the general outline for restructuring the Soviet Army Air Force. Appointed commander-in-chief of VVS KA on 11 April 1942, Novikov put before the *Stavka* the final proposal for the new VVS structure: the merging of the front air forces and the ground army air forces into air armies – *Vozdushnye Armii* (VA) – which would provide a centralised command over all aviation units in operation over a certain army front.

The *Stavka* approved the plan and, on 5 May 1942, the first three air armies were formed:

1 VA, from VVS Western Front and the aviation commands of its ground armies 2 VA, from VVS Bryansk Front and the aviation commands of its ground armies 3 VA, from VVS Kalinin Front and the aviation commands of its ground armies.

During the next few weeks identical structural changes took place within the air forces deployed on the Southern Front (the new 4 VA), the South-western Front (the new 8 VA), the North Caucasus Front (the new 5 VA), and the North-western Front (the new 6 VA). Usually, the VAs were operationally linked to the ground forces, with each army front possessing its own operational VA.

Also of great importance was the progressive introduction of new tactics. Under Novikov's influence, the VVS accepted the superiority of the German *Schwarm* (four-plane section) and *Rotte* (two-plane section) formations as the basic fighting elements and abolished the previous 'Vic' or *Kette* three-plane-section. That this had been demanded in vain by Soviet fighter pilots returning from the Spanish Civil War in the late thirties, and again by fighter pilots such as *St.Lt.* Aleksandr Pokryshkin during the fall of 1941, underlines the conservatism which had hindered the Red Army for so long.

Paralleling the implementation of these structural changes, obsolete I-153s, I-16s, and SBs were gradually rooted out – by the *Luftwaffe* in many instances. From the summer of 1942, the only replacements at hand for the Soviet aviation units operating by day were more modern aircraft.

These then were the elements of the new air force structure with which the Soviets would eventually defeat the *Luftwaffe.* But in 1942 the most crucial factor – the men to fly the new aircraft and implement the new tactics – was also the Soviet Achilles heel. Moreover, increasing demands for replacement personnel shortened the time pilots spent in training courses; thus, from the spring of 1942 most new VVS airmen were inadequately trained. Difficulties such as these were exacerbated by the teething problems encountered during the introduction of new aircraft types – the difficult combat situation forced the Soviets to send pilots into action in aircraft types with which they were not completely acquainted. Poorly trained Soviet airmen piloting new aircraft types (with as little as eight hours on type in their logs), clashing with well-trained German fighter pilots with experience gained from hundreds of combat sorties on the same type – such was the essence defining the air war in the spring and summer of 1942.

---

VVS North-western Front aircraft were lost for every German transport aircraft destroyed. In March 1942, fifty-four Ju 52s, two Ju 86s and an He 111 transport aircraft were either shot down by the Soviets or lost due to unknown circumstances in the Demyansk - Kholm area,[20] while VVS North-western Front registered 110 combat losses.[21] But displaying the usual Soviet resolve, the airmen of VVS North-western Front relentlessly mounted their attacks on the transports regardless of any hardships.

Badly depleted VVS units were also pulled back from front line service and replaced with fresh units. Thus, while VVS Western Front's 12 IAP, 169 IAP and 739 IAP were shifted to the rear in March, the new special aviation group, 6 UAG, was deployed to the Demyansk sector on the last day of March. This unit included one bomber, heavy bomber and *Shturmovik* regiment and four fighter regiments – 238 IAP, 295 IAP, 485 IAP and 580 IAP. Not surprisingly the month of April opened with intense Soviet air activity over the Demyansk battlefield and, according to German sources, the two *Jagdgruppen* shot down 21 Soviet aircraft on 1 April alone for no losses. 5 April was another major day of fighting in the air over Demyansk, with the German fighter units bringing home eleven victory claims for no losses. Nonetheless, four Ju 52s were shot down by Soviet fighters.

It was only when *Oberst* Morzik drew the correct conclusions from the previous weeks of aerial resupply flights and started to bring the transport aircraft together into larger formations which could be easily escorted, that the real shift took place. This immediately reduced losses dramatically. On 6 April, the Bf 109s escorted 360 Ju 52 sorties to and from Demyansk without a single loss. On 8 April *St.Lt.* Andrey Dekhtyarenko of 580 IAP claimed to have shot down four Ju 52s – three Ju 52s actually were registered lost by KGrzbV 800 and 900 that day. This would prove to be the last success of its kind achieved by Soviet fighters against the Demyansk transports. During the remainder of April no more than five Ju 52s were lost to enemy action. On the other hand, VVS North-western Front registered 168 combat losses in April 1942.

Thus, when Demyansk was relieved through a German ground offensive on 20 April, the *Luftwaffe* had won a convincing victory in the battle to secure the air bridge.

During the airlift operations to Demyansk and Kholm from February through May 1942, a total of 265 transport aircraft were destroyed or severely damaged from all causes, including 125 total losses due to enemy action or unknown reasons – 106 Ju 52s, 17 He 111s and two Ju 86s.[22] In addition, 387 airmen were lost.

VVS North-western Front sustained 408 aircraft losses, including 243 fighters, on operations from February through May 1942.[23]

*Oberst* Morzik, *Reichsmarschall* Göring and Hitler had reason to believe that they had developed the methods and tactics which would guarantee any effective airlift operation on the Eastern Front. This self-assured attitude would prove fateful at Stalingrad six months later, when conditions were quite different.

# Chapter Three

# The German offensive plan

Even at the height of the crisis in the winter of 1941/1942, Hitler had begun to lay his plans for the forthcoming summer offensive on the Eastern Front. Although this might have seemed out of touch with the realities at the time, Hitler at least realized that the crippling losses which his armed forces had sustained in the war in the East would not allow another general offensive along the entire front line as in the summer of 1941. *Heeresgruppe Mitte,* which had suffered the heaviest blows at the hands of the Red Army, would be confined to a defensive role. On 3 January 1942, Hitler told the Japanese ambassador Oshima that the main attack would be undertaken on the southern combat zone, towards the Caucasus. According to Hitler's statement to Oshima, the main goal was to reach "the oil [fields] and Iran and Iraq."[24]

In purely economic terms, Germany – despite its control of most of Europe – was inferior to the USSR. The Soviets had not only managed to dismantle and transfer the bulk of their industry from the western regions of the country to the east, out of reach of the Germans; they were also soon out-producing Germany. The *Abwehr,* Germany's intelligence service, reported that the Soviets were constructing 600 - 700 tanks per month. The actual figure in fact was three times higher – a monthly average of 1,863 Soviet tanks were produced during the first six months of 1942.

As far as aircraft production was concerned, 895 German and 627 Soviet aircraft were produced in November 1941 – when the Soviet production crisis bottomed out due to the evacuation. But from that low point, the Soviet figures rose sharply. In the period January - March 1942, both countries produced around 3,300 aircraft each. From the spring of 1942, the Soviet aviation industry was increasingly out-producing its German counterpart: Between April - June 1942, the Soviets produced nearly 5,000 aircraft while Germany only managed to manufacture 3,900. In addition to this, Soviet war materiel generally made a great qualitative leap forward compared to the previous year – although Germany still held the technological advantage, Soviet technology advanced at a far greater pace – and this all boded badly for Germany, even if the winter crisis was overcome.

Soviet industry had one Achilles heel and that was oil. The USSR was a major oil producer, but 86 per cent of Soviet oil came from the Caucasian oil fields at Baku, Grozny and Maykop. Hitler reckoned that if his armed forces could occupy these oil fields, Soviet industry would be strangled.

Moreover, it would also solve one of Germany's largest strategic problems – namely, its difficulty in securing crude oil supplies.

Once the Germans had managed to overcome the worst crisis on the Eastern Front, they began planning for the summer offensive according to Hitler's general ideas. On 28 March 1942, the OKW presented a general outline for an offensive on the Eastern Front. Hitler accepted the broad outlines, but subjected the plan to an overhaul which on 5 April 1942 was presented as the *Führer's* Directive No. 41, *Führerweisung* Nr. 41.

Under the code-name *Unternehmen Blau* (Operation 'Blue'), it presented the general plan for the great summer offensive. It would open with an encirclement operation from the Orel-Kursk and Kharkov areas, with one force – eventually *Heeresgruppe von Kleist* – in the north forming the northern jaw of a pincer, striking between the Don and the Donets ('Blue I'). Having occupied the city of Voronezh, this force would veer southwards, along the Don. Simultaneously, a southern pincer – (eventually VI. *Armee*) – would advance towards the north-east across the Donets from Volchansk ('Blue II'). The goal was to envelop and annihilate Soviet South-western Front and the northern flank of the Southern Front, after which a general thrust towards the Caucasus would be carried out.

In order to obtain a better staging area for Operation 'Blue', three smaller offensives were planned.

The first of these was Operation '*Fridericus* I', for which *Heeresgruppe von Kleist* and VI. *Armee* were to be concentrated south of Kharkov.

The second preparatory attack was dubbed Operation '*Wilhelm*', and was to be executed by VI. *Armee* from the area east of Kharkov against Volchansk in early June 1942.

The third operation, '*Fridericus* II', would simply spread the Operation '*Wilhelm*' attack southwards, aimed at occupying the Kupyansk sector. Thus, '*Wilhelm*' and '*Fridericus* II' would place VI. *Armee* in a perfect staging area for the pincer movement towards the north according to Operation 'Blue II'.

But before any of this could be undertaken, it was deemed necessary to 'clear up' the Crimea – for several reasons, not only because of the potential threat from the Soviet troops on the Kerch Peninsula and at Sevastopol and the fact that this tied up considerable German forces (the whole of XI. *Armee*), but also because the Crimea in itself was an important staging area for the upcoming offensive against the Caucasus.

*A Ju 87 D is made ready for another combat mission. With the Ju 87 D, which was introduced into service on the Eastern Front in early 1942, the old Ju 87 B Stuka had been considerably improved.*

On 12 February, the Operations Section of the OKH presented a plan which aimed at the re-conquest of the Kerch Peninsula and Sevastopol on the Crimea, and an envelopment operation directed against the bulge at Izyum south of Kharkov. On 16 April, *Generaloberst* Erich von Manstein, the brilliant commander of XI. *Armee*, visited Hitler to present his plan for the re-conquest of the Kerch Peninsula. He called the plan *Unternehmen Trappenjagd* ('Bustard Hunt'). Hitler approved of the ground operations element, but intervened to secure 'stronger air support'.

The experience of the war in the East during the past months clearly had taught Hitler the importance of air support. "The *Führer* was by experience and inclination an 'army man' who . . . lacked the experience in air tactics and strategy. During the successful first years of the war, he had rarely meddled in air force affairs."[25] But now Hitler strongly emphasised the decisive role of the *Luftwaffe* and he guaranteed von Manstein that he would personally ensure reinforcement of the *Luftwaffe* in the Crimea.[26] This, however, was not entirely necessary, since *Luftwaffe* commander, *Reichsmarschall* Göring, had, as a consequence of the general outlines in 'Directive No. 41', ordered *Generaloberst* Löhr to shift the focus of *Luftflotte* 4's operations to the Crimea just one week previously.[27]

Göring also took several measures to reinforce the weakened *Luftwaffe* forces in the East. Several units in the Mediterranean area or in reserve in Germany were prepared for transfer to *Luftflotte* 4. In order to increase the number of airmen in depleted air units, the *Reichsmarschall* also ordered that experienced airmen from *Ergänzungsgruppen* throughout the *Luftwaffe* would be earmarked for *Luftflotte* 4 units.

Hitler's attention was increasingly focused on the crucial air support for the new offensive operations. On 17 April he held a conference with the OKL to work out the nature and level of 'massed air power'. The following

day, Hitler personally ordered *Generaloberst* Wolfram *Freiherr* von Richthofen – the commander of VIII. *Fliegerkorps* and one of the *Luftwaffe's* most able close-support leaders – to assume command of the air support for the two Crimean offensives.

On 20 April, the War Diary of the OKW noted:

"The *Führer* stressed that massed air power will be decisive to the Army groups. Only the *Luftwaffe* will be able to decide the outcome of a battle."[28] The next day, Hitler emphasised the importance of establishing closer cooperation between the *Heeresgruppen* and the *Luftflotten*.

Typically for Hitler, his interest in technical details came to the fore – he became preoccupied with the weapons which could be deployed by the *Luftwaffe* with greatest efficiency. In his discussions on the forthcoming offensive, Hitler emphasised the need for large numbers of SD 2 anti-personnel cluster bombs, and ordered that "the equipping of *Luftflotte* 4 bomber units with these bombs was to be speeded up"[29]. The *Führer* also saw the great demand for very heavy bombs for the purpose of breaching the Soviet defence lines at the Kerch Peninsula and Sevastopol.

The offensives against Kerch and Sevastopol indeed were "preparatory measures" before the major offensive, but they also demanded a certain 'softening up measure' – which Hitler described in the following words:

"During the period until the attack itself begins, the supply of the Kerch Peninsula must be interrupted in the strongest manner. Because of the short travel time of the ships between Novorossiysk and Kerch, it will often be impossible to attack them at sea. The point of main effort of the fight against supplies will therefore be the harbours of Kerch and Kamysh-Burun as well as Novorossiysk and Tuapse."[30]

Thus, the focus of the air war decisively shifted towards the southernmost combat zone of the Eastern Front.

# *Fuhrerweisung* Nr.41

The winter battle in Russia is drawing to a close. As a result of the unparalleled courage and self-sacrificing devotion of our soldiers on the Eastern Front, German arms have achieved a great defensive success.

The enemy has sustained severe losses in men and equipment. In an effort to exploit what appeared to him to be early successes, he has expended during the winter the bulk of his reserves intended for later operations.

As soon as the weather and the state of the terrain allows, we must seize the initiative again, and force our will upon the enemy through the superiority of German leadership and the German soldier.

The aim is to once and for all annihilate what remains of the Soviet defensive potential, and, as far as possible, deprive it of its most important centres of war industry.

The German *Wehrmacht* and our allies must employ all available forces for this purpose. At the same time, the security of occupied territories in Western and Northern Europe, especially the coastal areas, has to be safeguarded in all circumstances.

### I. The General Plan

While maintaining the groundwork of the original plan for the Eastern campaign, the armies of the central combat zone will remain in position. In the North, Leningrad will be seized and an overland connection will be established with the Finns, while in the southern combat zone a breakthrough into the Caucasus will be achieved.

In view of the present conditions at the end of winter – the availability of troops and resources, along with transport problems – these goals can be met only in one combat zone at a time.

Hence, firstly, all available forces shall be concentrated in the southern combat zone, with the aim of destroying the enemy before the Don, followed by the occupation of the Caucasian oilfields and an advance through the Caucasus.

The final isolation of Leningrad and the occupation of Ingermanland may be undertaken when conditions in that area are favourable, or when sufficient forces can be made available from other combat zones.

### II. Conduct of Operations

**A.** The first task of the *Heer* and the *Luftwaffe*, when the period of thaw of its muddy ground conditions is over, will be to establish the pre-conditions necessary for carrying out our main operation.

This calls for mopping-up and consolidation on the whole Eastern Front and in the rear areas so that the greatest possible forces may be released for the main operation. The other sectors of the Front must be able to counter any attack with the smallest possible expenditure of manpower.

Wherever offensive operations with limited objectives are to be carried out for this purpose, in accordance with my orders, every effort will be made to ensure that all available forces of the *Heer* and the *Luftwaffe* are ready to go into action in overwhelming strength, in order to achieve rapid and decisive success. Only thus will we be able – prior to the launch of the big spring offensive – to imbue our troops with confidence in the certainty of victory, and to instil into the enemy a sense of his own hopeless inferiority.

**B.** Our next mission is to deal with the Crimea, and then the mopping-up of the Kerch Peninsula, the Crimea and the capture of Sevastopol. The *Luftwaffe*, and later the Navy, will have the task of preparing these operations and blocking enemy supply traffic in the Black Sea and the Kerch Straits as energetically as possible.

In the southern sector, the enemy forces which have broken through on both sides of Izyum will be cut off along the Donets River and destroyed.

A final directive concerning the mopping-up in the Central and Northern sectors of the Eastern Front must await the conclusion of the present fighting and of the muddy season. However, the necessary forces must be provided, as soon as the situation allows, by thinning out front line troops.

**C.** The Main Operation on the Eastern Front:
The purpose, as already stated, is to occupy the Caucasus Front by decisively attacking and destroying Russian forces which are employed in the Voronezh area to the south, west, or north of the Don River. Because of the manner in which the units available for this operation are employed, this operation can only be carried out as a series of successive, but coordinated and complementary,

attacks. Thus, these attacks must be so synchronised from north to south that each individual offensive is carried out by the largest possible concentration of the army, and particularly of air forces which can be deployed at the decisive points.

There is sufficient evidence – as in the double battle of Vyazma-Bryansk – to show that the Russians are not very vulnerable to encirclement operations. Hence, it is of decisive importance that individual breaches of the Front take the form of close pincer movements.

We must avoid closing the pincers too late, allowing the enemy to escape destruction. At the same time, a situation must be avoided where armoured and motorised formations advance so quickly that they lose connection with the infantry following, or that they fail to support the hard-pressed, advancing infantry through direct attacks on the rear of the encircled Russian armies. Thus, apart from the main object of the operation, in each individual case we must be absolutely sure to annihilate the enemy by the method of attack and by the direction of the forces used.

Operations in the centre will open with a major attack and, if possible, a breakthrough from the area south of Orel in the direction of Voronezh. Of the two armoured and motorised formations forming the pincers, the northern must be stronger than the southern. The goal of this breakthrough is the seizure of Voronezh. The task of certain infantry divisions is to establish a strong defensive front between the Orel area, from which the attack will be launched, and Voronezh. Meanwhile, the armoured and motorised formations will continue the attack towards the south from Voronezh, with their left flank on the Don River, in support of a second breakthrough which will take place towards the east, from the general area of Kharkov. Here, too, the primary objective is not to penetrate the Russian Front as such but, in cooperation with the motorised forces advancing down the Don, to destroy the enemy armies.

The third attack in the course of these operations will be so conducted that formations advancing down the Don can link up in the Stalingrad area with forces advancing from the Taganrog - Artemovsk area between the lower Don and Voroshilovgrad across the Donets to the east. Finally, these forces will establish contact with the *Panzer* Army which is marching towards Stalingrad.

Should these operations be able to establish bridgeheads to the east or south of the Don, particularly through the capture of intact bridges, advantage should be taken of such opportunities. In any case, every effort will be made to reach Stalingrad itself, or at least to bring the city under fire from heavy artillery so that it may no longer serve as an industrial or communications centre. It would be particularly desirable if we could secure either intact bridges in Rostov itself or other bridgeheads south of the Don for later operations.

In order to prevent large numbers of Russian forces north of the Don from withdrawing southwards across the river, the right flank of our forces advancing east from the Taganrog area must be reinforced by armoured and motorised troops which, if necessary, will have to be formed from improvised units.

According to the progress made in these attacks, we must not only provide strong protection for the north-east flank of the operation. We must also immediately set about establishing positions along the Don. In this matter, anti-tank defences are of particular importance. These positions will from the onset be prepared and fully equipped in view of their possible occupation in winter.

The Don Front, which will become more and more extended as the attack proceeds, will mainly be held by units of our allies, with German forces providing a powerful supporting force between Orel and the Don River, and in the Stalingrad strip. Elsewhere, individual German divisions will remain available as reserves behind the Don Front.

Allied troops will be deployed with the Hungarians farthest north, followed by the Italians, and the Rumanians farthest to the south-east.

**D.** In consideration of the season swift progress of the movements across the Don River to the south is essential in order to attain the operational objectives.

### III. The *Luftwaffe*

Apart from giving direct support to the Army, the task of the *Luftwaffe* is to cover the deployment of forces of Army Group South by reinforcing air defences. This applies, above all, to railway bridges across the Dnyiepr River.

If enemy forces are seen to be concentrating, the main roads and railways serving the concentration area in the enemy's rear will be subjected to continuous air attacks. A first priority will be the destruction of railway bridges across the Don River. On the opening of operations, the enemy air force and its ground organisation in the combat zone in question will be attacked and destroyed through a concentrated effort of all available forces.

The possibility of a rapid transfer of *Luftwaffe* units to the central and northern combat zones must be borne in mind, and the necessary ground organisation for this maintained as far as possible.

### IV. The Navy

In the Black Sea, the Navy's principal task, as far as our combat and escort forces and our tonnage allow, will be to supply the *Heer* and the *Luftwaffe*.

Because the great power of the Russian Black Sea fleet still is unbroken, it is particularly important that the light naval forces are moved to the Black Sea and made ready for action there as soon as possible.

The Baltic Sea will be protected by blockading Russian naval forces in the inner waters of the Gulf of Finland.

### V.

The need to ensure secrecy is once again to be brought to the attention of all staff concerned in these preparations. In this connection the attitude to be adopted towards our Allies will be laid down in special instructions.

### VI.

The preparations planned by the various branches of the Armed Forces, and their timetables, will be notified to me through the OKW.


Signed: Adolf Hitler


## *Fliegerführer Ostsee* versus the Black Sea Fleet

Throughout the war, the powerful Soviet Black Sea Fleet dominated the Black Sea. In early 1942, commanded by *Vitse-Admiral* Filipp Oktyabrskiy, this fleet could muster the battleship *Sevastopol* (previously named *Pariskaya Kommuna*), the heavy cruisers *Molotov, Voroshilov* and *Krasnyy Kavkaz*, the light cruisers *Krasnyy Krym* and *Komintern*, 15 to 20 destroyers and around 50 submarines.

Axis forces were able to challenge this formidable force only from the air, albeit with some success. However, the successful Soviet evacuation of Odessa in October 1941 was a slap in the face for *Luftflotte* 4, responsible for air attacks against Soviet shipping in the Black Sea. In order to render air operations over the Black Sea more effective, the *Luftwaffe* organized a special anti-shipping command based in the Crimea – *Fliegerführer Süd*. This office was established through the transfer of *Oberst* Wolfgang von Wild's *Fliegerführer Ostsee*, which had organized anti-shipping operations in the Baltic Sea with some success.

Initially, the main component of *Fliegerführer Süd* was *Seeaufklärungsgruppe* 125, equipped with Ar 196, He 114 and BV 138 reconnaissance seaplanes.

With the Soviet landings on the Kerch Peninsula in late December 1941 and the besieged port city of Sevastopol holding out longer than had been anticipated, attacks against Soviet supply shipping across the Black Sea suddenly received high priority.

*Oberst* von Wild received considerable reinforcement when the He 111-equipped I./KG 100 *Wiking* was shifted from Kirovograd in the Ukraine to Saki in the Crimea on 29 January, where it was subordinated to *Fliegerführer Süd*. *Kampfgeschwader* 100 had recently been activated and established from a nucleus originally designated KGr 100. Nothing could be more appropriate for its next combat task – to raid Soviet shipping in the Black Sea – than its unit name and crest, a Viking ship in full sail.

However, I./KG 100 was far from being a fully-fledged anti-shipping *Gruppe*. The chronic supply shortage on the Eastern Front had left the unit in poor condition. There were no more than eight serviceable He 111s at hand, while the aircrew were trained for minelaying and had no experience in anti-shipping attacks.

Things did not start well for I./KG 100. On 29 January one of its He 111s was lost on a mission over the Straits of Kerch – probably to a Soviet fighter.[1]

Had it not been for the exploits of the twenty-eight-year-old *Staffelkapitän* of 1./KG 100, *Oblt*. Hansgeorg Bätcher, the assignment of this *Kampfgruppe* to the Crimea would likely have passed with little note.

During one of his first days in Saki, the commander of I./KG 100 received a teleprinter message from headquarters: air reconnaissance had spotted a 7,500-ton Soviet tanker bringing in fuel for the entire Soviet army at Kerch. Löhr demanded that this ship be destroyed, and he specifically requested that the *Kommandeur* of I./KG 100 select *Oblt*. Bätcher's crew for this task. As Bätcher recalled;

"The *Kommandeur* had particularly mentioned which crew he wanted to fulfil this task. I briefed my crew with little fuss and simply told them: 'Tonight, lads, we're going to sink this tanker.' We took off late at night and were soon approaching Kerch. I decided to make one pass at high altitude to see if it was possible to make a high-altitude bombing run, and the Russians immediately opened up with fierce fire. There was an enormous amount of flak in the port. "It can't be done like that," I told my crew, "We have to do it in another way." I

flew out over the sea, hauled around and let down to low altitude, almost skimming the waves. We headed in against Kerch again. Approaching the target area, I throttled back so that the Russians wouldn't detect us from the sound of the engines, and, gliding in over the port, I caught sight of the tanker in front of me. I leaned toward my observer and said, 'I'll release the bombs myself,' since I figured I was best placed to take the decision in this situation. Flying straight toward the tanker, I threw open the throttles and dropped the bombs. With my engines roaring, my Heinkel flashed over the tanker and out of the port area. My SC 500 bomb hit square on, exploding amidships. We fled the scene at high speed, before the Russians had even managed to fire a single shot against us."

The date this raid took place has not been exactly established. The corresponding pages in Bätcher's logbook are missing but, according to German historians Ulf Balke and Georg Brütting, it is likely this mission was flown on 6 February 1942.[2] Nevertheless, Soviet records show no bomb damage on any large vessel in this area for this date. It is possible that the tanker hit by *Oblt*. Bätcher was the *Emba*, which was severely damaged on 29 January by a German bomber at Kamysh-Burun, the port seven miles to the south of Kerch.

Adverse weather conditions reduced flight activity to a minimum during I./KG 100´s first weeks in the Crimea.

Apart from *Oblt*. Bätcher's achievements, I./KG 100 was able to accomplish relatively little during the first weeks of its operations against Soviet shipping in the Black Sea and the Straits of Kerch. Meanwhile the Soviets had managed to bring almost 100,000 troops and hundreds of artillery pieces across the Straits of Kerch between 20 January and 11 February. Similarly, the resupply operations into Sevastopol went on unabated. On 12 February, four transport ships brought 4,987 troops, 764 tons of fuel and 1700 tons of other supplies to Sevastopol. The next day the cruiser *Komintern* and the destroyer *Shaumyan* arrived at the same destination with 1,034 troops and 200 tons of other supplies. This continued on 14 February, with the cruiser *Krasny Krym* and the destroyer *Dzerzhinskiy* bringing in 1,075 troops, and on 15 February, with the flotilla leader *Kharkov* and the minesweeper *T410* bringing in 650 troops and evacuating 152 injured. On 17 February, the transport ship *Belostok* brought an additional 871 troops to Sevastopol. In addition to this, the naval vessels of the Soviet Black Sea fleet regularly subjected German troops in the coastal areas to shelling using their heavy guns.

*Fliegerführer Süd* was further reinforced when the units previously under the command of *Sonderstab Krim* were subordinated to *Oberst* Wild on 18 February. As a consequence, *Oberst* Wild was able to deploy the Ju 88s of *Stab*, I. and III./KG 51 and the He 111s of I./KG 27 against the ports of Sevastopol and Kerch in the Crimea, and Anapa, Tuapse and Novorossiysk on the Caucasian Black Sea coast. But these operations were met both by the fighters of VVS ChF – which were described as 'most alert' by the German bomber airmen[3] – and, above all, by concentrated anti-aircraft fire. A German report read: "Due to strong anti-aircraft fire, heavy evasive action had to be taken in the target area, which often made it impossible to use the bombsights."[4]

*Oblt*. Bätcher was responsible for the bulk of German successes against Soviet shipping in the Black Sea. On 20 February, Bätcher attacked and destroyed what he reported to be "a loaded 2,000-ton freighter" – probably the 1,900-ton steamer *Kommunist*, which disappeared *en route* from Novorossiysk to Sevastopol.

Only with the arrival of the He 111 torpedo bombers of II./KG 26 in late February, was the *Luftwaffe* able to pose a serious threat to the ships of the ChF.

*Soviet LaGG-3 and La-5 fighters on the assembly line at State Production Plant No. 21 in Gorkiy in 1942 under the watchful eyes of Vladimir Ilyich Lenin. Production of the La-5 – a considerable modification of the LaGG-3 – commenced at Gorkiy in June 1942, and by August almost 300 La-5s had been manufactured. (Drabkin)*

The first result was achieved as early as the night of 1-2 March, when a II./KG 26 crew hit and severely damaged the 2,434-ton steamer *Fabritsius*. The ship was grounded at Cape Tuzla, where it was later destroyed in a storm.

*Vitse-Admiral* Oktyabrskiy was conscious of the threat posed by the torpedo bombers and immediately decided to restrict the bombardment of enemy troops to destroyers and flotilla leaders. Heavier vessels were held back unless guarded by powerful escort forces acting as an anti-aircraft deterrent. He also ordered resupply shipping operations to be provided with stronger escort.

This latter tactic resulted in the success achieved on 9 March, when all German torpedo attacks against the transport ship *Krasnaya Kuban* were repulsed by the escort. Nevertheless, March marked a turning point in the air-sea battle in the Black Sea, which would also have dire consequences for Soviet fighting capabilities in the Crimea.

On 3 March *Luftwaffe* bombers hit and damaged the tanker *Kuybyshev* (4629 GRT) in the port of Kamysh-Burun south of Kerch, thus depriving the Crimean Front of much of its fuel. The damaged ship was towed back to the Caucasian port of Novorossiysk, where it again was hit and damaged by Ju 88s of III./KG 51 on 17 March.

On 18 March, the escorting cruiser *Krasnyy Krym* and the destroyer *Nezamozhnik* managed to repulse twelve German air attacks against the transport ships *Sergo* and *Peredovik* in open sea, but two days later the *Sergo* was hit and damaged during a German air raid against the port of Sevastopol. The next day, nine Ju 88s of KG 51 hit and sunk the transport ship *Georgiy Dimitrov* (3689 GRT) in the port of Sevastopol, while six He 111s of I./KG 27 damaged one transport ship and a floating battery in the port of Kerch.[5]

On 23 March, nine KG 51 Ju 88s appeared over Tuapse and sank the two minelayers *Ostrovskiy* and *GS-13* and one motor torpedo boat, and damaged two submarines (*S-33* and *D-5*). That evening a II./KG 26 He 111 reportedly destroyed one 5,000-ton and two 2,000-ton merchant ships. According to Soviet accounts the 2,690-ton steamer *V. Chapayev* was sunk after being hit by an aerial torpedo some forty miles to the south of Khersones on 23 March. Sixteeen members of the crew and 86 soldiers were lost, but 173 men were rescued from the sea.[6]

KG 51 returned to raid the port of Tuapse on 24 March, sinking the transport ship *Yalta* and the depot ship *Neva*. Two days later nine Ju 88s of KG 51 returned to Tuapse and damaged the tanker *Sovneft* and the tug *SP-44*. Soviet flak claimed one Ju 88 shot down, confirmed in the III./KG 51 loss records. On 28 March, the transport ship *Akhilleon* was damaged at Novorossiysk. The next day, four He 111 torpedo bombers from II./KG 26 hit and damaged the transport ship *Voroshilov*.

On 2 April a German reconnaissance aircraft spotted the large tanker *Kuybyshev* off Kerch. It had been repaired after suffering bomb damage two weeks earlier and was now heading for Kamysh-Burun with 4,600 tons of badly needed fuel for the Crimean Front. A MiG-3 pilot from 7 IAP/VVS ChF managed to shoot down the reconnaissance aircraft, but its radio message had already

reached *Fliegerführer Süd*. An hour later *Kapitan* Vasiliy Chernopashchyenko of the same fighter unit reportedly brought down both the bombers that were launched against the tanker – the second through a *taran*, which also killed the Soviet pilot. But this would not save the tanker. Hit by a torpedo in the stern, *Kuybyshev* blazed furiously and went down in the shallow waters of the Mariya Maddalina sand bank. There, the half-sunk tanker continued to burn for almost a week. This was such a terrible blow that the Crimean Front had to discontinue the entire offensive.

The transport capacity of the Soviet Black Sea Fleet had been reduced from 43,200 tons at the beginning of February 1942 to 27,400 tons at the end of March. Six transports had been lost and another six were under repair.[7]

By way of riposte, on 2 April VVS ChF bombers hit and damaged the Rumanian auxiliary cruiser *Dachia* and a torpedo boat.

The next *Luftwaffe* unit to intervene in the battle of the Crimea was I./KG 55, which bombed Tuapse on 10 April, scoring hits on the destroyer *Sposobnyy* and the uncompleted cruiser *Frunze*. Intercepting Soviet fighters shot down one of the He 111s. On 17 April, II./KG 26 scored another important success when two torpedo strikes sank the 4,125-ton steamship *Svanetiya* between Sevastopol and Novorossiysk. Five hundred and thirty-five men were lost in this disaster.

German air raids against the ports of Kerch, Novorossiysk, and Tuapse on 19 April resulted in bomb strikes on the tanker *I. Stalin* and three transport ships. Two days later, II./KG 51 sank a transport and damaged the mineship *Komintern* in the same area. Against Soviet claims of seven Ju 88s shot down, only one Ju 88 was lost to fighter interception, according to German records.[8]

By this time, the Black Sea Fleet's capacity to supply the Soviet troops on the Kerch Peninsula and in Sevastopol had been badly curtailed. The Soviets were in dire straits, and this was demonstrated through a blow of almost symbolic dimensions on 24 April. That day, the Ju 87 Stukas of III./St.G 77 struck the ChF's 36th Aviation Repair Shop in Kruglaya Bay near Sevastopol. Among the forty-eight men killed here were *General-Mayor* Nikolay Ostryakov, the commander of VVS ChF, and the deputy commander of VVS VMF, *General-Mayor* F.G. Korobkov.

1. Via Hansgeorg Bätcher.
2. Balke, *Kampfgeschwader 100 Wiking*, p. 102; Brütting, *Das waren die deutschen Kampffliegerasse 1939-1945*, p. 150.
3. Waiss, *Chronik Kampfgeschwader Nr. 27 Boelcke*, Band IV, p. 40
4. Dierich, *Kampfgeschwader 51 'Edelweiss'*, p. 172
5. *Velikaya Otechestvenaya den' za dnyom*, in *Morskoy Sbornik*, 3/1992.
6. Morozov, *Morskaya aviatsiya Germanii 1939-1945. Chast 1. Torpedonostysy*, p. 17.
7. *Velikaya Otechestvenaya den' za dnyom*, in *Morskoy Sbornik*, 3/1992.
8. *Flugzeugunfälle und Verluste bei den Verbänden (täglich)*, Ob.d.L. Gen.Qu. Gen. 6. Abt. Bundesarchiv/Militärarchiv RL 2 III/1180.

# Chapter Four

# The Battle for the Kerch Peninsula

To the Soviets, who had made a successful invasion of the Kerch Peninsula at the turn of the year but had become bogged down, it was obvious that their only chance of achieving victory in the Crimea was through a swift outcome. Their German opponents enjoyed an important advantage – supplies and reinforcements could be brought in overland, while the Soviets were restricted to a seaborne resupply effort. Thus, the Soviets concentrated on hurriedly reinforcing the troops on the Kerch Peninsula. On 28 January 1942 these troops were organized into the newly formed Crimean Front, commanded by *General-Leytenant* Dmitriy Kozlov.

VVS Crimean Front was rapidly built into one of the largest air commands of the entire Soviet Air Force. But it was beset by several disadvantages. There had been little time to prepare the airfields on the small Kerch Peninsula, and aircraft from four or five aviation regiments were crowded into each base. Furthermore, the bulk of VVS Crimean Front was composed of obsolete Polikarpov fighters and SB bombers.

Meanwhile, *Reichsmarschall* Göring had ordered the dissolution of *Sonderstab Krim* on 11 February. Another assignment awaited *General* von Greim – the command of the *Luftwaffe* in the central combat zone. On 18 February, the *Luftwaffe* units operating over the Crimea were brought under command of *Oberst* Wolfgang von Wild's *Fliegerführer Süd*.

The Germans were still superior in the air as discovered by the Crimean Front's first attempt to achieve a major breakthrough on 27 February. Air attacks broke up the Soviet assault columns and the offensive stalled after only a few days.

Discontented with this meagre performance, Josef Stalin ordered VVS Crimean Front to be reinforced and sent one of his harshest senior political commissars, *Armeyskiy Komissar Pervogo Ranga* Lev Mekhlis, to the Crimea.

Disregarding the actual situation, Mekhlis demanded that all attention be redirected to the offensive, and completely ignored defensive measures. While he kept the commanders of the aviation units occupied with preparing three detailed reports each day, he ordered an all-out effort by the airmen.

The exhausted airmen were ordered into constant low-level and horizontal bombing attacks along the entire front. Mekhlis also had the fighters scrambled against every single report of *Luftwaffe* intrusions over the front line, which had been going on since early March. *General-Mayor*

Nikolay Skripko, the deputy commander of ADD, who arrived at this sector in early May 1942, later wrote: "The aviation of the Front wasted its service life under relatively quiet conditions, and when it shortly afterwards became necessary to fly in full strength, a large number of the fighters were unserviceable due to engine failures."[31]

As a measurement of this extreme activity, 743 IAP conducted 2,160 combat sorties between 12 February and 7 May, which resulted in 28 victory claims against losses of 11 aircraft and six pilots.[32]

From the first week of March, VVS Crimean Front and VVS ChF – the Black Sea Fleet's Air Force – initiated an air offensive against German troop concentrations, artillery positions, and airfields. On 8 March, VVS ChF mounted its strongest air attack to date against Saki aerodrome, the home of II./KG 26 and I./KG 100; the raiders dropped more than 400 bombs. During a follow-up raid against the same target on 9 March, five He 111s of I./KG 100 were severely damaged on the ground.

The Soviet 44th and 51st armies reopened the ground offensive on the Kerch Peninsula on Friday, 13 March. By then, VVS Crimean Front had been reinforced to number 581 aircraft.

Both sides launched everything they could into the air. In the middle of this battle, III./JG 77 – which had been the main German *Jagdgruppe* in the Crimea for five months – was pulled out of combat. It had sustained fairly high losses over the previous weeks, and the pilots showed signs of battle fatigue. It was replaced with II./JG 77, which arrived after a long and well-deserved period of rest in Germany.

The arrival of II./JG 77 had an immediate impact. On 19 March, the unit claimed 21 victories for no losses. Although the number of claims was exaggerated, Soviet losses were indeed severe. On 23 March, *Mayor* Mikhail Fedoseyev, the commander of Yak-1-equipped 247 IAP, was killed in a clash with II./JG 77. With 22 victories to his name, Fedoseyev was the top-scoring Soviet fighter ace at that time.

Vasiliy Shevchuk, who served as *Eskadrilya* commissar in 247 IAP at that time, described Fedoseyev's last fight:

"On that day, *Mayor* Fedoseyev sent two pairs of fighters – which was almost all that remained of his unit – into the air. Stepan Karnach [*Kapitan* and the commander of an *Eskadrilya*] and his wingman, Aleksey Shmyryov, comprised the first pair. I led the second pair.

Shortly after take-off, Aleksey Shmyryov started lagging behind. He radioed that his right undercarriage leg would not retract. At this moment, six 'Messers' bounced the three remaining Yaks. We were engaged in a most difficult combat.

Following our radio transmissions, *Mayor* Fedoseyev immediately realized that we were in a difficult situation. As soon as Shmyryov had landed, the CO dashed to the cockpit of his fighter and went into the air. He was certain that his skills would outweigh our numerical disadvantage. As he approached us, a pair of Messerschmitts veered towards him.

At that moment, Stepan Karnach, covered by Viktor Golovko and myself, managed to bring down one of the Fascists with an accurate burst of fire. It soon stood clear that we had to come to our commander's rescue. But then my aircraft was damaged. Bullets slammed into the engine and pierced the oil lines. Hot oil covered the windscreen and flooded into the cockpit, scalding my face and hands. The engine seized. I had to make a forced landing in friendly territory, next to our front line. The soldiers in the trenches called out and warned me not to get out of the cockpit. It turned out that I had landed in the middle of a minefield, miraculously avoiding being blown to pieces. Soon some sappers arrived and cleared a path, through which they brought me out. They salvaged the aircraft under the cover of darkness.

But the minefield, the possibility of a sudden explosion, and the enemy artillery fire was not what startled me most. The greatest tragedy took place in front of my eyes.

Another eight Bf 109s arrived to reinforce the Fascists. Stepan Karnach attempted to come to Fedoseyev's assistance, but in vain. Karnach, Golovko, and Fedoseyev were locked into an unequal combat. Our commander managed to evade several enemy attacks, and he even made a couple of attacks against the Messerschmitts. But finally several bursts from a Messerschmitt pierced the fuselage and wings of his aircraft. The engine emitted smoke and the machine was losing control. But as long as the pilot was alive, he kept on fighting. He fought until the end.

War puts the individual into many serious and hard situations. But nothing is worse than when you find yourself unable to help a friend in a mortal fight. With fists clenched and teeth gritted in frustration, the only thought was: "Bale out! Bale out!"

Our regiment had suffered heavily since the beginning of the war. But this was an irreplaceable loss. Few unit commanders in the muddle of the first days of the war had managed to organize resistance like *Mayor* Fedoseyev."[33]

Under these circumstances, the effect of Soviet air operations against German ground troops was fairly limited and in no way decisive – in contrast to the shock and awe from the air which the Crimean Front troops had to endure – the attacks by St.G 77's Stukas against Soviet armour being a particular case in point. Generally, Soviet tanks were able to withstand most attacks by Ju 87s – which by this time had not yet acquired sufficiently

effective anti-tank weapons. But the majority of the tanks which had been shipped over to the Kerch Peninsula were obsolescent types with thin armour, which were easy prey for the pin-point attacks by the German dive-bombers. Due to II./JG 77's effective cover, St.G 77 could carry out these attacks without much interference from Soviet fighters.

The air war over the Crimea cost VVS Crimean Front 70 aircraft in March 1942.[34] Meanwhile, the *Luftwaffe* sustained 21 combat losses in the Crimea.[35]

Inevitably, all Soviet attempts to achieve a major breakthrough failed.

While the Air Force of the Crimean Front fared badly against II./JG 77, the more experienced airmen of the Black Sea Fleet's Air Force proved to be a more deadly adversary for the Germans. In recognition of the courageous fighting in the air over the Crimea since the autumn of 1941, the first two aviation regiments of VVS ChF were adopted as Guards regiments on 3 April. 2 MTAP was re-designated as 5 GMTAP/VVS VMF and 8 IAP became 6 GIAP/VVS VMF.

Each day from 4 to 8 April, the new Guards regiments and other VVS ChF units raided the airbases at Saki and Sarabuz. The difference between VVS Crimean Front and VVS ChF is symbolically captured by two events during those days: On 4 April, *Ofw.* Rudolf Schmidt of II./JG 77 scored his 42nd victory by shooting down an RZ biplane bomber of VVS Crimean Front. The next day, II./JG 77's *Uffz.* Ernst Thoma shot down a Soviet aircraft which he identified as an 'I-153'. In reality, it was a UTI-1 – a two-seat trainer and liaison version of the obsolescent I-5 biplane fighter – flown by 743 IAP's C.O., *Kapitan* Sergey Ivanov, who was killed.[36] Then on 6 April, the ace *Ofw.* Rudolf Schmidt was shot down when he intercepted a group of incoming 40 BAP/VVS ChF Pe-2s between Yevpatoriya and Saki in western Crimea. Schmidt was listed as missing.

On 28 April, MiG-3s of 7 IAP/VVS ChF intercepted 33 Ju 88 crews of I./KG 51 who were attempting to attack the port of Novorossiysk. As the pale-faced and exhausted German survivors returned to base afterwards, they described one of the fiercest Soviet fighter attacks they had ever encountered on the Eastern Front. The MiG-3s brought down two Ju 88s and several returned with battle damage and injured crewmen. One of the missing Ju 88s was destroyed in an air-to-air ramming by *Serzh.* Leonid Sevryukov – the second *taran* driven home by a 7 IAP/VVS ChF pilot in less than a month. Soviet fighters and AAA claimed ten victories against only one loss, *Serzh.* Sevryukov's MiG-3.

This increasingly effective Soviet air activity compelled *Luftflotte* 4's *Generaloberst* Löhr to deploy another *Jagdgruppe* – III./JG 52 – to the Crimea. On 29 April, this unit took off from Kharkov for a transfer flight to Zürichtal, 25 miles to the west of the front lines on the Kerch Peninsula.

The Soviets gave the airmen of III./JG 52 a warm welcome. During their transfer to Zürichtal they had made an intermediary landing at Grammatikovo in northern Crimea to refuel and had been struck by a group of Pe-2s from 40 BAP/VVS ChF which made a swift hit-and-run attack against the airfield. The Germans were fortunate to avoid any losses during this attack.

Fifteen minutes later, III./JG 52 took off for the final flight that would take them to Zürichtal. This flight also would lead to a confrontation with Soviet airmen – which was quite different to what the pilots of this *Jagdgruppe* had grown used to. The logbook of one of the unit's pilots, *Fw.* Alfred Grislawski, shows that his last encounter with enemy airmen in the Kharkov area had taken place on 28 March.[37] However, on this their second flight in Crimean air space, on 29 April 1942, the pilots of III./JG 52 came across 247 IAP's Yak-1s. In the ensuing *mêlée*, the Germans claimed to have shot down five of these for no losses. When they finally landed at Zürichtal, *Lt.* Hermann Graf, the *Staffelkapitän* of 9./JG 52, reported his 61st victory, while his wingman, *Fw.* Grislawski, was to file his 18th.

The next day, Graf, Grislawski and two other pilots of III./JG 52 were dispatched on an escort mission for Stukas of St.G 77. They had barely crossed the front line before a formation of I-153 biplanes of VVS Crimean Front's 743 IAP appeared. In an extended air combat, in which

*A Yak-7V (tandem two-seat variant) at an airfield during the thaw. The primitive conditions of airfields in the Stalingrad area posed great problems to both sides in the winter of 1942/1943. (Viktor Kulikov Photograph Collection)*

*A Ju 88 A-4 of KG 51, possibly of 6. Staffel, prepares for take-off. The aircraft carries the yellow Eastern Front fuselage theatre band and yellow spinners.*

six I-16s of 36 IAP and two Yak-1s of 247 IAP also intervened, the Germans claimed to have shot down four biplanes, a Yak-1 and an I-16. The latter – registered as *Lt.* Graf's 65th victory – was piloted by *Mayor* Kartuzov, 36 IAP's C.O., who was injured by shrapnel in his leg.[38]

In all III./JG 52 claimed 71 Soviet aircraft shot down between 29 April and 2 May 1942. Although this was an exaggerated estimation of actual Soviet losses, III./JG 52 undoubtedly contributed substantially to weaken VVS Crimean Front. The Soviets were quite aware of the arrival of this *Jagdgruppe*. *M.Lt.* Petr Polyam of 743 IAP wrote in his memoirs: "Germany's best aces were brought together from all parts of Europe and sent to the Crimea on 1 May. Each of these had at least 100 victories on his scoreboard."[39]

There were several reasons for III./JG 52's almost unequalled successes in the Crimean skies. The large numbers of inexperienced Soviet airmen sent to the newly formed VVS Crimean Front, and the many obsolescent aircraft they were flying was the basis for the apparent inequality in air combat. But III./JG 52's results were definitely above the average. Through April 1942, the other *Jagdgruppe* in the Crimea, II./JG 77, had chalked up 44 victories against eight Bf 109s shot down.

The extent to which these German claims match actual Soviet losses is evident through Soviet records. Through April 1942, VVS Crimean Front recorded 30 aircraft shot down in air combat or missing in action, while VVS ChF lost at least 20 aircraft in combat.[40] This should be compared with the total claims by III./JG 52 and II./JG 77 over the Crimea in that month – 94 victories.

An important element in III./JG 52's achievements was the competition between some of the aces in the unit. *Lt.* Gerhard Köppen was the leading scorer but Graf was increasingly outscoring him. Among III./JG 52's seventy-one victories cited above, Graf was responsible for sixteen, and Köppen for eleven. Thus, Graf's tally stood at 76, only eight short of Köppen's 84.

This competition drove the young sharpshooters to take high risks, and one of III./JG 52's few combat losses in the Crimea in the spring of 1942 occurred when *Lt.* Köppen made a reckless attack against a Pe-2 over the Sea of Azov on 5 May. Hit by a burst of fire from the Soviet rear gunner, Köppen's Bf 109 went down in the sea and the pilot was listed as missing.

5 May was originally chosen as the day for the launching of Operation 'Bustard Hunt', the German attack aimed at 'clearing up' the Kerch Peninsula, but in order to give more time for preparations, this was moved to 8 May. On 28 April, the staff of VIII. *Fliegerkorps* arrived in the Crimea,

followed two days later by the commander, *Generaloberst* Wolfram *Freiherr* von Richthofen. A formidable force was placed under his command; bombers of KG 51, KG 55, KG 76, and I./KG 100; torpedo aircraft of II./KG 26; dive-bombers of St.G 77; fighters of I./JG 3, II., III., and 15.(Kroat)/JG 52, and I. and II./JG 77; and the new SchG 1. The latter unit was the *Luftwaffe's* first close-support *Geschwader*. Commanded by *Obstlt.* Otto Weiss, its I. *Gruppe* was equipped with Bf 109 E fighter-bombers; II. *Gruppe* was equipped with the new twin-engined ground-attack aircraft Hs 129; and 8./SchG 1 flew Hs 123 ground-attack biplanes.

The Soviets were totally unprepared for this rapid reinforcement of the *Luftwaffe* in the Crimea. Soviet Air Force *General-Mayor* Nikolay Skripko wrote: "The command of VVS Crimean Front did not take into consideration that the numerical strength of *Luftflotte* 4 was by no means fixed; it could be considerably increased when the enemy prepared a large offensive operation. And that is exactly what happened at Kerch."[41]

The position of the Soviet armies in the Kerch Peninsula had become extremely compromised. By late April 1942, local food and other resources were completely exhausted. Everything needed by the armies, down to fire wood, had to be transported by sea – a complicated process as a result of the mounting pressure from the *Luftwaffe*. Drawing the consequences of this situation, the *Stavka* proposed an evacuation of the Crimean Front from its obviously hopeless position back to the north-western Caucasus. But Stalin refused to countenance such a move. On the contrary, on 21 April he instructed the Crimean Front to prepare another major offensive aimed at liberating all of the Crimea.

To make things even worse, Stalin changed his mind on 6 May and issued Order No. 170357 which read: "The Crimean Front will not be further reinforced. The armies of the Crimean Front shall shift to the defensive and maintain positions, restricting offensive operations only for the sake of improving their tactical position – particularly by capturing Oi-Asanom."

Thus, on 7 May, instead of organizing a defence against the impending German onslaught – which the Front's intelligence officer had reported signs of – *General-Leytenant* Dmitriy Kozlov, the Crimean Front's C.O., held a conference to study plans for an attack against Oi-Asanom.

On the same day, XXX. *Armeekorps* of *General* Erich von Manstein's German XI. *Armee* was in position to launch Operation 'Bustard Hunt'. Following artillery preparation and attacks by St.G 77 against Soviet fortifications, XXX. *Armeekorps* opened its assault in the early morning hours of 8 May. During most of the day, von Richthofen concentrated his

The Ju 87 Stukas of St.G 77 carried out twenty-three separate operations on 8 May 1942, dropping 193 tons of bombs, mainly on Soviet 44th Army positions on the southern flank. All of this was achieved with just a single loss, the Ju 87 B-1 piloted by Fw. Otto Marschner with Uffz. Gerhard Hübner as radio operator – both of whom were killed. This photograph probably shows Marschner and Hübner in the Crimea, possibly only a few days earlier. (Mombeeck)

close-support units against the Soviet 44th Army on the southern flank. After only a few hours, the Soviet command had been deprived of most of its lines of communication with the troops at the Front.

Meanwhile, SchG 1 and the bomber units of VIII. *Fliegerkorps* went out against the airfields of VVS Crimean Front and achieved outstanding success. Following the experience in January, when Soviet ground operations were hampered because most of the aviation was based in the Taman area on the eastern side of the Straits of Kerch, most of the 176 fighters and 225 bombers assigned to VVS Crimean Front had been deployed to a few hurriedly constructed airfields on the Kerch Peninsula. With striking similarities to the first day of the war with the USSR, VIII. *Fliegerkorps* easily wrecked most of these overcrowded airfields during the early morning hours of 8 May. 743 IAP's airfield west of Kerch was subjected to an hour long aerial bombardment which destroyed all of the unit's I-153s except for one.

"After dealing heavy strikes against our airfields, the enemy's aviation started blocking them – preventing our fighters from taking off and intercepting its bombers," wrote *General-Mayor* Skripko.[42]

Soviet fighter pilots who attempted to take off from the forward airfields repeatedly found themselves subjected to attacks from Bf 109s diving down from the sky above. Apart from scattered aircraft that managed to take to the air during brief intervals in the German air assault, VVS Crimean Front could launch only one large mission on 8 May. Eight 36 IAP I-16s picked up the 214 ShAP I-153 Chayka ground-attack planes over Marfovka aerodrome, 25 miles south-west of Kerch, and headed for the front line. 36 IAP's *Lt.* Anatoliy Ivanov describes this mission:

"As we were approaching Marfovka's airfield we met a large number of Fascist bombers, flying considerably higher. They were heading eastward, in several groups of eighteen to twenty planes each. We hadn't seen such quantities since February. The Messerschmitts, divided into separate pairs or in groups of four, flashed past us. They didn't seem to care about us. Apparently their task was to provide the bombers with escort. But a second group of Messerschmitts attacked us immediately above the airfield at Marfovka. By that time the *Chaykas* were taking off and we took them under our wings. We attempted to fly in the direction of Vladislavovka, but there we were also confronted by a large group of Fascist fighters."[43]

*Lt.* Hermann Graf, who participated in the interception of this formation, wrote: "Units from three *Geschwader* were airborne in the hazy sky over the front line. We forced the bombers to jettison their bombs. My *Staffel* was positioned low, and we drew plentiful ground fire while the fighter combat took place above our heads. Two Me 109s collided and fell in flames to the ground. The pilots baled out and landed in enemy territory. Then I could see a Russian aircraft going down."

At the outcome of this air battle, III./JG 52 claimed 17 Soviet aircraft shot down, five of which were credited to *Lt.* Graf.

Of this mission, *General-Mayor* Skripko concluded laconically: "Heavily outnumbered, the I-153 unit suffered severe losses."[44]

At noon on 8 May, seven Il-2s of 103 ShAP, commanded by the regimental commander *Podpolkovnik* Pavel Mironenko, managed to take off for an attack against German troops who had landed on the eastern shore of the bay at Feodosiya. Escort was provided by six Yak-1s of 795 IAP, led by *Kapitan* Dmitriy Kalarash. The Soviet airmen managed to reach the target area, but there they were attacked by Bf 109s of JG 52 and JG 77 and they were able to make just one swift pass at the troops on the ground. In the subsequent combat, three Il-2s and five Yak-1s were shot down. *Podpolkovnik* Mironenko survived being shot down and returned to the regiment on foot that evening, but *Starshiy Politruk* Ivan Aladinskiy and *M.Lt.* Iosif Shkinder were killed. Among the fighter pilots, only *Kapitan* Kalarash returned from that mission.

Soviet command and control was in a chaotic situation even before *Luftwaffe* bombs made things utterly disastrous. *General-Leytenant* Dmitriy Kozlov was the commander of the Crimean Front, but he was de facto controlled by Stalin's representative, the ruthless *Komissar Pervogo Ranga* Lev Mekhlis. In addition to this, *Marshal* Semyon Budyonny exerted overall control as C-in-C of the North Caucasus Theatre, to which the Crimean Front was subordinate. Also, the aviation of VVS ChF operated independently and was divided between 3 OAG in Sevastopol with the remainder at the Caucasian Black Sea ports.

As a consequence of this, Soviet air operations lacked any coordination. While VVS Crimean Front largely was kept on the ground through *Luftwaffe* activity over the Kerch Peninsula, VVS ChF's 3 OAG carried out "business as usual" – launching small groups of aircraft for nuisance raids against the airfields at Saki and Yevpatoria in the western Crimea, against German troop positions at Sevastopol, and against German floating vessels in the Budyonnovka area. At the same time, the Air Force of North Caucasus Front did not intervene at all in the Crimea, because Budyonny – apparently underestimating the severity of the situation – had ordered its units to focus on attacks against targets in the Mariupol area north of the Sea of Azov from 7 to 9 May. According to the official Soviet version, "the Command of the [Crimean] Front absolutely failed to effect coordination of ground and air forces. Our aviation operated outside the general plan of the defensive operation."[45]

When Budyonny learned of the German offensive at the Kerch Peninsula, he calmly ordered a counter-attack with four divisions supported by armour. But, as historian John Erickson points out, "there was no hope of carrying this out since the forward HQs, exposed and uncamouflaged, were obliterated by *Luftwaffe* dive-bombers."[46]

The 44th Army's attempts to regroup were completely shattered – the army front collapsed under the weight of this onslaught on the first day and fell back in headlong flight, while the German breakthrough forces turned north in order to surround Soviet 47th and 51st armies, which remained in position on the northern flank.

That evening, the staff of III./JG 52 drew up an astonishing summary of the achievement of their *Gruppe* on the first day of the offensive; it had lost only one Bf 109 – *Fw.* Alfred Grislawski had made a forced landing[47] – but had contributed no less than 47 kills to VIII. *Fliegerkorps*' total of 57 aerial victories on 8 May. Hermann Graf alone chalked up seven of these victories. The neighbouring *Gruppe*, *Hptm.* Johannes Steinhoff's II./JG 52, was less

Soviet fighter pilots in front of their I-16. Polikarpov's I-16 fighter earned itself several unofficial names. Called 'Ishak' ('Jackass') by the Soviets, the Germans knew it as the 'Rata' ('Rat') – a nickname it had obtained with the Nationalist forces during the Civil War in Spain in the late 1930s. The Republican pilots who flew it in the Spanish Civil War called it 'Mosca' ('Fly'). Although still fairly modern by world standards, the Soviets had initiated an extensive re-equipment programme to phase out the I-16 for more modern fighters just at the time when the German invasion struck in 1941. After mid-1942 only few Soviet fighter regiments retained the I-16. But it remained popular among the pilots who flew it. (Petrov)

fortunate: for only three victories, it lost five aircraft and three pilots on 8 May, including two in a mid-air collision during the combat with 36 IAP. In total, VIII. *Fliegerkorps* sustained a loss of 14 aircraft destroyed or damaged on 8 May. One of them, an He 111 of I./KG 55, was destroyed through a *taran*.

VIII. *Fliegerkorps* carried out 2,100 sorties over this small area on 8 May.

At midday on 9 May when German 28th Light Division seized Arma Eli, a stronghold six miles into the Soviet lines, the Crimean Front commanders realized that the situation was grave. All available tanks were pulled together and launched in a desperate counter-attack. VVS Crimean Front contributed with a mixed formation of twenty I-153s and I-15bis fighter-bombers, six MiG-3s, and a few I-16s and LaGG-3s. According to 36 IAP's Anatoliy Ivanov, "the entire aviation was launched to support our troops" at Arma Eli.[48]

Just as the biplane pilots initiated their individual low-level attacks, they were attacked from above by several formations of Bf 109s coming in from all directions: about forty Bf 109s from JG 52 and JG 77 intercepted the Soviet airmen in successive waves. "One could see '109s everywhere," Lt. Armin Köhler of I./JG 77 noted.[49]

The outcome of this encounter was another heavy defeat, with JG 52 and JG 77 claiming 22 victories without any losses.

Meanwhile, the ground-attack machines of SchG 1 went after anything that moved on the ground in the Soviet rear area. The Soviet armoured counter-attack was blown apart by Stuka attacks, and the SD 2 cluster bombs, which Hitler had instructed be used massively, mowed down large numbers of Red Army troops. The *Luftwaffe* airmen pressed home their attacks with such vigour that they struck at some of their own forwardmost troops – in error – at noon on 9 May.

"The sky was filled with [German] aircraft," Lt. Ivanov recalls. "The Fascist aviation kept coming in over our territory, bombing and strafing the ground troops." Since *Fliegerkorps* VIII had to concentrate more on supporting its ground troops on 9 May, small groups of Soviet fighters managed to take off throughout the day, and they inflicted mounting casualties on the *Luftwaffe* formations. "Two or four at a time, we were waging a desperate struggle with the enemy's fighters and bombers," in the words of Lt. Ivanov.[50]

Hence, seven I-16s of 486 IAP violently pounced on a group of Bf 109s and claimed five shot down. I./SchG 1 and II./JG 52 lost one Bf 109 apiece while Hptm. Johannes Steinhoff claimed an I-16 – his second victory of the day. I./JG 3 was hit even harder; four of its Bf 109s were shot down or made forced landings without any successes of its own. In II./St.G 77, two Ju 87s were knocked down, possibly by 45 IAP's Lt. Dmitriy Glinka, who claimed three Ju 87s on 9 May. The first Hs 129 B-1 to be lost in action was the aircraft piloted by Hptm. Max Eck, which was destroyed by AAA on 9 May.

The Soviet report of 35 German aircraft shot down on these two days is not far from reality: VIII. *Fliegerkorps* filed 23 total losses, plus 14 severely damaged on 8 and 9 May. In return, the Germans claimed 99 Soviet aircraft shot down during the same period. VVS Crimean Front's actual losses on 8-9 May were 48 aircraft.

But the Soviet air effort was negligible compared to the 1,700 sorties carried out by VIII. *Fliegerkorps* on 9 May. Moreover, VVS Crimean Front's C.O., *General-Major* Yevgeniy Nikolayenko – who had established his command post in a cave near Kerch – lost all radio contact with his units.

Supported by intense air attacks, an advance group of the German 132nd Infantry Division was able to race 30 miles to the east. It passed several shattered groups of retreating Soviet troops and reached Marfovka aerodrome in the afternoon of 9 May. A group of Hs 129s struck the airfield, destroying five aircraft on the ground. Hptm. Bruno Meyer, the *Staffelkapitän* of 4./SchG 1, described this attack:

"Our low-level strafing attacks left about forty aircraft blazing wrecks. One Hs 129 was even successful in aerial combat when for the first time an Hs 129 shot down an I-16. The remaining Soviet fighters, about thirty in all, were unable to get away before they were overrun by an advance party from a motorised brigade which had made a surprise push forward deep into enemy territory".[51]

*An I-16 comes in to land. The I-16 combined relatively high speed with a tremendous manoeuvrability. However, the Bf 109 was considerably faster, and the Soviets had already realized the need for a new generation of faster fighters prior to the German offensive. (Petrov)*

*The I-15bis, or I-152, was already obsolescent when it entered service in 1937. Reaching a top speed of 371 kph at 2,896 metres altitude, it was outclassed by most other fighters which went into production at that time. Thus it was soon succeeded by the modified I-153, which due to its retractable landing gear became one of the fastest biplane fighters ever. This photograph shows one of the I-15bis which remained in service in early 1942. (Karlenko)*

The 132nd Infantry Division was able to take advantage of the confusion which reigned on the Soviet side to seize the airfield, capturing thirty Soviet aircraft in the process. The attack came so unexpectedly that the Soviets believed paratroopers had been dropped.

Late in the afternoon of 9 May, the skies darkened and a heavy downfall started, saving the Soviets from German air strikes – but only temporarily. Instead, the rain turned all roads into quagmires, which hampered the retreat movements.

Reflecting the desperation on the Soviet side, 119 MRAP/VVS ChF despatched three MBR-2 flying boats to raid the German troops on 10 May. But when they reached the target area, the rain had stopped and the naval pilots were met by four Bf 109s. Only one MBR-2, piloted by the commander *Kapitan* Ilya Ilyin (later appointed Hero of the Soviet Union), returned to base.

From noon on 10 May, when the downfall had stopped, von Richthofen ordered an all-out attack against the congested Soviet columns that were stuck in the mud on the roads leading to the east. But the airfields in the Crimea had not dried up, so most units could only put a few aircraft into the air. In this situation, von Richthofen instructed the bomber units – which operated from airbases with concrete runways farther in the rear – to carry out low-level attacks. *Obstlt.* Benno Kosch, the *Geschwaderkommodore* of KG 55, knew that this was a very dangerous task. The slow and large He 111s offered good targets to ground fire, but the mission had to be carried out.

Trapped with their backs against the wall, the Soviet troops opened up with all they had against the swarms of He 111s that came droning in literally feet above their heads. The bombers flew into a veritable wall of bullets. *General* von Manstein noted that von Richthofen indeed "made terrific demands on the units under his command." KG 55 lost eight He 111s to ground fire on 10 May. But the situation was immensely worse on the ground, as the SD-2s dropped by the He 111s rained down. "The horrendous low-level

attacks turned the awesome confusion into regular panic," a Soviet report read.[52]

Flying in his Fi 156 Storch over the same area on the next day, when it was in German hands, *Generaloberst* von Richthofen was stunned by the level of destruction. "Terrible," he noted in his diary: "Corpse-strewn fields . . . I have never seen anything of the kind in this war."

Many years after the war, 743 IAP's *Mladshiy Lt.* Petr Polyam wrote, reflecting the bitterness which he still felt from those days at the Kerch Peninsula:

"The wounded men damned and cursed Kozlov and Mekhlis, who had sent them and their comrades to certain death and destruction only to please and report to Stalin that the armies were counter-attacking. I don't know who gave these orders, and who approved them, but in the eyes of these men I could see what they had gone through, and I could imagine the terrible nightmare on the open highway. Those responsible for the senseless butchering of the men of the Crimean Front should have deserved to be executed."[53]

Other German bombers attacked Soviet shipping in the Straits of Kerch and sank the transport ship *Chernomorets* (1048 GRT).

The pilots of VVS Crimean Front fought hard to the end. "Early in the morning we were already in the air," *Lt.* Ivanov described the action on 11 May. "Just as we were taking off we were caught up in combat with ten or twenty enemy aircraft. That day we fought particularly fiercely to defend the retreating ground troops." 4./JG 52 lost three pilots in combat on 11 May, while II./JG 77 had three Bf 109Fs shot down or force-landed.

On 12 May *Lt.* Hermann Graf scored his 90th victory on his last mission over the Crimea. Later that day his 9./JG 52 was shifted to the Kharkov area to help counter the powerful Soviet tank offensive that had been launched in this area. In two weeks of action in the Crimean skies, this *Staffel* had scored 93 victories without loss.

By 14 May the Soviet troops were squeezed into an increasingly narrow area at Kerch. *Lt.* Ivanov describes the situation:

"In the harbour at Kerch there was such congestion of troops that there was hardly any space to move. Along a ten-mile stretch, the coast was littered with men and equipment. There were very few regular ships available, so tugs, barges, motor boats, and small craft arrived and lay waiting 100 to 200 yards from the docks. The soldiers jumped into the water and started swimming.

Several men made primitive rafts or used tyre inner tubes in attempting to cross the straits, but the current carried them to Kamysh-Burun, where the Germans were. Wave after wave of Fascist aircraft bombed and strafed the crossings without interruption."

Following bitter house-to-house fighting with heavy losses on both sides, Kerch finally fell into German hands on 20 May.

A total of 116,405 Soviets would be evacuated across the Straits of Kerch, but another 162,282 were left behind – dead or captured.[54]

## Aces over the Straits of Kerch

A major reason for the very heavy losses inflicted on the Soviet Air Force in World War II was the large number of exceptionally experienced German fighter pilots serving on the Eastern Front. This was particularly the case during the final battle of Kerch in the latter half of May 1942, when two young fighter pilots of I./JG 77 – *Hptm.* Gordon Gollob and *Hptm.* Heinz Bär – together racked up virtually half the Soviet losses in the air. Their achievements occurred as the bulk of the German fighter units in the Crimea – I./JG 3 and all of JG 52 – had been shifted to the Kharkov area, and the Soviets made determined efforts to take control of the air over Kerch.

On 12 May Josef Stalin called *General-Mayor* Nikolay Skripko, the deputy commander of the ADD, and ordered him to assume command of what remained of VVS Crimean Front. VVS Crimean Front's C.O., *General-Mayor* Yevgeniy Nikolayenko was removed from his command. Skripko's task was to organize the elements of VVS Crimean Front which had managed to escape to the eastern side of the Straits of Kerch into an air offensive over Kerch. For this purpose, he also was assigned with two ADD *Divizii* for nocturnal missions, and 113 AD – equipped with 45 Il-4s and around 20 I-16s for operations by day.

Stalin feared that the Germans would follow up their success on the Kerch Peninsula with an immediate landing on the other side of the Straits of Kerch, thus threatening the Caucasian oil fields. He could not know that in accordance with German planning, this would not follow until much later. Skripko's air offensive over the Straits of Kerch was launched on 15 May and its impact was immediately felt by the Germans. On 15 May KG 55 lost three He 111s, and a Ju 88 of II./KG 51 was badly shot-up by Soviet fighters.

This was the situation when *Hptm.* Gordon Gollob and *Hptm.* Heinz Bär began their run of success. Both were very experienced veterans and arrived from other sectors of the Eastern Front. In April 1942, Gollob had been tutored in the role of *Geschwaderkommodore* by JG 54's *Major* Hannes Trautloft, and had achieved his 86th victory on 30 April.[1] His previous victories had been attained with ZG 76 and II./JG 3 between 1939 and 1941. In October 1941 Gollob had been awarded the Oak Leaves to the Knight's Cross. Without question, he was one of the *Luftwaffe's* most skilful fighter aces of the entire war. The same can be said of Heinz Bär, who was likewise an Oak Leaves recipient. Bär's victory tally stood at 91 when he was posted from IV./JG 51 on the Moscow Front to take charge of I./JG 77 in the Crimea.

Bär arrived on 11 May, and two days later Gollob was introduced to the front by JG 77's departing *Geschwaderkommodore, Major* Gotthard Handrick – who in turn was sent to Norway to assume command of JG 5.[2] On 14 May, Gollob wrote in his diary:

"Together with Handrick, I flew to several airfields close to the front line. A fierce battle is raging in the Kerch area! The sweetish stench of dead bodies makes a terrible smell even high in the air in our Fieseler Storch. … We are met with a view of the most terrible destruction on the ground."

On 16 May Gollob and Bär displayed their abilities by respectively shooting down three and two LaGG-3s – Gollob taking his victory total to 89 and Bär to 93.

During the following night, Skripko's bombers subjected JG 77's airfield at Bagerovo to a heavy attack. "A dreadful night", wrote *Lt.* Armin Köhler of I./JG 77 in his diary. "The Russians are bombing us from dusk to dawn."[3]

But by day the German fighters were without peer. On 17 May Gollob claimed three R-5 biplanes. Soon afterwards, he and his wingman came across a formation of Soviet fighters.

In contrast to the common fighter tactic of attacking from above, Gollob preferred low-side attacks – as a means of ensuring that no one tried to attack him from the blind spot beneath his fighter. An anonymous pilot of JG 77 wrote the following account after witnessing Gollob and his wingman applying this tactic: "They positioned themselves at a low altitude beneath the Russian formation.

Then they started climbing in spirals, carefully maintaining their position beneath the enemy formation. Before the Russians even suspected any mischief, the two aircraft at the bottom of their formation had been shot down and the two Germans were gone."[4]

Gollob hit the Soviet fighter – a LaGG, he thought – in the belly, saw it go down, and returned home to report his 93rd victory. When Gollob returned to base, he learned that Bär meanwhile had bagged an I-16 and two Polikarpov fighter biplanes.

The next night, Skripko's bombers were in action against German airfields again. However, with their inadequate night bombing aids they failed to inflict any serious material damage on the ground. But they did manage to deprive the German airmen of their sleep, and with intense Soviet air activity around the clock, this wore down many of the *Luftwaffe* pilots. On 18 May, *Lt.* Köhler penned the following entry in his diary;

"We are airborne for our first mission as early as 03:30 hrs. We fly all day long and at night there is no sleep. I can't take much more of this – It's like I'm being driven mad. During my last mission today we came across twelve MiGs and *Ratas*. A fierce combat ensued which raged all the way across the Tamanskaya Straits and down to just above the waves."[5]

By this stage the ground battle was concentrated in the north-eastern tip of the Kerch Peninsula and around the city of Kerch itself. All available Soviet aircraft, including many R-5 and R-Z biplanes intended for night operations, crossed the Straits to intervene against the victorious Germans. Gollob was in constant action over the Straits, bringing down six of these same biplanes on 18 and 19 May.

It was evident that Gollob and Bär would soon become the next German fighter pilots to reach their 100-victory milestone. In order to be present to celebrate these events, *Oberst* Adolf Galland, the inspector of the *Jagdwaffe*, arrived at Bagerovo on 18 May. Galland had personally recommended that Gollob be appointed a *Geschwaderkommodore* – although he only held the rank of a *Hptm.* – and he was a personal friend of 'Pritzl' Bär.

Unusually for the *Luftwaffe's* top aces, who were fiercely competitive, Gollob allowed Bär to surpass him and enter the records as the ninth fighter pilot to reach the 100-victory mark. As Gollob recorded in his diary: "I refrained from reporting four victories – I'm not keen on reaching my hundredth so fast, since I fear that my superiors are likely to ground me afterwards."[6]

On 19 May Bär claimed an R-5 biplane during a morning sortie. This was recorded as his 99th victory. Immediately his Bf 109 F-4 was replenished with fuel and ammunition and he took off again. He spotted a formation of I-16s, and in less than ten minutes he claimed four of these shot down – for victories 100 to 103. Gollob was pleased to note that his JG 77 surpassed its 2,000-victory mark the same day. On 20 May, Gollob set out for a free hunt sortie over the Taman Peninsula on the opposite side of the Straits of Kerch, and blew up an Il-4 of 113 AD and a LaGG-3 out of the sky, and finally 'filed' his 100th and 101st victories. Quite symbolically, this marked the end of the battle of Kerch. The entry in Gollob's personal diary for the next day reads:

"It seems to be over at Kerch. XI. *Armee* is regrouping for the attack on Sevastopol." On 21 May, Gollob was summoned to Saki to discuss the air-support operation for the coming offensive against Sevastopol with *Oberst* Wolfgang von Wild, the commander of *Fliegerführer Süd*.

[1.] Hannes Trautloft, Personal Diary, 30 April 1942.
[2.] Gordon Gollob, Personal Diary, 13 May 1942.
[3.] Quoted in Prien, *Geschichte des Jagdgeschwaders 77*, p. 1012.
[4.] Ibid., p. 1018
[5.] Quoted in Ibid., p. 1018.
[6.] Gordon Gollob, Personal diary, 21 June 1942.

The Germans reported that 170,000 prisoners had been taken, but this figures includes a large number of civilians.

Soviet aircraft losses during the Battle of the Kerch Peninsula in May 1942 amounted to 417.[55] VVS Crimean Front recorded 315 aircraft lost in May 1942 – including 148 shot down or missing in action, eight in accidents and the remainder either destroyed on airfields or abandoned during the retreat.[56]

The disaster was the combined result of Stalin's refusal to evacuate the impossible positions on the Kerch Peninsula in time in combination with the confusion which prevailed in Soviet command and control plus, of course, inferior equipment and the crisis of resupply on the Soviet side. But instead of admitting his own responsibility, Stalin reacted by turning his fury against the military commanders. He immediately dropped Mekhlis, who had been one of the Soviet dictator's favourites, and demoted him to corps commissar. *General-Mayor* Kozlov and the Crimean Front's VVS commander, *General-Mayor* Nikolayenko, also were demoted and dismissed.

Hitler now was free to concentrate all his forces on the next preparatory steps before Operation 'Blue'.

# Chapter Five

# The Kharkov Cauldron

A cursory study of the war in the East may give the impression that the Germans were forced to rapidly shift a large part of the *Luftwaffe* presence in the Crimea to the Kharkov area when the Soviets launched their offensive in this sector. This is true only to a limited extent. In fact, even prior to the launch of the offensive against the Kerch Peninsula, the Germans had prepared the transfer of these units to the Kharkov area on 17 May. The only difference was that the Soviet offensive forced the first of these units to be moved northwards five days earlier.

As has already been discussed, the Germans planned a preparatory offensive in the Izyum sector following the successful conclusion of the 'mopping-up' operation in the Kerch Peninsula. But they also were aware of Soviet plans to stage a major attack in this area.

On 1 May, the OKW's intelligence organization for the Eastern Front, *Fremde Heere Ost,* submitted a report pointing out that the movements of the Soviet 28th Army and the development of the Soviet 6th and 38th Armies seemed to indicate an imminent Soviet attack against Kharkov and in the Izyum bulge.

At a conference with his highest military commanders in late March 1942, Stalin complained about the reluctance of the western Allies to open a 'second front' and foresaw a new German major offensive after the spring thaws – the conference discussed means of countering this offensive.

*Marshal Sovetskogo Soyuza* Boris Shaposhnikov, the *Stavka* chief-of-staff, was of the opinion that the defence needed to be flexible and that the bulk of the reserves should be grouped around Voronezh. *General Armii* Georgiy Zhukov repeated what he had proposed in January – concentrate the core of the Red Army for an offensive to the west of Moscow while the rest of the front line maintained a defensive posture. But Stalin did not want to listen to Zhukov, and sneered: "We can't remain on the defensive and only wait for the enemy to strike; we have to launch a preventive offensive on a broad front!"

*Marshal Sovetskogo Soyuza* Semyon Timoshenko seized the opportunity to propose a South-western Front offensive and had the backing of Peoples' Commissar *Marshal Sovetskogo Soyuza* Kliment Voroshilov. This was what the Soviet dictator wished to hear, and he instructed Timoshenko to develop a plan for such an offensive.

On 10 April Timoshenko sent a proposal for the operation to the *Stavka*, which adopted a revised version on 28 April. This plan called for a pincer movement against the German positions around Kharkov. The northern pincer would be formed by the South-western Front's 21st and 28th Armies which would attack from the bridgehead across the Donets which had been established to the east of Kharkov. The southern pincer would consist of the 6th Army and the ad hoc army-sized group called 'Army Group Bobkin', which would strike from within the 80-mile deep westward bulge which had been created to the south of Kharkov through the January offensive. These forces of the South-western Front would be supported by the Southern Front's 9th and 57th Armies, which were tasked to tie up the German troops south of the bulge.

To carry out the operation, the South-western and Southern Fronts received considerable reinforcements. These included a new so-called 'Manoeuvrable Air Group' (*Manyovrennaya Aviagruppa*), which enabled a more flexible use of the air assets. Fedor Falaleyev, the commander of VVS South-western Front, who had recently been promoted to *General-Leytenant,* had seen the effect of the improvised cooperation between elements of his Air Force and the aviation of the Southern Front during the offensive which led to the liberation of Rostov in November 1941. He had proposed the forming of an air groupment which was not so strictly tied to individual ground armies or even a certain Front.[57] Thus the Manoeuvrable Air Group preceded the reformation which VVS KA went through in May 1942. (See page 23 Restructuring the Soviet Air Force.)

On the eve of the offensive, the attack forces mustered a total of 640,000 men, 1,200 tanks, 13,000 guns and mortars and 926 aircraft. For the first time, Soviet armour would operate in tight armoured formations, similar to the German Panzer spearheads, and these would be provided with massive support from Il-2 *Shturmoviks.*

12 May was set for the opening day for the offensive. Soviet aviation would play an important role from the onset. On 9 May, the ADD initiated a series of night attacks against German rail junctions – starting with an attack by 55 bombers against the railway junction at Kharkov. This was repeated the following night, when Il-4 crews of the ADD's 3 AD, 17 AD and 24 AD, and heavy bombers of 717 TBAP and 746 TBAP went into action against the same target.

## Reinforcing VVS South-western Front

In April 1942 *General-Mayor* Vasiliy Ryazanov's Manoeuvrable Air Group (MAG YuZF; *Manyovrennaya Aviagruppa Yugo-Zapadnogo Fronta*) was set up to reinforce VVS South-western Front. MAG YuZF was composed of four fighter regiments (6 IAP, 186 IAP, 273 IAP and 512 IAP), two *Shturmovik* regiments (285 ShAP and 619 ShAP), and two bomber regiments (10 GBAP and 52 BAP). All of these were new in VVS South-western Front.

In addition to MAG YuZF, *General-Leytenant* Fedor Falaleyev's VVS South-western Front was composed of the following units on 1 May 1942:

*Polkovnik* Mikhail Borisenko's 4 RAG (Reserve Aviation Group) with three regiments (148 IAP, 431 ShAP and 99 BAP).
VVS 6th Army with four fighter regiments (23, 92, 181 and 296 IAP), 134 GBAP and the two light bomber regiments 623 and 633 LBAP.

VVS 21st Army with four regiments (43 IAP, 135 BBAP, 596 LBAP and 47 OKAE).
VVS 28th Army with 2 IAP and 709 LBAP.
VVS 38th Army with three regiments (164 IAP, 282 IAP and 598 LBAP).
In addition, the headquarters of the South-western Front had the two reconnaissance regiments 90 OKAE and 91 OKAE.

The next stage in these preparatory air attacks started on 11 May, through a series of air strikes against German airfields in the Kharkov area. These were carried out by Il-2s and Pe-2s of MAG YuZF and 4 RAG throughout the day. By that time, the *Luftwaffe* had only one *Jagdgruppe* in the Ukraine, III./JG 77, and its Bf 109s were unable to penetrate the strong shield offered by the escorting Soviet fighters. A formation of 282 IAP I-16s came under violent attack by the Bf 109s of III./JG 77 and lost five aircraft, but these were the only losses sustained during all Soviet air operations over Kharkov on 11 May.[58]

At 07.30 hrs early the next day, 12 May, the Soviet ground offensive was launched, supported throughout the day by 563 combat sorties by the aviation of the South-western Front. Heavily outnumbered, the Bf 109 pilots of III./JG 77 fought desperately to relieve their ground troops from incessant attacks from the air. Near Tetlega, ten Bf 109s attacked 282 IAP and shot down two I-16s.[59] But apart from this, III./JG 77's results were meagre on 12 May – two LaGG-3s from 2 IAP and a LaGG-3 from 512 IAP shot down, against its own losses of three Bf 109s and two pilots. The Soviets were easily able to take control of the skies above the battle area.

In particular the repeated *Shturmovik* attacks against the German front lines during the first days of the Soviet offensive had a negative impact on the morale of the German ground troops.[60] At this stage, the Germans had only the bombers of KG 51 and II./KG 55 of *General* Kurt Pflugbeil's IV. *Fliegerkorps* for air support against the Soviet ground troops. Between Kharkov and Belgorod on the northern flank – with Staryy Saltov as the crucial centre – Soviet 21st, 28th and 38th Armies penetrated the German lines and advanced between three and ten miles. Inside the bulge south of Kharkov the attack forces broke through the German lines at Bereka, halfway between Krasnograd and Balakleya.

From 13 May, strong *Luftwaffe* reinforcements started to arrive from the Crimea. Among the first was III./JG 52, which included *Lt.* Hermann Graf's élite *Karayastaffel*, 9./JG 52. Within 48 hours, the pilots of III./JG 52 were able to completely alter the situation in the air. That morning, a group of 8./JG 52 pilots came across the I-16s of 282 IAP and LaGG-3s of 164 IAP and claimed five shot down for no losses – four of which were recorded as *Lt.* Adolf Dickfeld's 76th through 79th victories. Actual Soviet losses were three aircraft. Two hours later, *Lt.* Hermann Graf led his 9./JG 52 *Schwarm* on a free hunt mission and they reported seven victories – four by Graf and three by *Lt.* Fritz Brückmann.

Two hours later, the 7./JG 52 *Rotte* of *Ofw.* Josef Zwernemann and *Uffz.* Hans Dammers engaged a group of Soviet fighters and claimed two each shot down – filed as Zwernemann's 46th and 47th and Dammers' 20th and 21st victories. Soviet records show that their opponents were LaGG-3s of 512 IAP, and *Starshiy Leytenants* Gennadiy Dubenok, Ivan Motornyy and Valentin Makarov were shot down.[61]

In total, III./JG 52 claimed to have shot down 42 Soviet aircraft on 13 May 1942. By bagging six each, Graf and Dickfeld reached a total of 97

and 81 respectively. Actual Soviet losses were only about half the total claimed by III./JG 52 but still represented a mauling for the VVS units. Quite interestingly, 512 IAP's *St.Lt.* Gennadiy Dubenok, who survived being shot down by either *Ofw.* Zwernemann or *Uffz.* Dammers of 7./JG 52, was downed again the following day[62] – apparently by *Uffz.* Dammers, as a comparison between Soviet and German records shows.

During the hours of darkness, Soviet aircraft continued to operate, with Il-4 crews of the ADD's 24 AD and 50 AD defying adverse meteorological conditions the following night to bomb concentrations of German armour and motorised infantry.

On 14 May, *Marshal* Timoshenko had all of Soviet 6th Army's aviation transferred towards the northern flank in an attempt to use concentrated air power to achieve a quick decision. But 14 May was the day when the situation in the air over the Kharkov area definitely swung in the Germans' favour. For III./JG 52, the day opened with Stuka escort missions and low-level attacks against Soviet artillery positions at dawn.[63] Shortly afterward, *Lt.* Graf reported two Su-2s shot down – of which one, from 13 GBAP, can be confirmed through Soviet documents.[64] Thus Graf achieved his 100th victory, becoming the seventh pilot of the war to reach this mark.

The operational records for *Lt.* Dickfeld on 14 May are quite indicative of the ferocity of the fighting in the air on 14 May. The Soviet combat report for Dickfeld's first combat on 14 May reads: "At 10.45 hrs in the Staryy Saltov area, five Yak-1s led by *Eskadrilya* commander *Kapitan* Gusarov [of 6 IAP] clashed with [eight Bf 109s] at an altitude of 2,000 metres."[65] During this combat, Dickfeld recorded his 82nd and 83rd victories (erroneously identified as 'MiG-1s', while the Soviets mistook the Bf 109s for 'He 113' and 'Me 115').

Shortly afterwards, *Lt.* Dickfeld took off for a fighter sweep in his 'White 13' with *Uffz.* Johannes Noe as wingman in 'White 3'. Over the front line they spotted four Il-2s attacking German troop positions and, according to his own account, Dickfeld shot down two. (Although another source asserts that these aircraft were claimed as 'MiG-1s',[66] this is probably incorrect, since the loss of these Il-2s can be confirmed through Soviet records.[67]) Prien goes on to assert in his *Die Jagdfliegerverbände der Deutschen Luftwaffe*, that this was the end of the mission, but Dickfeld's own account described how he continued his fighter patrol and came across a single-engined Soviet biplane which he set burning for his 86th victory. Again, this can be matched with Soviet records – which show the loss of an R-5,[68] although Dickfeld erroneously identified it as an 'I-153'.

Turning for home, Dickfeld and Noe spotted an SB which Dickfeld promptly shot down. Dickfeld had barely made his report after landing at Kharkov-Rogan before a Soviet air attack struck the base. "Overhead was a swarm of aircraft, Tupolev SB 2 bombers, I-16 *Rata* fighters and then, at low level, a gaggle of Il-2s," recalled Dickfeld. "The air was filled with howling and screaming aircraft which raced over the airfield. I lay on the ground and made myself as flat as possible. More than anything I would like to have disappeared into the earth. Only now did our alarm sirens begin to howl. The idiots had been asleep; even our quadruple Flak remained silent. *Ofw.* Steinbatz's machine blazed fiercely."[69]

That afternoon, the four aces *Lt.* Adolf Dickfeld, *Lt.* Hermann Graf, *Lt.* Fritz Brückmann and *Fw.* Alfred Grislawski took off for a free hunt sortie. Hermann Graf later wrote this account: "At around 2,000 metres altitude we spotted a bomber formation consisted of Pe-2s escorted by about eight MiG-1s. We immediately attacked the enemy formation. I saw *Fw.* Grislawski position himself behind a MiG-1 and then he opened fire obliquely from the rear. The MiG-1 went down in a shallow dive and crashed into the ground, exploding on impact."[70]

Dickfeld, Graf and Brückmann each claimed two Soviet aircraft shot down. "As the air combat continued, I saw a MiG-1 which tried to escape towards the east," Alfred Grislawski recalled. "Following my first burst of fire obliquely from above, parts were torn off from the aircraft. After my second burst it descended and crashed into the ground."[71]

Most Soviet air units were handicapped by the low training standards of novice pilots, and this was particularly felt when the opponents were of such quality as in the combat described above. Afterwards, the Pe-2 crews of 99 BBAP reported that seeking refuge in the clouds offered more reliable protection against German fighters than the cover which the escorting MiG-3s of 148 IAP were able to provide.[72]

More *Luftwaffe* reinforcements arrived from the Crimea and immediately went into action. Ju 87s of St.G 77, Ju 88s and He 111s of KG 51, KG 55, I./KG 76 and I./KG 77, and the ground-attack aircraft of

On 19 May 1942 III./JG 3 scored its first two victories against Soviet fighters in the Battle of Kharkov. These were claimed by the aces Oblt. Viktor Bauer, the 9. Staffel's

commander, and Ofw. Georg Schentke, who scored their 52nd and 45th victories respectively. This photograph shows Bauer's Bf 109 F-4, 'Yellow 7', probably in May 1942.

SchG 1 began to fill the skies above the battlefield. On 15 May, the Chief of the *General* Staff of the German Army, *Generaloberst* Franz Halder, wrote in his diary that "the force of the attack appears to have been broken by the efforts of our *Luftwaffe*."[73]

Following desperate calls from hard-pressed ground troops, the Soviet fighter units were instructed on 15 May to "clear the skies from German bombers." When, early on 15 May, 9./JG 52's *Fw.* Alfred Grislawski and *Uffz.* Fritz Hahn escorted a small group of four II./KG 51 Ju 88s towards Novaya Vodolaga, they found themselves the target of an unusually strong Soviet fighter interception – carried out by eight LaGG-3s of 181 IAP. In their first surprise strike, the Soviets managed to score hits on one of the Ju 88s, killing one of the gunners and causing the Germans to jettison their bombs. In a matter of moments, the two German fighter pilots had turned the tables. Grislawski and Hahn each shot down one of the

Lt. Adolf Dickfeld of III./JG 52 was one of the most successful German fighter aces on the Eastern Front in 1942 and is photographed on 14 May that year, when he shot down nine enemy aircraft. On 18 May, he destroyed 11 aircraft, bringing his score to 100 victories. He was a strong rival to Lt. Hermann Graf in terms of aerial victories. Following the Battle at the Kharkov Cauldron in May 1942, both were called to meet Hitler, where Graf was awarded with the Swords and Dickfeld with the Oak Leaves to the Knight's Cross.

LaGG-3s – with *M.Lt.* A. Sayko and *Starshina* F. Ponomarev baling out of their blazing fighters.

Led by *Kapitan* Ivan Pilipenko, six I-16s from 40 IAP subjected I./KG 55's He 111s to a violent attack on the *Kampfgruppe's* very first mission in the Kharkov area. As a result of the 20-minute combat, the Soviet pilots claimed to have shot down six He 111s, while the Germans recorded three He 111s shot down.[74] The war diary of I./KG 55 noted that "Russian fighters had rarely appeared in such force as they had over this sector of the front."[75]

However, due to the past days' heavy losses, the Soviet air units had become pretty worn down at this stage. Thus, for instance, 164 IAP had only three serviceable LaGG-3s on 15 May – a reduction from 12 five days before – and 282 IAP had six serviceable I-16s. The Soviet commanders tried to compensate for the diminishing number of serviceable aircraft by forcing the pilots to fly more missions, but this only further increased the severe strain on the airmen's nerves.[76]

That the increasing burden on the Soviet airmen also took a toll on their stamina was witnessed by 16 GIAP's *Kapitan* Aleksandr Pokryshkin during a mission at that time. On this occasion, 16 GIAP was instructed to escort nine Su-2s against German troop positions at Izyum. Pokryshkin led two Yak-1s as close escort to the bombers, while another four were placed as top cover. To his despair, Pokryshkin saw that the Su-2s dispersed their formation after completing their bombing attack. In that moment, eight Bf 109s emerged from the cloud cover to perform a diving attack against the Soviet aircraft.

The Soviet pilots panicked, for the nine Su-2s scattered in all directions, while the four Yak-1s of the top cover formation vanished. Pokryshkin and his wingman were left alone to defend a widely separated group of departing bombers. Only by recklessly charging the Bf 109s were the two Yak-1s able to save the Su-2s. Pokryshkin managed to knock down what he assumed was the German unit leader's Bf 109. According to Pokryshkin´s account, the other Bf 109s chose to disengage.

After his return to base, the furious Pokryshkin sought out the four top cover pilots. "What were you doing hiding in the clouds?" he exclaimed. "We were looking for the Messerschmitts," one of the pale-faced pilots replied. "Next time anyone leaves his position during a combat he will be punished severely," Pokryshkin yelled. "I promise you that I will deal with him as a traitor!"

"This could not continue," Pokryshkin later wrote. "The poor performance of my *Eskadrilya* today was far from the courage and determination with which we had fought in 1941."[77]

Meanwhile, the German fighter force was further reinforced through II./JG 52 – which on 14 May was transferred from the Crimea via Zaporozhye to Kharkov-Voychen. *Kommandeur* of this unit was *Hptm.* Johannes Steinhoff, a veteran with 53 kills on his scoreboard. At 04.40 hrs on 15 May, Steinhoff took off for his first combat mission in the Kharkov sector, and shot down *St. Lt.* Zakhar Semenyuk's 512 IAP LaGG-3 in a combat at 2000 metres altitude, thus recording his 54th victory.[78]

On 16 May, the next German *Jagdgruppe*, I./JG 3, became operational in the Kharkov area. The *Luftwaffe* was in almost total control of the air when the Germans launched their counter-attack – in reality the planned Operation 'Fridericus I' – on 17 May. The provisional Army Group Kleist – the 1st *Panzerarmee* and the 17th Army – struck against Soviet 9th Army on the southern shoulder of the Soviet bulge at Slavyansk, and advanced towards the north.

While Army Group Kleist attacked from the south, German VI. *Armee* attacked on the opposite side of the bulge in a classic pincer operation. A large tank battle developed in the Volchansk area, north-east of Kharkov. Inside the bulge, Krasnograd became the focus for ground combat. Thus, four major battles were fought simultaneously. In each sector, German counter-attacks with strong backing by Stukas and ground-attack aircraft forced the Red Army on to the back foot. On 17 May alone, the Stukas claimed the destruction of 54 Soviet tanks. Meanwhile, the bomber crews of IV. *Fliegerkorps* carried out an average of seven daily sorties against supply lines from the Kupyansk area. These air attacks not only blocked the Soviet supply lines across the Donets River between Izyum and Balakleya, but also severed all telephone communications between the South-western Front's headquarters and the 9th and 57th Armies. Thus the preconditions were created for a successful envelopment of Timoshenko's forces inside the bulge.

VVS South-western Front was reinforced through the arrival of *General-Mayor* Aleksandr Borman's new 220 IAD with 429 IAP, 791 IAP and 792 IAP. *General-Leytenant* Falaleyev, the commander of VVS South-western Front, realized that the weakness of his forces was the lack of bombers. Also, the *Shturmovik* units were too few and were hampered by low serviceability. In this situation, he saw no other option but to deploy his fighter planes on ground-attack missions against the advancing German troops who threatened to envelop elements of South-western Front. For this purpose Falaleyev ordered the fighters to be equipped with RS-82 rocket projectiles. But also there were too few fighters available – and, above all, too many German fighters in the skies! The rocket projectiles and their racks underneath the wings of the aircraft made the Soviet fighters heavy and cumbersome in combat with the Bf 109s.

On 17 May, the Bf 109 pilots of III./JG 52 claimed 12 Soviet fighters shot down for no losses other than a damaged Bf 109. In II./JG 52, *Gruppenkommandeur Hptm.* Steinhoff, attained his 55th kill by shooting down a 'MiG-1' from 2,500 metres altitude at 09.27 hrs.[79] Five of the claims can be identified as LaGG-3s of 791 IAP.

The ADD was brought in as a kind of 'fire brigade', and around 70 night bombers of 3 AD and 17 AD were dispatched against the railway junctions at Poltava, Kharkov, Vyazma and Smolensk on the night of 18 May. Meanwhile 24 AD attacked the German airfield at Stalino, and 50 AD bombed the port installations at Mariupol. But since these operations were carried out in darkness, with the still inadequate night bombing devices, none of the operations had any decisive influence on the German offensive.

The Soviet air attacks had to be carried out in daylight if there was to be any hope of bombing accuracy, but the *Luftwaffe's* supremacy in the air

*The fighter pilot Ganichkin of 18 IAP climbs out of his LaGG-3 following a combat mission. The strain of combat is clearly visible in the airman's face. (Karlenko)*

made this task extremely difficult. At this stage, South-western Front's aviation was hunted both in the air and on the ground. The records of VVS 6th Army show two air attacks against Malaya Kamyshevakha aerodrome on 15 and 17 May, one against the airfield at Brigadirovka on 18 May, and a series of daily Ju 88 dive-bombings of Levkovka aerodrome from 16 May to 19 May.

The German aim to envelop the Red Army forces in the bulge were greatly aided by Stalin's inability to realize that the South-western Front rapidly had to switch to the defensive. Instead, the Soviet dictator demanded that the armies continued their offensive operations, while becoming increasingly outflanked by the advancing German troops. Throughout 18 May, the Soviet troops were subjected to an intense bombardment from the air, and the *Luftwaffe* units reportedly put 130 tanks and 500 other vehicles out of commission. The next day, the air units of IV. *Fliegerkorps* were reported to have destroyed or damaged 29 tanks.

The Soviet efforts to support their hard-pressed troops from the air became increasingly hopeless. Early on 19 May, twelve Yak-1s of 429 IAP took off to escort the Su-2s of 13 GBAP on a mission against the German troops. Before they had even reached the front lines, the Soviet airmen were attacked by several formations of Bf 109s. The subsequent combat dispersed the Su 2 formation and cost 429 IAP the loss of four Yak-1s.

The German fighters were from II. and III./JG 52, where *Hptm.* Johannes Steinhoff claimed two 'MiG-1s' and *Fw.* Willi Nemitz and *Uffz.* Hans Dammers bagged one each.[80] Note: This contradicts Prien et al, *Die Jagdfliegerverbände der Deutschen Luftwaffe, Teil 9/II,* p. 481, which asserts that Steinhoff claimed a 'MiG-1' at 08.35 hrs and an Il-2 at 14.55 hrs. However, the entries in Steinhoff's logbook show that he landed at 08.15 hrs, following a free hunt sortie which resulted in "air combat with 10 MiG-1s" and "2 MiG-1s shot down".

That day, too, *Jagdgruppe,* III./JG 3, drew its first blood in the Battle of Kharkov.

With VVS South-western Front in shambles, 4 VA – formerly VVS Southern Front – was called in. But 4 VA's units were in no better shape. By this time 4 VA's *Shturmovik* regiments – 7 GShAP, 210 ShAP and 590 ShAP – could muster altogether less than 20 serviceable Il-2s.[81]

Furthermore, the actions suffered from lack of coordination. 4 VA's poor contribution is revealed in its own statistics: between 1 and 20 May, its units claimed to have shot down 27 enemy aircraft and lost 32 of its own aircraft.[82]

On 20 May, von Kleist's attack force had reduced the mouth of the bulge to less than 15 miles. From that day on, the *Luftwaffe* raids against the Donets River crossings in the area were intensified in order to block the evacuation of the Soviet troops from the bulge. On 20 May alone, the Ju 87s of St.G 77 blew up five of the main Donets bridges in this area and damaged another four. Ju 88s of KG 3 also participated in these raids, leaving scores of burned-out vehicles on the roads in this area.

On 21 May Timoshenko made a desperate attempt to halt the German advance from the south by launching a strike against von Kleist's flank at Izyum. All available Soviet fighters were concentrated in an effort to break the *Luftwaffe's* dominance in the air, but with JG 52's *Stabsstaffel* and another two German *Jagdgruppen* joining the battle – II./JG 3 and I./JG 52 – this task was doomed to failure. IV. *Fliegerkorps* sustained no more than six aircraft losses on both 21 and 22 May.

On 23 May the gates closed behind the Soviet 6th and 57th Armies, plus the army-sized 'Operation Group Bobkin,' in the bulge to the south of Kharkov. Increased *Luftwaffe* activity, rather than improved Soviet resistance in the air, explains the slight rise to eleven aircraft losses sustained by IV. *Fliegerkorps* on that day.

*Three pilots of 2 IAP in early May 1942:*
*P. I. Dzyuba, I. I. Mogilevits and A. V.Shashko.*
*Commanded by Podpolkovnik Aleksandr*
*Grisenko, 2 IAP was subordinated to VVS*
*South-western Front and saw extensive*
*action during the Battle of Kharkov.*
*I. I. Mogilevits was killed in combat on*
*29 May 1942. Dzyuba survived and was*
*credited with one individual and six shared*
*victories and was appointed a Hero of the*
*Soviet Union in 1943. (Karlenko)*

suffer. By 23 May, the three regiments of 4 RAG (148 IAP, 431 ShAP and 99 BAP) had lost 27 aircraft and 35 airmen since the opening of the battle.

On 25 May, the Germans noted a markedly increased presence of Il-2s in the battle. 820 ShAP was instructed to commit all aircraft to attacks against German troops in the Barvenkovo - Maryovka - Petrovskaya area, and 429 IAP provided fighter escort. During these attacks, 820 ShAP claimed to have destroyed or damaged ten tanks and around 100 other motor vehicles.[84]

II./SchG 1 lost four of its new Hs 129s to Soviet ground fire on 23 May 1942, but this did not prevent the unit from taking part with great success in what was to be "one of the bloodiest actions of the whole war in the East"[83] on 24-25 May, as the Soviet forces tried to break out of their encirclement. Caught in the open fields, the Soviet troops were mowed down in masses. "Even when we flew at 4,000 metres altitude above the battlefield we could feel the stench of decaying corpses on the battlefield below," recalled 9./JG 52's *Fw.* Alfred Grislawski.

The Soviets renewed their attempts to save the situation through intensified air operations, and 820 ShAP and 94 BAP arrived to reinforce 220 IAD. The *Stavka* also ordered the new 2 VA – formerly VVS Bryansk Front – to intervene in the Kharkov area. This was imperative, due to the heavy losses which all units of VVS South-western Front continued to

7 GShAP from 4 VA attacked the German airfield at Konstantinovka and, although all participating Il-2 *Shturmoviks* were either shot down or damaged, the Soviets claimed to have knocked out 26 German aircraft on the ground. This, however, proved to be a vast exaggeration since no German aircraft losses were recorded at Konstantinovka that day.[85] In his monograph on the Hs 129, historian Martin Pegg points out that "at Konstantinovka, II./SchG 1 was bombed several times but thanks to the Henschel's rugged construction, these particular attacks were not successful."[86]

Hunting these *Shturmoviks*, the German fighter pilots claimed to have shot down thirteen Il-2s on 25 May, the bulk of which were due to I./JG 52.

In order to support the South-western Front, 2 VA was assigned with the new 223 BAD. Commanded by *Podpolkovnik* Ivan Kosenko, 223 BAD was based at Zadonsk far to the north. According to the plan, its Pe-2s were to be provided with fighter escort from regiments of VVS South-western Front in the area east of Kharkov. But due to inadequate coordination of the two aviation commands, the escort failed to turn up on several occasions, which resulted in heavy bomber losses to the Bf 109 pilots. The first mission ended in a disaster. Shortly after 15.30 hrs on 26 May, several Bf 109s from JG 52 hacked a formation of 223 BAD's bombers to pieces, shooting down eleven according to German claims. Thus, I./JG 52 reached its 300th aerial victory.[87] Shortly afterwards, 9./JG 52's *Fw.* Alfred Grislawski and his wingman *Gefr.* Wilhelm Giesselmann bounced three Pe-2s to the west of Savintsy and shot down one each.[88]

27 May was another day of fierce aerial combat. At sunrise, six Il-2s from 431 ShAP and seven Yak-1s from 273 IAP launched a surprise attack against the large airfield at Chuguyev, where *Obstlt.* Günther Lützow's JG 3 was stationed. "The day opened with a low-level attack by Russian fighters against the airfield at Chuguyev, which resulted in two lightly damaged Messerschmitts," a German account reads.[89] "The attack struck so unexpectedly at the enemy that his anti-aircraft batteries opened fire only when our *Shturmoviks* turned for home," the corresponding Soviet combat report noted: "Two Me-109s that scrambled immediately were shot down by our fighters. As our attack commenced, the enemy flight personnel were standing in groups in front of their aircraft, apparently being briefed for a mission. The attack was carried out at treetop level along the dispersals. Each crew made individual passes against the target."[90] Quite optimistically, the Soviets claimed to have destroyed about 20 German aircraft on the ground.

A large undertaking by 2 VA's 223 BAD against German tank spearheads a few hours later ended in another disaster for the bomber *Diviziya*. Once more the Pe-2 airmen found that they had to carry out the mission without fighter escort. *Starshina* Ivan Kazakov, the radio operator in the crew of *Mayor* Yuriy Gorbko, Hero of the Soviet Union and commander of 24 BAP/223 BAD, recalls: "As we were approaching the target, the German anti-aircraft artillery opened a barrage of fire. But we broke through the flak and bombed the tanks successfully. After the bombing run we started to manoeuvre and our formation split up."

At that moment, I./JG 52, which had been scrambled against this large bomber formation, fell upon the Pe-2s. The German fighter pilots attacked with eagerness. "My wingman took off a half minute later. But I couldn´t wait for him, since I was pursuing a withdrawing bomber formation," wrote *Hptm.* Helmut Bennemann, the *Staffelkapitän* of 3./JG 52.[91] *Starshina* Kazakov continues: "The German anti-aircraft fire silenced and in the next moment Messerschmitts came diving against us. We had no fighter cover, and the Fascists could benefit from this. One of our aircraft caught fire, then another fell to the ground, followed by a third…"

*Lt.* Friedrich-Karl Bachmann, Bennemann's wingman whose take-off was delayed for technical reasons, pursued and caught the dispersed Pe-2s. "After about six minutes, I spotted a section of Pe-2s at an altitude of about 4,500 feet. Having shot down one of them, I turned against the leading aircraft," Bachmann's combat report reads. "I silenced the rear gunner with several bursts of fire. His right engine caught fire and the machine descended steeply and exploded on impact."[92]

Ivan Kazakov adds: "I watched as the Germans first shot down the right wingman of our *Zveno*. Then they dispatched the left wingman, and finally seven fighters were concentrated against our plane. *Mayor* Alkhovatskiy and I fired with our ShKASes. But after a short while, the *Mayor's* machine gun was silenced. Gorbko went down to treetop level, which made it impossible for me to defend us with my lower machine gun. The Fascists were circling above us, so I detached my machine gun and installed it on the upper side. I blasted away a few short bursts at the 'Messers' with the last remaining ammunition. At first the 'Messers' were reluctant to approach within short distance, but when they realized that I had ceased my fire definitely, one of them came very close from the right side and shot a long burst. Our left engine and left wing caught fire.

Assuming that we were finished, the Fascists disengaged. Remaining at the controls of our burning aircraft, *Mayor* Gorbko started looking for somewhere to put us down. Suddenly our plane flew straight into the wires over a railway line and was violently torn apart. I was in the rear cockpit. The front cockpit, where Gorbko and Alkhovatskiy were, went down not far from me. Fortunately, the peat marsh below us softened the crash.

My right leg was stuck in the lower gunport and my left arm was jammed in the hole in the fuselage. The cockpit was on fire and I struggled to release myself. I saw the navigator struggling to pull *Mayor* Gorbko out of the front cockpit. Having got free, I hurried to assist him.

Our commander sat in the marsh mud and the water reached up to his chest. We started to pull and he groaned with pain. It turned out that both his legs were stuck. It was impossible to pull him out of the cockpit. By now, the flames had reached the navigator's position and the ammunition started exploding. But we didn't care, the life of our commander was more important than anything else. Then the flames reached the cockpit.

"Well, that's it," Gorbko sighed and a harsh curse escaped his lips.

He took his documents from his pocket and handed them over to the navigator. Then he also gave him the Golden Star. It was a terrible moment – the man was alive but there was nothing that we could do to help him. "Now get away!" He looked at us with eyes filled with determination and pain. Before we could realize what he was up to, he pulled out his pistol and shot himself in the head. In an instant. We were shocked….by now the fire was approaching the fuel tanks, but we couldn't leave. We were absolutely paralysed. I had never felt like that before, not even in air combat.

Eventually we were able to pull the body of our dead commander from the cockpit. We carried him to the shore of a small lake, washed his head of blood and mud and wept together. . ."[93]

The *Eskadrilya* to which Kazakov belonged lost six Pe-2s during this action. It was a terrible blow to the entire 223 BAD. "Gorbko was very popular with all the airmen. His death and the tragic carnage on 223 BAD brought the entire personnel staff down," wrote *General-Mayor* Fyodor Polynin, the commander of 2 VA.[94] Included among other losses sustained by 223 BAD on 27 May 1942 was the Pe-2 flown by the *Diviziya* commander, *Podpolkovnik* Ivan Kosenko, who was lost.

By 28 May, the annihilation of all Soviet troops in the bulge to the south of Kharkov was completed. According to German estimations, 75,000 Soviet troops were killed, while 239,000 ended up in German captivity. South-western and Southern Fronts registered 170,958 men killed or missing between 12 and 29 May. The materiel losses sustained by the Red Army numbered 542 aircraft, 775 tanks and more than 5,000 artillery pieces and mortars. It was a classic battle of encirclement, and one of tremendous strategic importance. The *Luftwaffe* had made a decisive contribution to this. *Oberst* Hermann Plocher noted: "The Soviet capability to resist in the pocket west of Izyum was greatly influenced by the concentrated and devastating aerial attacks of the IV (reinforced) Air Corps. Extremely heavy losses in men and materiel were inflicted upon these Russian units by the almost round-the-clock assaults from the air."[95]

IV. *Fliegerkorps* claimed the destruction of 596 Soviet aircraft in the air and 19 on the ground, plus 227 tanks, 3,038 motor vehicles, 24 artillery batteries and two flak batteries, 49 separate artillery pieces, 22 railway engines and six complete trains. The cost for all of this was limited to 49 aircraft.

As usual, Josef Stalin searched for scapegoats to offload his burden of responsibility. *Marshal* Timoshenko, who was one of the Soviet dictator's favourites, managed to retain his position as the South-western Front's commander despite this gigantic failure for his proposed offensive. However, instead, his aviation commander, *General-Leytenant* Fedor Falaleyev, shouldered most of the blame. In spite of his many far-sighted ideas – such as the Manoeuvrable Aviation Group – Falaleyev was strongly criticised for having caused heavy losses among his fighters by ordering the mass use of RS-82 rocket projectiles. In early June 1942, Falaleyev was removed from command of VVS South-western Front.

Thus, a most able Soviet aviation commander was sacked. Falaleyev had led the Air Force of the South-western Direction with considerable skill during the difficult defensive battles in 1941. His greatest feat was his direction of air operations through the autumn of 1941 which contributed greatly to slowing down the German advance towards the industrial areas around Kharkov and in the Donets region. This enabled the Soviets to evacuate the bulk of this industry before the German troops arrived.

Nevertheless, *General-Leytenant* Aleksandr Novikov, the new Commander-in-Chief of VVS KA, was able to intervene to neutralise the effect of the removal of such a fine air commander. He could not alter Stalin's decision, but was able to place Falaleyev as Chief-of-Staff of VVS KA about a month after Falaleyev's humiliating dismissal. Moreover, Novikov ensured that the vacant position in charge of VVS South-western Front was filled by another very able commander – the 32-year old *General-Mayor* Timofey Khryukin.

# Chapter Six

# The Battle of Sevastopol

When the Kerch Peninsula had been 'cleared', VIII. *Fliegerkorps* and German XI. *Armee* immediately began preparations for the final assault against Sevastopol. As we have seen, because of the valuable time gained by the Soviets through their landings on the Kerch Peninsula in late December 1941, the defences of Sevastopol had been reinforced. *General-Mayor* Ivan Petrov's Soviet Coastal Army had fortified its positions and was determined to put up a stiff fight. The Soviet defence of Sevastopol was organized into the Sevastopol Defence District (SOR), which included the air group 3 OAG from VVS ChF. By 20 May, 3 OAG could muster 98 aircraft, of which 53 were serviceable. This force could be supplemented by VVS ChF units based in the north-western Caucasus and parts of 5 VA in the same area, but only on a limited scale, and almost exclusively during the hours of darkness.

On 1 June *Generaloberst* Wolfram *Freiherr* von Richthofen's *Fliegerkorps* VIII could line up the following forces against Sevastopol:

six *Kampfgruppen* from KG 51, KG 76, KG 100 and III./LG 1

three *Stukagruppen* from St.G 77

three *Jagdgruppen* and a *Jagdstaffel* from III./JG 3, Stab/JG 77, II./JG 77 and III./JG 77

two *Heeresaufklärungsstaffeln*, 3.(H)/11 and 3.(H)/13

In total, 600 aircraft of VIII. *Fliegerkorps* were ready to be launched on Sevastopol's defenders. In addition, the units of *Fliegerführer Süd* – notably II./KG 26 – would continue to be dispatched against the Soviet seaborne supply route to Sevastopol.

Clearly, German numerical superiority in the air was completely crushing, which was absolutely vital if the attack against Sevastopol was to have any chance of meeting with success. The 106,000-men strong Coastal Army was deployed in a network of hundreds of concrete and armoured gun positions, supported by very heavy artillery batteries. German and Rumanian anxiety at the prospect of storming such a formidable fortress was tangible.

Thus, XI. *Armee* demanded a five-day all-out air offensive, supplemented with a massive artillery barrage, against the Soviet defence positions before the ground assault could be launched. Von Richthofen prepared his units, and early on 2 June the 'softening up' attacks started.

Opening at 06.00 hrs, the first air attacks were directed against troop barracks and mobilisation points. For thirty minutes, Ju 87s, Ju 88s and He 111s of St.G 77, KG 76 and I./KG 100 dropped hundreds of bombs on these targets. *Hptm.* Hansgeorg Bätcher, the *Staffelkapitän* of 1./KG 100, noted in his logbook: "No defensive action."[96] Then von Richthofen's units shifted their attention to the city itself which, during the next twelve hours was subjected to a relentless aerial bombardment by all the units of VIII. *Fliegerkorps*. These aircraft dropped a total of 570 tons of bombs on 2 June, and German fighters unloaded some five hundred SC 50 splinter bombs. Meanwhile, more than 1,300 artillery pieces went into action against Sevastopol's defenders. Among these guns was the world's largest cannon, the 800mm 'Dora', which fired 7,000 kg shells.

3 OAG was also in action to support its ground troops – with Il-2s attacking German troop positions while the fighters attempted to intercept large formations of German aircraft. But all the odds were against the Soviets. On 2 June VIII. *Fliegerkorps* conducted 723 sorties, while 3 OAG could fly no more than seventy. The German fighters – which were commanded by *Hptm.* Gordon Gollob – also operated from a forward airfield from which the Soviet aircraft taking off in Sevastopol could be observed.

While most of VIII. *Fliegerkorps* was occupied against Sevastopol, the He 111 torpedo aircraft of II./KG 26 were directed against the seaborne supply route from the Caucasus ports to Sevastopol. In the evening of 2 June they sank the tanker *Mikhail Gromov* en route to Sevastopol. But the flotilla leader *Tashkent*, the destroyer *Bezuprechnyy*, and the transport ship *Abkhaziya* escaped destruction and brought military equipment and 2,785 soldiers into the besieged fortress.

The intense air and artillery bombardment continued with 643 sorties by VIII. *Fliegerkorps* on 3 June, 585 on 4 June and 555 the next day. But the Soviets fought back gallantly. A well-aimed bombardment forced the German fighters to abandon their forward airbase. In the hours of darkness, biplane light bombers of 23 AP/VVS ChF subjected the headquarters of XI. *Armee* at Yukhariy Karales to repeated attacks. The Army commander, *Generaloberst* Erich von Manstein, himself barely survived a Soviet air attack. On 5 June the Soviet flotilla leader *Kharkov* reached Sevastopol, bringing in 270 fresh troops.

The Bf 109s led by Hptm. Gordon Gollob commanded the skies over Sevastopol. This photograph shows a Bf 109 F of III./JG 77 in the Crimea in early summer 1942 shortly before the Gruppe converted to the Bf 109 G. Note the all-yellow cowling is unusual as, by mid-1942, most units had camouflaged the cowling top and sides leaving only the underside yellow as an identity marking.

On 7 June von Manstein hurled his ground troops against the Soviet lines. By that time, 3,069 *Luftwaffe* sorties had been made against Sevastopol over the previous five days, and a total of 2,264 tons of explosives and 23,800 incendiary bombs had been dropped. Many of these were of the heaviest calibre, aimed at knocking out the concrete bunkers from where the Soviets would be able to spray the attacking German ground troops with fire. The entries in *Hptm*. Bätcher's logbooks show that his He 111 was loaded with 1,000-kg SC 1000 bombs, 1,400-kg SC 1400 bombs and even 2,500-kg SC 2500 bombs during operations on these days.[97]

Individual German bomber crews made up to eighteen sorties daily. Historian Joel Hayward noted that "this hellish blitz was far more ferocious than those inflicted thus far in the war on Warsaw, Rotterdam, London, or Malta."[98] *Polkovnik* Ivan Laskin, who commanded the Soviet 172nd Rifle Division in the northern defence sector of Sevastopol, recalled: "Bombers in groups of twenty to thirty attacked us without caring for their targets. They came in, wave after wave and literally ploughed up the earth throughout our defence area."[99]

While German LIV. *Armeekorps* attacked from the north, XXX. *Armeekorps* struck from the east. *Generaloberst* von Richthofen demanded the utmost of his crews, who flew a record 1,368 sorties on 7 June, dropping 1,300 tons of bombs. But this obviously had no decisive impact on the Soviets, who continued to offer tenacious resistance. "Earth, water, rock fragments, steel, and cement were intermingled with bleeding corpses," recalled *Hptm*. Werner Baumbach, a bomber expert who had been brought in from KG 30 in the Far North. "And yet, the Russians continued to cling to their ground, their native soil, with unequalled tenacity."

The advancing German troops were mowed down in their hundreds, and after a few hours the Soviets had halted the Germans along the entire line.

On 8 June *Generaloberst* von Manstein received worrying reports that his 132nd Division was approaching "the end of its strength."

The Army turned to von Richthofen, who was asked to carry out another 'softening up' offensive. Another series of intense air attacks thus commenced. On 8 June German bombers were able to sink the destroyer *Sovershennyy* and the survey vessel *Gyuys* in the port of Sevastopol. Two days later, the crew of I./KG 100's *Lt*. Herbert Klein scored a direct bomb hit on the large transport ship *Abkhaziya* (4,727 tons), which immediately exploded and sank. Other He 111s managed to sink the destroyer *Svobodnyy*, also on 10 June.

Provided with close support by St.G 77, the German XXX. *Armeekorps* re-opened its assault on the southern flank at daybreak on 11 June. The Stukas were in action over the Soviet positions throughout the day. A report from II./St.G 77 on 11 June reads: "Enemy infantry positions on the

Zinnober Height were bombed between three and five times by each *Staffel* from 14.30 hrs to 14.45 hrs. In addition, two *Ketten* carried out machine gun strafing runs against enemy positions immediately ahead of our attacking infantry." A total of 1,070 *Luftwaffe* flights were made against Sevastopol on that day, and around 1,000 tons of bombs were dropped. But the Soviets not only halted the German offensive, they even launched local counter-attacks. And in the hours of darkness, Soviet bombers carried out quite successful raids against German rear areas.

The Soviet Black Sea Fleet continued to defy the menace from the air, and on 12 June the cruiser *Molotov* and the destroyer *Bditel'nyy* ran the German air blockade and delivered 3,341 soldiers, 28 artillery pieces, and 190 tons of ammunition and medical supplies to Sevastopol. As a result, the *Luftwaffe* concentrated much of their efforts on 13 June against supply shipping to Sevastopol and sank the transport *Gruziya*, the trawler *TShch-27*, patrol boat *SKA-092*, motorboat *SP-40*, five barges, and a floating crane in the port of Sevastopol.

But fuel and munitions stocks husbanded by VIII. *Fliegerkorps* for the assault were diminishing rapidly. The number of sorties flown decreased from a daily average of around 1,000 between 8 and 11 June to 780 from 13 to 17 June. Sevastopol's defenders were reinforced by another 3,400 soldiers, 442 tons of ammunitions, 30 tons of fuel, and 12 tons of provisions which arrived with the minesweepers *Molotov* and *Bditel'nyy*, and three submarines on 15 June. The next day the Soviet troops withstood five concentrated Stuka attacks and halted the offensive launched by German XXX. *Armeekorps*. "The German soldiers suffer from combat fatigue and are badly demoralised," reported *General-Major* Petrov.

To the Germans, everything now depended more than ever on the *Luftwaffe*. Von Richthofen decided to concentrate the main concentration of air attacks against the northern sector of the front, where LIV. *Armeekorps* was still attacking. The main target was the Soviet Coastal Battery 30, known to the Germans as Fortress *Maksim Gorkiy I* – the key to the Soviet defence in the north. Between 15.15 hrs and 15.30 hrs on 17 June, twenty-seven Ju 87s of *Hptm*. Alfons Orthofer's II./St.G 77 struck at the fortress. A German infantry *Leutnant* later wrote: "Our Stukas come swarming in overhead. They dive away over their wings and descend toward 'M.G.' with screaming engines. Over and over again! Their machine guns are spitting small flames. The air trembles from the bomb detonations. Dark smoke and gigantic dust clouds spiral skywards. . . ."

Stuka pilot *Oblt*. Maué scored a direct bomb hit on one of the gun towers of the fortress – Coastal Battery 30 fell silent. The Germans assumed that Maué had put the guns out of action, but Soviet records show that the fortress withstood all bomb hits – even by 1,000-kg bombs – without suffering internal damage. The battery had simply run out of ammunition.

*Bombs lie ready to be loaded into He 111s. Between 8 and 10 June, VIII. Fliegerkorps carried out nearly 3,000 combat flights and dropped around 2,800 tons of bombs. But the last air offensive also put a severe strain on the German supply system. Von Richthofen warned his colleague von Manstein that at the present pace of operations, his air units would run out of bombs and fuel in a matter of a few days. (Vollmer)*

In the event, this proved to be the turning point of the entire battle. With Coastal Battery 30 inactive, LIV. *Armeekorps* was able to open a breach into the Soviet lines north of Severnaya Bay, which lay opposite the city of Sevastopol.

A series of Soviet setbacks now followed in quick succession, mainly due to the *Luftwaffe*. On 18 June the flotilla leader *Kharkov* was severely damaged when a bomb exploded close to the ship in the waters off Khersones. The next day German ground troops reached the northern shore of Severnaya Bay and were able to subject the Soviet airfields to intense artillery fire. The effect of this is evident from the report from German LIV. *Armeekorps* for 19 June: "No enemy air activity."

During a dive-bombing attack in the evening of 19 June, 2./KG 51's *Oblt.* Ernst Hinrich managed to destroy the large anti-aircraft raft PZB-3

(Floating Anti-aircraft Battery No 3) – known to the Soviets as *Ne tron' menya* ("Don't touch me") – in Severnaya Bay. *Generaloberst* von Richthofen, who personally witnessed the conspicuous explosion of the anti-aircraft raft from the cockpit of his Fieseler Storch, immediately called Hinrich's commander and told him that the successful pilot would be awarded the Knight's Cross.

On 20 June the lack of anti-aircraft cover made it impossible for the minelayer *Komintern* to enter the port of Sevastopol with its cargo of supplies. This failure brought on the rapid deterioration of the SOR's already desperate shortage of both ammunition and fuel.

But the Germans were also at the end of their resources. The bitter fighting had completely worn down their ground troops; several XI. *Armee* regiments were down to a few hundred men each. Indeed, von Manstein recalled that one regiment reported a strength of one officer and eight men![100] The *Luftwaffe* units had been saved from heavy losses, but the long period of intense combat activity was taking a severe toll on the airmen. The situation for VIII. *Fliegerkorps* was further complicated by mounting supply shortages. The average number of sorties now carried out each day had gone down by some 40 per cent.

Referring to KG 51, historian Wolfgang Dierich wrote; "Because of shortages of ordnance, every bomb was now dropped individually. This meant that each crew had to carry out some 25-30 dive-bombings daily, plunging from 11,000 feet down to 2,500 feet. In the hot summer temperatures this resulted in great physical strain."[101]

The OKH also was growing impatient, demanding that VIII. *Fliegerkorps* should be shifted north to participate in Operation *'Blau'* – a move described by von Manstein as "a precondition for victory".[102] A compromise was achieved; the staff of VIII. *Fliegerkorps* and several aviation units were shifted to the Ukraine on 23 June, while some units were left in the Crimea under the new *Fliegerführer Krim*, commanded by *Fliegerführer Süd, Oberst* Wolfgang von Wild.

Von Manstein opted for a decision through an amphibious landing on the southern shore of Severnaya Bay on the outskirts of Sevastopol. In preparation, von Wild dispatched his units in a concentrated bombardment against Sevastopol's inner fortification belt. While the German troops lay waiting in their trenches, the *Luftwaffe* bombers and Stukas kept coming throughout 23 June, unloading their deadly cargoes over a small area. "The thick smoke that rose from Sevastopol completely obscured the horizon," JG 77's *Hptm.* Gollob wrote in his diary.

*The Junkers Ju 87 constituted the backbone of the Blitzkrieg in the early years of the war. It also proved most efficient for undertaking pin-point attacks against enemy shipping. St.G 77 operated Ju 87 Rs (R = 'Reichweite', 'long-range'), equipped with auxiliary tanks, with great success against Soviet shipping in the Black Sea in 1942. (Mombeeck)*

But by this time, shortages in fuel deliveries to the Crimean airfields cut the number of sorties carried out each day in half compared with the opening phase of the offensive. With von Manstein pressing hard for increased air support, *Oberst* von Wild flew from airfield to airfield, accusing the aviation unit commanders of slacking off.[103] On 26 June von Wild succeeded in reinforcing *Luftwaffe* activity bringing it up to levels not seen since the opening days of the offensive. The fortifications on the Sapun hills, which had blocked the advance of XXX. *Armeekorps* on the southern flank for so long, were completely devastated through air attack that day.

German aircraft were also launched against Soviet supply shipping. The flotilla leader *Tashkent* was able to evade the attacks by I./KG 100 and arrived with badly needed reinforcements, but the destroyer *Bezuprechnyy, en route* to Sevastopol with 320 soldiers, did not enjoy the same fortune. The combat report filed by II./St.G 77 for 26 June read: "Eight Ju 87s attacked the destroyer . . . Two direct hits were scored. The destroyer sank after two minutes. The decisive hit – splitting the vessel in two – was registered by *Oberfeldwebel* [Werner] Haugk. The second hit was scored by *Stabsfeldwebel* Bartle."

Early the next morning, III./St.G 77 and I./KG 100 pursued *Tashkent* as she withdrew from Sevastopol with 2,100 injured soldiers on board. Soviet journalist Yevgeniy Petrov, who experienced the struggle between the *Luftwaffe* pilots and the commander of the ship, *Kapitan 3-go Ranga* Vasiliy Yeroshenko, recalled: "Yeroshenko rushed from one side of the bridge to the other throughout the entire air attack. Peering up at the diving aircraft, and his voice increasingly hoarse, he yelled his instructions just at the right moment : 'Shift the helm to port! Shift the helm to starboard!' On occasion, he even waved to me by way of encouragement."[104]

Only after some four hours, during which time around 335 bombs had been dropped against the ship, did *Ofw.* Herbert Dawedeit of 8./St.G 77 manage to score a near miss which caused severe damage to the ship. But the *Tashkent* survived and was towed back to Novorossiysk.

Following the attacks against the *Bezuprechnyy* and *Tashkent,* the Soviets decided to stop sending large vessels to Sevastopol. A final effort to supply the badly mauled defenders was made by twenty PS-84 transport planes of MAGON GVF carrying out 288 night supply flights between 21 June and 1 July. But this effort was totally in vain since Sevastopol's fate was already settled.

On 28 June the *Luftwaffe's* bombings of the city drowned the sound of assault boats that had been brought forward. The amphibious landing was carried out the following night. The Soviets were caught completely by surprise, and the Germans managed to gain a foothold. Early the next morning *Oberst* von Wild ordered his units to conduct 'rolling attacks' to the east of Sevastopol, where the XXX. *Armeekorps* launched yet another offensive. "Everything on the ground below seemed to be on fire", recalled *Hptm.* Hansgeorg Bätcher, who made six combat missions and dropped seven tons of bombs on 29 June.[105] Von Wild's units managed to accomplish no less than 1,329 sorties on 29 June. That was the end of Sevastopol's defence.

"Approximately 300 Stukas are launched in merciless, deafening attacks against the Sapun Heights," wrote a German infantry *Oberstleutnant:* "Never ever – neither previously, nor later – did the men of Infantry Regiment 42 experience anything like this."

With almost all artillery ammunition spent and no hope of any significant reinforcement or resupply, the Soviet forces withdrew towards Cape Khersones. "Panic is spreading, particularly among the officers," wrote *General-Mayor* Petrov.

Realising that all hope had vanished, the *Stavka* agreed to abandon Sevastopol. A PS-84 from MAGON GVF picked up the commander of the Black Sea Fleet, *Vitse-Admiral* Filipp Oktyabrskiy, and flew him to safety in the Caucasus. *General-Mayor* Petrov and other commanders of the Coastal Army were evacuated aboard the submarines Shch-209 and L-23. But most of the troops of the SOR were left to their own fate. *General-Mayor* Petr Novikov, who assumed command of the SOR, saw no point in further resistance.

*Kapitan* Mikhail Avdeyev of 6 GIAP/VVS ChF penned the following lines from within the besieged area:

"Our last aircraft flew out from Khersonesskiy Mayak on 30 June. Sevastopol was at the mercy of the Germans. The Soviet troops streamed down onto the Khersones Peninsula. We were subjected to a terrible and relentless aerial bombardment from five in the morning until nine in the evening. Bombs of all calibres rained down. It was painful to watch the sky

Werner Baumbach (left) belonged to the group of Ju 88 pioneer pilots who flew the type shortly before the outbreak of the war. He developed particular skills in dive-bombing the Ju 88 against enemy ships. One of his first feats was to damage a French cruiser, for which he was awarded the Knight's Cross in May 1940. By August 1941, Baumbach had been credited with the sinking of 300,000 GRT of enemy shipping. He already carried the Oak Leaves to his Knight's Cross. Having served with KG 30 since the beginning of the war, Baumbach was sent to the Crimea in late spring 1942 to supervise the Luftwaffe's attacks on the Soviet ships which brought supplies to Sevastopol. On 1 August 1942, Baumbach became the first German bomber pilot to be awarded with the Swords to the Oak Leaves. He ended the war as Geschwaderkommodore of KG 200. Baumbach was killed in a flying accident on 20 October 1953. (Mombeeck)

continuously filled with enemy aircraft. I can only describe the situation as a living hell. Never ever during the entire war have I seen as many killed and wounded men as during the last days on the the Khersones Peninsula. There were not even enough dressings for all the wounded men – they had to be bandaged with torn up sheets. I lack the words to describe all the horrors during the last days of our defence at Sevastopol. It tormented us to see the injured men begging for something to eat, while we had nothing to give them. The wells and the supply stores had been destroyed through the bombing. We were an army without food, without water, and most important of all – without ammunition. The army had even lost the possibility of shooting back at the enemy!"

"The Russian will to resist is broken," the diary of German XXX. *Armeekorps* triumphantly recorded on 30 June. But von Manstein still shuddered at the prospect of drawn-out and merciless street fighting inside the city. "In order to avoid that," he wrote, "I instructed the artillery and [the *Luftwaffe*] to have a word once again."[106]

All available bombers and Stukas, along with the entire German artillery establishment, opened a massive bombardment against the city itself early on 1 July. *Lt.* Herbert Kuntz of I./KG 100 recalls: "The impact of our heaviest bombs is terrible. Entire blocks of houses disintegrate. Rocks, parts of roofs, and rafters are flung 3,000 feet high."[107] The assault "met with complete

*A scene of utter carnage at the Crimean town of Sevastopol in July 1942 inflicted by the bombers of General Wolfram von Richthofen's VIII. Fliegerkorps.*

*General-Mayor* Novikov, the last commander of the SOR, was among the 95,000 Soviet troops captured during the battle of Sevastopol; he was eventually executed by the SS at the Flossenburg concentration camp.

The Sevastopol defenders indeed stunned the world by their indefatigable will to resist. They had held out for more than eight months, tying up considerable German forces. This would eventually have important repercussions for the German summer offensive.

The final battle of Sevastopol cost the German XI. *Armee* more than 24,000 casualties, while participating Rumanian units lost approximately 4,000 men. Undoubtedly, the German victory at Sevastopol could not have been achieved without the contribution made by VIII. *Fliegerkorps* and its successor, *Fliegerführer Krim*, which conducted 23,751 sorties between 2 June and 3 July 1942, during which time the German bombers dropped 20,529 tons of bombs. According to German sources, 123 Soviet aircraft were destroyed in the air (including 118 by German fighters) and another 18 were destroyed on the ground. St.G 77 alone carried out 7,708 combat sorties and dropped 3,537 tons of bombs. Total *Luftwaffe* combat losses over and around Sevastopol were limited to 23 aircraft destroyed and seven damaged.[108]

As usual, the most outstanding fighter pilots received the highest awards: *Hptm.* Gollob was awarded the Swords to his Knight's Cross with Oak Leaves and *Oblt.* Heinrich Setz and *Oblt.* Friedrich Geisshardt – both from JG 77 – received the Oak Leaves to their Knight's Crosses. The commander of XI. *Armee*, Erich von Manstein, was not even awarded the Oak Leaves to his Knight's Cross following the victory at Sevastopol, although he was promoted to *Generalfeldmarschall.*

For the Soviet defenders, the eight-month defensive battle for Sevastopol had laid down a marker for the forthcoming battle for Stalingrad. By the time the exhausted troops of XI. *Armee* raised their flag over Sevastopol, the *Wehrmacht* had already embarked upon its rendezvous with destiny at Stalin's city.

success," von Manstein noted laconically. At 13.15 hrs on 1 July, the German flag was raised over the ruins of Sevastopol.

Fearing a last-minute intervention by the Soviet Black Sea Fleet with its powerful ship guns, *Oberst* von Wild sent 78 bombers of I./KG 76 and elements of I./KG 100 plus 40 Ju 87s of St.G 77, escorted by 40 Bf 109s of JG 77, against the Caucasus ports of Taman, Anapa, and Novorossiysk. For the loss of only one bomber, several Soviet ships were sunk: the flotilla leader *Tashkent* and the destroyer *Bditelnyy;* the transport ships *Ukraina, Proletariy,* and *Elbrus;* the salvage vessel *Chernomor;* the schooner *Dnestr;* two torpedo boats; and a patrol boat. In addition, the minelayer *Komintern,* the destroyers *Soobrazitelnyy* and *Nezamozhnik,* the patrol vessels *Shkval* and *Shtorm,* one gunboat, one torpedo boat, two transports, and a floating dock all sustained varying degrees of bomb damage.

Other German aircraft were sent into action against the dispersed Soviet troops at Cape Khersones. *Hptm.* Hansgeorg Bätcher of I./KG 100 flew his 300th bombing sortie against these troops on 2 July.

Over the following days, Coastal Army collapsed. The main German operation was over by 4 July. Five days later the last sporadic fighting ended.

## Aces over Sevastopol

While hundreds of *Luftwaffe* bombers and Stukas pounded Sevastopol, an air duel was waged between very skilful fighter pilots on both sides in the skies high above. As we have seen previously, the naval aviators of VVS ChF were among the best Soviet airmen in 1942.

In 3 OAG, the fighter pilots of 6 GIAP/VVS ChF stood out particularly. The most famous pilot of this unit was *Kapitan* Mikhail Avdeyev, an excellent marksman who commanded 1 AE (formerly 5 AE of 32 IAP/VVS ChF).

On 1 June Avdeyev and his wingman, *St.Lt.* Danilko, came close to killing *Generaloberst* Erich von Manstein, the commander of XI. *Armee*. As the two Soviet pilots returned from a reconnaissance mission over the road to Yalta, they spotted a lone motor torpedo boat. Disregarding orders to avoid combat, they immediately put down the noses of their Yak-1s and dived with guns blazing.

Von Manstein had boarded the Italian motor torpedo boat in order to check if the strategically important road from Sevastopol to Yalta could be controlled from the sea. Suddenly machine gun bullets crashed into the deck. The two Yak-1s dived out of the sun, undetected by the enemy. To the left and right of von Manstein, the port commander of Yalta, Kapitän Joachim von Wedel, the Italian commander of the torpedo boat, and the *Generaloberst's* faithful driver, *Ofw.* Fritz Nagal, fell dead. Von Manstein escaped without injury.[1]

As already described there were some very skilful aces on the German side

in the Crimea. Most notable amongst these during the battle of Sevastopol were JG 77's *Hptm.* Gordon Gollob, *Oberleutnante* Anton Hackl and Heinrich Setz, and *Fw.* Ernst-Wilhelm Reinert. Due to the quite limited geographical area of aerial operations during the battle of Sevastopol, these veterans encountered the same faces on the Soviet side each day – among whom *Kapitans* Mikhail Avdeyev, Konstantin Alekseyev and Boris Babayev of 6 GIAP/VVS ChF were the most noteworthy.

Both sides learned to treat their adversaries with great respect. Heinrich Setz, the *Staffelkapitän* of 4./JG 77, described the initial air combat with "most experienced" Soviet fighter pilots over Sevastopol as "extremely hard."[2] On 3 June VVS ChF performed 99 sorties over Sevastopol, including 48 from bases in the north-western Caucasus, and claimed eight German aircraft shot down. Although only two were actually destroyed (for the loss of four Soviet naval fighters),[3] the fighting that day showed the Germans that they were up against very skilful and dangerous opponents. In consequence, *Hptm.* Gollob – who commanded the German fighters in VIII. *Fliegerkorps* – instructed his fighter pilots to avoid "turning combats at low flight altitude."

On the Soviet side, *Kapitan* Mikhail Avdeyev devoted an entire chapter of his memoirs to the German ace over Sevastopol whom the Soviet pilots referred to as '*Zet*' - their interpretation of the call sign on the fuselage of this Bf 109 F – a black Latin character 'Z'. Avdeyev wrote:

"'*Zet*' appeared every day, always with his back protected by other fighters.

Usually, he picked his victims carefully and only rarely were his attacks without success. More than once, I tried to pursue this Fascist, but this proved to be a most difficult undertaking. . . .

It was clear that '*Zet*' was an outstanding pilot, definitely somebody from von Richthofen's inner circle, or maybe even von Richthofen himself. . . .

That damned '*Zet*' deprived us of our sleep and never left us in peace. It was as if he was mocking us. A hundred times I racked my brains to think up different ways to attack him – from above, from below, from the clouds, or from the sun. But these fine theories always came to nothing in practice. '*Zet*' wasn't someone whom you could lure into a trap, or who could be made to lose his nerve through a frontal attack. He was a worthy opponent, and he definitely gave us a lot of headaches.." [4]

There appears to have been no Bf 109 marked with a 'Z' at Sevastopol in 1942. The German pilot identified as '*Zet*' appears to be a combination of *Oblt.* Anton Hackl, the *Staffelkapitän* of 5./JG 77, and *Hptm* Gollob. The latter's aircraft carried a horizontal black zigzag marking which could be the explanation for the 'Z', while some of Avdeyev's descriptions of '*Zet*' appear to be encounters with *Oblt.* Hackl. Roaming the skies above Sevastopol in his Bf 109 F-4, 'Black 5' during June 1942, 'Toni' Hackl would bring down a total of eleven Soviet aircraft during the battle, becoming the most successful German fighter pilot during the operation in the process. On 3 June a LaGG-3 fell to his guns, bringing his total score to 51. On 4 June Hackl claimed another Soviet fighter, and on the 7th he bagged an Il-2. Mikhail Avdeyev was a stunned witness to the rapier thrust with which 'Z' downed an Il-2 of 18 ShAP/VVS ChF:

"The fighters of the 1st *Eskadrilya* took off first. Three or four minutes later, a dozen Messerschmitts appeared. In that moment, *Mayor* Gubriy's *Shturmoviks* were taking off.

Eight Yaks met the Messerschmitts over the sea. Our fast, sudden attack and precisely gauged manoeuvres drew the Messerschmitts into combat and prevented them from engaging the Shturmoviks. Then, from somewhere high above, beyond the dogfight, a lone Messerschmitt, undetected by anyone, came screaming down like a bird of prey. It set one of the *Shturmoviks* on fire and disappeared at treetop level. Together with Danilko, I tried to pursue him as he levelled out from the dive, but we were intercepted by four Messerschmitts. We caught a quick glimpse of a black 'Z' on the fuselage of the hunter."

The same determination was displayed by the airmen of 3 OAG. Mikhail Avdeyev described how the Yak-1s of 6 GIAP/VVS ChF tied up the Bf 109s that attempted to close with a formation of 18 ShAP/VVS ChF Il-2s: "Suddenly one of the Messerschmitts broke away from the fighter tussle and headed for the Il-2s, but [*Kapitan* Konstantin] Alekseyev saw it in time and shot down the German. A second Me 109 was shot down by myself and one more Me 109 fell burning toward the mountains."

During the evening of 7 June *Hptm.* Gordon Gollob wrote in his diary: "My fighters achieved nine victories, while one officer and an *Uffz.* are reported missing. The Russians are putting up a desperate – and quite skilful – fight. I shot down a LaGG-3, which plunged straight into the ground at Sevastopol IV aerodrome and burst into flames. But I was also close to being shot down myself. I barely managed to reach our own lines with a shot-up radiator." One of the missing pilots, *Lt.* Wolfgang Werhagen, an eleven-victory ace in 4./JG 77, was captured after being shot down.

"Defying our air superiority, the enemy's air force intervened in the ground combat with ground-attack aircraft and fighters," noted a report from LIV. *Armeekorps.*

However, the veterans of 6 GIAP were unable indefinitely to oppose the overwhelming German numerical superiority in the air. 8 June was a particularly difficult day for Avdeyev and his compatriots. "For several hours the skies were buzzing, howling, and thundering; there was no way for us to repulse the masses of enemy aircraft arriving in wave after wave," Avdeyev recalled. "There were not enough fighters or anti-aircraft artillery."

In the whirling air combats, both sides inevitably overclaimed; there was no time to confirm whether an enemy aircraft seemingly knocked down smashed into the ground or plunged into the sea. In addition, visibility was hampered by the thick columns of smoke from the raging fires on the ground below.

6 GIAP/VVS ChF claimed nine victories on 8 June while in fact not a single German aircraft was actually lost. Meanwhile II./JG 77 claimed nine 'LaGG-3s' or 'MiG-1s' shot down while IAP VVS/ChF lost three Yak-1s. Anton Hackl was credited with three victories in these engagements.

One of the Soviet pilots shot down on 8 June was 6 GIAP's *Kapitan* Konstantin Alekseyev, who baled out with severe wounds. 'Kostya' Alekseyev's

score stood at eleven personal and six group victories, which made him the top ace of the Soviet Black Sea Fleet Air Force at the time. Mikhail Avdeyev recalled the fateful mistake made by *Kapitan* Alekseyev's wingman: "Together with his wingman, Katrov, he was caught up in a prolonged dogfight with six Messerschmitts, attempting to break through to our *Shturmoviks*. Here the primary task was holding the enemy at bay, not shooting them down. But Katrov couldn't resist and went after a Messerschmitt that appeared in front of him. This was exactly what the Germans had been waiting for. A pair of Messerschmitts came racing in to attack Katrov. Alekseyev tried to overtake them but was himself caught between two other fighters, one from each side, which set his aircraft on fire." [5]

*Oblt.* Heinrich Setz described the combat in his diary: "I managed to position myself behind one of these pilots several times. My cannon wouldn't fire, and with only the machine guns I didn't have sufficient fire power. The Russians proved to be very skilful airmen and I found myself coming under continual attack. After a prolonged dogfight, I suddenly saw a Yak climbing after a Messerschmitt. I went after him. While turning, I came so close that I almost rammed him. The burst from my machine guns hit his engine and cockpit. He went down and crashed right next to his own airfield." [6]

The next day, 9 June, it was Boris Babayev's turn. That morning, the three Yak-1 sections which remained in Mikhail Avdeyev's 1 AE of 6 GIAP/VVS ChF took off to clear a corridor through the Bf 109s for *Mayor* Gubriy's 18 ShAP/VVS ChF Il-2s. Since the German forward command kept the Soviet airfields inside the fortress under constant surveillance, *Generaloberst* von Richthofen – from an observation tower located in the front line – could personally direct the JG 77 fighters against the Yak-1s when he spotted the dust that was blown up as the Soviet pilots started their engines. Mikhail Avdeyev was first to race across the runway with his wingman, Katrov, and as soon as the undercarriage of his fighter left the ground he was attacked from above by two Bf 109 pilots. Both Soviet pilots engaged the enemy while Boris Babayev and three other Yak pilots took to the air. Shortly, German reinforcements were called in. The Yak-1 pilots were locked into a severe combat with a large number of German fighter pilots who included Anton Hackl, Heinrich Setz, and *Fw.* Ernst-Wilhelm Reinert.

The Il-2s and three I-16s of 6 GIAP/VVS ChF took off just as a formation of Ju 88s was approaching with the obvious intention of bombing the airfield. The Bf 109s were occupied with the Yak-1s, so the *Shturmoviks* and I-16s managed to slip away to carry out a swift low-level attack against German troops a few miles away.

Boris Babayev baled out of his blazing Yakovlev, became entangled with the rigging lines of his parachute, and fell head downwards, smashing his front teeth and fracturing his skull when he hit the ground. The combat was still raging when one of the German pilots caught sight of the Il-2s and I-16s as they returned from their strafing attack. Several Bf 109s turned to intercept them and the Yak-1s followed to protect their comrades – but in vain. Avdeyev's wingman, Katrov, was shot down and fell to a certain death.

By comparing Soviet and German sources, the Yak-1s of Babayev and Katrov were probably shot down by *Fw.* Franz Schulte (who claimed his 22nd victory against a 'LaGG-') and 'Toni' Hackl – who claimed a 'MiG-1' for his 58th kill. Although *Oblt.* Setz was not credited for his claim, he seems likely to have participated in the shooting down of Babayev – as indicated in his personal diary:

"I dived against a 'bird', large areas of which were painted red," Heinrich Setz recalled. "I gave him a burst from my cannon and he exploded in a huge cascade of fire directly in front of me." [7]

From his observation tower, *Generaloberst* von Richthofen saw the Soviet aircraft go down in flames. "This is great fun!" he chuckled. Next, two I-16s were knocked down by Setz and Reinert (the latter's forty-ninth victory). The sheer toughness of the fighting was indicated by that day's entry in Gordon Gollob's diary: "We fought at altitudes of between 1,500 feet and ground level. I shot down an I-153, but I was also hit myself and landed close behind our own lines with one of my tyres burning..."

In total, 3 OAG/VVS ChF managed to carry out 144 sorties on 9 June, but lost eleven of its own aircraft.[8] By now, 6 GIAP/VVS ChF had only four Yak-1s remaining.

The next morning twenty Yak-1s of 45 IAP/5 VA arrived in Sevastopol from the north-western Caucasus. On 11 June a group of eight VVS ChF Yak-1s followed to reinforce 3 OAG. However, the largely inexperienced Soviet replacement airmen were no substitute for veterans like Babayev and Alekseyev. The air combat situation grew steadily more unequal. On 12 June the four 'old' Yak-1s and seven of the 'new' were subjected to an attack by at least thirty JG 77 Bf 109s.

Mikhail Avdeyev barely managed to escape by means of a daring low-level flight between the houses on both sides of a Sevastopol street. When he returned to base, he learned that only three of the 'new' navy Yakovlev pilots – the unit's political commissar and two inexperienced *Serzhs.* – had survived that day's air fighting, and a 45 IAP pilot had managed to bale out when he was shot down. In his memoirs, Avdeyev wrote laconically: "And next day, the Commissar and his wingmen were no more. . . ." That evening *Hptm.* Gollob noted in his diary: "An average of 700 sorties are carried out each day, with approximately 600 tons of bombs dropped. The losses in our air units have declined and are now very limited."

On 14 June II./JG 77 claimed fourteen Soviet aircraft shot down – two of which marked Hackl's 60th and 61st victories. VVS ChF meanwhile recorded the loss of seven of its own aircraft over Sevastopol, for only two victory claims on 13 June.[9] Three 45 IAP pilots were also shot down. In a matter of days, 45 IAP lost nine Yak-1s, and most of its novice pilots had been killed.

The Soviet fighter pilots adopted a new tactic in response to German fighter attacks from above. After taking off as fast as they could, they raced out over the sea at low level. Once out of sight of Sevastopol, they climbed high and turned back, diving against the enemy bombers. "Three attacks were made by strong Il-2 formations," an astounded Gordon Gollob wrote on 14 June.

During an air combat on 15 June, Mikhail Avdeyev finally managed to ease the feared '*Zet*' into his gunsight:

"The sun was already sinking below the horizon. Suddenly I spotted the hated reddish-brown ['carrot-coloured'] aircraft over the airfield. I called upon all the Gods to ensure that my engine and guns would not fail and that my speed wouldn't decrease, so that nothing would go wrong. The matter had become personal: '*Zet*' had become my nightmare, my fixation, the symbol of everything that I hated ferociously. . . . I still don't know the reason for this – either '*Zet*' made a blunder, or my swift attack caught him by surprise – but finally, and not without sensing a fiendish pleasure, I saw 'my' *ryzhyy* ['carrot'] fly into the bead of my gunsight. I fired one burst. A second. A third. The fighter shot past. I turned my head and looked back: Trailing smoke, '*Zet*' raced towards [German] territory. I turned to follow him, but too late; a pack of Messerschmitts intercepted me. . . .

Until today, I don't know if I managed to shoot him down or not, nor do I know if it was *General* von Richthofen himself, or one of his favourites. But we never saw '*Zet*' again. In vain we looked for his dirty reddish-brown machine in the sky."[10]

Although Avdeyev may have come out with a 'moral victory' from his last engagement with the infamous '*Zet*,' it is clear that neither 'Toni' Hackl nor any other German fighter pilot was shot down over Sevastopol on 15 June. Nevertheless, Avdeyev's observation that Hackl disappeared from the skies in this area is correct. On 14 June he received the Knight's Cross during a ceremony led by Gordon Gollob. After that he left for a well-deserved spell of home leave. (Coincidentally Mikhail Avdeyev and Konstantin Alekseyev were appointed Heroes of the Soviet Union on the very same day.)

The Germans soon countered the new Soviet tactics when becoming airborne from Sevastopol by dispatching standing fighter patrols over the airfield. On 18 June, Gordon Gollob led one of these patrols when eight 18 ShAP Il-2s and some escort fighters took to the air from Sevastopol's airbase at Khersonesskiy Mayak. Within minutes Gordon Gollob sent one Il-2 and one LaGG-3 tumbling earthwards. Since Gollob earlier had refrained from reporting four of his victories, his two kills on 18 June were officially recognized as his 100th and 101st victories – which earned him a mention in the OKW Bulletin the following day.

On 19 June German ground troops stood on the northern shore of Severnaya Bay and started shelling the Soviet airfields. This had the effect of almost completely paralysing Soviet air activity, although only four of 3 OAG's aircraft were destroyed on the ground. That day, *Oblt.* Heinrich Setz patrolled above Sevastopol together with his *Schwarm* from 03.00 hrs, searching for an opportunity to achieve his 80th victory. Only after some twelve hours did the Bf 109 pilots spot the first Soviet aircraft. Setz dived on a group of Soviet fighters that were taking off and unleashed a burst at an I-16 which crashed straight onto Khersonesskiy Mayak Aerodrome. Setz then made a quick escape.

The next day all Soviet seaplanes and bombers from Sevastopol were ordered to leave. A GST (a licence-built American Catalina) from 80 AE/VVS ChF, based in the north-western Caucasus, was shot down by Bf 109s near the Kerch Peninsula. Thus *Kapitan* Chebanik died, the commander of 80 AE/VVS ChF.

But still 3 OAG's remaining airmen kept offering frantic resistance in the air, as Gollob noted in his diary on 23 June: "We drop bombs against ships and quays in the western part of the bay, and strafe vehicles and other targets of

opportunity. But although the Sevastopol IV airfield is subjected to continuous shelling from our anti-aircraft artillery, Russian aircraft continue to take off and land at this place." *Oblt.* Setz was amazed to see a lone I-153 carrying out what he thought of as 'aerobatics' above Khersonesskiy Mayak aerodrome. "One minute later, I destroyed the biplane," Setz wrote – his 81st victory, which can be confirmed in Soviet loss records.[11]

6 GIAP/VVS ChF fought its final combat – for almost two years – over Sevastopol on 24 June. The next day, when only 32 aircraft remained in 3 OAG, the decision was taken to evacuate all airmen of 6 GIAP/VVS ChF, 247 IAP, and a few other *Eskadrilya*s. The Yak-1s of these units were handed over to 9 IAP/VVS ChF and 45 IAP.

Four Soviet aircraft were destroyed and twelve were damaged at Khersonneskiy Mayak aerodrome on 26 June.[12] But that was not yet the end of Soviet resistance in the air over Sevastopol. Although the blazing city was obviously doomed, the VVS fighter pilots kept fighting to the bitter end. On 29 June eight 45 IAP Yak-1s attacked a formation of St.G 77 Stukas. *Kapitan* L. Saprykin and *Lt.* Nikolay Lavitsky reportedly teamed up to destroy one of the Ju 87s. In fact, a Ju 87 of Stab/St.G 77 was the only *Luftwaffe* loss over Sevastopol on 29 June. Also, 3.(H)/12 reported that one of its Hs 126s was damaged during a fighter interception.[13]

Even on the last day of June, 3 OAG flew 22 combat sorties. During the following night, all remaining aircraft – eleven Yak-1s, seven Il-2s, four I-16s, four U-2s, three I-153s, one LaGG-3, and one I-15bis – flew to Anapa in the north-western Caucasus. Thirty aircraft, which for various reasons could not get into the air, were set on fire. But the U-2s and UT-1s from 23 AP/VVS ChF remained in the besieged territory, and the biplane pilots continued to carry out night raids against the Germans over the following two nights.

Testifying to his unbreakable do-or-die determination, *Kapitan* Mikhail Avdeyev – who had remained in place when most of 3 OAG's airmen were evacuated – set out to swim out into the open sea rather than to stay and wait for the German troops to capture him. At 05.00 hrs on 4 July, after spending three hours in the sea, he was miraculously spotted and picked up by a Soviet patrol boat.

The tenacious Soviet resistance on the ground at Sevastopol may have only few parallels in military history, but obviously it pales when compared with the determination with which the airmen of 3 OAG fought. "These guys have some nerves," Heinrich Setz noted in his diary: "Each day they see their friends go down in flames and yet they're back in the air with the same enthusiasm the next day."[14]

Between 25 May and 1 July 1942, 3 OAG carried out 3,144 sorties, including 1,621 ground-attack sorties. According to Soviet accounts, they destroyed 57 tanks, 60 enemy aircraft in the air, and 43 enemy aircraft on the ground. They lost 69 aircraft and 50 airmen in the process. Afterwards, 6 GIAP/VVS ChF received the name of honour, *Sevastopolskiy*.

The Soviet airmen actually had the last word in the battle of Sevastopol. On 5 July 1942, the Germans held a victory banquet in the old Czar castle, *Livadia*, at Yalta. All XI. *Armee* unit commanders, from battalion commanders up, and several *Luftwaffe* unit commanders, took part. The entertainment had just reached a climax when Soviet aviators gate-crashed the party. Based on information from partisans, SB bombers of 5 VA's 6 BAP carried out a surprise raid in the middle of the night, which sent the festively dressed officers tumbling toward the basement and caused severe bloodshed among their drivers waiting outside. This in itself was a foretaste of what lay ahead for the Germans.

1.  Manstein, *Verlorene Siege*, p. 269; Avdeyev, *U samogo Chyornogo morya*, p.138; Dorokhov, *Geroi chernomorskogo neba*, p. 77.
2.  Prien, *Geschichte des Jagdgeschwaders 77*, p. 1057.
3.  *Velikaya Otechestvenaya den' za dnyom, in Morskoy Sbornik*, 5-6/1992.
4.  Avdeyev, *U samogo Chyornogo morya*, p. 177.
5.  Ibid., p. 180.
6.  Quoted in Prien, *Geschichte des Jagdgeschwaders 77*, p. 1050.
7.  Quoted in Ibid., p. 1056.
8.  *Velikaya Otechestvenaya den' za dnyom, in Morskoy Sbornik*, 5-6/1992.
9.  Ibid.
10. Avdeyev, p. 182.
11. *Velikaya Otechestvenaya den' za dnyom, in Morskoy Sbornik*, 5-6/1992.
12. Ibid.
13. *Flugzeugunfälle und Verluste bei den Verbänden (täglich), Ob.d.L. Gen.Qu. Gen. 6. Abt.* Bundesarchiv/Militärarchiv RL 2 III/1181.
14. Quoted in Prien, *Geschichte des Jagdgeschwaders 77*, p. 1061.

# Chapter Seven

# Izyum – the final preparations

## The Build-Up

For Operation 'Blue', 41 army divisions, including 21 from Germany's Axis allies, were transferred to *Heeresgruppe Süd* in May – June 1942. Thus, *Heeresgruppe Süd* was boosted to a total of between 65 and 67 divisions. Altogether, around 1.3 million soldiers and 1,495 serviceable tanks could be mustered on the eve of the offensive.

The Axis air forces in the Ukraine, tasked with providing the offensive with air support, were reinforced by the arrival of units from all over Europe during May and June 1942:

From Germany these units were St.G 2 with the *Stab* and three *Gruppen*; SchG 1 with the *Stab*, two *Gruppen* and 8. *Staffel*; ZG 1 with the *Stab* and three *Gruppen*; ZG 2 with its *Stab* and three *Gruppen*; the *Stab*, I. and III./JG 3 and the *Stab*, I. and II./JG 52. I./JG 53 also arrived from Germany. Units arriving from France included the *Stab*, II. and III./KG 55, and I./KG 77, while II./JG3 flew in from the Mediterranean area. Units shifting into this theatre included II./KG 27 (*Luftflotte 1*) and II./KG 54 and II./KG 76 from *Luftwaffenkommando Ost*. Elsewhere III./KG 27, I./KG 55, the Stab./KG 76, III./KG 76 and III./JG 52 arrived from the Crimea.

On 23 June the staff of *Generaloberst* von Richthofen's VIII. *Fliegerkorps* flew in from the Crimea to supplement *General* Kurt Pflugbeil's IV. *Fliegerkorps*. While the latter took charge mainly of semi-strategic bomber operations with the aim of isolating the battlefield, VIII. *Fliegerkorps* would organise close support for the offensive.

Through these reinforcements, around 1,700 German combat aircraft were ready to support Operation 'Blue'. Among these, about 1,200 were operational – around 350 bombers, 211 fighters, 161 *Zerstörer*, over 150 Stukas, 91 *Schlacht* aircraft, approximately 150 tactical reconnaissance aircraft and 51 strategic reconnaissance aircraft.

Additionally, other Axis States sent elements of their air forces to support the operation they hoped would deal the final blow to the Soviet Union:

Hungary sent its 1st *Repülöcsoport* (aviation detachment) with 51 aircraft, including Reggiane Re. 2000 fighters and bombers and reconnaissance aircraft.

Italy's Eastern Front expedition corps, the ARMIR (Armata Italiana in Russia), contributed an air force of 66 aircraft – Macchi C.200 Saetta fighters of 21 *Gruppo Autonomo* and Caproni Ca.311 and Fiat BR.20 reconnaisance aircraft of 71 *Gruppo O.A.*

All of these units were subordinated to *Generaloberst* Alexander Löhr's *Luftflotte* 4.

On the Soviet side, the South-western Front was rapidly rebuilt following the disaster in the Kharkov Bulge. Many new and rested units arrived to bolster the aviation of the South-western Front. 4 RAG, which had played an important role in the Battle of Kharkov, was reorganised into 270 BAD. The South-western Front's ground-attack units were organised into the new 228 ShAD, and the fighter arm meanwhile was brought together into the new 268 IAD and 269 IAD. By this time, the so-called light night bombers – single-engined biplane trainers or reconnaissance planes converted into bombers – formed a vital part of the VVS. In late May, the South-western Front's aviation was equipped with two whole *Diviziyas* of such aircraft, 271 and 272 NBAD. In addition, VVS South-western Front received three new *Diviziyas* – 206 and 220 IAD, and 226 ShAD.

The new commander, *General-Mayor* Timofey Khryukin, was one of the most able air commanders in the VVS. On 9 June, VVS South-western Front was reorganised into the air army 8 VA. 8 VA was further reinforced on 12-13 June, through the arrival of 235 IAD and six independent fighter regiments. In total, 8 VA received no less than 49 new air regiments in early June, and was able to muster 596 combat aircraft and 240 liaison or transport planes at that stage.

On 12 June, 8 VA consisted of 49 aviation regiments with a total of 596 combat aircraft, 116 auxiliary aircraft and 124 transport aircraft. On 24 June, 8 VA received 221 BAD. This *Diviziya* had four regiments – 57 BAP, 745 BAP, 794 BAP and 860 BAP – equipped with American Douglas Boston bombers. To the north of 8 VA's area was *General-Mayor* Stepan Krasovskiy's 2 VA, which was tasked with supporting the Bryansk Front. 2 VA mustered 503 aircraft (including 374 serviceable), based in the Livny - Staryy Oskol area east of Kursk by 28 June 1942. In the Voronezh area, *General-Mayor* Ivan Yevsevyev's 101 IAD/PVO lay in wait. To *Continued on page 50*

*Continued from page 49*
the south of 8 VA's area was *General-Mayor* Konstantin Vershinin's 4 VA, which was tasked with supporting the Southern Front. 4 VA mustered around 200 aircraft, based between Izyum and Rostov. Farther to the south, *General-Mayor* Sergey Goryunov's 5 VA was stationed in the north-western Caucasus. Tasked

with supporting the North Caucasus Front, 5 VA reported a strength of 134 combat aircraft by 10 June 1942. Along the Caucasian coastal area, VVS ChF also was active, mustering around 200 aircraft. These forces were supplemented by elements of the ADD.

## The Commander of VIII. *Fliegerkorps* and *Luftflotte* 4 - Wolfram *Freiherr* von Richthofen

Several misconceptions surround 'Wulf' von Richthofen, who was born on 10 October 1895. First of all, he was not the cousin of the famous World War One fighter ace, Manfred von Richthofen. However, they were distantly related, and 'Wulf' was a pilot in the same fighter unit, achieving eight aerial victories. Secondly, he was not the 'founder' of the revolutionary Stuka dive-bomber concept. In fact, serving as chief of the development staff of the *Luftwaffe's* Technical Department in the mid-1930s, von Richthofen fell out with Göring and Ernst Udet, who by that time were more far-sighted regarding the potency of the new dive-bomber tactic.

Von Richthofen was quite outspoken and not at all the diplomat. Removed from the *Luftwaffe's* Technical Department and sent to Spain, where he was appointed Chief-of-Staff of the *Legion Condor* in Spain, he clashed with his commanding officer, *Generalmajor* Hugo Sperrle. In October 1937 von Richthofen was sent back to Germany where he was appointed *Geschwaderkommodore* of KG 257.

However, while in Spain, von Richthofen had cooperated with Adolf Galland in developing the close-support tactics which were pioneered by Galland's He 51-equipped 3./J 88. In November 1938, von Richthofen returned to Spain – this time to lead the *Legion Condor* – with a further remit to refine close-support tactics. This time, the method of providing ground troops with close air support merged with the proven success of the Ju 87 Stuka. Von Richthofen was 'converted' and henceforth became a determined advocate of the Stuka.

In 1940 - 1941, *Generalmajor* von Richthofen led the specialised close-support air corps VIII. *Fliegerkorps* with outstanding success during the campaigns in the West, in the Balkans and against the Soviet Union. He was awarded the Knight's Cross on 18 May 1940 and the Oak Leaves on 17 July 1941.

In the winter of 1941/1942, von Richthofen organized the *Luftwaffe* air operations which halted the Soviet offensive that threatened to annihilate *Heeresgruppe Mitte*. Having completed this task, von Richthofen – promoted to *Generaloberst* on 1 February 1942 – and his VIII. *Fliegerkorps* were subsequently moved to the Crimea, where they played a vital role in the German victories at the

Kerch Peninsula and Sevastopol. From 4 July 1942, von Richthofen headed *Luftflotte* 4, which was responsible for the air support of Germany's summer offensive in 1942.

On 16 February 1943, at the age of forty-seven, von Richthofen became the youngest *Generalfeldmarschall* in the history of Germany and Prussia. Four months later he left the Eastern Front to assume command of *Luftflotte* 2. Due to health reasons, von Richthofen retired in October 1944 and died in July 1945.

*At the time of the Stalingrad airlift, Luftflotte 4 was commanded by General Wolfram Freiherr von Richthofen, on the right, who held this position from July 1942 until September 1943.*

## The Commander of 8 VA - Timofey Khryukin

*General-Mayor* Timofey Khryukin was barely 32 years old when he was appointed commander of VVS South-western Front in early June 1942. Born on 21 June 1910 in Yeysk in the north-western Caucasus, he had graduated from the Lugansk flight school in 1933. Five years later Khryukov earned fame when he successfully led a volunteer bomber group in China's defensive war against Japan in 1938. On 22 February 1939, Khryukin was appointed a Hero of the Soviet Union.

In the Winter War against Finland, Khryukin commanded the aviation of Soviet 14th Army. The opening of the German attack on the USSR in June 1941 saw him serving as the aviation commander in South-western Front's 12th Army, with the rank of a *General-Mayor*. The main element of VVS 12th Army, 64 SAD, was badly depleted during the surprising German onslaught on 22 June and lost no less than 125 aircraft, most of them on the ground. In this situation, there was not much the aviation under Khryukin's command could do to prevent the rapidly advancing German pincers from closing around the 12th Army, which was annihilated during the encirclement battle of Uman in August 1941.

Following this tragedy, Khryukin was sent north to the new Karelian Front, where he received the task of organising the air defence of the vital Kirov railway – which connects Murmansk with the Soviet hinterland. In this position, Khryukin

again displayed excellent organisational and tactical talents. By developing a network of airbases, and improving the use of radio navigation and light beacons for nocturnal operations, he managed to provide the long rail line with effective air cover despite the meagre resources to hand. The inability to sever the Kirov railway for any prolonged period of time was one of the *Luftwaffe's* most important tactical failures during Operation 'Barbarossa'. In the meantime, much valuable Lend-Lease materiel rolled into the Soviet Union on the Kirov railway.

Following the disastrous defeat of the South-western Front and its aviation during the Battle of Kharkov in May 1942, Khryukin was called back to VVS South-western Front. He replaced his former commander, *General-Leytenant* Fedor Falaleyev as the commander of the Front's aviation and oversaw its organisation into the new 8 VA.

Khryukin introduced many new tactics and took the initiative of remodelling 9 GIAP as the Soviet Air Force's first 'all ace unit'. He continued to lead 8 VA until July 1944, when he was appointed commander of 1 VA, which played an important role in the major Soviet offensive in Belarus, Operation 'Bagration'. On 19 April 1945, Khryukin became one of the few Soviet citizens to be appointed Hero of the Soviet Union for a second time. In 1953 Khryukin passed away as a result of injuries sustained in a car accident.

*Hptm. Helmut Bennemann, the Gruppenkommandeur of I./JG 52 (with his back against the camera), supervises the repainting of his Bf 109 F. Shortly after I./JG 52 had arrived at the Eastern Front in May 1942, the upper section of the yellow cowlings were painted in a camouflage colour. Note that this aircraft carries a pair of underwing MG 151 machine guns.*

The German summer offensive in 1942 should not have come as a surprise to the Soviets. During the weeks preceding the attack, the airmen of the new Soviet air armies in the Donets combat zone – 2 VA assigned to the Bryansk Front and 8 VA assigned to the South-western Front – were able to follow the build-up of German forces in the sector from Izyum in the south to Kursk in the north.

A major offensive of such magnitude had often been preceded by a period of relative tranquility, but this was not the case in the Donets sector prior to Operation 'Blau'. Following the bitter defeat during the Battle of Kharkov in May 1942, the *Stavka* had rapidly reinforced the Red Army forces east of the Donets River, fearing that the Germans might otherwise be able to develop the counter-offensive at Kharkov into a successful drive across the Donets, maybe towards Moscow from the south-east. Above all, the battered VVS South-western Front was reinforced, and, together with ADD forces, was immediately hurled into continuous attacks against the German air and ground forces which were gathering on the western side of the Donets. The large airbase at Kursk was subjected to an attack by six Il-2s from 800 ShAP, escorted by ten 31 IAP LaGG-3s, at dawn on 30 May. When I. and II./JG 52 were transferred to Grakovo on 1 June, these units were immediately subjected to repeated air attacks, mainly by Il-2s in groups of ten to twenty at a time. Intercepting one of those raids, *Uffz.* Johannes Noe was killed on 2 June. That day, too, JG 52 lost its *Geschwaderkommodore, Major* Wilhelm Lessmann, when his Bf 109 was shot down near Brigadirovka.

Meanwhile, the German long-range reconnaissance airmen who carried out regular missions over the Soviet rear area noted increasing opposition from the PVO *Diviziya* in the area, 101 IAD. One of the *Fernaufklärungsstaffeln* in the Ukraine, 3.(F)/10, lost two crews to air-to-air rammings in a short space of time – the crew of *Fw.* Kurt Stepatat to

591 IAP's *Lt.* Viktor Barkovskiy on 20 May, and the crew of *Lt.* Dietrich Pütter to 587 IAP's *Lt.* Mikhail Proskurin on 3 June.[109]

Operation 'Wilhelm' was launched on 10 June 1942 – German VI. *Armee* attacked Volchansk with the aim of securing a better staging area for Operation 'Blau'. German tactical air support for Operation 'Wilhelm' was provided by II./St.G 1, SchG 1, ZG 1, ZG 2, KG 27, elements of KG 51 and KG 55. The Ju 88s of KG 51 *Edelweiss* conducted more than 300 sorties during the first four days of the offensive. However, during their missions in this area, the German aviators encountered many fresh VVS units which had been brought in as reinforcements. Operation 'Wilhelm' was launched only one day after the air forces of VVS South-western Front were restructured into the new 8 VA on 9 June. Appointed as the new commander was *General-Mayor* Timofey Khryukin. On the first day of the offensive, 20 German aircraft were destroyed or severely damaged in this sector. Ten of these were from the two *Zerstörergeschwader*.[110] Meanwhile, the German fighters recorded only half that number of shot-down Soviet aircraft.

The German attack, which struck at the junction of the South-western and Southern Fronts, was opposed in the air by both 8 VA and 4 VA – the latter the former VVS Southern Front. As early as 11 June, the German Army Headquarter's Situation Report noted heavy Soviet air attacks in the Artemovsk region. During an aerial combat on 11 June, the *Staffelkapitän* of 3./JG 3, *Oblt.* Alfons Raich, was shot down, while *Lt.* Ernst Quasinowski of 6./JG 52 was injured in another clash. Hermann Graf's wingman, *Stab's Fw.* Alfred Emberger (credited with 25 kills) of 9./JG 52 was killed in action on the following day.

On 13-14 June, 8 VA carried out 605 combat sorties.[111] 13 June marked the climax of the air battle, with the German fighters recording over 20 victories in the area. 206 IAD, one of the new units which had arrived to support South-western Front in late May 1942, was rapidly worn down.

Among several reinforcements to arrive at VVS South-western Front (later 8 VA) in late May 1942 was 504 ShAP. In this photograph, a group of pilots pose before the camera shortly after having arrived for first-line service in May 1942. Sitting from left to right: deputy Eskadrilya commander V. K.Batrakov (KIA on 15 September 1942), G. K. Zotov, F. V.Yanchenko, Gonta, and I. F.Pilipenko. Standing from left to right: Yu. N. Lyapin, Koryazhkin, Y. V.Orlov, Ivan Pstygo, P. I. Malinin, and F.V. Rybin. Led by the Shturmovik ace Mayor Fyodor Boldyrikhin, 504 ShAP was relatively successful during the air fighting in the Izyum area in June 1942. On 4 June, nine Il-2s of 504 ShAP, led by Mayor Boldyrikhin, attacked Grakovo's airfield, where they put several aircraft out of commission, shot down one of the intercepting German fighters (from I./JG 52), caused another to crash during take-off (with the pilot, Uffz. Viktor Petermann, escaping without injury), and returned to base without having sustained any losses. (Karlenko)

Eight of its fighters – half of them from 427 IAP – were lost on 14 June.

For the Germans, Operation 'Blue' was preceded by a period of bad luck. The *Luftwaffe's* superiority relied quite heavily on a number of very experienced veterans. One of the most successful fighter pilots in service with *Luftflotte* 4 was 9./JG 52's *Fw.* Leopold Steinbatz. He was lost on 15 June, less than a fortnight prior to Operation 'Blue'.

Having returned from a long leave of absence following his 42nd victory in January 1942, Steinbatz had displayed a combat fever which shocked even the die-hard *Karaya*-veterans. His *Staffelkapitän Oblt.* Hermann Graf later wrote:

"After his return he proved to be absolutely reckless. (...) He entered upon an unparalleled victory march, scoring one victory after another! As he had achieved his No. 80 and was expected to be awarded with the Oak Leaves (2 June 1942 – author's comment), I urged him to take some leave. The combats had put a tremendous strain on his nerves. This was shown on several occasions. I grounded him for a couple of days, but then he requested that I allow him to start flying combat sorties again. As I was called to the *Führer's* Headquarters (24 May 1942 – author's comment), I exhorted him to 'cool down' a bit. But I knew that his goal was to reach his '100'."[112]

On what was to become his last combat mission, on 15 June 1942 *Fw.* Steinbatz engaged a numerically superior formation of enemy aircraft and shot down three – for victories 97, 98 and 99. During the return flight, his Bf 109 F-4 sustained a direct flak hit. The fighter went down in dense forest, never to be found by the Germans. A week later, Leopold Steinbatz was posthumously awarded the Swords – the first NCO of the *Wehrmacht* to be so honoured.

Four days later, on 19 June 1942, *Major* Joachim Reichel of German 23rd *Panzer* Division was instructed to deliver the operational orders for the first phase of Operation '*Blau* I' to the headquarters of XXXX. Motorised Corps. Contrary to clear instructions against carrying orders in this way, Reichel decided to travel by air. Tactical reconnaissance unit 6.(H)/13 put a Fi 156 Storch at the *Major's* disposal. But *en route* to their destination, the Fi 156's pilot, *Oblt.* Hermann Dochant, made a navigational error. East of Belgorod, the aircraft drifted across the front line and immediately came under ground fire. The aircraft came down at Nezhegol, some 20 miles east of Belgorod. This was a disaster for the Germans – the men on board the aircraft were all killed before they had a chance to destroy the valuable documents.

Hitler was furious and sacked all Reichel's closest superiors, including the corps commander. But it was decided to carry on with the operation as planned. On 20 June, the *Führer* ordered Operation '*Fridericus* II' to be launched the following day.

The Germans sustained another hard blow on 21 June, when JG 52's *Geschwaderkommodore, Obstlt.* Friedrich Beckh, was lost. 34-year old Beckh was one of the most famous unit commander veterans of the *Luftwaffe.* At the same time, he was a skilful and daring fighter pilot. After Werner Mölders' appointment to Inspector of the Fighter Air Arm in July 1941, Beckh rose from *Gruppenkommandeur* of IV./JG 51 to *Geschwaderkommodore.* He remained in this position until 3 June 1942, when he took charge of JG 52 after the death of *Major* Leesmann. By that time, he wore the Knight's Cross and had been credited with more than 40 aerial victories – plus more than a dozen other aircraft destroyed on the ground. The men in JG 52

Fähnrich Cvitan Gali of 15.(Kroat)/JG 52 in the Caucasus in 1942. In this photograph, the rudder of Gali's Bf 109 G-2 W.Nr. 13432 ('Black 2' with white outline) sports 15 victory markings, indicating that it was taken between 20 and 25 June 1942. At the end of 1942, Gali had amassed a total of 29 victories, which made him the leading Croatian ace by that time. (Marko Jeras)

Yak-1 fighters taxiing out on the runway for another combat mission. From mid-1942 the Yak-1 became the VVS standard fighter, which constituted a great qualitative leap forward compared with only six months previously. (Drabkin)

called him '*Lokomotiv-Beckh*' due to his rather unusual liking for strafing railway engines. In the end he made one too many of these low-level strafing passes. Hit in the radiator, his 'White 4' came down in a marsh near Valuyki. The body of Friedrich Beckh was found when the aircraft was excavated sixty years later.[113]

The Soviet commanders, with Reichel's papers in their hands, ordered their aviation to intensify air attacks against the German build-up areas. On 22 June, when 1. *Panzerarmee* launched Operation '*Fridericus* II' after one day's delay, the German Army Headquarters reported heavy Soviet air attacks against German troop assembly areas south of Izyum and south-east of Kharkov.[114]

The Soviet troops were overwhelmed by the mass of armoured forces – from both VI. *Armee* and I. *Panzerarmee* – which the Germans thrust against Volchansk and Kupyansk. With Operation '*Wilhelm*' leading to a German foothold on the eastern side of the Donets, the final assault against Kupyansk could be initiated on 24 June. At that stage, two weeks of intense air action had worn down much of the reinforcements which 8 VA had received, but 24 June would represent a highpoint in the air war in the weeks preceding Operation 'Blue'.

On 24 June, 206 IAD was assigned to provide a vital Soviet radio station near Kupyansk with air cover. Since late May, this *Diviziya* had lost 34 fighters, but it dispatched nine Yak-1s of 427 IAP and five Yak-1s of 515 IAP for the mission. Suddenly a large formation of Bf 110s and Bf 109s dived out from the clouds – I./ZG 2 escorted by I./JG 52. The war diary of 206 IAD reads: "We engaged a large formation of approximately forty German fighters. Our formation disintegrated during the course of the combat – it was every man for himself, twisting and turning with three or four enemy aircraft. As a result of the air combat, six Yak-1s of 427 IAP and two Yak-1s

of 515 IAP were shot down while another two were damaged." Another five Yak-1s made belly-landings or force-landed at other airfields. The only Soviet fighter that returned to base after this engagement was piloted by Hero of the Soviet Union *Mayor* Anton Yakimenko, who was credited with all three victories claimed by the Soviets in this combat. The scene was just as chaotic from the German point of view. Two Bf 110s of 2./ZG 2 collided and crashed, and both crews were lost. Another Bf 110 was shot down, while a fourth barely managed to return to base with very heavy battle damage. In I./JG 52, which was responsible for the bulk of the Soviet losses, *Ofw.* Oskar Wunder, an ace with 14 victories, was shot down and listed as missing. It may be assumed that Wunder was shot down by 131 IAP's *Mayor* Viktor Davidkov, who claimed a Bf 109 whose pilot baled out and was captured.

## Chapter Eight

# The Big Summer Offensive

On 24 June, with I. *Panzerarmee* lined up along the Oskol River from its inlet into the Donets to a point east of Kupyansk, Operation 'Fridericus II' was successfully concluded. Hitler ordered Operation 'Blue' to commence on 27 June but, on the day itself, bad weather with low clouds and heavy rainfall caused a postponement until the next day. Nevertheless, this failed to prevent Soviet bombers and ground-attack aircraft from carrying out their attacks. "Heavy enemy air activity against our divisions which are re-grouping north of Izyum," reported the German Army Headquarters.[115]

German fighters scrambled to intercept these attacks. In the bad visibility, this led a *Schwarm* from JG 52 to attack two He 111s of 8./KG 55. Historian Wolfgang Dierich wrote:

"It was not until flares had been fired off that the fighters realized their mistake and left. The crew of G1 + BS, piloted by *Lt.* Heinz Moldenhauer, made a forced landing near Volczhansk. The radio operator *Obgefr.* Leopold Horchy and the gunner *Obergefr.* Konrad Skraitzke were killed. *Fw.* Karl Hiltner's crew in G1 + LS fared little better: the flight engineer and one of the gunners was killed. Unfortunately, such events struck other *Kampfgeschwader* now and again. The bomber pilots were committed to combat missions from dawn to dusk, even if they were totally exhausted from the strain of operations. This also applied to the fighter units. Every airman gave his all."[116]

The Soviet air attacks continued with increased intensity during the following night, when the final preparations for Operation 'Blue' were made. In these final hours, *Division Grossdeutschland* – part of XXXXVIII. *Panzerkorps* of *Heeresgruppe von Kleist* in the Kursk sector – suffered badly from these air attacks. The *Panzer* battalion's entire fuel dump was destroyed.

But with clearing weather, *Luftflotte* 4's bombers also were in full action throughout that night, striking at rail lines and roads leading to the Front from the Soviet rear area. While their bombs rained down on the railway junctions at Voronezh, Michurinsk, Svoboda, and Valuyki, the soldiers of German II. *Armee*, IV. *Panzerarmee* and the Hungarian 2nd Army opened the offensive. It was 02.15 hrs on the morning of 28 June and above the heads of the advancing ground troops, German aircraft of all kinds swarmed eastward. Operation 'Blue' had begun.

For many German airmen who took off in the early hours of 28 June, it was the beginning of anything from 12 to 17 hours of uninterrupted combat action. *Fw.* Hermann Buchner of III./SchG 1 flew six combat missions between 03.05 and 17.05 hrs. The logbook of III./JG 52's *Fw.* Edmund Rossmann shows combat missions from 03.40 to 18.40 hrs.[117] An airman from I./KG 27 recalled: "We took off for the day's first mission at 03.25 hrs, and at 20.12 hrs we returned from our fifth combat flight of the day."[118]

At various places, such as Novoalekseyevskiy and Plotovskie Vyselki, Soviet field positions had to endure aerial attacks lasting for three hours. The *Luftwaffe* held a convincing numerical superiority from the onset. Still, 2 VA and 8 VA fought back both skilfully and with great tenacity. The first day of the offensive, 28 June, cost *Luftflotte* 4 a loss of 15 aircraft against 32 victory claims by its fighters.[119] Actual Soviet losses were 20 aircraft by 2 VA and three by 8 VA.[120]

Soviet 40th Army, which bore the brunt of the German onslaught, was forced into a rapid withdrawal. The *Stavka* sent 4th and 24th Soviet tank corps from the South-western Front northwards. On 30 June both sides sent most of their aviation to the Staryy Oskol area, where a large tank battle developed when Soviet 4th and 24th Tank Corps attempted to halt IV. *Panzerarmee* through a counter-attack. 2 VA's files for this day are missing in the archives, but 8 VA recorded 14 aircraft lost on 30 June 1942.[121]

While South-western Front sent 4th and 24th Tank Corps northwards, the Germans initiated Operation 'Blue II' – with VI. *Armee* striking against South-western Front's 21st Army and surging towards the north-east.

Realizing the German intention to surround large bodies of the Bryansk and South-western Fronts to the west of the Don, the *Stavka* ordered the left and right wing formations of these Fronts respectively to pull back behind the Don. Meanwhile, two reserve armies, the 6th and the 60th, were hastily sent to Voronezh. These troop movements were immediately discovered by the *Luftwaffe*. On 1 July the entire bomber force of IV. *Fliegerkorps* went into action against the Voronezh area. This resulted in heavy clashes with the Soviet fighters of 101 IAD, which was assigned to protect Voronezh from the air. During one of these engagements, *M.Lt.* Vasiliy Kolesnichenko of 101 IAD's 573 IAP destroyed a Bf 110 of I./ZG 1 through a mid-air ramming, and was killed in the process.

*In the second phase of the German 1942 Summer offensive, Generalfeldmarschall Fedor von Bock's Army Group B was ordered to clear the west bank of the Don and take the city of Voronezh. Here, German infantry move through a wheat field in the River Don area.*

The Red Army was forced to withdraw under a hellish rain of bombs. In this situation, the Soviets dispatched all available aircraft to attack the advancing German troops. Fighters were temporarily stood down from their regular duties and instead were sent into the battle as fighter-bombers, each loaded with FAB-50 bombs.

Although 2 VA's records for these days have been lost, the notes of 2 VA's deputy commander, *General* Fyodor Polynin, indicate that the *Shturmovik* units were badly depleted on 1 July.[122] JG 3 was credited with the destruction of ten Il-2s during its patrols over the German *Panzer* spearheads on 1 July – all for no losses. Nevertheless, the Soviet air attacks appear to have slowed down the German advance to such an extent that the Soviet troops were able to avoid encirclement. On 2 July, the VVS conducted 570 combat sorties against *Heeresgruppe von Kleist* in the north and VI. *Armee* in the south. "Heavy enemy air activity at Artemovsk and in the Izyum region," was noted in the German Army Headquarter's daily report.[123]

*Luftwaffe* reconnaissance crews reported large concentrations of Soviet troops retreating across the Don at Voronezh. VIII. *Fliegerkorps* shifted its attention to these river crossings. They inflicted heavy losses on the Soviet troop and vehicle columns, but were unable to prevent the general withdrawal across the Don.

The *Stavka*, which feared that Voronezh would be used as the springboard for an offensive from the south towards Moscow, sent all kinds of reinforcements to the Voronezh sector. As usual, this was detected by the effective German air reconnaissance. "Heavy traffic on the railway at Yelets", was reported from the *Luftwaffe*.[124]

These reinforcements included a whole fighter air army – a new tactical formation. Under the command of *General-Mayor* Yevgeniy Beletskiy, 1 IA was hastily and prematurely formed on 1 July, mustering 231 fighter planes. Before the command structures had been properly set, and with many inadequately trained pilots and inexperienced unit commanders, 1 IA was sent into combat. Another new unit which was sent to the Voronezh area was 153 IAP, which was equipped with the American Airacobra fighter.

Aware of the build-up of new Soviet air units, *Generaloberst* von Richthofen sent the Ju 88s of KG 51 and II./KG 54 to bomb the Soviet airfields in the Voronezh area on 4 July. He issued this order as commander of *Luftflotte* 4; on the same day von Richthofen was appointed commander of the air fleet. *Generalleutnant* Martin Fiebig succeeded him as the chief of VIII. *Fliegerkorps*.

On 4 July the first German bridgehead was established on the eastern bank of the Don. The next day, von Richthofen ordered up *Luftflotte* 4 in its entirety to support the ground offensive against Voronezh, east of the river. Bombers and Stukas attacked the city itself, and *Zerstörer* and *Schlacht* aircraft paved the way for the advancing *Panzer* troops. The skies were the

scene of a huge air battle as 1 IA and 101 IAD tried to ward off these *Luftwaffe* attacks. The inexperienced and poorly trained airmen of 1 IA proved to be no match for the Bf 109 veterans of *Luftflotte* 4. On 5 July alone, *Luftflotte* 4's fighter units claimed to have shot down 48 Soviet aircraft for only two losses.

Meanwhile, German VI. *Armee* made a rapid advance from its positions east of Kharkov. This forced not only the ground troops of the South-western Front into a hasty retreat, but the units of 8 VA also had to 'hedgehop' back from airfield to airfield. Thus, 268 IAD was shifted from Viktoropol to Rovenki on 4 July. The next day it moved to Rzhevka, and on 6 July to Kopenki. On the latter day, German troops reached the outskirts of Rossosh, some 90 miles to the east of VI. *Armee's* point of departure. On 7 July 268 IAD was pulled back to the eastern side of the Don. However, despite this difficult situation, 268 IAD was able to conduct 342 combat sorties between 4 and 8 July, and reported 17 enemy aircraft shot down.[125]

To the north, the battle became harder when Soviet 5th Tank Army, mustering more than 600 modern tanks, launched a counter-attack against von Kleist's flank from the area south of Yelets. On 7 July, the Bryansk Front was divided in two by the creation of the new Voronezh Front, commanded by *General-Leytenant* Nikolay Vatutin. 2 VA was assigned to the latter, while a new 15 VA was formed for the Bryansk Front farther to the north.

As had been the case the previous summer, the *Luftwaffe* scored immense numerical successes. *Luftflotte* 4 claimed to have shot down 540 Soviet aircraft in the Kursk - Voronezh area between 28 June and 9 July. Meanwhile, the German bombers subjected the Soviet rail network to relentless attacks. On 9 July, KG 76 was reported to have carried out particularly devastating attacks against Yelets and the rail junctions at Tambov and Povorino.

But the flow of Soviet reinforcements could not be halted, and the Germans inevitably became bogged down in Voronezh.

On 9 July, the bulk of *Generalfeldmarschall* von Bock's forces – both *Panzer* armies and VI. *Armee* – were ordered out of the Voronezh sector and sent southwards. Thus, Operation 'Blue' was succeeded by Operation 'Clausewitz'. In the Voronezh sector, the Axis shifted from the offensive to the defensive – leaving German II. *Armee* and the Hungarian 2nd Army to guard the northern flank. The situation in the air also shifted, with the Soviets – in spite of the heavy beating they had taken over the previous two weeks – seizing the initiative. Most of *Luftflotte* 4 was used to support the drive south. The only *Luftwaffe* units left to operate in the Voronezh sector were KG 27, KG 76, an *Aufklärungsgruppe*, and II./JG 77. These were brought together into *Gefechtsverband Nord*, commanded by *Oberst* Alfred Bülowius. In addition to these few *Luftwaffe* units, he was also assigned the Hungarian Air Force's 1st *Repülöcsoport*.

## Soviet Boston bombers into the fire

On 24 June 1942, 8 VA received a new bomber *Diviziya*, 221 BAD. Commanded by Hero of the Soviet Union *Polkovnik* Ivan Antoshkin, it mustered three regiments – 57 BAP, 794 BAP and 860 BAP. All of these were equipped with the US-designed twin-engine Douglas Boston bomber. Designated 'B-3' by the Soviets, these Lend-Lease aircraft joined the battle with 2 VA's 244 BAD and 8 VA's 221 BAD.

When the German troops on 30 June established a bridgehead on the eastern side of the River Olym near Kastornoye, north-east of Staryy Oskol, 221 BAD's Boston B-3s were sent to attack the bridgehead. This resulted in the first encounter between Bf 109s and Soviet Bostons. Three of the latter were shot down, and JG 3's *Lt.* Hans Fuss claimed two and *Oblt.* Helmut Mertens one of these aircraft.

On 2 July 221 BAD's 57 BAP reported four successful attacks against German ferries on the River Oskol and troop concentrations in the vicinity. This time the intercepting German fighters failed to bring down any of the Soviet bombers. Between 29 June and 4 July 221 BAD's operations cost a loss of 13 Bostons, but the bomber gunners claimed eight German fighters shot down.

On 4 July the first German bridgehead was established on the eastern bank of the Don. The Bostons of 221 BAD went into action against this sector on 5 July. During their return flight after an attack against the German Don bridgehead on 5 July, the 221 BAD Bostons were attacked by Bf 109s which tore up the bomber formation. *Fw.* Georg Schwientek of I./JG 52 gave the following account of the air combat:

"Four aircraft were dispatched against Russians who were bombing our front zone. It didn't take long before we spotted a group of Bostons with fighter escort. *Lt.* [Paul-Heinrich] Dähne's *Rotte*, which flew to the right in our formation, went after the Bostons, but they went into the clouds. Beneath the cloud cover, two [Soviet] fighters made for the east.

*Hptm.* [Johannes] Wiese positioned himself behind the last one and attempted to shoot. I remained 100 metres behind him and watched. But then the Russian turned slightly to the left. I immediately recalled everything I had learned about deflection shooting, turn radius and ballistics. I switched on my reflector gunsight and depressed the firing button. Excited, I followed the tracers with my eyes and saw them tear into the engine, the cockpit and the fuselage of the Russian fighter – it went down in flames. I was terrified; I had stolen a certain victory from my commander. All that I had wanted to do was to test what I had learned as a trainee fighter pilot. Furthermore, the Russian was dead, there was no parachute in sight. As I walked to the debrief after landing, I felt most distressed. But before I had even started my explanation, *Hptm.* Wiese patted me on the back and said that he would like to keep such an excellent wingman, who could shoot and score when his own guns refused to work!"[1]

On 10 July, 221 BAD dispatched six Bostons of 57 BAP for an attack against the airfield at Marfovka, 20 miles north-west of Rossosh, where a *Luftwaffe* unit was due to be stationed according to an intelligence report. The Boston crews encountered the German unit in question – JG 3 – but in the air, not on the ground. When the Soviet airmen reached Marfovka, they found it deserted. Instead they dropped their bombs on a motorised column of 15 tanks and 30 other motor vehicles. Next they strafed the German troops with their forward-firing machine guns. It was during this action that II./JG 3 dived down on the Bostons. Several bombers were hit, but only one was shot down, and a second crashed at its own base. In return the bomber gunners Sergakov and Yerokhin shot down a Bf 109. The German pilot was the ace *Lt.* Wolf Ettel. He survived by taking to his parachute, came down in Soviet-held territory and managed to evade capture for four days, when he finally made it back to his own lines. His compatriots in JG 3 exaggeratedly reported nine Bostons shot down in the same combat – including three by the *Geschwaderkommodore, Hptm.* Wolf-Dietrich Wilcke (who thus reached a total score of 61) and four by II./JG 3's *Ofw.* Alfred Heckmann.

Intelligence information such as the report of JG 3's imminent transfer to Marfovka was quite commonly received on the Soviet side. The Germans regularly used Soviet 'volunteers' as helpers in *Wehrmacht* units, and many of these were Soviet agents and delivered valuable reports. 221 BAD and JG 3 would meet again the next day, on 11 July – and this time when JG 3 had actually been transferred to the airfield at Marfovka. The Soviet attack was skilfully conducted and caught the Germans totally unaware. It opened with four Bostons of 57 BAP's 1st *Eskadrilya*, which claimed to have destroyed two German aircraft on the ground. This strike was immediately followed up by three Bostons from the 2nd *Eskadrilya* and their bombs reportedly knocked out another three German aircraft. The attack succeeded in killing and injuring both pilots and men of JG 3's ground crew, as well as putting several Bf 109s out of action. The scrambling German fighters managed to shoot down only one of the attackers. However, during other operations on 11 July, 221 BAD lost three more Bostons. The next day, the unit's own airfield was subjected to a German air attack which destroyed four Bostons. Having lost 22 Bostons in combat, 221 BAD was pulled out of combat on 23 July. Following four months of training, it returned to front line service in November 1942 to support the Soviet counter-offensive at Stalingrad.

[1] Fast, *Das Jagdgeschwader 52*, vol. II, pp. 345-346.

---

On 10 July, *Heeresgruppe Süd* was split – *Heeresgruppe A* was established under *Generalfeldmarschall* Wilhelm List's command. This new army group comprised XVII. *Armee* and I. *Panzerarmee*. This left von Bock with VI. *Armee*, the 2nd Hungarian, the 8th Italian and the 3rd Rumanian armies and IV. *Panzerarmee* in the new *Heeresgruppe B*. While List's forces attacked eastwards from Izyum and the Mius River farther south, von Bock's infantry units advanced along the Don. The aim of Operation '*Clausewitz*' was to envelop the South-western Front on the right banks of the Don, and then continue towards Stalingrad on the Volga.

But the Soviet South-western and Southern Fronts kept withdrawing and thus eluding the German plans for a gigantic encirclement. By this time, two weeks of intense fighting had also worn down both sides. Between 28 June and 10 July, the close-support units of VIII. *Fliegerkorps* had lost 110 aircraft alone.[126] 8 VA recorded 91 losses between 1 and 11 July.[127] The fresh 1 IA suffered far worse, losing 93 fighters – with another 23 sustaining severe damage – during the seven days from 5 to 11 July.

Adapting their organization to the new strategic situation, the *Stavka* reorganized the South-western Front into the Stalingrad Front on 12 July. Commanded by *Marshal* Timoshenko, this was composed of South-western Front's old 21st Army, plus the 62nd, 63rd and 64th Armies from the *Stavka* reserve. 8 VA, which had no more than 138 serviceable aircraft on 11 July, was responsible for the new Front's air support.

While their enemy was withdrawing as rapidly as possible, the progress of the German forces racing across the steppe southwards became increasingly hampered by shortages of fuel. Having arched over a wide eastern - southern bend, the forward elements of *Heeresgruppe B* found themselves to be more than 300 miles from their supply bases. With the few non-asphalt roads in this sparsely populated area in appalling condition – the result of hundreds of tanks ploughing over them and the continuous downfalls of rain – the mainly horse-drawn supply columns could advance only slowly and with great difficulty. Because of the need to pursue the retreating enemy with the highest possible speed, the *Panzer* spearheads inevitably outran their own supply columns. In consequence, two entire divisions – *Grossdeutschland* and the 24th *Panzerdivision* – became helplessly stranded for two days. Air transportation saved other units from the same fate. On 12 July alone, Ju 52s flew in over 200 tons of fuel to the *Panzer* units. The He 111-equipped III./KG 4 was also assigned to fly in supplies.

In the meantime, German ground troops endured repeated Soviet air attacks. From 1 to 11 July, 8 VA performed 3,546 combat sorties. The Germans simply could not understand how the Soviets were still capable of mounting such air activity, in the face of the huge losses they had apparently sustained. However, most German estimates of the damage being inflicted on the VVS were exaggerated. Thus, when SchG 1 claimed the destruction of 20 Soviet aircraft during an attack against the airfield at Kamensk on 13 July, Soviet records show that no more than one Pe-2 and a Su-2 of 270 BAD were in fact destroyed.[128]

Owing in part to Soviet air activity against their marching columns, the German forces failed to outrun their retreating enemy. When the pincers of *Heeresgruppen A* and B met at Millerovo on 14 July, no more than 14,000 Soviet soldiers were captured. In his frustration, Hitler changed the operational target. He decided to concentrate against Rostov in the south instead of Stalingrad in the south-east. For this aim, IV. *Panzerarmee* was shifted to *Heeresgruppe A*, which was instructed to launch all of its forces against Rostov. On 15 July, Hitler also sent von Bock into retirement and appointed *Generaloberst* Maximilian von Weichs as *Heeresgruppe B's* new commander.

*Oblt. Viktor Bauer, the Staffelkapitän of 9./JG 3 'Udet', was among the most successful German fighter aces on the Eastern Front. This photograph was taken on 30 June 1942 and shows Bauer and a group from the ground crew next to his Bf 109 F-4, W.Nr. 13325, 'Yellow 7', on 30 June 1942.*

*On 24 July 1942, Oblt. Viktor Bauer, the Staffelkapitän of 9./JG 3, claimed to have shot down three Il-2s and a Soviet fighter. One of the former proved to be piloted by the well-known Soviet Shturmovik ace Lt. Boris Yemelyanenko – who nevertheless survived to tell the story in his memoirs, which have been translated into English.*

New VVS units were hurled into combat to fill in the gaps which had been created through the losses. One of these units was the elite special air group 1 OAG. This consisted of the Pe-2 equipped 150 SBAP and Yak-1 equipped 434 IAP. The former was commanded by *Podpolkovnik* Ivan Polbin, one of the most outstanding Soviet bomber pilots and tacticians. 434 IAP was led by the ace *Mayor* Ivan Kleshchyov and its pilot roster included some very experienced flight trainers from the Kacha Flight Training School. However, none of these were of the quality of the leading fighter aces of the *Luftwaffe*.

When 150 SBAP attacked JG 3's new airfield at Millerovo on 16 July, its bombers were intercepted by the *Jagdgruppe*, and within a short space of time six of the Soviet unit's Pe-2s had been shot down for a single German loss.

206 ShAD was another new Soviet unit which entered combat with 8 VA on 16 July. As the former 206 IAD, badly mauled in May and June, it had been converted into a *Shturmovik Diviziya* bringing four brand new *Shturmovik* regiments – 621 ShAP, 686 ShAP, 766 ShAP and 811 ShAP – into action. The first operation cost 621 ShAP the loss of its *Eskadrilya* commander *Mayor* Mikhail Dmitriyev: his Il-2 was filed as the 91st victory on the tally of 9./JG 3's *Oblt*. Viktor Bauer.

However, Soviet air attacks – in particular a strike by 150 SBAP against a fuel dump near Morozovsk on 15 July – continued to put a brake on the German offensive across the sparsely populated and desert-like steppe between the Rivers Donets and Don. Lack of fuel forced IV. *Panzerarmee's* XLVIII. *Panzerkorps* to halt once it had reached the Don at Tsimlyansk, halfway between Rostov and Stalingrad. Farther to the north-east, in the Don Bend, fuel shortages in the face of stiffening Soviet resistance halted VI. *Armee* at the River Chir.

*Luftflotte* 4's strength report on 20 July reveals that the number of serviceable aircraft had decreased by 45 per cent – to just 718. The ground attack units had been hardest hit. SchG 1 had no more than 36 combat-ready aircraft. The two *Zerstörer Geschwader* could muster only 86 serviceable Bf 110s between them.

With no large reinforcements in sight, harsh measures had to be taken. ZG 2 was withdrawn from combat, handing over all of its aircraft to ZG 1. Above all, von Richthofen was forced to prioritise his forces at the most critical combat sectors by expedient measures – the so-called *Schwerpunktbildung*, individual points of maximum strength – even if this meant leaving other areas with only weak air support.

From 21 July he pulled together the major part of *Luftflotte* 4 into a *Schwerpunkt* in the south-western sector. The purpose of this was to support *Heeresgruppe A* in its attack against Rostov, the gateway to the Caucasus.

The Germans wished to avoid difficult street fighting at all costs and so von Richthofen had all his *Kampfgruppen* subject the city of Rostov itself to all-out indiscriminate bombing. Even the anti-shipping units of *Fliegerführer Süd* in the Crimea were instructed to participate in these attacks. Thus, He 111s of the torpedo *Gruppe* II./KG 26 dropped SC 1800 bombs over Rostov on 21 July.

On 22 July, the German ground assault against Rostov commenced. "The *Luftwaffe* provided excellent support for the attack during the entire

When the German Panzer forces veered southwards from Voronezh on 9-10 July 1942, only limited Axis forces remained to fight 2 VA and 1 IA in the Voronezh area. The former included the Hungarian Air Force's 1st Repülöcsoport. This photograph shows one of the He 46E-2/Un of the Hungarian tactical reconnaissance squadron 3/2. közelfelderítöszázad in the summer of 1942. (Becze)

The great, flat steppe between the Donets and the Don could be used as one huge airfield when the ground was dry in the summer of 1942 – as can be seen in this photograph. The aircraft is a Bf 109 F-4, 'Yellow 2', of 3./JG 3 Udet.

day. Not one target was overlooked. Heavy attacks were already launched against Rostov. The cooperation between the ground troops and *Luftwaffe*, guided by the air liaison officer (known as *Flivo* for short) was exceptional."[129]

When the *Luftwaffe* was able to concentrate its forces in such a manner, it was totally without compare. A few days later, Rostov was in German hands.

On 23 July Hitler issued his Directive No. 45, which ordered German forces to achieve two different aims simultaneously – the attacks against Stalingrad and against the Caucasus. This was completely in contradiction to von Richthofen's own conclusion that all-out efforts could be directed only against one sector at a time.

While *Generaloberst* von Richthofen concentrated *Luftflotte* 4 against Rostov in the west, his opponents placed the emphasis farther to the east.

By 22 July, 8 VA had been brought up to muster 337 serviceable aircraft – twice the number available to 4 VA and 5 VA in the Caucasus. With most of *Luftflotte* 4's Bf 109 units committed to the air over Rostov, the Ju 87s of

I. and II./St.G 2 were furnished with cover from Macchi C. 200s of the Italian 21 *Gruppo* Autonomo C.T. during their operations in support of VI. *Armee*. This proved to be an inadequate arrangement.

On 25 July 434 IAP attacked 4./St.G 2 and shot down four Ju 87s. The *Staffelkapitän*, Knight's Cross holder *Oblt*. Martin Möbus, was wounded and another Stuka pilot was reported missing. 434 IAP's *Lt*. Nikolay Karnachyonok was credited with the destruction of two Ju 87s in this combat. The next day, 434 IAP chalked up 18 victory claims – including double or triple victories by *Kapitan*s Vasiliy Babkov and Ivan Izbinskiy, and *Leytenants* Nikolay Karnachyonok and Vasiliy Savel'yev. Meanwhile 512 reportedly shot down 12 enemy aircraft. Although these claims were overstated, 21 *Gruppo* lost three Macchi C. 200s.

Once Rostov had been captured, von Richthofen immediately sent the bulk of *Luftflotte* 4 to support VI. *Armee* inside the so-called Don Bend. Less than a month after the German summer offensive had commenced, *Luftflotte* 4 had thus again assumed the role of 'fire brigade' which had so worn down the *Luftwaffe* on the Eastern Front during the past year.

A LaGG-3 in the air. In the spring of 1942, the Soviets modified the LaGG-3 into a 'light weight' version. Thus the manoeuvrability of this fighter – which previously had presented a great problem to the Soviet pilots – was considerably improved. The modified LaGG-3s in 1942 were definitely far better than some of the worst serial produced aircraft of 1941. (Drabkin)

Obstlt. Günther Lützow commanded JG 3 'Udet' during the Battle of Britain and the invasion of the USSR. On 11 August 1942 he was appointed Inspector of Day Fighters in the West. The position of Geschwaderkommodore of JG 3 was assumed by Hptm. Wolf-Dietrich Wilcke. Lützow was known as both an able and very popular unit commander. Following his 100th victory – which he achieved as the second fighter pilot to do so (following Werner Mölders) on 24 October 1941 – the Luftwaffe's Commander-in-Chief, Reichsmarschall Göring had Lützow grounded from flying any further combat missions. The reason was simple: the Third Reich could not afford losing such a public war hero. Nevertheless, later in the war, Lützow fell out with Göring and was threatened with execution. Günther Lützow was posted as missing after a mission in an Me 262 jet fighter whilst flying with Jagdverband 44 on 24 April 1945.

Loading the guns of a Lend-Lease P-39 Airacobra. A substantial share of the ground crew in Soviet air units was constituted of female technicians. (Viktor Kulikov Photograph Collection)

# Chapter Nine

# The Battle of the Don Bend

During the first four weeks of air combat following the launch of the German summer offensive, Soviet losses had been far higher than those on the German side – as had been the case since the *Luftwaffe* had launched its assault on the USSR. Between 28 June and 24 July 1942, a total of 783 Soviet aircraft were lost in the Donets - Don region. During the same time frame, the units under the command of *Luftflotte* 4 had reported a total of 175 of their own aircraft destroyed through hostile activity or lost to unknown causes.[130]

In the event, one of the most decisive advantages enjoyed by the Soviets was their superior ability to make good these losses. While the Soviets could exert an even pressure in the air along the entire front line, *Generaloberst* von Richthofen, the commander of *Luftflotte* 4, had little choice but to concentrate the bulk of his air units to a certain front sector, the so-called *Schwerpunktbildung*. Having used most of *Luftflotte* 4 to ensure a German victory at Rostov in the third week of July, von Richthofen shifted his main attention towards the eastern flank, where VI. *Armee* had become bogged down inside the Don Bend in its advance against Stalingrad on the Volga. But von Richthofen's *Schwerpunktbildung* in this sector was thwarted for a number of reasons.

At Voronezh, farther up the Don, a considerably reinforced Soviet Voronezh Front, supported by the Bryansk Front on its northern flank, engaged in relentless offensive action, mainly to relieve the pressure farther down the Don River. This placed German II. *Armee* and the Hungarian 2nd Army in a difficult situation. A particularly strong Soviet offensive opened against the German positions at Voronezh on 20 July. These attacks were reinforced three days later, resulting in a 15-mile deep breakthrough into the German lines.

As a result, bombers of *Gefechtsverband Nord's* KG 27 and KG 76 – which days earlier had been sent southwards to participate in the Rostov offensive – were brought back into action in the Voronezh sector. The Soviet aviation in this sector – mainly 2 VA, but also elements of 15 VA and the ADD as well as 1 IA and 101 IAD – also were very active, attacking German troop columns, encampments, gun positions and airfields both day and night. An account from KG 27 read:

"The area 40 - 50 km was the front sector which was subject to the greatest threat. We flew up to four combat flights each day. (…) The Russian air force was also up in force. They attacked our airfield day and night although mostly without inflicting any important damage. But now and then they scored some good hits. (…) During one of their attacks in the evening of 25 July, the last aircraft of the attack force hit a large fuel dump at the far end of the airfield and set it ablaze. During a daylight raid on 28 July, one aircraft on the ground was hit which exploded in a ball offire."[131]

This made it imperative to keep the only *Luftwaffe* fighter unit in the area in place. Counting aces such as *Oblt.* Heinrich Setz, *Oblt.* Anton Hackl, *Oblt.* Erwin Clausen and *Fw.* Ernst-Wilhelm Reinert amongst its ranks, II./JG 77 largely managed to maintain German air supremacy. Of 283 aircraft lost by 2 VA during the period 28 June - 31 July 1942,[132] the majority fell to this single German *Jagdgruppe*. In the meantime, II./JG 77's own combat losses were limited to only eight Bf 109s.[133]

At the beginning of August, 2 VA was down at a strength of 280 aircraft – including 197 in operational condition (30 fighters, 23 Il-2s and 144 bombers).[134] But this was still a force to reckon with for the Axis in the Voronezh sector, and the calm which had set in on this front was only temporary.

Combined with the need to maintain a *Luftwaffe* detachment at Voronezh, Hitler's Directive No. 45 of 23 July – outlining the simultaneous capture of Stalingrad and the Caucasus – made it impossible for von Richthofen to create the *Schwerpunkt* he wished in the Don Bend area. Directive No. 45 included an explicit order that the *Luftwaffe* was to provide "close and strong support to both army groups", i.e. *Heeresgruppe B* in the Don area and *Heeresgruppe A* during its advance into the Caucasus. Hence, von Richthofen was forced to divide his *Luftflotte* into three separate parts – which actually meant spreading it out instead of concentrating the forces.

*Generalmajor* Günther Korten – one of the *Luftwaffe's* most able senior commanders – was called in from *Luftflotte* 1 in the Leningrad sector, where he had successfully commanded I. *Fliegerkorps* for more than a year. On 28 July, Korten (who was promoted to *Generalleutnant* on 1 August 1942) and the staff of his *Fliegerkorps* took command of operations in the Voronezh – Kursk sector, where the new *Luftwaffenkommando Don* was formed, taking over the responsibilities of the ad hoc command *Gefechtsverband Nord* under *Oberst* Bülowius.

*An excellent in-flight view of Bf 110 C-7, S9+AN, of 5./ZG 1 on a mission to attack a Russian target. An armoured windscreen is fitted, and the undersurface wing tip is yellow.*

To the south, *Heeresgruppe A* – mainly German XVII. *Armee* and IV. *Panzerarmee* – was streaming across the lower Don and into the vast steppe in the northern Caucasus immediately following the conquest of Rostov. This was the sector where the Soviets offered the lightest opposition. The remnants of the battered Soviet Southern Front had little prospect of creating a defensive line, and were integrated into *Marshal* Semyon Budyonny's North Caucasus Front. But this too was incomparably weaker than List's forces, and fielded no more than 71 tanks by 28 July. For air support, Budyonny's troops could count on only around 200 aircraft: On 28 July, 4 VA was down to 126 serviceable aircraft – of which almost half were U-2 and R-5 biplanes for night missions. 5 VA, based on 4 VA's south-western flank, had less than 100 serviceable aircraft. In addition to this, however, VVS ChF had 216 combat aircraft for the air defence of the Caucasian Black Sea ports.

However, the vast distances which had to be covered in order to reach the oil fields in the southern Caucasus complicated *Heeresgruppe A's* task. This being one of the main goals for the German summer offensive, von Richthofen simply could not leave the Caucasus operation with too limited *Luftwaffe* forces. He decided to put *General* Kurt Pflugbeil, commander of IV. *Fliegerkorps,* in charge of air support for *Heeresgruppe A*. For this task, *General* Pflugbeil would command the bombers of KG 51 and KG 55, together with the Stukas of I. and II./St.G 77, the Bf 110 *Zerstörer* of ZG 1, and the Bf 109s of JG 52 and I./JG 53.

With these forces employed on what von Richthofen regarded as the 'flanks', the core of *Luftflotte* 4 – VIII. *Fliegerkorps* – was tasked with providing VI. *Armee* in the Don Bend sector with air support. By late July 1942, the units available to *Generalleutnant* Martin Fiebig's VIII. *Fliegerkorps* were St.G 2 with around 80 Ju 87s, SchG 1 with around 70 ground-attack planes, and JG 3 with 74 Bf 109s, plus reconnaissance units. But of these, less than half were serviceable. Even though the *Luftwaffe* aircraft were supplemented by a few dozen *Regia Aeronautica* aircraft, the Soviets enjoyed a numerical superiority in the air over the Don Bend in late July 1942. *General-Mayor* Timofey Khryukin's 8 VA could muster a total of 337 serviceable aircraft on 22 July – 85 fighters, 48 Il-2s, 88 day bombers, and 116 night bombers. These forces were supplemented by around 50 fighters of the Stalingrad Air Defence's 102 IAD PVO.

Relieved from the tasks over Rostov, the Bf 109s of *Obstlt.* Günther Lützow's JG 3 immediately set about clearing the skies of Il-2s and bombers – which were exerting heavy pressure on the German ground troops – and the modern Soviet fighters which were starting to take a heavy toll on both the Stukas and the Italian escort fighters.

On 27 July 8 VA recorded a loss of 26 aircraft. Fifteen of these were destroyed on the airfield at Illarionovskoye, 15 miles to the east of the Don Bend, during an attack by SchG 1. The next day, II. and III./JG 3 hacked down a formation of Il-2, claiming six victories – including three by *Fw.* Leopold Münster – without suffering any losses. The Soviets actually lost seven Il-2s.

But JG 3's Bf 109s were too few in number to provide the German ground troops with continuous air cover. Other VVS units slipped through and caused havoc among vehicle columns, claiming to have destroyed or damaged 30 tanks, 30 armoured vehicles, and two anti-aircraft batteries on 28 July.

On the same day, Stalin issued his famous order No. 227, which soon became known as *"Ni shagu nazad!",* "Not One Step Backwards". In harsh words, it called for the "elimination" of "the retreat mentality". Indeed, the new order signalled an even tougher stand against any Soviet serviceman suspected of cowardice, but above all it drummed into the Soviet troops that the period of retreat was over, and that they now were fighting with their backs to the wall. The impact of this order should not be underestimated. Clearly, from late July, the battle grew in intensity. On 30 July, *Heeresgruppe B* reported:

"North of Chirskaya an enemy attack was repulsed, resulting in 800 Russians killed. To the west of Kalach, motorised and armoured forces are locked into combat with around 100 enemy tanks. Farther north, about 40 Russian tanks broke through from the west and managed to overrun the headquarters of XIV. *Panzerkorps.*"[135]

8 VA and VIII. *Fliegerkorps* sent in all available aircraft. With only relatively few aircraft still serviceable on each side, these operations did not result in many clashes in the air. According to each side's loss records, operations over the Don Bend on 30 July cost six German and eleven Soviet aircraft However, in most cases when Bf 109s came across any opponents, the technical superiority of the German fighter and the much greater experience of the German pilots placed the Soviets in a situation of considerable disadvantage. As usual, a handful of German fighter aces played a considerable role in the outcome of the air battles as was the case on this date – II./JG 3's *Lt.* Ludwig Häfner was credited with the destruction of four Soviet aircraft.

Not least as a result of their support from the air the Soviets were able to continue to hold down VI. *Armee* in the Don Bend. Reacting to the stalemate inside the Don Bend, Hitler again changed the plan of operations. On 31 July he instructed IV. *Panzerarmee* to veer to the east from its position in the northern Caucasus south of the Don River, heading directly for Stalingrad in order to support VI. *Armee*. This gave von Richthofen the

*When I./JG 53 was sent into action over the Don Bend with its new Bf 109 G-2s – one of which, 'Black 3', is seen in this photograph – the situation in the air tilted dramatically to the German advantage.*

green light to divert more *Luftwaffe* units to the Don Bend area. He had already ordered the bomber units of IV. *Fliegerkorps* to divide their missions between the Caucasus and the Stalingrad sector, and on 31 July he diverted I./JG 53 from the northern Caucasus to the Don Bend sector.

I./JG 53 *Pik As* had recently returned to front line service after a rapid conversion onto the new Bf 109 G-2 '*Gustav*' fighters. This new Bf 109 variant, equipped with a more powerful engine, was unrivalled in the skies over the Eastern Front during the summer of 1942. Although the Soviets had improved the performance of their Yak-1s and LaGG-3s through the installation of better engines, and also introduced two new fighters – the Yak-7B and the La-5 – no VVS fighter could compete on terms with the Bf 109 G-2. In addition, I./JG 53 was noted for its very high combat morale and resolve, comparable only with that displayed by the toughest Soviet fighting men.

I./JG 53's arrival in theatre had an immediate impact on 8 VA. From 31 July onwards, its airmen could no longer count on being able to slip through to perform their attacks unnoticed by German fighters. *Oblt.* Wolfgang Tonne opened I./JG 53's account over the Don Bend at noon on 31 July. The 109s of I./JG 53 mounted an extra pair of 20mm cannon in detachable housings underneath the wings – so called 'gondolas'. This installation provided heightened effectiveness against the heavily armoured Il-2, and Tonne's victim at 11.40 hrs on 31 July was one of these *Shturmoviks*. From midday on 31 July and for a further five hours through the afternoon, Bf 109s were continuously on patrol in the air over the Don Bend, and repeatedly dived down on formations of five to fifteen Soviet aircraft attempting to attack targets on the ground. When the day was over, these air combats had cost 8 VA 27 aircraft, including 18 Il-2s.[136] This is well in line with the victory claims submitted by the German fighters – 32 in total, with no losses sustained.

*General-Mayor* Khryukin made absolutely ruthless demands on his airmen who, in spite of growing hardship flew nearly 1,000 combat sorties on the first two days of August. Owing much to the support from the air, a Soviet counter-attack succeeded in slicing through the German Front and surrounding parts of 16. *Panzerdivision* south-east of Kletskaya in the northern part of the Don Bend. German aircraft swarmed to this sector in large numbers and, on 3 August, no less than 60 Soviet tanks were reported destroyed. During this battle, the *Rotte* of *Uffz.* Wilhelm Crinius and *Uffz.* Heinz Golinski of I./JG 53 shot down five Il-2s in a single engagement at low altitude north of Kalach.

Despite the efforts of the bombers, Stukas, *Schlachtflieger* and fighters of VIII. *Fliegerkorps*, von Richthofen's greatest contribution to the German thrust against Stalingrad was possibly his strong measures to improve the

supply situation in the Don Bend area. One of the main reasons why the Germans were unable to make further headway towards Stalingrad was the poor state of the roads in the area, which created logistical bottlenecks and caused desperate shortages in fuel, ammunition, spare parts and other vital requirements at the Front. The real *Schwerpunkt* formed by von Richthofen against Stalingrad comprised transport aircraft. Most of the Ju 52s in *Luftflotte* 4 – altogether more than 300 aircraft – were concentrated in this sector. III./KG 4, whose He 111s had converted from bomber operations to mainly transport flights, was also sent southwards from Kharkov to Makeyevka. All of these were brought together into the so-called 'Stalingrad Transport Region'.

Supplies which were rapidly flown in to improvised landing strips on the flat and almost treeless steppe enabled IV. *Panzerarmee* to surge rapidly forward in the area immediately to the south of the Don. On 2 August, XLVIII. *Panzerkorps*, which attacked in IV. *Panzerarmee*'s centre along the rail line to Stalingrad, seized Kotelnikovo. From this point it progressed rapidly towards Stalingrad, 90 miles farther to the north-west, encountering little organized resistance. The advance from the south was facilitated by Soviet command and control difficulties. *Heeresgruppe B's* combined attacks had caused the Soviet Stalingrad Front to become spread out across over 400 miles – from Pavlovsk, 90 miles south-east of Voronezh, all the way down to the area south of Stalingrad.

On 4 August, the tanks of XLVIII. *Panzerkorps* had reached the Aksay River, just 60 miles south-west of Stalingrad. News of this quickly reached Stalingrad and caused panic among the population in the city.

In order to improve command and control of the operations against *Heeresgruppe B*, the *Stavka* decided to divide the Stalingrad Front in two. On 5 August, the 51st, 57th, 64th Armies and 1st Guards Army were placed under a new command, the South-eastern Front. One of the Red Army's best generals, *General-Polkovnik* Andrey Yeremenko, was flown in to assume command of the new Front. The 21st, 62nd and 63rd Armies and 4th Tank Army remained in *General-Leytenant* Vasiliy Gordov's Stalingrad Front. The city of Stalingrad itself marked the border between the two Fronts, with the Stalingrad Front's 62nd Army at Kalach, west of Stalingrad, and the South-eastern Front's 64th Army placed just south-west of Stalingrad.

Khryukin's 8 VA also was prepared to be divided in two, with the units based from Stalingrad and to the north-west earmarked for a brand new air army, 16 VA. However, the forming of 16 VA was delayed by several weeks.

On 5 August, Khryukin ordered most of his air units to strike against the threat on the southern flank, i.e. IV. *Panzerarmee*. LaGG-3s equipped with 37mm cannon were employed against the German armour, and reportedly knocked out four tanks, six armoured vehicles and a fuel dump on 5 August. In total, 8 VA conducted 265 sorties on this day, but suffered heavy losses at the hands of the German fighters – who claimed 31 aircraft shot down in the sector south-west of Stalingrad on 5 August. A low-level attack by seven fighters of 268 IAD against the German fighter base at Frolov on the same day was without any effect.

By this time, the German fighters in the Don Bend area – placed under the command of *Hptm.* Wolf-Dietrich Wilcke – had managed to seize control of the air. This fact was admitted in period Soviet accounts, which described "a clear and massive German air superiority". But the Soviets kept challenging the *Luftwaffe* with unbending tenacity.

On 6 August, one of the best Soviet fighter aces in the area – 183 IAP's *St.Lt.* Mikhail Baranov, who had been credited with 21 victories – was badly wounded in combat with I./JG 53. However, Baranov was not shot down: after claiming two Bf 109s and a Ju 87, Baranov was locked into an

The sorrowful remnants of German Flak vehicles following a raid by Il-2s in the Don Bend area in the summer of 1942. (Becze)

Bombs exploding among Soviet tanks during a Stuka attack by II./St.G 2 'Immelmann' in the Don Bend. (Taghon)

uneven combat with several Bf 109s of I./JG 53. When his Yak-1 ran out of ammunition, Baranov rammed one of the enemy fighters – possibly the one flown by *Lt.* Hans Roehrig, one of the aces in I./JG 53, who barely survived.

Although most of 8 VA's air units at this stage were in a shambles due to heavy losses, the Soviets managed to overcome some of these problems by bringing together aircraft of the same kind from various units for concentrated operations. The surviving Soviet airmen, and those who arrived as replacements, continued to offer stiff resistance. A letter written by an aviator from 270 BAD on 7 August 1942 well illustrates this: "Each one of us is absolutely aware of the great responsibility which we have for our people and for the destiny of our country. Our task is to rout the German army in southern Russia. We know that the struggle will be difficult and hard and that it will cost the lives of many of us. But we also know that it depends on us, our generation, if this deadly threat to our native land is to be overcome. Because of that we have to fight to the last drop of blood. Now it literally is a question of victory or death. Others may retreat, but we don't have that alternative."[137]

In order to relieve the pressure against Stalingrad, the Voronezh Front prepared an attack with Soviet 6th Army at Korotoyak, farther upstream the Don River, 50 miles south of Voronezh. In this sector the Hungarian 2nd Army secured the flanks of the German advance to the south. For air

A shot-down Su-2. The Su-2 light bomber was vulnerable to German fighter interception, but no more than other light bombers. The Su-2 was, in fact, a quite successful type. However, the Il-2 proved to be superior in carrying out similar tasks, and thus production of the Su-2 was discontinued. The Su-2 in this photograph, which belonged to 52 BAP, is being examined by soldiers of the Italian Expeditionary Force. (Karlenko)

A shot-down Pe-2. (Broschwitz – TG JG 52)

support, the *Stavka* reserve assigned the 6th Army with 291 ShAD, led by the *Shturmovik* 'ace' and Hero of the Soviet Union *Podpolkovnik* Andrey Vitruk. The Soviet attack opened on 6 August, with a 30-minute preparatory artillery shelling. Then the troops crossed the river, while the Il-2s of 291 ShAD held down the Hungarian defenders. Meanwhile, the whole of 244 BAD was dispatched to attack II./JG 77's airbase at Kastornoye. The German fighters scrambled and subjected the Soviets to a terrible massacre in the air. When the air battle was over, the pilots of II./JG 77 counted 21 victories, seven of which were against Bostons and four against 153 IAP's Airacobras. The price for all of this was a single Bf 109 shot down, with the pilot surviving, albeit with injuries.

But the Soviet 6th Army succeeded in establishing a bridgehead on the western bank of the Don and, on 8 August, a second crossing of the river was made. This time too, 291 ShAD provided valuable support from the air. The Soviet attack provided the new *Luftwaffenkommando Ost* with its baptism of fire. A pilot of I./KG 27 wrote: "From 8 August, the short period of calm which we were blessed with by the Russians in the Voronezh area is over. Up to 17 August we were again in intense action, flying up to four missions per day, attacking tanks and troop positions."[138]

This forced the Germans to divert the 336th Division from VI. *Armee* to bolster the bulging Hungarian defence, and bought the Stalingrad Front valuable time.

South-west of Stalingrad, *General-Polkovnik* Yeremenko's South-eastern Front thrust a powerful armoured counter-attack against IV. *Panzerarmee*

which was less than 30 miles from the city on 8 August. On the wide steppe in the Abganerovo - Tinguta area, a fierce tank battle developed. This succeeded in tying down IV. *Panzerarmee* at the Myshkova River. Meanwhile, in the subsequent air fighting, the Bf 109 *Gustav* pilots of I./JG 53 continued to score heavily and chalked up another sixteen victories for no losses on 8 August. *Polkovnik* Aleksandr Grisenko, commander of 2 IAP, was severely injured at the controls of one of the LaGG-3s shot down.

The pressure – in the air, from the air and on the ground – was too intense for the Soviets to be able to hold their own. Between 7 and 12 August, units of VI. *Armee* occupied the right banks of the northern part of the Don River bend north of Kalach, and surrounded elements of Soviet 62nd Army to the west of the Don at Kalach on 9 August. That marked a shifting in the air operations, with both sides turning their greatest attention to the Kalach sector.

9 August saw an increase in 8 VA's operations against German ground troops, mainly VI. *Armee*. Throughout the day, 8 VA's airmen performed 231 fighter sorties, 74 *Shturmovik* sorties and 51 sorties with bombers. As a result, they claimed to have destroyed or damaged around 50 tanks and 160 other motor vehicles.[139] But all of these air operations had to run the gauntlet of the fighters of VIII. *Fliegerkorps* which, on 9 August, reportedly shot down no less than 50 Soviet aircraft. This was the result of an endless series of small engagements between mostly four to six German fighters and maybe twice that number of Soviet aircraft. Meanwhile, the *Luftwaffe's* bombers, Stukas and *Schlacht* aircraft were generally saved from attacks from Soviet fighters because most Soviet fighters were either used in escort missions or simply tied up in fights with free-hunting Bf 109s. VIII. *Fliegerkorps'* own losses in air combat on 9 August were limited to two aircraft, both Bf 109s.[140]

The *Jagdwaffe's* own losses were more a result of the intensity of the air fighting than any severe opposition in the air. 10 August was a particularly bleak day – I./JG 53 lost two aces, *Lt.* Helmut Macher and *Ofw.* Heinrich Leschert, each with a personal score of 23 kills. Even worse, on the same day, *Oblt.* Viktor Bauer, the 106-victory ace who led 9./JG 3, was so badly injured during a force landing that he never returned to the Front. Bauer's successor as 9./JG 3's *Staffelkapitän*, *Lt.* Rolf Diergardt (30 victories), was killed in air combat as early as the next day. That such a high percentage of the German fighter pilot losses in the Don Bend area were aces is explained by the fact that even though fuel was scarce – which it often was due to the rapid German advance – the most experienced pilots were always in the air, with the other pilots flying sorties only as far as fuel allowed. This is another explanation for the high scores which were racked up by the *Experten* of VIII. *Fliegerkorps* during these weeks.

A Yak-1 revs up its engines prior to take-off. Test flights with serial produced Yak-1s in June 1942 rated the top speed of the aircraft at 218 kmh at 3657 metres altitude – which was quite inferior to the Bf 109 F-4 or G-2. (Petrov)

Bf 109 G-2s belonging to II./JG 52, photographed in the summer of 1942. All aircraft have mottled cowlings, presumably to tone down the earlier yellow finish. This seems to have been a characteristic of this unit's aircraft.

Another very important German fighter pilot left the combat zone on 11 August, when *Obstlt.* Günther Lützow, who had led JG 3 *Udet* with great success for two years, was called to France to become Inspector of day fighters in the West. Lützow was one of the most able unit commanders in the *Jagdwaffe* but his successor, Wolf-Dietrich Wilcke, was a talented leader and fighter pilot. Although he only held the rank of *Hauptmann,* Wilcke was appointed *Geschwaderkommodore* of JG 3. Under his leadership, JG 3 would continue to perform as one of the best German *Jagdgeschwader,* and Wilcke was soon assigned the task of leading all German fighter units in VIII. *Fliegerkorps.*

By that stage, VIII. *Fliegerkorps* had claimed nearly 600 Soviet aircraft shot down during the battle in the Don Bend. Although these figures were inflated – 8 VA recorded 230 aircraft losses (114 fighters, 70 *Shturmoviks,* 29 Pe-2s, four Su-2s, and 13 night bombers) between 20 July and 10 August – they nevertheless testified to a marked German superiority in the air.

In an effort to cripple the German fighters on the ground, Khryukov ordered renewed attacks against their forward airfields. This nevertheless failed completely. On 12 August, eight Il-2s from 686 ShAP tried to attack the German airfield at Tusov, near Kalach, but were attacked by Bf 109s of both I./JG 53 and JG 3 and lost all eight *Shturmoviks,* plus seven of the escorting fighters (from 235 and 269 IAD). The cost for all this was only one shot-down Bf 109. I./JG 53's *Fw.* Wilhelm Crinius, who claimed three 'MiG-3s' (probably LaGG-3s) during the air battle, wrote:

"The Russians attacked our base with a large number of fighters. Several of our *Gruppe*'s aircraft were in the air and the enemy formation was attacked before it reached the field. As I recall, the aircraft still on the ground were able to become airborne without difficulty.

The dogfight extended over many kilometres. I still remember my third victory very precisely. I overtook a MiG-3 from behind and below and immediately scored hits. I sideslipped to lose airspeed and then took up position above and to the right of the Russian. From only a few metres away I could see the Russian pilot slumped over the stick. The enemy's canopy was open. The MiG made a steep reversal and then went almost straight down, crashed and burned. I was so unnerved by this experience that I flew home without watching my tail. I was unable to fly any more that day."[141]

In the Voronezh - Korotoyak sector, 12 August saw heavy fighting between II./JG 77 and the attacking units of 2 VA. When the day was over, II./JG 77 had recorded 31 victories against six losses of its own. One of the pilots lost was *Fw.* Franz Schulte, credited with 46 victories.

On 13 August, JG 3 and I./JG 53 thwarted another Soviet attempt to strike at Tusov's airfield, shooting down seven Il-2s (although the Germans claimed 19) for no losses. II./JG 77 also had a field day on the 13th, bagging 29 Soviet planes, again for no losses.

On 17 August German VI. *Armee* managed to gain its first foothold on the left bank of the Don, north-west of Stalingrad. *General-Major* Khryukin immediately received an order to direct the main focus of his 8 VA to attack and destroy the German bridge heads across the Don. But the resources at his disposal were too weak. Either the units were severely battered, or they were newly arrived and thus lacked the necessary experience. Nevertheless, 270 BAD was thrust in full force against the bridges.

The first attack was made by the newly arrived 86 BAP in the evening of 19 August. The next day a group of Bf 109s from *Stab* and II./JG 3 attacked 779 BAP's Pe-2s before they had a chance to perform their bombing. Nine Pe-2s were shot down, one of them piloted by the unit commander, *Podpolkovnik* Bystrov (who nevertheless survived). The Germans also claimed nine victories in this engagement, including five by *Fw.* Werner Lucas and three by the new *Geschwaderkommodore, Hptm.* Wilcke.

Both sides received important fighter reinforcements on 20 August. 8 VA was bolstered through the arrival of 287 IAD with four regiments – 27 IAP, 240 IAP, 297 IAP and 437 IAP – equipped with the new Lavochkin La-5 fighter. On the German side, *Hptm.* Johannes Steinhoff's II./JG 52 arrived at Tusov, bringing in its new Bf 109 G-2s. However, II./JG 52's operations over the Don Bend started badly. On the following day, this *Gruppe*'s *Lt.* Waldemar Semelka, credited with 65 aerial victories, was shot down and killed by one of 86 BAP's Pe-2s. But in general, the German fighters managed to score excessively for limited losses. On 22 August, II./JG 52 paid back 86 BAP by shooting down three of its handful of remaining Pe-2s – all of which were claimed by *Lt.* Heinz 'Johnny' Schmidt. The next day, the main German assault across the Don and towards Stalingrad opened. The scene was set for one of the most famous battles in history…

This damaged Bf 109 G-2 was flown by Uffz. Hans Waldmann, who flew his first combat mission with Stab II./JG 52 on 31 August 1942; he was wingman to Hptm. Steinhoff, the Gruppenkommandeur. Waldmann claimed his first two victories on 2 and 3 November 1942 and subsequently became very successful as a fighter pilot, later flying with 6./JG 52 before transferring to the West. He claimed a total of 134 victories, including two with the Me 262, and was decorated with the Oak Leaves in March 1945. This photograph shows Waldmann's aircraft, W.Nr. 13566, in September 1942 after Soviet anti-aircraft fire had damaged its rudder.

21-year old St.Lt. Mikhail Baranov posing in front of his Yak-1 in the summer of 1942. 183 IAP's Mikhail Baranov was one of the Luftwaffe's most dangerous adversaries during the air battle in the summer of 1942. However, after scoring 21 victories, Baranov fell prey to overwhelming German air superiority. On 6 August 1942 he was badly injured after ramming a Bf 109 of I./JG 53. Eager to return to combat, Baranov took up flying again before he was fully recovered and perished in a flying accident on 17 January 1943.

# Chapter Ten

# The Offensive into the Caucasus

ollowing the fall of Rostov on 25 July, the Caucasus with its flat steppe and oil fields lay open to German *Heeresgruppe A*. Marshal Semyon Budyonny's weak North Caucasus Front was in no position to offer any lasting resistance, and resorted to the same tactic as had saved the South-western Front from annihilation between the Rivers Donets and Don – a rapid withdrawal.

As we have seen, Hitler had explicitly demanded that *Generalfeldmarschall* Wilhelm List's *Heeresgruppe A* should be provided with strong air support. Thus the Ju 88s and He 111s of III./LG 1, KG 51, KG 55 and I./KG 100 were brought to bear on Soviet road transport, railways and bridges, while the Bf 110s of ZG 1 provided the advancing troops with close support. Bf 109 fighters from the *Gruppen* of JG 52 – including the Croatian 15./JG 52 – and I./JG 53 meanwhile roamed the skies, hunting for the poor remnants of 4 VA. Commanded by *General* Kurt Pflugbeil, the commander of IV. *Fliegerkorps*, more than 500 German aircraft supported the initial attack against the Caucasus.

This was more than sufficient, since 4 VA was in a shambles and could only fight delaying actions with small forces. By 29 July, the *Luftwaffe* reported: "The Russian air force facing Army Group South's right flank is very weak. Stukas carry out their attacks without fighter escort. The Russian fighters are not attacking the Stukas and only intercept single German aircraft."[142]

Acknowledging the weakness of the Soviet resistance in the Caucasus – in stark contrast to the bitter fighting in the  – Hitler redirected IV. *Panzerarmee* from *Heeresgruppe A* back to *Heeresgruppe B*. I./JG 53 also was sent eastward. But this had no immediate impact on the speed with which *Generalfeldmarschall* List's forces continued their advance. On 1 August, I. *Panzerarmee* stood at the Krasnodar - Stalingrad railway at Salsk, 80 miles south of the Don. Two days later, the 3rd *Panzerdivision* occupied Voroshilovsk. The 3rd *Panzerdivision* continued towards Mozdok and the Grozny oil fields far to the south-east, and LVII. *Panzerkorps* was assigned the task of seizing the Maykop oil fields and the port of Tuapse in the south-west. On 9 August Maykop was overrun by the LVII. *Panzerkorps* – the oil fields had nonetheless been sabotaged by the retreating Soviet troops and could not be exploited for several weeks.

In the skies the *Luftwaffe* was in total control. Only at the Black Sea coast in the west, where VVS ChF operated, did the German airmen encounter any serious opposition. When 59 *Luftwaffe* bombers and 20 escort fighters were sent to attack the port installations at Novorossiysk and Tuapse on 10 August, fighters from VVS ChF rose in force and knocked down five of the German bombers – including two KG 55 machines lost following a ramming attack flown by *M.Lt*. Mikhail Borisov of 62 IAP/VVS ChF.

But in general, the Germans were more or less alone in the air over the Caucasus. Thus, more elements of the *Luftwaffe* forces which had supported the Caucasus offensive started to be diverted to other sectors. On 14 August, I./JG 52 was sent to *Luftwaffenkommando Ost* in the central combat zone – where the Soviets had initiated very strong relief offensives. A few days later, the main body of IV. *Fliegerkorps* was transferred north-eastwards to bolster the air support being assembled for the forthcoming final assault towards Stalingrad.

However, this coincided with a general Soviet regroupment. Along the mountain ridge which bars the Caucasian Steppe in the west from the Black Sea coast, and in the Terek River area at Mozdok in the south, the Soviet forces halted their retreat and turned to fight *Heeresgruppe A*. In the Terek River area, fresh troops from the Transcaucasian Front joined the North Caucasian Front to form strong defence positions. Led by *General-Mayor* Konstantin Vershinin, 4 VA opened an air offensive against the advancing columns of I. *Panzerarmee*. In a matter of days, the triumphant German offensive stalled in bitter fighting. Shortages in fuel and ammunition due to the extended supply lines contributed to German difficulties, but the effect of Soviet air attacks should not be underestimated. Although 4 VA mustered only slightly more than 100 aircraft, these played a vital role – testified by numerous German accounts – to the successful Soviet defence in the Terek area.

Through the *Schwerpunktbildung* in the Stalingrad area, the fighter units available to cover the whole Caucasian air space for the Germans were only 15.(Kroat)/JG 52 against 5 VA and VVS ChF in the west, and two-thirds of a *Jagdgruppe* – III./JG 52 – and *Major* Gordon Gollob's *Stabsstaffel* of JG 52 in the south-east.

The German fighter pilots gave a good account of themselves. On 29 August, *Major* Gollob became the first pilot ever to reach a score of 150

A scene of destruction on a Soviet country road in the Caucasus in the summer of 1942. The effect of German Zerstörer attacks is evident. (Broschwitz)

The commander of the Croatian 15.(Kroat)/JG 52, Obstlt. Franjo Dzal, and Hptm. Josip Helebrant of the same Staffel, next to Dzal's Bf 109 G-2, W.Nr. 13619. (Marko Jeras)

aircraft downed. Other notable *Jagdwaffe* aces who fought against 4 VA in the summer and autumn of 1942 were *Oblt.* Adolf Dickfeld, *Oblt.* Günther Rall, *Ofw.* Josef Zwernemann, *Fw.* Alfred Grislawski and *Fw.* Edmund Rossmann. They dominated the sky wherever they appeared, and frequently inflicted absolutely crippling losses on formations of 4 VA aircraft. With 4 VA combat losses numbering 149 aircraft through September 1942,[143] the average airman in 4 VA could expect to fly no more than four weeks before being shot down. But the German aces were too few in number to be able to control such a vast area and the VVS exerted mounting pressure on the German ground troops, who frequently spoke of 'Soviet air superiority'.

With the exception of some local territorial gains, the combat zone in the Caucasus froze into positional warfare. While the main battle at Stalingrad was being fought out, both sides kept their forces in the Caucasus at a mimimum, allowing neither side to achieve a decision. The Caucasus

operation in the summer and autumn of 1942 was a major success for the new elastic Soviet tactic of evading when at disadvantage, sacrificing 'empty land' for the purpose of gathering their forces farther back and when their opponent had his supply lines strung out. 4 VA also demonstrated stiff-necked resolve and skilful command – whether led by *General-Mayor* Vershinin or his successor from 8 September, *General-Mayor* Nikolay Naumenko.

On the German side, the dismal end to the Caucasus offensive was the consequence of Hitler's decision to split his limited resources between two geographical goals which lay hundreds of miles apart. Typically for the self-minded *Führer*, he put the blame on *Generalfeldmarschall* List, who was dismissed on 9 September. Instead, direct command of *Heeresgruppe A* was assumed by the *Führer* himself.

# The Night Witches

Possibly the most well known Soviet air unit during the Battle of the Caucasus was the all-female 588 NBAP. Throughout the Battle of the Caucasus, the young women of this unit flew their U-2 biplanes on regular night harassment sorties, bombing encampments, airfields, supply depots, headquarters, etc in the German rear areas. They carried out this with such élan that they earned a special soubriquet among the Germans in the Caucasus – *Nachthexen* or 'Night witches' – the name soon spread throughout the Axis armed forces on the Eastern Front.

After the war, it was widely assumed that the term 'Night Witches' was a Soviet propaganda invention, but German servicemen who were stationed in the Caucasus assert that the nickname originated with them. "It was we pilots in III./JG 52 who invented the name", confirmed Alfred Grislawski, who served as an *Ofw.* in the Caucasus in 1942: "And I can assure you that it was an expression of the respect we felt towards those courageous women."[1]

*Hptm.* Johannes Steinhoff, *Kommandeur* of II./JG 52 – which operated in the Caucasus between September and November 1942 – recalled the attitude among the German airmen: "We simply couldn't grasp that the Soviet airmen that caused us the greatest trouble were in fact women. These women feared nothing. They came night after night in their very slow biplanes and for some periods they wouldn't give us any sleep at all."[2]

*St.Lt.* Serafima Amosova-Taranenko, one of the pilots in 588 NBAP, told American author Anne Noggle about her experiences in the Caucasus during this period:

"On one airfield where we were stationed there were two regiments, one female and one male. We had the same missions, the same aircraft, and the same targets, so we worked together. The female regiment performed better and made more combat flights each night than the male regiment. … Once one of the German prisoners said, 'When the women started bombing our trenches we [Germans] had a number of radio nets, and the radio stations on this line warned all their troops, "Attention. Attention. The ladies are in the air; stay in your shelter."

"Nobody knows the exact date when they started calling us night witches. We were fighting in the Caucasus near the city of Mozdok; on one side of this city were Soviet troops and on the other, German. We were bombing the German positions nearly every night…"[3]

Early in the war, Marina Raskova – one of the world's pioneer aviatrices – had managed to persuade Stalin to agree to the formation of all-women air combat units. The result was an order by the Soviet Peoples' Defence Committee on 8 October 1941, according to which three all-women air combat units would be formed: 586th IAP, 587th BAP and 588th NBAP. Raskova took command of 587 BAP, and handed over command of 588 NBAP to *Mayor* Yevdokiya Bershanskaya. On 27 May 1942, 588 NBAP was declared operational and assigned to 218 NBAD. Sixteen days later, the unit carried out its first operations.

The presence of 588 NBAP was soon noticed by the Germans. While other night harassment units conducted their operations by aircraft flying singly, the female regiment flew in groups of three. Two of these went in first, attracting the attention of the German searchlights and anti-aircraft fire, while a third would sneak in undetected and drop its bombs.

On most occasions, the U-2's poor bombing and navigational devices prevented the 'Night Witches' from dealing any heavy material damage to the enemy, but the relentless night raids wore down the Germans by depriving them of their sleep.

The Germans had great trouble in adopting any effective countermeasures against the U-2s, whose cruising speed was below that of the Bf 109. Alfred Grislawski recounts how the newcomer *Lt.* Erich Hartmann once set up a 20mm-anti-aircraft gun against the U-2 intruders – with the only result that the gun's muzzle fire served as an aiming point for the U-2 crew, and Hartmann barely escaped being killed by the bombs which were dropped.[4]

IV. *Fliegerkorps* eventually organized improvised night fighter units with He 111s from *Kampfgeschwader* and Bf 110s from 10./ZG 1. Operating with the support of searchlights, these night fighters occasionally took a heavy toll of the biplanes. When hit, the U-2 aircraft was easily set on fire and the aircraft was almost always doomed. The crew could not escape because parachutes were not provided until the summer of 1944.

Serafima Amosova recalled one very harsh event:

"One night, as our aircraft passed over the target, the searchlights came on, anti-aircraft guns were firing, and then a green rocket was fired from the ground. The flak ceased firing and a German fighter plane arrived on the scene and shot down four of our aircraft as each one came over the target. Our aircraft were burning like candles. We all witnessed this scene. When we landed and reported that we were being attacked by German fighters, they would not let us fly again that night. We lived in a school building and slept on camp beds. You can imagine our feelings when we returned to our quarters and saw eight beds folded, knowing that these were the cots of our friends who had perished a few hours ago."[5]

However, the U-2 – later designated Po-2 – had the lowest loss rate among all Soviet combat aircraft during World War II. In spite of the hazardous nature of 588 NBAP's missions, the unit lost only 30 aircrew members during the war. Thus, with 23,672 combat sorties carried out by 588 NBAP throughout the war, 789 combat sorties were flown for each fatal loss. It should be kept in mind that when a U-2/Po-2 was lost, it often meant the loss of both crew members in the aircraft. In recognition of the unit's feats during the Battle of the Caucasus, 588 NBAP was adopted as the 46th Guards Regiment of VVS KA in February 1943. The Po-2 later served with success during the Korean War, providing the Americans with the same difficulties that the Germans had experienced ten years previously.

[1] Interview with Alfred Grislawski.
[2] Interview with Johannes Steinhoff.
[3] Noggle, *A Dance with Death: Soviet Airwomen in World War II*, p. 46.
[4] Bergström and Antipov with Grislawski, *Graf & Grislawski: A Pair of Aces*, pp. 142-143.
[5] Noggle, p. 46.

# Air War over the Desert

One of the least known chapters of the air war was the fighting – with very small but decisive forces – over the desert-like Kalmyk Steppe in the summer and autumn of 1942. As the German VI. *Armee* began to advance into the Don Bend, *Generaloberst* von Richthofen instructed the bombers of IV. *Fliegerkorps* to open up attacks against Soviet shipping from Astrakhan upstream on the Volga. Astrakhan, on the northern shore of the Caspian Sea, was the connection between the seaborne oil deliveries from the Baku and Grozny oil fields in the south and the Soviet mainland – via the Volga River. These attacks opened quite successfully on 25 July, when two tankers were set ablaze on the Volga near Stalingrad and three barges were sunk. The next day, the *Luftwaffe* bombers reported the destruction of two tankers, a 1,200-ton steamer, five barges and one tug boat on the Volga. On 27 July, the German bombers returned to sink the passenger ship Aleksandr Nevskiy, three transport ships, three oil barges and four other barges on the Volga.[1] The greatest successes were achieved on the night of 30-31 July, when *Luftflotte* 4 reported the following results:

Sunk on River Volga:
One large transport ship
Three oil barges
One 1,000-ton barge
Two 300-ton barges
One 800-ton tanker
Damaged on River Volga:
Seven 500-ton barges
One 1,500-ton transport ship
One 1,000-ton transport ship[2]

Following these attacks, the vital oil supplies to Stalingrad and the Soviet hinterland were more or less brought to a complete standstill. As a result, hundreds of thousands of tons of oil was accumulated in large oil stores in Astrakhan. Naturally, this became a tempting target for the Germans. Initially, the Germans planned the seizure of these rich oil reserves rather than aerial bombardment. But just as the Soviets lacked troops to defend this vital city, the

Germans had minimal resources available for the the long march to Astrakhan –
300 miles east of *Heeresgruppe* A's base at Salsk in the Caucasus.

Indeed, as *Heeresgruppe* A surged southward, deep into the Caucasus, and
*Heeresgruppe* B was locked into the difficult battle at Stalingrad – with the Soviet
South-eastern and North Caucasus Fronts tied to these battles – a huge gap
opened in the vast and sparsely populated Kalmyk Steppe between those two
battlefields.

The German advance towards Astrakhan started as a flank securing operation.
Moving towards the east from Salsk, the Germans reached Remontnaya on
9 August, 100 miles to the east of Salsk, in a raging sandstorm and broiling 52-
degree Celsius heat. The advance was virtually unopposed. In fact, the Soviets had
been compelled to shift the bulk of their 51st Army, responsible for this sector,
farther to the north to help counter German IV. *Panzerarmee* as it threatened
Stalingrad from the south. This gave the Germans the idea of pushing forward into
the desert-like Kalmyk Steppe. On 12 August, the small town of Elista – the Kalmyk
Soviet Socialist Republic's capital – was occupied.

The Soviets hurriedly brought military reinforcements to the area.
On 17 August, *General-Leytenant* V. F. Gerasimenko was instructed to organize the
defence of Astrakhan. Subordinated to the South-eastern Front, he received one
division and three brigades from the *Stavka* Reserve to form the new 28th Army.
In addition to these ground forces, Gerasimenko was supplied with 289 SAD.
Led by *Polkovnik* Leonid Reyko, the *Diviziya* consisted of 20 Il-2s, divided between
232 and 806 ShAP. Stationed at the airfields at Nachalovo and Ivanovo near
Astrakhan, the Il-2s commenced operations on 18 August.

The Germans countered by dispatching Ju 88s and He 111s of
IV. *Fliegerkorps* against Soviet military installations in the northern parts of
Astrakhan on 19 August. However, 289 SAD was saved from any destruction and
soon the regular attacks by the *Shturmoviks* became the main obstacle to the
German advance against Astrakhan. Since there was initially neither fighter
opposition nor any anti-aircraft artillery worth mentioning in this area, the main
problem for the Il-2 pilots of 289 SAD was navigation. In the huge desert area with
its monotonous landscape and very few inhabited settlements, the Soviet pilots
had to navigate to their target by dead reckoning.[3]

On 23 August, the Germans subordinated the 16th Motorised Division to
*Heeresgruppe* B and assigned to this unit the task of advancing towards
Astrakhan. Although lacking adequate fuel supplies, the motorised columns
started moving along the only earth road in the area, seizing Yashkul, 60 miles
east of Elista, on 29 August. The following day, the Utta oasis was occupied
without opposition – another 25 miles farther to the east. That left Soviet 107th
Guards Rifle Regiment cut off at Yashkul. Only under cover of six attacking Il-2s,
led by *Kapitan* V. L. Kiriyevskiy, were the Soviet troops able to break through and
link up with the Soviet main line.

German 16th Motorised Division advanced to Khalkhuta, just 75 miles from
Astrakhan, but there the offensive ground to a halt. This was not least due to
289 SAD's increasingly effective attacks against the troop columns out on the flat
steppe. According to 289 SAD's own reports, 20 motor vehicles and 50 horse-
drawn carts were destroyed during a few days of attacks by 289 SAD's Il-2s.

The Germans responded by dispatching a *Schwarm* from I./JG 53, led by
*Lt.* Hans Roehrig, to an improvised airfield at Utta. As early as their first mission
on 4 September, the Bf 109 fighters shot down three Il-2s, two of them achieved
by Roehrig. One of the downed Il-2s, piloted by 806 ShAP's *Kapitan* Vsevolod
Shiryayov, crashed straight into a fuel truck at Khalkhuta, causing a raging fire
which reportedly could be seen in Utta. For this feat, reported as a 'fire *taran*',
Shiryayov was posthumously appointed a Hero of the Soviet Union.

From then on, I./JG 53 and III./JG 3 took turns to station a *Schwarm* in this
desert outpost. The Soviets countered by shifting *Mayor* Georgiy Zaytsev's Yak-1-
equipped 148 IAP to the area, but no encounters between Soviet and German
fighters are known in this area in the autumn of 1942.

Aided by Fw 189 crews from 5.(H)/12, which was also based at Utta, the
Germans started to send out motorised groups on armed reconnaissance towards
Astrakhan. On 15 September, one of these groups reached within less than
10 miles of Astrakhan. This of course provoked new Soviet counteractions.

289 SAD received a new and energetic commander in *Podpolkovnik* Mikhail
Avvakumov. On 19 September he sent two groups of Il-2s from 232 and 806 ShAP,
escorted by nine Yak-1s of 148 IAP, against the positions of German 156th
*Kradschützen* Batallion at Khalkhuta. The *Shturmoviks* carried out a 28-minute
bombardment which allowed Soviet troops to conduct a successful ground-
attack. Next, the two *Shturmovik* regiments teamed up to maintain six-plane

formations in continuous attacks for four hours, which forced the Germans onto
the defence.[4] This air operation was even mentioned in the German Army High
Command's daily report.[5]

The Soviet attack had struck at a time when there were no German fighters
available. But now an urgent request was sent to *Luftflotte* 4's headquarters, and
at Pitomnik near Stalingrad, *Hptm*. Wilcke was instructed to send a *Schwarm*
down to Utta. Wilcke decided to dispatch 9./JG 3's *Fw*. Siegfried Engfer and
*Fw*. Karl Schäuble with their respective wingmen. Engfer was a veteran with over
50 victories to his credit, and Schäuble was one of JG 3's most promising
newcomers. In only four weeks he had increased his victory tally from 4 to 18.
289 SAD's continued operations on 23 and 24 September cost six Il-2s – five of
which fell to Schäuble's guns. As a result, the 156th *Kradschützen* Batallion was
able to regain its positions. During those air combats, 232 ShAP's *St.Lt.*
K.P.Gaverdovskiy landed twice in no-man's land to pick up downed comrades,
while *St.Serzh.* L. S. Savelyov similarly flew *M.Lt.* Z. S. Khitalishviliy back to safety.

Nevertheless, a few days later the German fighters returned to Stalingrad –
leaving one Bf 109 behind which had crashed at Utta.[6] On 29 September 289 SAD
made four concentrated attacks against 156th *Kradschützen* Batallion.

A war of attrition continued during the remainder of the autumn, and aerial
reconnaissance played a particularly vital role to both sides. "Air reconnaissance
provided an inestimable service to the division," wrote *Oblt*. Damm, the Air liaison
officer in the German 16th Motorised Division. "Often, the aircraft would join in
the ground battle or engage enemy movements independently." In his chronicle
on the war in the Caucasus, Wilhelm Tieke describes one example of the often
decisive role played by air reconnaissance in the Kalmyk Steppe:

"At the end of October air reconnaissance reported enemy east to west
movement 20 kilometres south of Khalkhuta. According to the maps, this had to be
in the vicinity of a water station. A small combat formation from the II./60
*Pz.Gren.Rgt.* was committed. However, it missed its attack objective in the
steppes. The operation was repeated with the cooperation of two fighter aircraft.
The fighters led the ground formation to the objective. Over 100 Soviets, who
were establishing a supply point for a following enemy formation at an oasis,
were surprised and, after a short battle, captured. The water station and the
supply dump were blown and the area was mined."[7]

On the Soviet side, the successes achieved by the Il-2s owed much to the
excellent reconnaissance missions which were performed by Pe-2s of 86 BAP,
which had been brought in from 270 BAD. They flew 'shuttle' missions from
Vishnyovka near Stalingrad to Nachalovo near Astrakhan, where they refueled
and then flew their photo reconnaissance missions over the Elista - Utta area.
Afterwards, they would return to Vishnyovka via Nachalovo. It was noted that
especially successful reconnaissance missions were carried out by the Pe-2
crew of *Lt.* Leonid Bobrov, who later was to be appointed a Hero of the
Soviet Union.[8]

However, the operations in the hot and dry of the semi desert required a
special attentiveness from the men. This was painfully demonstrated to the
86 BAP Pe-2 crew of *St. Serzh.* Ivan Bespalov, shot down by a German fighter on
20 October. The crew force-landed in the middle of the waterless steppe, 90 miles
west of Astrakhan. The navigator, *M.Lt.* Borisov, was killed, but Bespalov and his
gunner, *Serzh.* Sapozhnikov, survived. The two men endured two days without
water before they managed to reach the State Farm Budyonnyy on foot.[9]

When it was clear that Astrakhan would remain in Soviet hands, *Luftflotte* 4
resumed its bombing operations against the city and the shipping in the Caspian
Sea. I./KG 100's He 111s carried out a first mission against ships in the Caspian
Sea on 26 October. That evening, *Hptm*. Hansgeorg Bätcher, 1./KG 100's
*Staffelkapitän*, located a tanker which he attacked six times during one and the
same mission. Finally he hit the fo'c'sle with an SC 250 bomb which set the ship
burning. When Bätcher landed in Armavir at 22.10 hrs he was feted by the entire
unit – he had just completed his 400th bombing mission.[10]

During the night of 26-27 October I./KG 100 carried out two more such
operations. Together with other participating *Kampfgruppen*, they claimed to have
sunk three freighters and set one tanker ablaze. On the night of 27-28 October
I./KG 100 attacked the city of Astrakhan. The next day IV. *Fliegerkorps* bombers
reported two freight ships of 3000 GRT tonnage sunk and two tankers and five
freight ships damaged in the Caspian Sea. During continued operations on the
night of 29-30 October, I./KG 100 reported the sinking of two tankers in the
Caspian Sea.[11] The following night four tankers and five freight ships were
damaged by *Luftwaffe* bombs. Meanwhile other bombers raided the rail line north
of Astrakhan and set thirteen tank cars burning.

All of these German bomber operations were met with only light opposition. No fighter interception was reported, and mostly the bombers were confronted with only light anti-aircraft fire. The first *Luftwaffe* loss during these operations over the Caspian Sea occurred on the night of 31 October - 1 November, when the crew of I./KG 100's *Uffz.* Hans Zehbe failed to return. By that time I./KG 100 had no more than seven operational He 111s.[12]

It would not be before mid-November until I./KG 100 made any further operations over the Caspian Sea, but on 15 November *Lt.* Herbert Kuntz's crew scored a bomb hit on a 1300-GRT transport ship. That was the end not only of *Luftwaffe* operations over the Caspian Sea, but it also marked the beginning of the end of the war in the Elista - Utta area. A *Schwarm* from III./JG 3 made a final appearance at Utta in the third week of November, with *Uffz.* Heinz Gosemann shooting down a U-2 and an Il-2 on 21 November. But at that stage the Soviets had already opened their large counter-attack at Stalingrad, and it would soon spread south. On 23 November one of III./JG 3's Bf 109s was destroyed by Soviet artillery fire at Utta.

1. *Chazanow, Nad Stalingradem*, p.10.
2. *Lagebericht OKH 1 August 1942: Eingegangene Meldungen Generalstab Luftwaffe während des 1.8.41. Kriegstagebuch des Oberkommandos der Wehrmacht*, Vol. III, p. 544.
3. Gubin and Kiselyov, *Vos'maya vozdushnaya*, p. 22.
4. TsAMO, f. 46, op. 5755, d. 8, l. 45.
5. *Lagebericht OKH, 21 September 1942. Kriegstagebuch des Oberkommandos der Wehrmacht;* Vol. III, p. 751.
6. *Flugzeugunfälle und Verluste bei den Verbänden (täglich)*, Ob.d.L. *Gen.Qu. Gen. 6. Abt.* Bundesarchiv/Militärarchiv RL 2 III/1183.
7. Tieke, *The Caucasus and the Oil*, pp. 133-134.
8. TsAMO, f..346, op. 5755, d.19, l. 131-132.
9. TsAMO, f. 134 GBAP.
10. Major Hansgeorg Bätcher, logbook.
11. Balke, *Kampfgeschwader 100 Wiking*, p. 122.
12. 12. Ibid., p. 124.

*Polikarpov's single-engined trainer biplane, the U-2, was brought into use as a light night bomber – a 'harassment bomber' – by the Soviets in 1941. Used in this role, it was so successful that the Germans later copied the method of using old trainer biplanes in nocturnal harassment missions in so-called 'Nachtschlachtgruppen'. (Drabkin)*

*This Fw 189 was shot down and barely managed to perform a belly-landing in the Caucasus in the summer of 1942. (Taghon)*

# Chapter Eleven

# The Drive towards Stalingrad

*Before the German invasion of Russia, Stalingrad ranked among the country's greatest industrial cities, but by the autumn of 1942 it was a battleground where every building was contested in bitter hand-to-hand fighting, after which the contestants fought for the rubble amidst devastated industrial suburbs, such as seen here.*

During the days preceding the final assault towards Stalingrad – which was initiated from VI. *Armee*'s bridgehead on the eastern side of the Don Bend – *Generaloberst* von Richthofen was finally able to assemble a *Schwerpunkt* of his *Luftflotte* 4 in this sector. KG 27 and KG 76 were brought in from *Luftwaffenkommando Don* in the north to support the Stalingrad offensive. In addition the bombers of KG 51, KG 55 and I./KG 100, the Stukas of I./St.G 77, and a fighter detachment from III./JG 52 arrived from the Caucasus.

As we have seen, the *Luftwaffe* already enjoyed a convincing supremacy in the air in this sector, but by now they had attained numerical superiority – 600 Axis aircraft were pitted against only slightly half that number in 8 VA and 102 IAD PVO, supported by around 100 aircraft of the ADD.

The German attack against Stalingrad opened early on 23 August with 16th *Panzerdivision* of *Generalleutnant* Hans Hube's XIV. *Panzerkorps* breaking out from its bridgehead across the Don north-west of Stalingrad, and pushing towards the east.

*Generaloberst* von Richthofen sent the following message to all his units:

"The battle of Stalingrad, the stronghold of the Reds, has begun. By dealing destructive blows against the enemy, the *Luftwaffe* will bring this battle to a victorious end. I expect all unit commanders in *Luftflotte* 4, in the air as well as on the ground, to give their utmost to bring us Final Victory."

While the *Panzer* troops raced across the steppe between the Don and the Volga, aircraft of VIII. *Fliegerkorps* swarmed in the air above, bombing and strafing Soviet pockets of resistance and warding off Soviet aircraft which tried to interfere. *Hptm.* Kurt Brändle, commanding II./JG 3, bagged three Soviet ground-attack planes – thus reaching a total score of 102 victories. This was his last achievement before his *Jagdgruppe* was pulled out of combat

for rest and refit in Germany, leaving its Bf 109s to the other elements of JG 3.

At 16.35 hrs on 23 August, Josef Stalin sent the following wire to the Stalingrad and South-eastern Fronts: "The enemy has broken through your front with [only] small forces. You have enough forces to destroy the enemy which has broken through. Assemble the aircraft of both fronts and attack the enemy." But that was precisely what *General-Mayor* Khryukin had been attempting to do for the previous ten hours, and by the time Stalin sent his wire, 8 VA's air units were hardly in a position to put more aircraft into the air. Since early that morning, the Soviet pilots had been shot out of skies swarming with Messerschmitt fighters.

## Excerpt from the initial Soviet report on the effects of the air raids against Stalingrad 23-26 August 1942

The initial Soviet report on the effects of the air raids against Stalingrad between 24 August (the evening of 23 August and the night of 23-24) and 26 August 1942 came to the following conclusions, in brief:

27 August 1942
No 411-A
The Urban Committee of Defence reports the following results of the German aerial attacks against Stalingrad on 24, 25, 26 and August

Traktorozovodskomiy area:
Number of dead: 68
Number of wounded: 247

Barrikadnomiy area:
Number of dead: 200
Number of wounded: 120

Krasno Oktaybrskomy area:
Number of dead: 62
Number of wounded: 126

Dzerzhinskiy area:
Number of dead: 70
Number of wounded: 68

Yermanskomiy area:
Number of dead: 302
Number of wounded: 157

Voroshilovskiy area:
Number of dead: 315
Number of wounded: 463
90 per cent of all buildings in the central Voroshilovskiy area have been burned down.

Throughout the city, the water supply has been knocked out as have the electricity grid and the city's telephone network. The railway station is completely destroyed.

The 955 dead and 1,181 injured were of course only preliminary figures. Due to the prolonged period of relentless and intensified fighting which opened with these aerial attacks, the actual number will never be known. The true number of victims was clearly higher than the figure that appeared in this initial Soviet report. However, post-war estimations ranging in the tens of thousands can barely be accepted as credible.

During the course of one day, the 16th *Panzerdivision* surged across the flat steppe between the Rivers Don and Volga and established positions just to the north of Stalingrad. All-out German air raids against Stalingrad followed. From 7.00 in the evening and throughout the night of 23-24 August, *Luftflotte* 4's bombers subjected Stalingrad to a hellish bombardment. *Generaloberst* von Richthofen had ordered these attacks to annihilate the Soviet defenders of Stalingrad. More than 1,000 tons of bombs were dropped, and Stalingrad was set ablaze from one end of the city to the other. Early the next day, the *Luftwaffe* bombers flew straight into the thick black columns of smoke spiralling upwards from the battered city and continued to unload their bombs into the destruction.

The bombs kept falling over Stalingrad throughout 24 August, during the following night, and with the same intensity on 25 August. On that day, Richthofen took his personal Fieseler Storch to study the destruction from the air. He saw the entire city on fire, thick smoke clouds obscuring the horizon. "Stalingrad is completely destroyed", he later noted in his diary, expressing full satisfaction.[144] To the inhabitants of the tormented city, it felt as if the end of the world had arrived.

But the ruthless air attacks were not sufficient to break the Soviet resistance on the ground. On 24 August the Stalingrad Front regrouped its 63rd Army to launch a counter-attack against *Generalleutnant* Hube's 16th *Panzerdivision* north of Stalingrad. Supported by the bulk of 8 VA, which conducted 265 sorties, these Soviet forces managed to surround the *Panzer* troops. When Hube's troops proved unable to withstand these attacks alone, von Richthofen ordered his air fleet to shift their focus from the bombardment of Stalingrad to direct support of the hard pressed *Panzer* troops. Thus the logbook of *Hptm.* Hansgeorg Bätcher, the *Staffelkapitän* of 1./KG 100, shows one mission against Stalingrad on the night of 23-24 August, three more missions against Stalingrad on the 24th, on the following night and at noon on 25 August – followed by an attack against Soviet troop positions in the afternoon of 25 August.[145] *Hptm.* Johannes Steinhoff sent the Bf 109 pilots of his II./JG 52 on repeated fighter sweeps in the air above 16th *Panzerdivision,* and they claimed to have shot down more than 20 Soviet aircraft on 25 August – of which Steinhoff himself contributed four, bringing his total victory tally to 90. In return, II./JG 52 lost no more than a single Messerschmitt.

For two consecutive days, heavy air battles raged in the area between the Don and the Volga north of Stalingrad. These combats were characterised by a tremendous German superiority, both in numbers and quality. In fact, VIII. *Fliegerkorps* did not lose a single aircraft to hostile action on 26 August.

At night the situation was somewhat different. On 24 August, the ADD transferred five more *Diviziyas* to bolster the activities of 50 AD against the German rear area in the Don Bend sector. Night after night these bombers were in action against German lines of communication, troop encampments, airfields and supply bases. On 26 August, *Generalmajor* Wolfgang Pickert, the commander of German 9th *Flakdivision* in the same sector, described a nocturnal journey to the front line in his diary:

"Our train made a stop for several hours, and we learned that the tracks behind us had been severed. I'd have preferred to stay at the front with the *Panzer* troops! Assigned to a wagon with 2cm *Flak*, we are able to continue our journey. Further on we come under bombing attack aimed at our troop columns; however, no harm is inflicted. At noon we meet Wietersheim and Hube. With the fall of darkness, almost uninterrupted air attacks begin again."[146]

But these Soviet nocturnal air attacks were hampered by the usual lack of precision. On 28 August, the strong German air support had tipped the scale in the ground battle, and a counter-strike relieved Hube's *Panzerdivision* from the encirclement. This made it possible for von Richthofen to shift the focus of VIII. *Fliegerkorps* to the south of Stalingrad, where IV. *Panzerarmee* manoeuvred in order to wheel around the strong Soviet defences. Early on 29 August, all of VIII. *Fliegerkorps'* Stukas were launched against the Soviet defence lines in this sector. Covered by these attacks, the tanks of *General* von Hauenschild's 24th *Panzerdivision* were hurled against the Gavrilovka sector, where there were only weak Soviet defences.

While Soviet South-eastern Front's positions crumbled south of Stalingrad, *Generaloberst* von Richthofen dispatched his air units on another massive air attack against the city on 30 August. *General-Major* Khryukin sent his air forces against the menacing *Panzer* columns of IV. *Panzerarmee* south of Stalingrad – only to find that these had been furnished with overwhelming fighter cover.

By this time the three Pe-2 regiments of 270 BAD which had carried out the attacks against the Don bridges ten days earlier – 86, 140 and 779 BAP – had been reduced to a combined strength of no more than 19 bombers.[147] Two of these were shot down by German fighters on 30 August – one of which became the 139th victory of 9./JG 52's *Oblt.* Hermann Graf.

In place of the Pe-2s, the Il-2s of 206, 226 and 228 ShAD were brought in *en masse* against the German armoured columns. On the previous day, two new *Shturmovik* regiments had been assigned to 8 VA, and these were immediately hurled into the fight. The *Shturmoviks* were intercepted by scores of Bf 109s – many of which were equipped with gondola-mounted underwing 20 mm cannon – and throughout the day bitter air fighting raged. "German infantrymen and *Panzer* crews alike would shade their eyes with a hand against the sun, peering up at the blue sky and vapour trails," wrote historian Anthony Beevor. "There were cheers whenever an enemy

Kurt Brändle had served as a fighter pilot since the outbreak of the war in 1939. He reached ace status during the Battle of Britain, but his main successes were scored on the Eastern Front in 1942 and 1943, when he commanded II./JG 3 'Udet'. When Brändle was killed in action on 3 November 1943, he had amassed a total score of 180 victories –

all but 25 on the Eastern Front. This photograph shows Brändle on the day he attained his 100th victory, 23 August 1942 – which also was the day the German advance towards the Volga north of Stalingrad was initiated.

machine was hit, and the stricken aircraft, pouring smoke, corkscrewed down and exploded on the ground. The reputation of star fighter pilots began to grow within the German Army as well as the *Luftwaffe*".[148] On 30 August, the fighter pilots of *Fliegerkorps* VIII were credited with the destruction of nineteen Il-2s.

Despite these losses, the surviving *Shturmoviks* were in the air over the battlefield on 31 August. German fighter pilots claimed another thirteen Il-2s shot down. One of these fell as the 100th victory of II./JG 52's *Hptm.* Johannes Steinhoff. Also that day a single Bf 110 of ZG 1 succeeded in destroying ten U-2s of 621 NBAP during an attack against the airfield at Novo Nikolskoye. Having lost 201 aircraft between 23 and 31 August, 8 VA's strength had rapidly dwindled to just 192 serviceable aircraft at the onset of September – 57 fighters, 38 day bombers, 51 night bombers, 32 Il-2s, 13 liaison aircraft and two reconnaissance aircraft.[149] It is easy to understand why the division of 8 VA into two, for the formation of the new 16 VA, was delayed.

Threatened with encirclement by IV. *Panzerarmee*'s attack from the south, the Soviet troops to the west of Stalingrad were rapidly pulled back. The retreating columns became congested on the narrow roads leading east, and offered an easy target to *Luftwaffe* bombers which harried them ceaselessly. A ridge of low pressure which shrouded the entire area in low clouds, rain and fog on 1 September brought some relief to the Red Army troops, but on 2 September the skies cleared again. On that day elements of German VI. *Armee*, advancing from the north, linked up with IV. *Panzerarmee* to the west of Stalingrad. Nine days after the 'main attack' against Stalingrad had been launched, it finally appeared as though the city bearing Stalin's name was on the brink of falling.

In his headquarters, Hitler issued an order that Stalingrad's entire male population was to be exterminated.[150] From Moscow, Josef Stalin wired:

"The situation in Stalingrad is deteriorating. The enemy has closed to within three *verst* [two miles] from Stalingrad. Stalingrad may fall today or tomorrow if the northern group is not provided with immediate support. Demand that the commanders of the forces to the north and north-west of Stalingrad strike against the enemy and come to the aid of the Stalingrad defenders. No delay can be tolerated. Delay at this moment is a crime.

Deploy all your aerial forces to the aid of Stalingrad. In Stalingrad itself only a handful of aircraft remain."

But neither Hitler's murderous intentions, nor Stalin's demands could render Soviet resistance more stubborn – airmen and ground troops were already giving their utmost in the defence of Stalingrad. Early on 2 September Bf 110s of ZG 1 strafed Soviet troops in the Kotluban sector, north-west of Stalingrad; the *Zerstörer* were subjected to a fierce attack by Yak-1s from 220 IAD and lost three Bf 110s for only one Soviet fighter shot down.[151] But this was the exception for the day.

Several German fighters were out over the Soviet rear area, blocking the VVS airfields. *Oblt.* Klaus Quaet-Faslem – who had just been appointed *Gruppenkommandeur* I./JG 3 – and his wingman, *Fw.* Willi Krug, flew a sweep of the region 50 miles north-east of Stalingrad and fell on seven Pe-2s of 779 BAP/270 BAD which had taken off from Stepnoye aerodrome. In just two minutes three Pe-2s were shot down – two by Quaet-Faslem and one by Krug. In addition, the Pe-2 flown by 779 BAP's commander, *Podpolkovnik* Bystrov, was so badly shot up that it crashed on landing. Thus 779 BAP was left with no more than two remaining Pe-2s.[152] In *Podpolkovnik* Bystrov's case, it was the second time in a fortnight that he had been shot down by Messerschmitts of JG 3 *Udet* – and he was lucky to survive on this occasion too.

During the afternoon of 2 September, 140 BAP/270 BAD sent out its seven last Pe-2s, but these were intercepted by 9./JG 3's *Oblt.* Emil Bitsch and *Ofw.* Walter Ohlrogge fifteen miles north-east of Stalingrad. Again, in two minutes, three Pe-2s were shot down. The remaining Pe-2s attempted to flee – only to run into two Bf 109s from I./JG 3, with *Fw.* Heinz Baum claiming two shot down. 140 BAP in fact lost five Pe-2s in this combat.[153]

The Soviet fighters not only failed to cover their bombers against German fighter attacks – they were also unable to protect themselves. Throughout 2 September, the fighters of VIII. *Fliegerkorps* and 8 VA clashed in ten combats altogether over or around Stalingrad. According to each side's loss records, this resulted in 16 Soviet fighters shot down – 12 Yaks, and two Kittyhawks and La-5s[154] against one damaged Bf 109.[155] The claims made by both sides were very different from the actual outcomes – the Germans claimed 19 Soviet fighters shot down (in fact, in addition to the 16 Soviet fighter losses, three of 288 IAD's Yak-7Bs belly-landed due to battle damage), and the Soviets reported ten Bf 109s and six Bf 110s shot down.

JG 3 Udet would deal another severe blow against 270 BAD's Pe-2s on 3 September. 284 BAP, which arrived with 18 brand new Pe-2s led by Hero of the Soviet Union *Mayor* Dmitriy Valentik, was attacked by I./JG 3 Bf 109s close to their field at Rakhinskiy on 3 September and lost three crews.[156] At least two of these fell to *Fw.* Heinz Baum again.

However, not even the overwhelming German superiority in both numbers and quality was able to crush the bitter Soviet resistance. When the Germans attacked in one sector, they were met with stiff resistance, and at another sector the Soviets launched relief offensives. On 3 September, the German Armed Forces' Headquarters reported: "At Serafimoivich the enemy managed to achieve a deep penetration into our own lines. The 22nd *Panzerdivision* has been dispatched against the enemy forces which have broken through. At Korotoyak the enemy still holds out in his Don bridgehead."[157] These Soviet bridgeheads in the northern part of the Don Bend – about 100 miles north-west of Stalingrad – would, two and a half months later, constitute the springboard from which the Soviet major relief offensive would be launched. On 4 September, the OKH's Situation Report read: "The enemy launched a counter-attack from the north with 150 tanks striking XIV. *Panzerkorps'* positions."[158]

In the central combat zone, *Heeresgruppe Mitte* had barely managed to withstand repeated Soviet offensives from late July and throughout August 1942. During the air battles which raged in conjunction with these operations, one *Jagdgeschwader*, JG 51, recorded 75 Bf 109s destroyed or damaged through enemy action in the month of August 1942 alone. This compelled the *Luftwaffe* High Command – the OKL – not only to divert I./JG 52 from *Luftflotte* 4 to *Luftwaffenkommando Ost* in this sector, but also made it imperative to send reinforcements from Germany to the central combat zone rather than to the Stalingrad sector.

This situation was further complicated through Hitler's unwise decision to send von Manstein's XI. *Armee* directly across the occupied Soviet Union – from the Crimea in the south to the Leningrad sector in the north. The aim was to deploy von Manstein's battle-hardened troops to capture the stubbornly resisting city of Leningrad. But instead of waging an offensive against this tenacious city, XI. *Armee* was immediately faced with a powerful Soviet offensive and was forced onto the defensive. Ground and air troops which could have been decisive in the Stalingrad battle were thus tied up at Leningrad, almost 1,000 miles to the north.

On 26 August, *General Armii* Georgiy Zhukov – who had led Soviet Western Front in the recent relief offensive against *Heeresgruppe Mitte* – was appointed vice supreme-commander of the Soviet Armed Forces. Three days later, he arrived at Stalingrad, where Josef Stalin had ordered him to support the planning of military operations. Zhukov coordinated the relief offensive which was initiated on 3 September when the Stalingrad Front's 1st Guards Army attacked XIV. *Panzerkorps* along the land bridge between the Don and the Volga north of Stalingrad. The next stage would see the 24th and 66th Soviet armies joining the offensive in the same area. For this purpose, it was necessary to provide the Stalingrad Front with an air force of its own, and hence the formation of 16 VA was hurriedly carried through.

On 4 September, 228 ShAD and 220 IAD – with 25 serviceable Il-2s and 42 serviceable Yak-1s – were shifted from 8 VA to the new air army. 16 VA was formally commanded by *General* Pavel Stepanov. However, in reality, 16 VA was led by Stepanov's deputy, the more experienced *General-Mayor* Stepan Rudenko. The decision to create a second air army in the Stalingrad sector was made in order to facilitate command and control. However, unusually for the VVS, a centralised command was established for both 8 VA and 16 VA – *General-Leytenant* Aleksandr Novikov, the new commander-in-chief of VVS KA who had arrived at the Stalingrad sector on 23 August, was in a position to concentrate the aviation – in particular the fighters – to any sector where they were needed.

16 VA had its baptism of fire on 4 September, when Il-2s from 688 ShAP and 783 ShAP and their escort of Yak-1s from 220 IAD performed 127 sorties against IV. *Panzerarmee* in the Voroponovo sector, some five miles west of Stalingrad's southern suburbs. The escorting Yak-1s managed to engage the intercepting German fighters – enabling the *Shturmoviks* to carry out their attacks successfully, claiming the destruction of 30 tanks and 40 other motor vehicles.[159] But the price for this achievement was heavy. No less than 20 of these Soviet aircraft were shot down, including 17 of 220 IAD's Yak-1s.[160] With one of these, 9./JG 52's *Oblt.* Hermann Graf achieved his 150th victory. The VVS also failed to prevent the *Luftwaffe* from launching

*Stalingrad's main airfield in late August 1942 – a scene of utter destruction. However, worse was to come.*

another heavy air attack against Stalingrad on 4 September. This time scores of civilians were killed when German aircraft attacked the boats being used to evacuate them across the Volga.

The aircraft losses at Stalingrad on 4 September again confirmed the inequality between the two sides: 23 Soviet aircraft (20 fighters and three Il-2s) and only four German aircraft were shot down, according to the loss records of each side.[161] The *Luftwaffe* also demonstrated a better accuracy in claiming enemy aircraft shot down – with German fighters submitting claims for 21 shot-down fighters and four Il-2s, while 8 VA and 16 VA claimed 13 victories.

16 VA also received 291 ShAD with 54 serviceable Il-2s from 2 VA. By bringing in a whole new *Shturmovik Diviziya*, the combined forces of 8 VA, 16 VA and 102 IAD/PVO at Stalingrad were increased to 738 aircraft – 313 fighters, 241 *Shturmoviks*, 113 day bombers and 71 night bombers – of which less than half were serviceable. However, an attacking Ju 88 *Gruppe* quickly reduced that number by attacking 291 ShAD's airbase early on 5 September, destroying half its aircraft on the ground.

16 VA's first major task was to support the counter-attack of 24th and 66th Armies against XIV. *Panzerkorps* on 5 September. With inadequately trained and poorly equipped troops launched against the *Panzer* troops, which were covered by a strong aerial umbrella, this Soviet attack broke down. The OKH's Situation Report read: "Massive [Soviet] attacks from the north, which were preceded by artillery fire, were repulsed by intense activity by our *Luftwaffe*. Of 120 attacking tanks, 30 had been destroyed by midday."[162]

But this unexpectedly strong resistance offered by the Soviets at Stalingrad compelled the Germans to dispatch more troops to this small sector, creating a situation where the Germans came to rely more heavily on their allies for flank protection of the Stalingrad sector. The Italian 8th Army marched up to take positions along the Don south of the Hungarian 2nd Army, which held the sector at Rossosh. In the Caucasus, the 3rd Rumanian Army was instructed to move northwards into the Don Bend, where it was assigned the task of covering the contested sector where the Soviets had established several bridgeheads to the south of the Don. The 4th Rumanian Army was lined up along a 170-mile front south of Stalingrad. All of this created a dangerous tactical situation – from the Axis point of view – which the Soviets would take advantage of when they launched their major attack in November.

Soviet fighter pilots study a flight map in front of one of their unit's La-5 fighters. The La-5 proved unable to fulfil expectations when it entered service in the summer of 1942. The first engagements with the Luftwaffe demonstrated that it was inferior to the latest versions of the Bf 109 in most aspects. However, in the hands of a skilful pilot, the La-5 was a deadly weapon. One of the most talented La-5 pilots during the battle of Stalingrad was 23-year old Lt. Yevgenniy Dranishchenko. He was posted to 437 IAP on 20 August 1942 and achieved his first victory against a Ju 88 only three days later.

By 13 September, Dranishchenko had participated in ten aerial combats and had already been credited with five victories – including two Ju 88s shot down in the same engagement on 8 September. Dranishchenko was killed in action on 20 August 1943, exactly one year to the day after he had been posted to first-line service. He scored a total of 21 individual and seven shared victories in just 120 combat missions and 50 air combats. (Viktor Kulikov Photograph Collection)

Meanwhile, the forces of German II. *Armee* were effectively tied to the Voronezh sector, 300 miles farther upstream the Don, where Soviet Voronezh Front supported by 2 VA was engaged in an incessant series of relief attacks. Thus, while 16 VA and the Stalingrad Front were launched in full force against XIV. *Panzerkorps* on 5 September, the aviation of 2 VA made a combined attack directed against the airfields of *Luftwaffenkommando Don*. While one of 2 VA's *Shturmovik Diviziyas* raided II./JG 77's field at Kastornoye, 205 IAD struck Rossosh airfield with both Il-2s and Hurricanes, just as KG 27's He 111s were being rolled out for an evening sortie. An airman of I./KG 27 recalled: "Once again, the Russians attacked our airfield with bombers, ground-attack aircraft and fighters – mainly Hurricanes flying low-level strafing passes. This time they were quite successful. One He 111 was totally burnt out, and several others sustained damage through shrapnel splinters or machine gun fire. Our two fighters which were stationed at the airfield came under heavy fire as they attempted to take off, but in spite of this managed to get their damaged aircraft airborne and shoot down one of the attackers."[163]

Anatoliy Kozhevnikov, who participated in the attack as an *M.Lt.*, flying a 438 IAP Hurricane, described the raid from the Soviet perspective:

"Our guns raked the airfield; bombs dropped by the *Shturmoviks* flung fountains of earth into the air and wrecked enemy aircraft. Burning aviation fuel spread out on the ground, and a black smoke cloud billowed from a blazing fuel dump and obscured the horizon. The enemy's anti-aircraft guns had no chance to open fire and were knocked out early in the attack.

While our fighters strafed the airfield, we failed to spot eight Messerschmitts which arrived on the scene. Just as he recovered his aircraft from a dive, *Lt.* Kudinov saw an aircraft with crosses and swastika directly ahead of him. Instinctively he pressed the firing button, saw flashes as his bullets hit the Messerschmitt, and then the enemy aircraft crashed into the ground.

*Serzh.* Olyenikov, part of the escort group, dived down and shot down a second enemy. This Fascist pilot apparently sought to place himself in a good position for an attack against our ground-attack group, and failed to detect our escort.

The other six Messerschmitts attempted to attack the *Shturmoviks*, but were immediately set upon by our second *Eskadrilya*. *Serzhs.* Khnylov and Oryol shot down two of them."

The German report indicates that there were in fact only two Bf 109s at Rossosh, and one of these was shot down.[164] On the other hand, all Soviet aircraft participating in the attack against Rossosh returned safely to base.[165]

The units which meanwhile attacked II./JG 77 at Kastornoye fared much worse. Although they succeeded in their task of preventing II./JG 77 from intervening against the Rossosh raid, the price paid for that accomplishment was dear – the German fighter pilots claimed to have shot down 24 of the attackers, including 17 Il-2s.

The latter operation captures the Soviet strategy in a nutshell. Albeit for a cost of extremely high losses, the Soviets managed to tie down considerable German forces, and in the long run to wear them down.

Having sustained 40 aircraft lost (destroyed or damaged due to all causes) and twelve pilot casualties since the opening of the German summer offensive, I./JG 3 was at the end of its strength and had to be pulled out of combat on 6 September for a period of rest and rehabilitation. Seventeen Bf 109s – all aircraft which remained in this *Jagdgruppe* (out of an assigned strength of forty) – were handed over to the *Geschwaderstab* and III./JG 3. The second *Gruppe* of JG 3 had already been sent to Germany for a period of rest on 23 August; when it returned to the Eastern Front in September, due to the relentless Soviet pressure against *Heeresgruppe Mitte,* the OKL was compelled to employ it in the central combat zone instead of at Stalingrad.

Thus, one week into September, the fighter force of VIII. *Fliegerkorps* was reduced to the equivalent of just one single *Geschwader* – the *Geschwaderstab* and III./JG 3, two-thirds of III./JG 52, and

*'Yellow 11', a Bf 109 G-2, W.Nr. 13670, of 9./JG 52, was sometimes flown by Hermann Graf in the late summer of 1942, and it is believed that he may have been flying this machine when he accounted for his 150th victory on 4 September 1942.*

I./JG 53. By the time I./JG 3 was sent to Germany, *Hptm.* Steinhoff's II./JG 52 had also departed the Stalingrad sector; on 1 September it had been shifted to the Caucasus – where the Axis forces had run into stiffened Soviet resistance.

I./JG 52, which had been sent from *Luftflotte* 4 to the central combat zone in August to help fight back the Soviet attacks against *Heeresgruppe Mitte,* was hurriedly instructed to transfer to Stalingrad. But clearly a single *Jagdgruppe* would not suffice. With fewer and fewer *Luftwaffe* units available to reinforce the forces at Stalingrad, the Rumanians were pressed to dispatch their air force to the Eastern Front again. This decision was probably taken with some hesitation from the Rumanians. Their Combat Air Group – *Gruparea Aeriană de Luptă* (GAL) – had taken a severe beating during Operation 'Barbarossa' in 1941 and had subsequently not seen further action against the VVS. But in view of the unflinching Soviet resistance in the air over Stalingrad, the GAL was re-activated at Stalingrad on 6 September 1942. Over the next two days, the GAL's two first combat units arrived at the front. *Grupul 7 Vânătoare,* equipped with 37 Bf 109 E fighters, was based at Karpovka, and *Grupul 8 Vânătoare,* with I.A.R. 80B fighters, landed at Tusov. Led by *General Aviator* Ermil Gheorghiue, the GAL's headquarters was established at Rostov.

But the Soviets had far greater means to bring in new reinforcements. 16 VA, which lost over 50 aircraft – one-third of all serviceable aircraft – during its first four days of operations, received 47 new aircraft on 8 September. The majority of these came with *Podpolkovnik* Vladimir Kitayev's 283 IAD, which was brought in from the *Stavka* reserve with three Yak-1-equipped regiments – 431, 520 and 563 IAP. Most of its pilots were thrown into battle before they had received a complete training. But what the Soviet rookies lacked in experience and flying skills, they tried to make up for with fighting stamina.

8 September would see some of the biggest air battles ever fought on the Eastern Front. *St.Lt.* Arkadiy Kostritsin, a pilot in 283 IAD's 431 IAP, managed to shoot down a Ju 88 and ram a Bf 109, but was killed in the process, on his first mission on 8 September 1942. Kostritsin's victims may be identified as the II./KG 76 Ju 88 piloted by *Fw.* Hans Nauroschat, and a Bf 109 of III./JG 3. It is also possible that the aircraft lost by II./KG 76 to Soviet fighters on 8 September was shot down by 437 IAP's *Lt.* Yevgenniy Dranishchenko, who reportedly bagged two Ju 88s at the controls of his La-5 on this day.

But III./JG 3 replied in kind, bagging six Soviet fighters during fighter sweeps in the morning of the same day. Meanwhile a group of I./JG 53 Bf 109s intercepted a formation of Il-2s at low altitude north of Stalingrad. Eight Il-2s were claimed shot down, including three by *Ofw.* Alfred Franke, while one of the Messerschmitt pilots was injured.

During the following hours, the Stukas, bombers and *Schlacht* aircraft of VIII. *Fliegerkorps* were continually launched against Soviet troop positions without interference from Soviet fighters. The German fighters were effectively screening the Soviet rear area, and when a formation of Il-2s with

escort of Yak-1s was sent in to the Kotluban sector by 16 VA, these Soviet airmen were hit by 3./JG 53 with the aces *Oblt.* Wolfgang Tonne and *Fw.* Wilhelm Crinius in the lead. The air fight developed into a one-sided slaughter, with the German aces hunting the Soviet aircraft as they sought to flee. When it was over, nine Soviet aircraft had been shot down. Tonne chalked up four, while Crinius claimed two victories.

To the Germans it was evident that the Soviets had reinforced their air strength. Such was definitely the view of the airmen of I./KG 100 when their He 111s were sent out against Kamyshin during the morning of 8 September. During the approach flight they were intercepted by what were reported as "12 to 15 Russian fighters".[166] These were in fact 520 IAP's Yak-1s on their transfer flight to the new front line airfield. Following a prolonged air combat, during which the fledgling Soviet pilots proved unable to achieve any results against the bombers, *St.Serzh.* Boris Gomolko dived his Yak fighter straight into *Lt.* Adolf Büsge's He 111. Both aircraft went down over Soviet-controlled territory, with the Soviet pilot baling out to safety.

Three He 111s were reported in the I./KG 100 loss files after this combat. In 520 IAP, *Mayor* Stepan Chirva, *Lt.* Nikolay Kharitonov, and *Serzh.* V. P. Vusikov returned to base each with one claim for an He 111.

The Soviet 'method' of substituting bravery for skill continually resulted in terrible losses. While the He 111s defended themselves against 520 IAP's Yak-1s, *Oblt.* Graf's *Schwarm* from 9./JG 52 attacked a group of 8 VA Il-2s, escorted by 287 IAD La-5s over Stalingrad's western outskirts. In the first attack, Graf sent a La-5 to the ground, with 27 IAP's *St.Serzh.* Anatoliy Yegoshin perishing.[167] Less than a minute later, an Il-2 fell to Graf's guns. This engagement cost the Soviets a loss of six aircraft, again for no losses on the German side.

These scenes were repeated throughout the day. In total, nearly 20 air combats were fought over or around Stalingrad on 8 September. When darkness fell, the Soviet commanders counted the results and paled at the figures. No less than 50 aircraft – 30 fighters, 19 Il-2s and a Pe-2 – were in fact shot down by the Germans at Stalingrad on 8 September 1942. Included among the personnel losses on this day was the Spanish volunteer *Lt.* José Pascual Santamaria, who flew with 788 IAP. Santamaria was shot down and killed by a Bf 109 shortly after he had achieved his 14th victory, thus becoming the most successful Spanish fighter pilot in World War II.

The loss rates in the Soviet units were appalling. In 16 VA, the average loss rate for 8 September was almost ten per cent – 283 combat sorties had been flown, and 27 aircraft were lost![168] *Fliegerkorps* VIII sustained six losses and its fighters reported 58 victories on 8 September 1942.

And still the Soviet airmen refused to yield! On 9 September, an Il-2 pilot attacked and managed to shoot down the Bf 109 piloted by I./JG 53's 59-victory ace *Ofw.* Alfred Franke, who was reported as missing.

Four of 629 IAP/102 IAD's I-153 pilots gave a good account of themselves on 9 September. Returning from a combat mission, the biplane pilots were approaching their own airfield when they were jumped by seven

*A shot-down Il-2. The Shturmovik Diviziyas of 8 VA sustained appalling losses in the summer of 1942. In July 1942, 8 VA's Shturmovik units registered at least 83 Il-2s lost. Between 6 August and 6 September, another 102 were lost. (Karlenko)*

Bf 109s which dropped out of the clouds. One of the *Chaykas* was hit in the initial attack, and went down trailing a banner of black smoke. Catching sight of the Bf 109s diving down, *M.Lt.* A. S. Shishatskiy pulled the stick of his I-153 and made a half loop to evade the attack. As he rolled over, he found himself nose to nose with two enemy fighters. Both Bf 109s broke off to the left and, in this situation, the highly manoeuvrable biplane had the advantage. Shishatskiy kicked the rudder pedal and the agile little *Chayka* rapidly turned straight into the two Germans' flight direction. All Shishatskiy had to do was press the trigger and keep it down until one of the Bf 109s flew into the shower of 7.62mm bullets at a distance of between 30 and 50 metres. Shishatskiy's victim possibly was the Bf 109 of 9./JG 3 which was reported to have carried out a belly-landing at Gorodishche with 30 per cent battle damage.

The first small contingent of I./JG 52 to arrive at the Stalingrad Front from the central combat zone soon learnt with what determination the Soviet airmen in this area fought. On 9 September, six Bf 109s of *Oblt.* Friedrich Bartels' 1./JG 52 made a high-side attack against two Yak-1s – 563 IAP's *Batalyonnyy Komissar* Aleksandr Oborin and his wingman. Certain of two victories, the skilfully flown evasive manoeuvres of the two Yaks caught the German pilots by surprise. Oborin locked the Messerschmitts into a sharp turning combat, and for almost 20 minutes, the combat was a draw. But it was an uneven dogfight – six against two – and the situation gradually worsened for the two increasingly tired Soviet pilots. With Oborin expending the last of his ammunition, he realized that he and his wingman would soon be shot down unless he took radical action. He threw open his throttles, aimed at the nearest Bf 109 and promptly flew straight into it. As he hit the Bf 109 from the rear, the collision was not violent enough to bring down both aircraft although they were severely damaged. But it saved Oborin. Obviously disheartened by what they had seen, the Bf 109s disengaged and escorted the damaged Bf 109 to the east. The German fighter went down at Tusov with damage assessed at 30 per cent.[169] Oborin also managed to nurse his crippled fighter back to base.[170]

However, in another engagement that day, *Oblt.* Hermann Graf led his *Schwarm* in a strike against a group of 27 IAP La-5s at 6,000 feet over central

Stalingrad. Witnessed by thousands of soldiers on the ground below, they bagged four for no losses of their own.[171] With two victories, Graf reached a personal tally of 160. In total, on 9 September 8 VA and 16 VA recorded 27 aircraft lost in combat, while the Soviets managed to bring down no more than three aircraft from *Fliegerkorps* VIII.

By this time, the accumulated losses had reduced the number of serviceable Il-2s in 16 VA to only 28.[172] Relieved from the incessantly attacking *Shturmoviks*, IV. *Panzerarmee* managed to reach the Volga south of Stalingrad on 10 September. Thus the connection between the Stalingrad and South-eastern Fronts was severed, with the former's 62nd Army isolated inside Stalingrad.

*Mayor* Dmitriy Valentik's 284 BAP – the only one of 270 BAD's bomber units still capable of fielding more than a dozen serviceable aircraft – attempted to come to the aid of the hard-pressed Soviet ground troops, but only ran into swarms of Bf 109s. Of the fifteen Pe-2s remaining in 284 BAP on the evening of 9 September, six were shot down on 10-11 September.[173] In addition to those losses, two of 275 BAP's Pe-2s were shot down by Bf 109s on 11 September – both falling to III./JG 3's *Fw.* Heinz Kemethmüller – leaving the regiment with only one operational Pe-2.

The VVS fighter units assigned to protect the bombers and *Shturmoviks* had also been bled white. On 11 September, I./JG 53 reported 17 Soviet aircraft shot down, 14 of which were fighters. By shooting down a La-5 for his 78th victory, *Oblt* Wolfgang Tonne killed 27 IAP's *Kapitan* Fyodor Chuykin, an ace with 11 individual and six shared victories to his tally.

Meanwhile, Soviet 62nd Army inside Stalingrad had been whittled down to around 50,000 men and 110 remaining tanks. They were still largely holding the German troops at bay. The Germans had not yet entered the city itself – they remained stuck in the suburbs, where the devastation caused by *Luftwaffe* bombing strikes made it difficult for the German tanks to move. And while the situation in Stalingrad continued to defy 'normal' military logic, the battle for Stalingrad would soon defy even more than that.

# Chapter Twelve

# The Indefatigable City

As the summer of 1942 drew to a close, Adolf Hitler was becoming increasingly concerned. Firstly the intended attack to be mounted by XI. *Armee* against Leningrad was stymied by a Soviet offensive which began on 27 August. Over the following days, the reports from both *Heeresgruppe A* in the Caucasus and *Heeresgruppe B* on the Don and at Stalingrad showed that the great summer offensive had bogged down in the face of Soviet resistance. On 9 September, a furious Hitler sacked *Generalfeldmarschall* List, the commander of *Heeresgruppe A*. Three days later, Hitler summoned *Generaloberst* Friedrich von Paulus – commander of VI. *Armee* and the Axis supreme commander at Stalingrad – to his Eastern Front headquarters in Vinnitsa. The *Generaloberst* was strongly reproached for having so far failed to take control of Stalingrad. Hitler's impression of von Paulus was not improved by von Richthofen, who phoned *Reichsmarschall* Göring and proposed that the 'uninspiring' von Paulus should be replaced as the supreme commander at Stalingrad.[174]

A pale von Paulus assured the *Führer* that he indeed was preparing another 'final offensive' against Stalingrad. This attack opened at 06.30 hrs on 13 September with a massive bombardment by the Stukas of St.G 2 and St.G 77. The ground-attack aircraft of SchG 1 spread death and devastation along the banks of the Volga and twin-engined Junkers and Heinkels unloaded their bombs over field positions inside the city and anti-aircraft nests and artillery positions on the eastern side of the Volga. German fighters swarmed through the skies. A small group of Il-2s tried to attack German vehicles at the outskirts of Stalingrad, but they were bounced by Bf 109s which shot down three of the Il-2s in quick succession. One of them crashed in the centre of the city.

Soviet fighters were scrambled from all airfields east of the Volga, and they hurled themselves against the mass of *Luftwaffe* aircraft, causing a multitude of air combats. Most of these took place at altitudes below 6,000 feet, since the Soviet fighters had no time to gain altitude before the Messerschmitts fell on them. *Oblt.* Hermann Graf sent his 9./JG 52 pilots to patrol the Kotluban area, resulting in the destruction of three of 220 IAD's Yak-1s early in the morning.[175] Nevertheless, some Soviet fighters broke through the German fighter shield and made furious attacks against the German bombers and *Schlacht* aircraft. Knight's Cross recipient *Lt.* Josef Menapace, 7./SchG 1's *Staffelkapitän*, was lucky to survive his aircraft being

shot up by a Soviet fighter right above Stalingrad. Five German bombers also limped back to base with battle damage and injured crew members on board.

Occasionally the tables were turned elsewhere, a group of 283 IAD Yak-1s attacking two I./JG 53 Bf 109s over Stalingrad and shooting down *Uffz.* Erwin Meyer. However, shortly afterwards these Yakovlevs were bounced by another *Rotte* of I./JG 53 and lost one of their number to *Uffz.* Heinz Golinski. One hour later, the same airmen clashed again, with Golinski shooting down a second 283 IAD Yak-1.

The *Luftwaffe's* concentrated air attacks had a terrible impact on the defenders. The hailstorm of bombs cut all telephone connections between Soviet 62nd Army's headquarters and the troops. Stalingrad's defenders had to resort to runners with messages. Meanwhile Soviet positions were overrun by a mass of German troops, who approached the centre of the city on a five-mile broad front. By the afternoon of 13 September, *Luftwaffe* pilots could see a large swastika banner hoisted above the huge *Dzherzhinskiy* tractor plant in the northern part of Stalingrad.

However, 13 September was a memorable date for another reason: That day, the *Stavka's* chief-of-staff, *General-Polkovnik* Aleksandr Vasilyevskiy, and *General Armii* Zhukov presented the main strategy at Stalingrad to Stalin – the city of Stalingrad would be held at all costs, sucking as large an Axis force as possible into this small sector. Meanwhile, large Soviet forces would secretly be marched up on both flanks of *Heeresgruppe B,* preparing for a great encirclement operation. The two generals had thus drawn the broad outlines of what would become the greatest military defeat in Germany's history.

The Soviets could hardly have found a more suitable commander to lead the difficult and self-sacrificing defence of Stalingrad than the harsh *General-Leytenant* Vasiliy Chuykov, who on 12 September arrived to replace *General* Lopatin as commander of the 62nd Army. *General-Leytenant* Vasiliy Chuykov was resolutely determined not to lose Stalingrad to the Germans. Relying on powerful support from 700 artillery pieces and mortars, most of which were placed on the other side of the Volga, he called upon his men to wage fanatical resistance.

While Chuykov imbued his soldiers with an unbreakable do-or-die mentality, Soviet airmen increasingly resorted to air-to-air rammings as a

## II./JG 77 versus Soviet Hurricanes

While Soviet 62nd Army locked the Germans into house-to-house fighting in Stalingrad, the Voronezh Front launched repeated relief offensives farther upstream on the Don. The Voronezh Front struck again on 15 September. 2 VA was dispatched en masse to support the offensive. But despite committing large numbers of fighters on escort missions, the Soviet fighters failed to ward off the interceptions by Bf 109s of II./JG 77. In bitter air fighting, II./JG 77 was able to protect the German ground troops from relentless attempts by Il-2s, Pe-2s and Bostons to attack them.

On the Soviet side the slow Hawker Hurricane had been found to be the fighter best suited to escort the Il-2s, since it could easily match its speed to that of the Il-2. Thus, 205 IAD's 438 IAP, equipped with these British Lend-Lease fighters, was most commonly used to escort *Shturmoviks*. But in reality, the inadequate training of the Soviet pilots often caused the fighters to lose contact with the Il-2s. This was the case during 2 VA's first operation early on 16 September. South-east of Voronezh, a group of 4./JG 77 Bf 109s struck these Il-2s. Taking advantage of the absence of fighter escort, the Bf 109 pilots managed

to shoot down three Il-2s in quick succession. Although the heavily armoured *Shturmoviks* went down low to protect their vulnerable bellies, this ultimately proved to be of little help. II./JG 77's pilots had refined a new tactic against the Il-2 – shooting up their tail fins, thus causing the heavy ground-attack aircraft to adopt a pronounced nose-down attitude and plunge out of control. The first Il-2 fell to the guns of 4./JG 77's *Staffelkapitän Oblt.* Heinrich Setz, and then *Fw.* Ernst-Wilhelm Reinert knocked down two more. Next the German fighters climbed to engage the Hurricanes. These had arrived on the scene only to become more fodder for the German aces. *M.Lt.* Anatoliy Kozhevnikov described the scene:

"The Messerschmitts were above us and dived through us with their superior speed, firing as they came. We could only form a defensive circle and try to repel them. Abaltusov's wingman, Zaborovskiy, was shot down. The second *Eskadrilya* lost [*Serzh.*] Khmylov while [*Serzh.*] Olyenikov baled out." The Germans claimed two Hurricanes, including two by Reinert, for one loss. As at Stalingrad, the Soviets were more successful on the ground, where the Voronezh Front succeeded in breaking through the German lines. The German positions in the city of Voronezh came under threat and only following attacks by Stukas and He 111 bombers were the Germans able to stabilise the situation.

means of overcoming the opponent's superiority in the air. On 14 September, 327 IAP's *M.Lt.* Ilya Chumbarov destroyed an Fw 189 of 1.(H)/10 in this manner. A 'Rumanian He 112' reportedly *taraned* by *St.Lt.* Sergey Luganskiy on 12 September was probably the Rumanian *Grupul* 8 *Vânătoare's* I.A.R. 80 piloted by *Adjutant Aviator* Vasile Teodorescu lost on the same day.

16 VA was replenished with 36 new aircraft, but was still not able to score any successes in air combat on 15 September.[176] Instead, when 8 VA's 206 ShAD and 226 ShAD tried to intervene on the battlefield north of Stalingrad that morning, these units took a heavy beating at the hands of JG 3, JG 52 and JG 53. Seven Il-2s failed to return from that mission (the German fighter pilots claimed exactly that number shot down) and another three limped back home badly damaged.[177]

Early on 15 September, 102 IAD's 629 IAP put a group of I-16s and I-153s into the air, commanded by *St.Lt.* Nikolay Lysenko. They intercepted a group of Ju 88s, but only to find themselves coming under attack from above by four Bf 109s from *Oblt.* Hermann Graf's *Schwarm* of *Experten*. *St.Lt.* Lysenko fell to the guns of Graf's Bf 109, and was recorded as the German ace's 170th victory. Next, Graf and his wingman, *Uffz.* Johann Kalb, claimed the destruction of one I-153 apiece before the remainder of the Soviet fighters were driven off. Shortly afterwards, the German pilots came across a formation of LaGG-3s, of which Graf dispatched one for his 172nd kill. On the following day Graf was awarded the Diamonds to his Knight's Cross with Oak Leaves and Swords.

On 16 September a sudden sandstorm which swept in over Stalingrad from the Kalmyk Steppe in the south brought some relief to the besieged troops of 62nd Soviet Army. The adverse weather also gave the Soviets an opportunity to replenish their losses. Between 13 and 16 September, 10,000 troops of Soviet 13th Guards Division were ferried across the Volga to join the battle. 16 VA received 28 new aircraft and managed to restore another 24 to serviceable condition on 16-17 September. With clearing skies on the 17th, the Soviets increased their activity in the air over Stalingrad and 16 VA managed to fly some 180 combat sorties.

I./JG 53's *Oblt.* Wolfgang Tonne and *Fw.* Wilhelm Crinius both reached their 90th aerial victories during the fighting on 17 September, while *Oblt.* Friedrich-Karl Müller of the same unit ran up his score to 93 by shooting down three enemy fighters.

*Hptm. Friedrich-Karl 'Tutti' Müller led I./JG 53 Pik As, undoubtedly the most successful Jagdgruppe during the battle for Stalingrad. This photograph shows Müller as he celebrated at Pitomnik after returning from the mission on 19 September 1942 in which he had scored his 100th victory. The primitive conditions at Pitomnik are clearly visible. On the 23rd, Müller received the Oak Leaves to his Knight's Cross.*

During the night of 17-18 September, Soviet night bombers were in relentless action against the German airfields at Tusov, Surovikino, Zryazhskiy, and Oblivskaya. This was the prelude to the next Soviet attempt to break the northern flank of German VI. *Armee*.

At dawn on 18 September, Soviet 1st Guards Army and 24th Army were launched in an attack against VIII. *Armeekorps* at Kotluban. It began with Il-2s of 688 ShAP dropping smoke bombs over the German lines, thus blinding the German ground troops. Bf 109s of both III./JG 3 and I./JG 53 fell upon these *Shturmoviks*, shooting down several. *Oblt.* Friedrich-Karl Müller even succeeded in bringing down four Il-2s in just five minutes. *Mayor* K. V. Yarovoy, 688 ShAP's commander was shot down himself. But the scores of Soviet heavy tanks which rolled out to attack managed to penetrate the German defence positions.

VIII. *Fliegerkorps* was immediately called in to concentrate its attacks against the Soviet breakthrough area. The airfield at Pitomnik came under artillery shelling, but this did not prevent the Bf 109s and Ju 87s from taking off in large numbers. Subjected to a methodical bombardment from the air, the Soviet offensive collapsed. Out of 106 Soviet tanks reportedly destroyed at Kotluban during the morning of 18 September, 41 were knocked out by Stuka attacks. Meanwhile the Bf 109s took a terrible toll on the Soviet aircraft.

In total, the fighter pilots of VIII. *Fliegerkorps* claimed to have shot down 77 Soviet aircraft without a single loss on 18 September. Of these, some 32 were Il-2s. Although the German fighter pilots exaggerated their successes by about two to one, actual Soviet losses were severe enough. 8 VA and 16 VA alone recorded 14 Il-2s lost on 18 September 1942.[178] 220 IAD claimed four Bf 109s but lost 12 Yak-1s, while 283 IAD registered six Yak-1s lost against reports of three Bf 109s shot down.[179] 434 IAP lost at least eight Yaks and five pilots on 18 September. *St.Lt.* Vladimir Mikoyan, the son of the premier aircraft designer of the USSR, Anastas Mikoyan, was killed in combat with Bf 109s. 434 IAP's *Lt.* Nikolay Shulzhenko was also shot down but survived with injuries. In 237 IAP, the commander, ten-victory ace *Mayor* Aleksandr Isayev, was shot down and was so severely wounded that he never returned to front line service. 296 IAP's Hero of the Soviet Union *St.Lt.* Aleksandr Martynov, credited with at least 17 individual and 16 shared victories, was injured during a combat with Bf 109s while escorting Pe-2s. It was clear that the Stalingrad Front and its air forces had sustained a

*A propeller is replaced on an Il-2 of 226 ShAD during the Battle of Stalingrad. Keeping aircraft in serviceable condition was a great problem for the VVS during the difficult air fighting over Stalingrad. Between one-third and half of the Il-2s at Stalingrad were unserviceable throughout September 1942. (Karlenko)*

major tactical defeat on 18 September, which was largely due to VIII. *Fliegerkorps*.

And yet the Soviets continued their attacks in the north on 19 September, although with far fewer Il-2s available to support the Soviet ground troops. The losses the previous day had reduced the number of serviceable Il-2s in 16 VA from 103 to 67. Instead, the Soviets dispatched all available fighters in an effort to ward off the Stuka attacks. But as usual these aircraft were forced to defend themselves against the Bf 109s which harried them continually. The aces of I./JG 53 were in the forefront of the dogfighting with *Oblt.* Friedrich-Karl Müller and *Lt.* Hans Roehrig claiming three each and Tonne and Crinius two Soviet fighters apiece. All of this took place during a series of fierce clashes in the morning hours – the sky was soon virtually devoid of Soviet aircraft. The Yak-1 which was bagged by Roehrig at 13.55 hrs for his fourth kill that day was one of the few exceptions.

At Pitomnik, *Oblt.* Friedrich-Karl Müller was feted – his last victories had taken his total past the magic 100-mark. At the airfields on the opposite side of the Volga there was not much cause to celebrate. 291 IAP – which had just arrived to reinforce 220 IAD – lost 10 LaGG-3s on its first day of action over Stalingrad.[180] In total, the fighter units of 16 VA recorded 17 losses on 19 September, while VIII. *Fliegerkorps* reported 24 Soviet fighters shot down. Only the veteran unit 434 IAP managed to restore some honour by claiming six Ju 88s, five Ju 87s, three Bf 109s and a Bf 110 shot down for two losses. Even though these success reports proved to be quite exaggerated, they included two Ju 87s of 3./St.G 2 and Knight's Cross holder *Lt.* Egbert Jaekel was wounded in the cockpit of one of them. In total, VIII. *Fliegerkorps* sustained 12 aircraft destroyed or severely damaged due to hostile action on 19 September.

What remained of the Soviet fighter force at Stalingrad took to the air again on 20 September, again mainly in order to try to bring some relief to the tormented ground troops. The day's fighting saw a 'clash of aces'. During seven separate engagements from early in the morning until late in the afternoon, three I./JG 53 pilots claimed to have shot down 12 Soviet fighters – *Lt.* Roehrig, five; *Fw.* Crinius, four; and *Oblt.* Tonne, three – of which all but three were identified as Yakovlevs. Of 16 Yakovlev fighters recorded as lost by 8 VA and 16 VA that day, five were Yak-7Bs from 434 IAP. Included among 434 IAP's four pilot casualties that day was *St.Lt.* Nikolay Garam – the second of the four Garam brothers (all of whom were fighter pilots) to fall prey to a Bf 109. *St.Lt.* Sergey Dolgushin from the same unit was shot down – by a Bf 109 – for the second time in two days, and once again managed to survive, albeit with severe injuries. In 296 IAP, the ace *Mayor* Boris Yeryomin had to take to his parachute after his Yak-7B was set ablaze by a German fighter. Against these losses, the Soviet fighter pilots managed to shoot down two Bf 109s, an Fw 189

and a Bf 110. In addition, II./St.G 1 lost two Ju 87s to Soviet anti-aircraft fire.[181]

On 21 September, 4 IAP's ace *Lt.* Sultan Amet-Khan was shot down by Bf 109s during an escort mission for Pe-2s, and had to bale out of his stricken Yak-1. On 22 September, Hero of the Soviet Union *Lt.* Nikolay Karnachyonok, one of the most experienced pilots in 434 IAP, was killed in action. It is possible that he fell prey to the German fighter commander at Stalingrad, *Hptm.* Wolf-Dietrich Wilcke, who claimed six Yak-1s in two separate engagements that day. With the loss of Karnachyonok, 434 IAP had lost nine pilots in combat during the past four days. In I./JG 53, *Oblt.* Wolfgang Tonne and *Fw.* Wilhelm Crinius became the next *Jagdwaffe* pilots to reach their 100th victories on 22 September. The three leading aces in I./JG 53 *Pik As* – Müller, Tonne, and Crinius – were all awarded with the Oak Leaves on 23 and 24 September, Crinius receiving both the Knight's Cross and the Oak Leaves simultaneously. The achievements of the three *Pik As* aces were astounding – since the opening of the offensive against Stalingrad one month previously, *Hptm.* Müller had increased his victory tally from 60 to 101; Tonne from 68 to 101; and Crinius from 44 to 101.

23 September became Hermann Graf's most successful day. On his first mission that day, he and his wingman came across two Il-2s and five Soviet fighters right above Stalingrad. Pursuing the escaping Soviet aircraft 20 miles to the north-west, the two Bf 109 pilots sent down five Soviet aircraft in flames – four of them by Graf. During his fourth sortie that day, Graf bagged a Yak-1 and two Su-2s near Kotluban in three minutes. Finally, during a mission in the same area two hours later, the German ace managed to knock down two Yak-1s and a LaGG-3 – reaching a tally of ten aircraft shot down in a single day. Hermann Graf's total tally now stood at 197.

But in the landscape of ruins on the ground below, no similar German victories were achieved. From their position high above in the air, the German airmen noted the conspicuous lack of progress on the ground. For the Stuka pilots, who were in action over Stalingrad day in and day out, dropping their bombs with pin-point accuracy at the Army's demands, the situation became increasingly frustrating. "We continue to pulverise a wasteland of torn-apart, burnt-out factory sheds in which not a wall is left standing, but the Army makes no progress", one of them wrote. "Eight sorties a day, from dawn to dusk", noted *Major* Paul-Werner Hozzel, the *Geschwaderkommodore* of St.G 2 *Immelmann*.

At German headquarters, the nervousness increased. Hozzel's commander-in-chief, *Generaloberst* von Richthofen, was infuriated at what he considered the indecisiveness of VI. *Armee* on the battlefield – in fact he employed the word 'constipation' to describe the lack of progress.[182] Hitler gave vent to frequent hysterical outbursts, and on 24 September he fired the OKW's Chief-of-Staff, *Generaloberst* Franz Halder. "Both of us have trouble with our nerves", Hitler told Halder, and continued: "Half my nervous

Hptm. Wolfgang Tonne led 3./JG 53 'Pik As' during the first stage of the Battle of Stalingrad. Tonne increased his victory tally on the Eastern Front from 13 to 101 between May and September 1942. In this photograph Tonne poses next to his rudder with 95 victory markings. His 95th victory was scored on 20 September 1942.

Maintenance of a La-5. On 18 August 1942, the La-5-equipped 27 IAP was transferred to 8 VA near Stalingrad. Until 24 December 1942, when the unit was pulled out of combat, it was credited with 60 aerial victories against a loss of 14 La-5s. The most successful pilots of this unit during the Battle of Stalingrad were Kapitan Fyodor Chuykin and St.Lt. Arkadiy Kovachevich. Chuykin was shot down and killed in combat with the German ace, Hptm. Wolfgang Tonne, on 11 September 1942. (Drabkin)

exhaustion is your fault. There is no use in continuing. What we need now is National Socialist enthusiasm, not professionalism. I can not expect this from a professional officer of the old school such as you."

But all of this was just a search for scapegoats. What caused von Richthofen's and Hitler's nervous outbursts was neither von Paulus' 'indecisiveness', nor Halder's personality – it was the unflinching Soviet resistance in the ruins of Stalingrad. Von Paulus' troops fought well, but they had become locked into what became popularly known as a *Rattenkrieg* – 'a rat's war' – where both sides fought for a street, a single house, or a small section of the underground sewage system.

At this stage, Chuykov's and his soldiers' successful defensive fight in the city – which had been waged in spite of the failure of the VVS to provide any effective support – convinced the Soviet commanders that the Soviet soldiers could actually do quite well even without the Air Force. In these

circumstances, it was decided to save the battered aviation for the upcoming major offensive at Stalingrad.

Soviet aircraft started to appear over Stalingrad with diminishing frequency by day. *Luftwaffe* bombers and Stukas increasingly had the skies to themselves and could carry out their operations mostly without disturbance from Soviet fighters. But at night the situation was different as Soviet night bombers were increasingly active. Between 17 July and 19 November 1942, the ADD flew 11,317 combat sorties in the Stalingrad – Don Bend sector – which amounts to 49 per cent of all ADD sorties in that period.[183]

Even Soviet night fighters started to achieve successes. A 7./KG 76 Ju 88 was shot down over Saratov on the night of 24 September. The victorious Soviet fighter pilot was a woman, *Lt.* Valeriya Khomyakova of the all-female 586 IAP.

Unlike the majority of Soviet aviation units at Stalingrad, 283 IAD was in action on 25 September. During various missions that morning, it

## First blood to the Soviet women fighter pilots

In October 1941 the well-known Soviet aviatrix Marina Raskova commanded three all-female air units, one of which was the fighter regiment 586 IAP. Officially activated on 9 December 1941, 586 IAP comprised 25 young women, led by Yevgeniya Prokhorova, who had earned fame for several record-breaking flights before the war. Eventually, she was succeeded by *Mayor* Tamara Kazarinova.

In late January 1942, the unit's flight training commenced – first on Yak-7 twin-seaters and eventually on standard Yak-1 fighters. One of the pilots, Valeria Khomyakova, stunned her trainers by being able to perform her first solo flight after only 52 minutes of flight training.

The unit flew its first operational mission on 23 February, when a number of pilots flew to cover a bridge across the Volga River. On that same day, the women of the unit swore their oath of allegiance – some of the servicewomen burst into tears with the emotion of the occasion.[1]

The female fighter pilots were eager to join combat, but the following months were filled with disappointments. After sustaining injury during a German bombing raid, 586 IAP's original commander, *Mayor* Tamara Kazarinova, was replaced by a male pilot, *Mayor* A. V. Gridnev. Only on 14 May 1942 was 586 IAP assigned to a combat unit, 144 IAD of the PVO, and tasked with providing the rail installations at Saratov with air cover. Apart from 586 IAP, the *Diviziya* was composed of the male unit 963 IAP.

Initially there was some reluctance at higher levels to accept that female pilots would be able to endure the hardships of the front line. But the rigours of the Battle of Stalingrad obviously forced these conservative thinkers to re-evaluate their opinions. On 10 September, eight pilots of 586 IAP's 1st *Eskadrilya*, commanded by *St.Lt.* Raisa Belyayeva, were transferred to the Stalingrad sector. The eight pilots were assigned to two male fighter regiments. Belyayeva's *Zveno* of four went to 287 IAD's 437 IAP at Verkhnyaya Akhtuba, and the four female pilots with *Lt.* Klavdiya Nechayeva were sent to the Yak-1-equipped elite unit 434 IAP at Ivanovka.

The male pilots' initial scornful attitude towards the women fighter pilots rapidly changed after a handful of mock combats. In 287 IAD, two La-5 piloted by 27 IAP's ace *St.Lt.* Arkadiy Kovachevich and his wingman met Belyayeva and *Lt.* Yekaterina Budanova in their Yak-1s.[2] In 434 IAP, Klavdiya Nechayeva was pitted against the commander *Mayor* Ivan Kleshchyov. Stepan Mikoyan of that unit recounted how amazed he was to see how the 19-year old female pilot got on the tail of Kleshchyov's fighter.[3]

But the fighting over Stalingrad was no easy game even for skilful female pilots. On 17 September, Nechayeva was killed when her Yak-1 was shot down by a Bf 109, possibly flown by one of the aces in I./JG 53. The first aerial victory attained by a female fighter pilot was achieved in the rear when 586 IAP's *Lt.* Valeriya Khomyakova shot down a Ju 88 flown by *Oblt.* Gerhard Maak of 7./KG 76 on the night of 24 September. On 27 September, the female pilot *Serzh.* Lilya Litvyak, who was among those who had been assigned to 437 IAP, scored her first victory against a Ju 88. During the next eleven months, Litvyak would amass a total of 12 individual and four shared victories. By the time she was killed in action in August 1943, she was the world's leading female fighter ace – a position she still holds.

[1.] Aviamaster 3/2000.
[2.] Bergström, Antipov and Dikov, *Black Cross/Red Star: Air War over the Eastern Front*, Vol. 3, p. 167.
[3.] Interview with Stepan Mikoyan.

claimed a Ju 88 shot down – confirmed by German records – but lost three Yak-1s, two of which fell to I./JG 53's *Uffz.* Heinz Golinski. In the afternoon, some twenty of its Yak-1s intercepted a large Ju 87 formation from II./St.G 1 and St.G 2 near Kotluban. For 20 minutes, the Soviet fighters carried out uninterrupted firing passes from all sides, from above and from below. Three Ju 87s were shot down, and another seven were damaged. Although badly injured by machine gun fire, Knight's Cross holder *Oblt.* Günther Schwärzel, the acting *Gruppenkommandeur* of III./St.G 2, managed to nurse his crippled Ju 87 back to base at Oblivskaya. Schwärzel died from his wounds two days later.

In total, 283 IAD was credited with the destruction of six Ju 87s, three Bf 109s and a Ju 88 for the loss of eight Yak-1s on 25 September 1942. Other units of 16 VA claimed altogether just three victories for the loss of two Yak-1s on the same day.

But on 26 September, the Germans barely saw any Soviet aircraft over Stalingrad. During one of the few encounters in the air on that day, Hermann Graf claimed his 200th victory. His opponents in this fight appear to have been three I-153s of 102 IAD's 629 IAP but, in spite of Graf's report, all Soviet aircraft returned home.[184] On 27 September Soviet 62nd Army launched a counter-attack inside Stalingrad. But they were beset by intense attacks from the air. Only a handful of Soviet fighter pilots rose to intercept the German bombers and Stukas. One of these was the female pilot *Serzh.* Lilya Litvyak, who scored her first victory against a Ju 88.

With the *Luftwaffe* fully in control of the air over Stalingrad, I./JG 53 and Graf's III./JG 52 detachment left the area. The former was sent back to Germany for a well-deserved period of rest and refit, while the III./JG 52 detachment was reunited with the rest of III./JG 52 farther south in the Caucasus. In return, I./JG 3 returned from its period of rest and refit. The Axis air forces at Stalingrad were also reinforced by the arrival of Rumanian GAL's *Grupul 5 Bombardament* with *Escadriles* 79 and 80 *Bombardament* on 25 September – both equipped mainly with He 111 H-3s. On 4 October, bomber groups *Grupul 1 Bombardament* (*Escadrilas 71* and 72 with Italian-designed Savoia 79s) and *Grupul 3 Bombardament* (equipped with Polish-designed P.Z.L. P.23s, and French Potez 633s and Potez 63.11s), also arrived – in addition to *Grupul 6 Bombardament în Picaj* (I.A.R. 81 dive-bombers).

The Soviet air forces had indeed been dealt a severe defeat at Stalingrad. On 28 September, *General* Pavel Stepanov was removed from command of 16 VA. His place was assumed by his former deputy, *General-Mayor* Stepan Rudenko, who had in reality been leading 16 VA since early September.

*A Rumanian anti-aircraft artillery position at a joint Rumanian-German airfield.*

But on the ground, the so-called *Rattenkrieg* continued to be waged with undiminished fierceness. In late September, the Soviets had completed their first bridge across the Volga. This bridge was built two feet below the surface of the water, which rendered it almost impossible to destroy through aerial bombardment. The Stukas were called upon to carry out pinpoint attacks. On 2 October, Stukas managed to locate and hit Chuykov's headquarters. The oil tank above the headquarters was hit by dozens of bombs and burst into flames. But von Richthofen was not satisfied, as his diary notes from these days reveal.[185]

On 5 October, von Richthofen's Stukas carried out more than 700 individual attacks against Soviet troops holding out at Stalingrad's Tractor Plant *Dzherzhinskiy*. The next day, a *Luftwaffe* raid wiped out the entire staff of Soviet 339th Infantry Regiment. But meanwhile, Soviet RS-132 *Katyusha* rocket-projectiles almost annihilated a whole battalion of German 60th Motorised Division inside Stalingrad.

*The Battle of Stalingrad as aircrew saw it. This photograph was taken by the radio operator of a Ju 87 of 6./St.G 2 at 300 metres altitude on 10 September 1942. (Taghon)*

On 8 October, a furious Hitler called for a renewed offensive effort in Stalingrad by no later than 14 October. But he also demanded that the *Luftwaffe* should strike against the oil installations at Grozny down south in the Caucasus. He thus demonstrated both his lack of resolve – after all, the seizure of the oil fields for German use was one of the main strategic goals on the Eastern Front – and his leaping focus from one sector to another.

Von Richthofen knew that success in Stalingrad would depend on air support. He nonetheless elected to dispatch some bomber units for attacks against the oil refinery at Grozny. The attacks were carried out on 10 and 12 October. Then, with just one day remaining before the Stalingrad offensive had to commence, he rushed his bomber units back north again. By the time the offensive began in Stalingrad on 14 October, *Luftflotte* 4 had been reinforced with the arrival of KG 1's three Ju 88 *Gruppen* from *Luftflotte* 1. Von Richthofen launched his armada of bombers into the air once again.

"The whole sky was full of aircraft," wrote a German soldier who witnessed the effect of von Richthofen's new *Schwerpunkt* as von Paulus' soldiers launched their attack against the factory settlements in the northern part of Stalingrad dominated by three huge factory buildings – the *Dzherzhinskiy* Tractor Plant, the *Barrikadiy* and the *Krasniy Oktyabr*. The

industrial rail line in this sector formed a great oval-shaped 'U', and from the air resembled a huge tennis racquet – thus the area became known to the German airmen as *der Tennisschläger*. Nearly 2,000 *Luftwaffe* sorties were flown on 14 October, and 600 tons of bombs were dropped, mainly in the *Tennisschläger* area. The Stukas of II./St.G 1, I. and II./St.G 2 and I./St.G 77 made 320 individual sorties in a total of 53 missions.[186] The German airmen met barely any opposition at all from Soviet fighters, which von Richthofen noted with great satisfaction in his diary.[187]

With Stukas and *Schlacht* aircraft blasting a path towards the massive concrete forms of the three great factories, the German troops managed not only to surround the Tractor Plant, but also to reach the Volga along a 2,000-yard front. On the following day, *Major* Hozzel, the Stuka *Kommodore,* first dispatched his Ju 87s against the Soviet artillery on the Volga's eastern bank.[188] Next, the Stukas went into action against the ferries on the Volga. This paralysed the flow of supplies to Chuykov's 62nd Army – which had been cut in two by the German advance to the Volga.

In this situation, *General-Leytenant* Aleksandr Novikov, the Commander-in-chief of VVS KA and the supreme aviation commander in the Stalingrad sector, decided to send Soviet aircraft into the battle again. Take-off orders went out to the airfields of 220 IAD and 228 ShAD. The Yak-1s, Yak-7Bs and Il-2s took off early on 16 October and flew into grey and rainy skies. Visibility was further reduced by billowing smoke clouds from the raging fires on the ground below. Above Stalingrad they spotted twelve Ju 87s, ten Ju 88s and four He 111s. The Soviet fighter pilots immediately attacked, but failed to notice several formations of Bf 109s which were patrolling high above. The latter dived down on the Soviet formations. In a bitter fight, the Messerschmitts of 9./JG 3 and 1./JG 52 claimed four Soviet fighters and four Il-2s shot down while the Soviet fighter pilots were credited with the destruction of nine German aircraft. The Germans actually lost three aircraft – Ju 88s from KG 1.

The *Dzherzhinskiy* Tractor Plant was captured by the Germans following an extremely bloody battle. The fighting reached the very walls of the *Barrikadiy* factory, which meant that the Soviet defenders were crammed into a 1,000-yard narrow strip of land on the western bank of the Volga. This small sector was subjected to an intense air and artillery bombardment which made even the attack against Sevastopol pale in comparison. *Major* Hozzel's Stukas made 230 individual sorties against this tiny piece of land on 23 October, 381 on the 24th, 329 on the 25th and 268 on the 26th.[189]

And still the Soviet defence would not budge! *General* Karl Strecker, who commanded XI. *Armeekorps,* wrote: "Factory walls, assembly lines, the whole superstructure collapses under the storm of bombs, but the enemy simply reappears and utilises these newly created ruins to fortify his defensive positions."[190]

By the evening of 29 October, the German attack was petering out. By this time, Soviet 62nd Army was down to just 47,000 men with 19 tanks, split into three separate groups.[191] The Germans simply could not grasp that the combined forces of VI. *Armee* and IV. *Panzerarmee* – with a numerical

*German soldiers in the ruins of Stalingrad. After a series of piecemeal attacks which the Soviets destroyed, a major German assault succeeded in reaching the suburbs, but once German troops attempted to move into the built-up areas, the battle developed into two months of bitter house-to-house fighting during which neither side gained any advantage. While holding off the German attack, the Soviets prepared a massive counter-attack.*

Ju 87s at a front line airstrip on the Eastern Front. Through September 1942, St.G 2 'Immelmann' recorded 25 Ju 87 D-1s or D-3s destroyed or severely damaged due to hostile action. All of these losses occurred over Stalingrad.

Hermann Graf, who commanded the III./JG 52 Detachment at Stalingrad in September 1942, flew almost to exhaustion. On 26 September 1942, Graf became the first pilot to reach a total of 200 victories and is seen here carried in celebration on the shoulders of his mechanics at Pitomnik on that occasion. Fatigue can be seen in the faces of these men, who had been fighting an incessant battle with the VVS for several months without any pause.

strength six times greater than the enemy in Stalingrad, subjected to tremendous aerial onslaught – were unable to seize the last small slice of land in the contested city.

On 1 November, *Generaloberst* von Richthofen again gave vent to his dissatisfaction with VI. *Armee*: "We drop our bombs on enemy positions less than a hand grenade's throw from the infantry, but they do nothing!"[192] But this was just another expression of the growing frustration on the German side. In fact, heavy Soviet artillery fire from across the Volga tore the attack forces to pieces where they stood. "The effect of massed enemy artillery has decisively weakened the division's attacking strength", noted German 79th Infantry Division.

With this going on, the build-up for the Soviet offensive in the rear of VI. *Armee* was in full swing. In early November, the 5th Tank Army was shipped across the Don to the bridgehead which the Soviets held at Serafimovich on the northern side of the Don Bend. In this sector, the Rumanian 3rd Army had proven unable to eradicate the Serafimovich bridgehead even before these Soviet reinforcements had arrived. Meanwhile, south-east of Stalingrad, 111,000 men, 420 tanks, 556 artillery pieces and 7,000 tons of ammunition were shipped across the Volga south-east of Stalingrad, and were lined up against the 4th Rumanian Army south of the city.

Hitler, in throes from his own deprecatory attitude towards the Russians, not only refused to acknowledge the mounting threat – he appears to have been certain that victory was within reach. His Operational Order No. 1, issued on 14 October 1942, read: "The Russians have been substantially weakened during the recent fighting and in the coming winter will not be able to assemble any large forces as they did in the previous winter."[193] Only five weeks later, these words rang very hollow for those Germans who were trapped at Stalingrad.

Clearing skies – and a subsequent cold spell that brought down temperatures to minus 15 degrees Celsius – during the second week of November, seemed to promise good flying weather during the Soviet offensive, which was scheduled for 19 November. But three days prior to that date, a warm front moving northward from the Caucasus resulted in inclement weather. Temperatures rose to around melting point. Rain and sleet increased the effects of thaw, and the collision between banks of warm and cold air created thick fog. All of this effectively grounded the air forces of both sides on the day that the offensive opened.

## The build-up for an offensive

Throughout the autumn of 1942, the Soviet plans for the upcoming major offensive were being methodically worked out. On 28 September, the Stalingrad Front was re-designated the Don Front. Shortly afterwards it was split in half, with the right (western) wing forming the new South-western Front under *General-Leytenant* Nikolay Vatutin – who until then had commanded the Voronezh Front. The old South-eastern Front was renamed the new Stalingrad Front; thus 8 VA was once again to be associated with Stalingrad. On 29 September, *General Armii* Zhukov returned to the Stalingrad area in a Li-2 transport aircraft. He brought along a dynamic senior officer of Polish origin, *General-Leytenant* Konstantin Rokossovskiy who would assume command of the new Don Front, replacing the old Stalingrad Front's commander, *General-Leytenant* Gordov. Rokossovskiy was briefed on the situation. He learned that the South-western Front would be launched in a major attack against the rear of the German troops in Stalingrad. This attack would begin in November.

While the bitter fighting continued inside Stalingrad, *General-Polkovnik* Andrey Yeremenko – who was the supreme commander of the Red Army in Stalingrad and to the south of that city – decided to test the strength of his opponent in the open steppe south of the city. On 29 September his 51st and 57th Armies launched some limited forces against the Rumanian 4th Army in the area around the Lakes Sarpa, Tsatsa and Barmantsak. The success was immediate. On 29 September the Rumanians were ousted from Sadovoye and, had it not been for the rapid deployment of German 14. *Panzerdivision,* the whole Rumanian Front could have crumbled. As a result of this experience, the *Stavka* decided to add a southern attack axis to the intended major offensive.

Shortly afterwards it was decided to shift the northern attack from the centre of Don to the Serafimovich bridgehead on the right bank of the Don in the northern Don Bend – where the other Rumanian army, the 3rd, was positioned. Thus, the northern attack would be carried out in cooperation between the South-western and Don Fronts.

The outlines for the offensive – Operation "*Uranus*" – had been drawn up by *General Armii* Zhukov and *General-Polkovnik* Vasilyevskiy on 13 September 1942 and in October the Soviets started to assemble their forces for the upcoming offensive.

On the eve of the offensive, Rokossovskiy's Don Front numbered more than 300,000 troops, 4,000 artillery pieces, and 161 tanks north and north-west of Stalingrad. On its western flank, *General-Leytenant* Vatutin's South-western Front mustered almost 400,000 soldiers, with over 4,000 artillery pieces and 400 tanks. With only the 62nd Army left fighting inside Stalingrad, the bulk of *General-Polkovnik* Yeremenko's Stalingrad Front – with a strength of 430,000 soldiers, 5,000 artillery pieces, and 323 tanks on the eve of Operation "*Uranus*" – was lined up along a 100-mile front line from Stalingrad and to the south.

About 60 per cent of the Red Army's tanks and nearly half the artillery was concentrated in the Stalingrad - Don sector.

The Soviet build-up did not pass unnoticed by the Germans. Aerial reconnaissance was a field where the Germans enjoyed one of their largest advantages over the Soviets. Despite all kinds of decoy attempts by the Soviets, *Luftwaffe* reconnaissance aircrews detected and mapped the general flow of Soviet supplies and reinforcements to the forces opposing the flanks of *Heeresgruppe B*. This was particularly the case at the bridgeheads across the Don which South-western Front had created at Serafimovich and Kletskaya, 80-100 miles north-west of Stalingrad. Rumanian 3rd Army proved to be too weak to prevent this and, day by day, these bridgeheads received more fresh Red Army troops. On 12 November 1942, it was noted in *Luftflotte* 4's war diary: "In front of the Rumanians the Russians are cold-bloodedly continuing their build-up. Parts of VIII. *Fliegerkorps*, the *Luftflotte*'s forces, and Rumanian aviation forces are in constant action against this. Ground troop reserves are brought together. *When are the Russians going to attack?*"[1]. Two days later, *Generaloberst* von Richthofen decided that he would assume personal command of *Fliegerkorps* VIII and the Rumanian Air Corps once the expected Soviet offensive was initiated.[2] On 17 November, the so-called *Gefechtsverband Hitschold* – one *Stukagruppe* and a *Zerstörergruppe* – was shifted to Rumanian 3rd Army's sector, north-west of Stalingrad.[3]

But for various reasons, *Luftflotte* 4 was unable to interfere decisively against the Soviet build-up. First of all, on Hitler's explicit instructions, the main target remained the last Soviet footholds inside Stalingrad, and not the dangerous bridgeheads at Serafimovich and Kletskaya. On 11 November, the Stukas of VIII. *Fliegerkorps* were brought in *en masse* to support another futile attempt by VI. *Armee* to achieve a decisive breakthrough in the city of Stalingrad. Bad weather also hampered flight activities on most days during the damp autumn. To this should be added the effect of six months of large-scale combat activity, which in combination with an inadequate supply system, ground down the efficiency of the German air fleet. As if this was not enough, *Luftflotte* 4 was forced to give up several units for the North African combat zone, in response to the Allied landings in Morocco and Algeria on 8 November 1942.

[1.] War Diary *Luftflotte* 4, 12 November 1942. Bundesarchiv/Militärarchiv, RL 7/482.
[2.] War Diary *Luftflotte* 4, 14 November 1942. Bundesarchiv/Militärarchiv, RL 7/482.
[3.] War Diary *Luftflotte* 4, 17 November 1942. Bundesarchiv/Militärarchiv, RL 7/482.

## The opposing air forces

The vast amount of military equipment employed by the Red Army in the Stalingrad – Don Bend area on the eve of Operation "*Uranus*" was possible through the amazing recovery of Soviet industry, which in late 1941 had largely been dismantled and transported eastwards to escape the German advance. Production figures rose from 11,000 tanks and 14,000 artillery pieces in the first half of 1942 to 13,600 tanks and 15,600 artillery pieces during the last six months of that year. But the most astonishing production increase was accomplished by the aviation industry, where the figures rose from 9,600 between January and June to 15,800 in the second half of the year. The cream of the latter figure went to the Stalingrad – Don Bend sector, where the numbers of aircraft available increased five-fold from August to November 1942. This is particularly remarkable in view of the fact that the Soviets recorded 2,846 aircraft lost during the battle in the Don - Stalingrad area from 28 June to 18 November 1942.

Soviet aviation in the Stalingrad - Don Bend area was centralised in command under VVS C-in-C, *General-Polkovnik* Aleksandr Novikov. Revealing renewed confidence in his air forces, Novikov had assigned the aviation arm an important role in the upcoming offensive. The bombers were tasked with attacking German airfields, headquarters and troop encampments in the rear.

The *Shturmoviks* were to support the infantry and tank attacks on the battlefield, with special orders issued for close support of the special breakthrough units which consisted of tank and cavalry forces. The concentration of 575 Il-2 ground-attack planes for Operation "*Uranus*" had no previous parallel in the VVS, and indeed constituted a tremendous strike force. Much emphasis was also given to the battle for air supremacy. Gaining control of the air was one of the major tasks assigned to Soviet air forces and here the fighters were to play the leading role.

Having been mostly spared large-scale daylight operations since the end of September, 8 VA – which was assigned to support the southern attack by *General-Polkovnik* Yeremenko's Stalingrad Front – was reinforced to muster 499 aircraft (267 serviceable) on the eve of Operation "*Uranus*".

*General-Leytenant* Rokossovskiy's new Don Front, which held positions from the north of Stalingrad and about 100 miles to the west, had the weakest aerial support in numerical terms; on 19 November 1942, *General* Sergey Rudenko's 16 VA reported a strength of 107 fighters (81 serviceable), 103 *Shturmoviks* (68 serviceable), and 93 light night bombers (80 serviceable). But the Don Front could also count on support from the Stalingrad air defence's 102 IAD PVO – with 88 aircraft (of which 23 were serviceable) – and the ADD.

Farther to the west, the South-western Front was supported by a brand new air army, 17 VA. Formed as late as 16 November, 17 VA could muster 423 aircraft

(372 serviceable). *General-Mayor* Stepan Krasovskiy, who previously had displayed good abilities leading 2 VA in the Voronezh area, was appointed commander of 17 VA.

Krasovskiy's "old" 2 VA, with 163 aircraft (139 serviceable) on the eve of Operation "*Uranus*", could also be used to support the South-western Front. *General-Mayor* Konstantin Smirnov, who previously had led the Air Force of the Volga Military District, became 2 VA's new commander.

Including ADD forces, Soviet air assets totalled well over 1,500 aircraft in the Stalingrad - Don Bend area on 19 November 1942. This gave the Soviets numerical superiority of two to one. Their quality had also improved. The period of reduced operations by day was utilised for intensive tactical training of the newer pilots. Several new tactical methods were also put into practice. The network of radio stations which had been brought into use during September 1942 to direct the aircraft from the ground was further extended, and the methods for ground-to-air radio communication were improved. Starting with improvised improvements at unit level, more and more Il-2s were also modified into two-seaters and equipped with a rear gun.

Perhaps the most important tactical reform was the implementation of the German *Rotte – Schwarm* fighter tactic – *Para - Zveno*, as it became called in the VVS – among the Soviet fighters.

German industry proved unable to compete with Soviet industrial output and managed to produce only about half as many aircraft as the USSR in the second half of 1942. The 8,314 aircraft which left German assembly plants between July and December 1942, were barely enough to maintain German first-line strength – taking into consideration that older aircraft had to be replaced with new models (such as the Ju 87 B and Bf 109 F superceded by the Ju 87 D and Bf 109 G).

Furthermore, in the Stalingrad - Don Bend sector, the *Luftwaffe's* strength was dwindling. This was the result mainly of two factors. First of all, the increased needs of other combat zones – above all the Mediterranean area, where the Allies had landed in Morocco and Algeria on 8 November 1942 – compelled the OKL to release units from *Luftflotte* 4. But another important factor was the appalling state of the German supply situation on the Eastern Front. Bottlenecks, strung out supply lines, too few railroads, bad road conditions, and even

corruption, contributed to wearing down the stream of supplies from Germany to a mere trickle at the war zone in the Don Bend 1,200 miles farther to the east.

Out of 732 combat aircraft reported by *Luftflotte* 4 with its *Fliegerkorps* IV and VIII on 20 November 1942, only 402 were serviceable.

*Luftflotte* 4 also had on strength the inadequately equipped aviation forces of a number of other Axis powers in the Stalingrad region – Rumanian, Italian, and Hungarian. *General Aviator* Ermil Gheorghiue's Rumanian *Gruparea Aeriană de Luptă* (GAL) – numbered around 100 aircraft, of which around half were bombers. They were divided into the fighter groups *Grupul* 7 *Vânătoare* (equipped with Bf 109 Es) and *Grupul* 8 *Vânătoare* (equipped with I.A.R. 80 fighters of Rumanian designation); and the bomber groups *Grupul* 1 *Bombardament* (*Escadrilas* 71 and 72 with Italian-designed Savoia 79s), *Grupul* 3 *Bombardament* (equipped with Polish-designed P.Z.L. P.23s, and Potez 633s and Potez 63.11s, the two latter of French designation), and *Grupul* 6 *Bombardament în Picaj* (I.A.R. 81 dive-bombers). All of these suffered from a supply situation which was even worse than among the German units.

German fighters on strength with *Luftflotte* 4 – which would remain the major threat against Soviet aerial operations – amounted to less than fifty Bf 109s in the Stalingrad region. Since the departure of the last remnants of JG 52, JG 53 and JG 77 (the latter two *Geschwader* leaving the Eastern Front for the Mediterranean area), the only *Jagdwaffe* units remaining in Stalingrad were *Stab*, I. and III./JG 3 *Udet*. They could count on support mainly from the Bf 109 Es of Rumanian *Grupul* 7 *Vânătoare*. The Italian and Hungarian aviation detachments, based farther up the Don, made a weak presence in the air. The two Hungarian fighter squadrons in the East, 1. and 2./I *Vádasz Osztály*, reported four aerial victories in October 1942 and one in November 1942, and were left with only nine serviceable Reggiane Re. 2000 fighters by that time. The aerial resources of the Italian ARMIR – 21 *Gruppo Autonomo Caccia* with approximately 50 Macchi C. 200 and C. 202 fighters and 71 *Gruppo* with approximately 50 Fiat BR.20M, Caproni Ca. 311, and SM. 81 bombers – suffered from shortages in supplies of all kinds and appear to have operated on a highly sporadic basis.

Il-2s of 226 ShAD being prepared for operations at an airfield near the front line in June 1942. Commanded by Podpolkovnik Mikhail Gorlachenko, 226 ShAD was transferred to 8 VA with a completely new complement of Il-2s on 24 June 1942. Following severe losses during the first days of action to repulse the German summer offensive, the Diviziya was pulled out of action for rest and refit on 5 July 1942. However, it soon returned to first-line service with 8 VA and, during the subsequent Battle of Stalingrad, it developed into one of the most successful VVS units. (Karlenko)

# Chapter Thirteen

# Into the Fog

A t 07.30 hrs on 19 November 1942, the artillery of *General-Leytenant* Nikolay Vatutin's South-western Front received the expected command: "*Ogon!*" (Fire!). Around 3,500 guns and mortars opened fire into the fog in the south, where the Rumanian 3rd Army had taken up positions. *General* Petre Dumitrescu, the commander of the Rumanian Army who had expected the attack for several weeks, immediately called for air support. But the thick white mist, the low cloud ceiling, and wet ice covering many runways on the airfields made take-offs impossible. One hour later, Soviet South-western Front's 21st Army and 5th Tank Army opened the attack against the Rumanians north-west of Stalingrad.

Contrary to most German accounts, the Rumanians put up a stiff fight and managed to ward off the first attack waves. At *General* Dumitrescu's disposal were 143,296 troops[194] equipped with 827 artillery or anti-tank pieces between 37mm and 75mm calibre, and 134 tanks.[195] When wind dispersed the fog a little in mid-morning, a handful of Il-2s from 17 VA's 267 ShAD were able to take to the air. These rocket-firing *Shturmoviks* added to the horror created by the artillery onslaught and formations of T-34 tanks, and morale collapsed among the Rumanians.

The Rumanian Combat Air Group GAL, which was assigned to cover the 3rd Army, failed to launch a single aircraft on this day. *Generaloberst* von Richthofen, who was supposed to assume personal command of the Axis counter-strike from the air, happened to be on an inspection tour down south in the Caucasus. *Generalleutnant* Martin Fiebig, who led *Luftflotte* 4's VIII. *Fliegerkorps*, ordered the commanders of his Stuka- and *Schlacht* units to put at least some small groups of aircraft on armed reconnaissance in the air above the Rumanian lines. *Oblt.* Hans-Ulrich Rudel, 1./St.G 2's *Staffelkapitän*, took off from Karpovka, some 20 miles west of Stalingrad. Rudel was one of the most experienced Stuka pilots. A Knight's Cross recipient, he had carried out more than 650 combat sorties on the Eastern Front, but the sight that he met when he flew towards Kletskaya early on 19 November was like no other he had yet experienced in the war:

"What troops are those coming toward us? We have not gone more than halfway. Masses in brown uniforms – are they Russians? No. Rumanians. Some of them are even throwing away their rifles in order to be able to run faster – a shocking sight, we are prepared for the worst. We fly the length of the column emplacements. The guns are abandoned, not destroyed. Their

ammunition lies beside them. We have passed some distance beyond them before we sight the first Soviet troops. They find the Rumanian positions in front of them deserted. We attack with bombs and gunfire – but how much use is that when there is no resistance on the ground?"[196]

Rudel was lucky that he managed to see anything at all on the ground. On 19 November visibility was so bad in places, shrouded in fog and swept by blizzards, that Soviet tank crews reportedly had to steer by compass.[197] *Luftflotte* 4 managed to conduct no more than 120 sorties on this day, while 17 VA performed 546,[198] and 16 VA's units flew just 82. Among the latter, crews of 54 aircraft failed to locate their targets, and lost five of their aircraft.

A frustrated *Generaloberst* Wolfram von Richthofen noted in his diary: "There is no possibility of aerial reconnaissance providing us with an overview of the situation." Thus the Germans and Rumanians failed to realize the full scope of the crisis until it was too late.

South-western Front's troops continued to push southwards and south-east inside the Don Bend while the Rumanian 3rd Army broke up in increasing disorder. 20 November dawned with the same weather prevailing, and still no clear picture in the Axis camp of what was going on. That day, *General-Polkovnik* Andrey Yeremenko's Stalingrad Front crashed through the Rumanian 4th Army's positions south of Stalingrad and dashed to the west across the steppe. With 63,958 troops at its disposal,[199] the Rumanian 4th Army was considerably weaker than the 3rd Army farther to the north.

The weather still prevented the air forces on both sides from interfering decisively in the confused ground battle. On the German side, KG 55's Chief Meteorologist wrote: "Despite terribly bad weather, *Major* [Hans-Joachim] Gabriel's and *Oblt.* [Hans] Neubert's crews take off. Both fail to return."[200] Onboard He 111 call-sign G1+HM, II./KG 55's *Gruppenkommandeur*, *Major* Hans-Joachim Gabriel was lost – as was the pilot, Knight's Cross holder *Lt.* Karl Lipp. Both were among the *Luftwaffe's* top aviators in the Stalingrad area. *Major* Gabriel was a veteran of the Battle of Britain in 1940, and Lipp had flown more than 400 bombing missions. On the Soviet side, only the most experienced pilots were picked to carry out armed reconnaissance in single flights or in pairs at almost zero level.

With slightly improved weather conditions in the afternoon of 21 November, the VVS made several attacks against Axis airfields in the

During the first years of the war, the Luftwaffe was significantly superior to its Soviet adversary in terms of aerial reconnaissance. This photograph shows an Fw 189, probably Germany's most successful reconnaissance aircraft during the Second World War. When the Luftwaffe was 'blinded' by thick fog as the Soviet winter offensive was opened in November 1942, it revealed just how much the German Army depended on aerial reconnaissance. (Mombeeck)

region. Six 285 ShAP Il-2s, led by Hero of the Soviet Union *Kapitan* Viktor Golubev, claimed to have destroyed eight enemy aircraft in one of these attacks. During their return flight the Il-2s were intercepted by Bf 109s, but reportedly shot down one of these and returned to base without losses. Meanwhile, *Lieutenant-General* Mihail Lascar's V Army Corps of Rumanian 3rd Army – which had become surrounded south of Serafimovich – also received badly needed support from both the GAL's bombers and fighters and *Luftwaffe* aircraft. I./KG 100 flew three missions in *Gruppe* strength against Soviet troop concentrations on 21 November,[201] and St.G 2 *Immelmann* conducted 141 sorties in support of both the Rumanian 3rd and 4th armies.[202] This cost the *Immelmanngeschwader* a loss of at least five Ju 87s.[203] *Hptm.* Joachim Langbehn, 5./St.G 2's *Staffelkapitän*, crashed his burning Stuka in no-man's land, but he and his radio operator were rescued by *Lt.* Teigler who landed alongside and picked them up.[204]

On the following day, 22 November, the weather deteriorated again, and *Luftflotte* 4 was not able to carry out more than 150 sorties in the Stalingrad - Don Bend area. Despite the increasingly desperate situation for Lascar's V Army Corps, Rumanian *Escadrila* 105 *Transport Greu* could dispatch only five Ju 52s to supply their surrounded troops at Serafimovich.[205] Meanwhile, Kalach, with its large Don Bridge on the main road from the west to Stalingrad, was seized by *General-Mayor* Rodin's Soviet 26th Tank Corps. This unit had dashed 70 miles to the south-east from the Serafimovich area. At Tusov aerodrome, 20 miles west of Kalach, St.G 2 and SchG 1 pilots panicked and took off in their Ju 87s, Bf 109s and Hs 123s as Soviet tanks rolled into view. At least six *Schlacht* aircraft were destroyed on the ground at Tusov, and KGrzbV 5 lost at least one of its He 111 transports. "..Only a weak *Gruppe* of St.G 2 managed to get out," was the laconic note in *Luftflotte* 4's War Diary.[206]

Another 30 miles farther to the south-west, at the Chir River, Oblivskaya came within reach of other elements of the Soviet 5th Tank Army. Oblivskaya was not only where the headquarters of VIII. *Fliegerkorps* was located and a vital German airfield, it also had an important rail bridge. By organizing his *Flakregiment* 99 into a makeshift ground defence force, *Luftwaffe Oberst* Reiner Stahel was able to keep the Soviets at bay at Oblivskaya.

A similar situation occurred at Karpovka aerodrome. *General-Mayor* Vasiliy Volskiy's Soviet 44th Mechanised Corps of the Stalingrad Front had sliced through all resistance south of Stalingrad and advanced rapidly towards the north-west, reaching the Karpovka region late in the evening of 22 November. *Căpitan Aviator* Alexandru Serbănescu, who commanded the Rumanian Bf 109 E-equipped *Grupul 7 Vânătoare*, improvised a rather unorthodox defence line – consisting of four 75mm anti-aircraft guns, and the guns of the parked aircraft! This nevertheless sufficed to hold the weak scouting elements of 44th Mechanised Corps at bay while an evacuation of the airfield could be organized.

On 23 November, all serviceable aircraft took off from Karpovka, transporting as many ground personnel as possible in their fuselages. Sixteen Rumanian Bf 109s made it to the airfields at Morozovsk and Tatsinskaya. Axis losses were nonetheless severe. Three Rumanian Bf 109s were shot down during the evacuation flight. Another twelve and at least one of

*Soviet Pe-2 bombers in hazy weather above front lines during the winter battle.*

SchG 1's aircraft were destroyed on the ground. The *Luftwaffe's* loss records from this period are incomplete and full of gaps. Historian Holger Nauroth's unit chronicle states that II./St.G 2 *Immelmann* lost around 20 men killed or injured at Karpovka.[207] In their monthly reports of aircraft strength, *Stab*, I., and II./St.G 2 reported a total of 40 aircraft written off – 17 to hostile activity, 11 to other causes, six sent for repair and six assigned to other units – through November 1942.[208] Of this total, 16 were not specified in the reports of individual aircraft losses to the *Generalquartiermeister der Luftwaffe*.[209] Nor is *Stukageschwader* 2's War Diary specific on losses at Karpovka on 23 November 1942.[210]

*Stukageschwader Immelmann* was dealt another significant setback when the veteran *Hptm.* Joachim Langbehn, who had conducted over 400 dive-bombing missions, was shot down early on 24 November – for the second time in just three days – during a mission to support Rumanian 3rd Army. This time, Langbehn would not survive.[211] He was posthumously awarded the Knight's Cross four months later.

Although dramatic, the evacuation of Karpovka was overshadowed by another event of much greater importance in the same area that same day – *General-Mayor* Volskiy's rapid advance saw the 44th Mechanised Corps establish contact with elements from South-western Front's 5th Tank Army. Thus the door closed behind a quarter of a million German troops in Stalingrad. The task of the commander of the surrounded force, *General* Friedrich von Paulus, rapidly switched from seizing "Stalin's City" to organizing the defence of a cauldron that extended 35 miles westward from the city of Stalingrad, and around 20 miles from the north to the south. As an indication of what awaited them, *General* Lascar's enveloped Rumanian V Army Corps surrendered that same evening. A total of 27,000 Rumanians marched into Soviet confinement.

During the five days over which these events had occurred, thick fog and low cloud ceilings had limited the Soviet air forces in the Stalingrad - Don Bend to a daily average of merely 200 combat sorties, while *Luftflotte* 4 could perform only slightly half that number. Air power indeed played almost no role at all during the initial onslaught of Operation 'Uranus', which led to the creation of the Stalingrad cauldron. All that was about to change.

# Chapter Fourteen

# Improvising an airlift

The leadership of the Third Reich proved to be totally unprepared for the implications of Operation "*Uranus*". Initially, both Hitler and *Luftwaffe* Commander-in-chief *Reichsmarschall* Hermann Göring, considered the Soviet envelopment of Stalingrad as a temporary setback. Hitler instructed *General* von Paulus to stay put with his forces at the Volga, and – supported in his view by Göring – promised that the *Luftwaffe* would supply the isolated army from the air. This provoked a short but heated debate in senior *Wehrmacht* command circles.

*Generaloberst* Wolfram *Freiherr* von Richthofen, commanding *Luftflotte* 4, and *Generalleutnant* Martin Fiebig, commander of VIII. *Fliegerkorps*, opposed the idea that an army of such dimensions could be supplied from the air. *Generalmajor* Wolfgang Pickert, who led the 9th *Flakdivision* inside the cauldron, was of the same opinion and proposed an immediate breakout to the south-west. But according to the Chief-of-Staff of the surrounded VI. *Armee*, *Generalmajor* Arthur Schmidt, fuel supplies inside the cauldron were simply insufficient for a successful breakout.

In any event, Hitler appeared to base his decision on two previous experiences. Firstly, he was conscious that *Heeresgruppe Mitte's* retreat west of Moscow in December 1941 had turned into a headlong flight that almost brought the entire army group to collapse. He had good reason to fear that the green light for an evacuation of Stalingrad would lead to a collapse of the entire Don Bend position. Thus, rather than VI. *Armee* being surrounded, the whole of *Heeresgruppe A* in the Caucasus risked isolation – a perspective much worse than the envelopment of Stalingrad. Secondly, as we have seen, the *Luftwaffe* had demonstrated a convincing airlift capability in sustaining the beleaguered 100,000-strong garrison at Demyansk from the air earlier in 1942.

So while *Reichsmarschall* Göring undertook an apparently carefree shopping trip to Paris, his OKL began the difficult task of improvising an air transport operation at Stalingrad. The German commanders inside the Stalingrad cauldron looked askance at the meagre results obtained during the initial days of the air bridge. A mere 32 transport planes landed in Stalingrad on 25 November – a day with clear skies.[212]

According to estimates made by the OKH on 27 November 1942, the Stalingrad garrison would need 700 tons of supplies each day.[213] Two days earlier, Göring had promised that a daily average of 500 tons would be

delivered by the *Luftwaffe*. In theory, this could be accomplished, even if around 280 Ju 52 transport planes were already engaged in the newly established air bridge to Tunisia. Of around 750 Ju 52s in service, 298 were reported as immediately available for the Stalingrad air supply operation on 27 November 1942.[214]

When various liaison and ambulance aircraft were added, a total of 320 Ju 52s were available for the Stalingrad operation in late November 1942,[215] and KGrzbV 5 reported a strength of 30 He 111s for transport tasks in the region.[216]

With the Ju 52 able to fly some two tons and the He 111 a total of 1.2 tons of goods into Stalingrad, simple arithmetic showed that each transport just had to make one flight per day to fulfil Göring's promises, and theoretically each aircraft had time to conduct at least two such flights per day. Initially, the Germans found some reason to be optimistic.

They also were able to stabilise the situation on the ground after a few days. VI. *Armee* and IV. *Panzerarmee*, plus the Rumanian 3rd and 4th Armies were organized into the new army group *Heeresgruppe Don*, with *Generalfeldmarschall* Erich von Manstein appointed its commander. The Axis troops formed a series of defence positions that acted as a breakwater against the Soviet offensive along the Chir River on the northern flank, and at Kotelnikovo on the southern flank. With improved weather conditions, *Luftflotte* 4 again went into action and brought about a decisive contribution to the German recovery:

"The soggy airfields were overcrowded and were virtually without wire communications, command being exercised by means of radio and liaison aircraft. The VIII. *Fliegerkorps*' command post was situated at Oblivskaya airfield, close behind the thinly-manned line of resistance. There, despite many difficulties, VIII. *Fliegerkorps* managed to reorganize its badly mixed up units, to establish new units, and to reinforce its organizations with highly qualified personnel (some of whom were brought in by air) from other combat areas. The corps was thus soon able to help slow down the Soviet advance all along the Chir River line, particularly around Kalach."[217]

Flying out in the clear blue skies on 25 November, *Luftwaffe* aerial reconnaissance was able to establish the exact positions of the Soviet main forces: "Enemy troop columns from the south-east on the road to Businovka and from the north-west on the road to the railway station at Chir."[218]

## Conditions during the Demyansk and Stalingrad Airlift Operations - a comparison

Of course the realities of the winter of 1942/1943 were different from those during the Demyansk airlift the previous winter. Not all of these were to the Germans' disadvantage at Stalingrad. Conditions in a number of areas had been worse at Demyansk, where there was only one airfield – a former advance Soviet tactical airfield with a single runway some 30 metres wide and 600 metres long with no other installations. Demyansk's airfield was capable of accepting no more than 20-30 aircraft at a time. Moreover, there were no navigational devices at Demyansk during the major part of the airlift operation. For a variety of reasons, it could only be used by day. In addition to this, the Germans lacked any experience of such a large-scale airlift operation, and, as we have seen, committed many mistakes before they perfected their procedures. In spite of all these difficulties, German transport aircraft were able to fly in an average of 273 tons of supplies per day to Demyansk.

In comparison with Demyansk, airfield conditions were much better inside Stalingrad. There were six airfields inside the cauldron – Pitomnik, Gumrak, Bolshaya Rossoshka, Basargino, Stalingradskiy, and Voroponovo. Although only Pitomnik, 12 miles west of the city of Stalingrad, was equipped to handle large-scale operations, the fact that there were six different airfields in such a relatively large area made the task of intervening against the transport planes more difficult for the Soviet fighters; at Demyansk, everyone knew where the German transports would arrive.

At Stalingrad, the Germans also had installed *X-Gerät* and *Y-Gerät* radio homing devices. Through these, the transport crews could home in on the radio beacons located at Pitomnik and were able to locate their landing area in darkness and in the most adverse weather conditions. Thus, flights to Stalingrad could be made around the clock.

Damp and cold weather causing aircraft to ice up, allied to a chronic shortage of spare parts and lack of heating equipment for the aircraft, have all been pointed out in German accounts as major obstacles hampering the Stalingrad airlift. But these factors were no less crucial during the Demyansk airlift. While airfields used in the Demyansk operation were permanent and located closer to major rail lines than those used for the Stalingrad airlift, air-bases such as Pskov, Riga and Daugavpils were incomparably better than the airfields of Tatsinskaya and Morozovsk in the sparsely populated steppe inside the Don Bend. Above all, when the Stalingrad airlift was launched, the Germans could rely on the experience gained during the Demyansk operation the previous winter.

One great disadvantage during aerial resupply operations into Stalingrad was the width of the Soviet wedge between the encircled troops and the main German front lines. At the onset of the airlift, the transports had to fly at least 75

miles across Soviet-held territory where they were subject to ground fire. When the airlift operation to Stalingrad commenced, the transports flew from Morozovsk and Tatsinskaya. No German fighter aircraft could operate closer to the front line than Morozovsk, 130 miles from the Stalingrad cauldron.

Under normal circumstances, a Bf 109 G-2 with its fuel capacity of 106 gallons had an average combat range of 300 to 400 miles, or a flight endurance of 60 to 80 minutes. But the Ju 52s made the trip to Stalingrad at a cruising speed of only slightly more than 100 miles per hour, which resulted in a flight time of at least 60 to 80 minutes. One of the features of the Bf 109 was its comparatively low stalling speed, but when escorting the slow Ju 52s, the Bf 109 pilots had to make use of all kinds of tricks to stay with the lumbering transports – turning into the wind, weaving to and fro, diving and climbing – in fact anything other than economic flight. This, and the various detours the transport flights had to undertake in order to avoid flak concentrations and Soviet fighters lying in wait, pushed many escort flights to Stalingrad right up to and even beyond the Bf 109's flight endurance. On 28 November 1942, II./JG 52 lost two Bf 109s when they ran out of fuel while escorting Ju 52s from Morozovsk to Pitomnik.

Drop tanks were available for Bf 109s, but one of the tragic realities of the Stalingrad airlift operation is that none of them, for unknown reasons, arrived at the *Jagdgeschwader* engaged in this campaign until late January 1943. But *Major* Wilcke, the German fighter commander in VIII. *Fliegerkorps*, took measures to overcome the problems resulting from the large distances to be covered. Led by *Hptm.* Rudolf Germeroth, the so-called *Platschutzstaffel Pitomnik* – a JG 3 detachment inside the cauldron – was established. Thus, at least in theory, German fighters could be present to cover the Ju 52s throughout their entire flight to and from Stalingrad. Of course this task was complicated by the fact that the *Luftwaffe* singularly failed to organize radio communications between Bf 109s and the aircraft they were supposed to escort. In the cloudy and hazy conditions in the Don Bend area that winter, this frequently resulted in the Bf 109s failing to locate the Ju 52s at the appointed rendezvous point. However, this was not a new problem – and it also had affected the Demyansk airlift operation.

Two *Jagdgruppen*, III./JG 3 and I./JG 51, had been available to provide the Demyansk airlift with fighter cover. When the Stalingrad airlift operation commenced, *Stab*, I., and III./JG 3 *Udet* were immediately available, and II./JG 52 arrived at Morozovsk from the Caucasus on 26 November, while II./JG 3 was underway from Smolensk. In addition to these units, the Rumanian Bf 109-equipped fighter group and ZG 1 with its long-range Bf 110s could also be used for escort missions.

The greatest difference between the Demyansk and the Stalingrad airlift operations was without doubt the quality of the opposition facing the *Luftwaffe*. When the Stalingrad airlift operation commenced in November 1942, the VVS fighter force had undergone a vast improvement from early 1942 and had become a singularly effective adversary.

## Ju 52 - equipped transport units available to *Luftflotte* 4 on 30 November 1942

| Unit | Commander | Base | Available aircraft | Serviceable aircraft |
|------|-----------|------|--------------------|-----------------------|
| KGrzbV 5 | *Oberst* Hans Förster | Makeyevka | 31 He 111s | 7 He 111s |
| KGrzbV 9 | *Obstlt.* Adolf Jäckel | Konstantinovka | 43 Ju 52s | 15 Ju 52s |
| KGrzbV 50 | *Major* Baumann | Tatsinskaya | 33 Ju 52s | 13 Ju 52s |
| KGrzbV 104 | | Kirovograd | 0 Go 244s | 0 Go 244s |
| KGrzbV 106 | | Kirovograd | 0 Go 244s | 0 Go 244s |
| I./KGzbV 172 | *Major* Zähr | Stalino - Nord | 29 Ju 52s | 11 Ju 52s |
| KGrzbV 500 | *Major* Beckmann | Tatsinskaya | 45 Ju 52s | 35 Ju 52s |
| KGrzbV 700 | | Taganrog | 53 Ju 52s | 53 Ju 52s |
| KGrzbV 900 | *Oberst* Wübben | Tatsinskaya | 41 Ju 52s | 12 Ju 52s |

*Generalleutnant* Fiebig's diary notes for 25 November describe the subsequent *Luftwaffe* action: "All units took part in the annihilation [of the Soviet troop columns]. *Schlacht* aircraft and Stukas at Oblivskaya perform ten to fourteen flights each. All the reports point to the massacre of horses and riders."[219]

Even the Bf 109s of JG 3 and II./JG 52 and the He 111s of KG 27, KG 55, and KG 100 participated in the devastating low-level attacks against

these cavalry forces. This also resulted in a string of losses among the relatively slow He 111s, which offered easy targets to Soviet ground fire. On 25 November, *Hptm.* Siegfried Scholz, *Staffelkapitän* of 2./KG 100, failed to return from his 410th combat sortie. Meanwhile, the He 111 piloted by the *Staffelkapitän* of 2./KG 55, *Oblt.* Werner Oberländer, was badly damaged by ground fire near Chernichevskaya. Oberländer, an experienced pilot who had flown 263 bomber missions since the beginning of the war, managed to nurse his crippled Heinkel on a single engine back to Morozovsk. The injuries he sustained on this mission rendered Oberländer unfit for operational duties for the remainder of the war. As 5./St.G 2's *Hptm.* Langbehn, these two veterans were awarded the Knight's Cross on 24 March 1943 – posthumously in the case of Scholz and Langbehn.

The VVS made a remarkably limited appearance over the battlefield on what was a bright 25 November. This was largely due to the limited amounts of aviation fuel and supplies available to the forward VVS airfields in the region. Hence, the Red Army had to continue its offensive with insufficient support from the air. When a force from Soviet 5th Tank Army's 8th Cavalry Corps managed to infiltrate through gaps in the still thin German defence lines to approach Oblivskaya on 26 November, this vital point was again saved by the *Luftwaffe*. The Soviet task force was first spotted by *Oblt.* Hans-Ulrich Rudel,

Aircraft of I./St.G 2
photographed while
returning from a mission
or while transferring base.
The formation is split into
separate elements, each
consisting of a Staffel,
with an aircraft of
1. Staffel in the
foreground.

1./St.G 2's *Staffelkapitän*. While the trenches around Oblivskaya were manned by personnel from SchG 1's and St.G 2's ground crew and from VIII. *Fliegerkorps* headquarters, Hs 123s, Hs 129s, and Ju 87s went into action against the Soviet task force. "There are virtually no Army troops in this sector, so we were in dire straits," Rudel wrote in his memoirs. "First of all I attack and wipe out the artillery with bombs and guns, before they can be lined up against us. Then we strike at the other elements of the attack force. A cavalry unit without horses loses its mobility and fighting strength, so there is no alternative but to shoot all the horses. We take off and land without interruption and in great haste. If we fail to annihilate the attack force before nightfall, we will be in great danger when darkness arrives."[220]

In the afternoon of 26 November, *General-Leytenant* Prokofiy Romanenko, 5th Tank Army's commander, dispatched a tank column against Oblivskaya. The Soviet tanks were immediately targeted individually by I./St.G 2's Stuka pilots. Rudel continued: "[The Soviet tanks] approach our airfield at full speed. If we fail to destroy them, we are lost. We attack them with bombs. They make evasive manoeuvres. The desperate situation gives us the power to drop our bombs with an unmatched precision."[221] During the course of the day, *Oblt.* Rudel took off seventeen times against the Soviet assault force. Another St.G 2 pilot, *Fw.* Hans Ludwig, flew six sorties and received a special honorary mention for this.[222] The Soviet tank force was completely obliterated, with the last tank being destroyed at the very edge of the airfield.

While *Generalfeldmarschall* von Manstein hastily organized new defence positions, the aircrews of VIII. *Fliegerkorps* gained the Germans valuable momentum. Soviet army commanders complained of "irreplaceable losses from German air attacks."[223]

Inside the *Kessel* cauldron, Friedrich von Paulus – who was promoted to *Generaloberst* on 1 December1942 – deployed his surrounded troops to hold the 120-mile circular front line. In doing so, they received invaluable assistance from the *Luftwaffe* ad-hoc unit *Aufklärungsgruppe Fleischmann* – which mustered eight tactical reconnaissance *Staffeln* at the large Pitomnik airbase. These reconnaissance airmen provided the ground troops with regular updates on the Soviet Don Front's troop movements, which allowed von Paulus to concentrate his troops at the most critical points. Apart from the reconnaissance aircraft and *Hptm.* Rudolf Germeroth's JG 3 detachment at Pitomnik, *Lt.* Heinz Jungclausen's St.G 2 *Stuka-Sonderstaffel* also was permanently based at Pitomnik, ready to operate against Soviet attacks. In fact, *General-Leytenant* Rokossovskiy – commanding the Don Front, which

manned the Soviet positions around the Stalingrad cauldron – came to the conclusion that it was impossible to annihilate the cauldron at this stage and refrained from any large-scale offensive.

The German airlift operation to Stalingrad was put on a more organized footing. The administrative command of the airlift was assigned to *Generalmajor* Viktor Carganico – the father of JG 5 fighter ace *Major* Horst Carganico – who was appointed *Luftversorgungsführer Stalingrad*. All Ju 52 units committed were concentrated at Tatsinskaya under *Oberst* Hans Förster's centralised command. However, on 26 November only 37 transports flew into Stalingrad, bringing in 50 tons of supplies.[224]

Simultaneously, on 26 November *General* Sergey Rudenko, 16 VA's commander, began organizing the interception of the German transport flights. It had been noted that the Ju 52s made their flights either singly without fighter escort, or in groups of three to ten with an escort of between two to six Bf 109s. The Yak-1-equipped 512 IAP, based at Kotluban, was the first fighter unit to focus on the transport flights.

VVS operations against the German air bridge intensified day by day. On 28 November, 16 VA made repeated attacks against the airfields in the Stalingrad cauldron, claiming 29 aircraft destroyed on the ground. *Hptm.* Germeroth's JG 3 Stalingrad detachment at Pitomnik had a busy day, claiming nine Soviet aircraft shot down for no losses. II./JG 52 added another twelve victories – *Gruppenkommandeur*, *Hptm.* Johannes Steinhoff, achieved his 113th and 114th victories by downing a P-40 and a Yak-1[225] and the *Staffelkapitän* of 4./JG 52, *Oblt.* Gerhard Barkhorn, shot down another P-40 for his 82nd kill.[226]

At least six transports were lost *en route* to Stalingrad on 28 November 1942.[227] On the Soviet side, *Lt.* Mikhail Mudrov of the recently arrived 3 GIAP claimed to have shot down three of those aircraft.

Between 25 and 29 November, the daily average of supplies flown in to Stalingrad amounted to no more than 53.8 tons. To improve these figures, it was decided to shift all of *Luftflotte* 4's He 111 bomber units to the air bridge. Oblivskaya was abandoned and the German flying units were shifted to Morozovsk. It was here that KG 55's *Geschwaderkommodore*, Knight's Cross holder *Obstlt.* Ernst Kühl, was appointed *Lufttransportführer 1* on 29 November. Kühl was responsible for managing the air bridge into Stalingrad, a task now also assigned to He 111 units of VIII. *Fliegerkorps*. Apart from KGrzbV 5 and the newly arrived KGrzbV 20, which were specialised He 111 transport units, the following units were instructed to

## Wilcke's Messerschmitts forced onto the defensive

Led by *Major* Wolf-Dietrich Wilcke, the German fighter units in the Stalingrad - Don Bend area were involved in an intense struggle to protect both the transport aircraft from Soviet fighter attacks and the Axis ground troops from the relentlessly attacking *Shturmoviks* and Soviet bombers.

Although the Soviet air forces had indeed undergone a qualitative improvement since the September battles, the German fighter pilots in their Bf 109 G-2s still enjoyed a marked superiority. *Hptm.* Germeroth's JG 3 Stalingrad detachment engaged numerous small groups of Il-2s which relentlessly came in to strafe Pitomnik's airfield during the morning of 30 November, and claimed eleven Il-2s. 8 VA's 622 ShAP alone lost six Il-2s during its operations on 30 November 1942, with another five receiving severe battle damage.[1]

*Hptm.* Johannes Steinhoff, II./JG 52's *Gruppenkommandeur*, knocked down two Yak-1s for his 115th and 116th victories during his first mission early on 30 November.[2] Meanwhile, *Oblt.* Gerhard Barkhorn, 4./JG 52's *Staffelkapitän*, brought down a P-40, a Yak-1 and a "LaGG" (LaGG-3 or La-5) for his 83rd through 85th victories.[3] A few hours later, Steinhoff was in the air again and bounced a Yak-1 which was flying with two P-40s and shot down the Yak and one of the P-40s,[4] leaving the remaining P-40 to be destroyed by his wingman, *Ofw.* Reinhardt. Flying from Morozovsk shortly after noon, the II./JG 52 *Rotte* of *Lt.* Gustav Denk and *Uffz.* Hans Waldmann engaged ten Il-2s escorted by six Yak-1s over Stalingrad, Waldmann destroying one of the Il-2s while his *Rottenführer* shot

down two of the Yak-1s above.[5] In total, the German fighters claimed to have shot down 34 Soviet aircraft in the Stalingrad - Don Bend area on the last day of November for a single loss.

The new month opened with II./JG 52 submitting claims for 14 victories for no losses in two days of action. Following four days of adverse weather, Wilcke's fighters were called upon to carry out low-level strafing attacks against Soviet troops threatening another breakthrough at the Chir River inside the Don Bend on 7 December. The following day the Bf 109s were forced to defend their own airfields against repeated air attacks by 17 VA's *Shturmoviks* and bombers. 221 BAD carried out these attacks without any fighter escort, with its Bostons flying singly and attempting to take advantage of the clouds to hide from the German fighters. This cost them dearly. 57 BAP lost two out of 18 Bostons dispatched. II./JG 52 reportedly shot down four Bostons in the morning and two at noon. In the afternoon, *Major* Wilcke intercepted raiding Il-2s and claimed three shot down. But these Soviet air attacks, which continued throughout the day, forced the bulk of the German fighters onto the defensive. Meanwhile, the transport flights into Stalingrad resulted in the destruction of 20 transport aircraft.

1. *Aviatsiya i Kosmonavtika*, May - June 2001.
2. Johannes Steinhoff, Logbook.
3. Gerhard Barkhorn, Logbook.
4. Via Johannes Steinhoff.
5. *Leistungsbuch für Hans Waldmann*

concentrate on transport flights: II. and III./KG 27; *Stab*, I. and II./KG 55; and *Stab* and I./KG 100. *Obstlt.* Kühl's own KG 55 registered six He 111s destroyed or severely damaged during the first transport missions on 29 November.[228]

On 30 November, VIII. *Fliegerkorps* was instructed to devote its activities exclusively to bringing in supplies to the besieged VI. *Armee* in Stalingrad. *Generalleutnant* Fiebig was appointed the new *LuftversorgungsFührer Stalingrad* or Air Supply Leader Stalingrad. But Fiebig's forces had to fight against both hostile weather conditions and increasingly strong Soviet resistance in the air.

The Soviet fighters continued to achieve mounting successes against the lumbering transport aircraft – with or without fighter escort. On the last day of November four Yak-1s commanded by 283 IAD's leader, *Polkovnik* Vladimir Kitayev, claimed five Ju 52s and a Bf 109 shot down out of a formation of 17 transports and four Bf 109s above Stalingrad. Other Yak pilots shot down an He 111 from Rumanian *Grupul* 5 *Bombardament* over Stalingrad on the same day.[229]

In fact, fighter escorts could even increase the risk of the Ju 52s being shot down. On their own, the Ju 52s flew as low as possible so that Soviet fighter pilots, perhaps 3,000 - 10,000 feet higher, were often unable to detect the camouflaged and slow transports against the ground and through the haze. But the escorting Bf 109s which conspicuously swung to and fro above the Ju 52s were as likely to draw the attention of hunting Soviet fighter pilots to the easy pickings below.

The seven Ju 52s lost on 30 November represented an appalling 23 per cent loss rate. The regular Soviet air raids against the airfields inside Stalingrad brought additional pressure on the transport airmen.

On 1 December, the transport flights had to be cancelled due to heavy snowfalls. *Luftflotte* 4's War Diary recorded a loss of seven transport planes[230] (only three of which can be found in the *Generalquartiermeister* der *Luftwaffe* files[231]) while fifteen Ju 52s and twenty-five He 111s landed in Stalingrad. A record 115 tons of supplies were flown in to the surrounded army on 2 December.[232] At the same time, 16 VA reported the destruction of 17 enemy aircraft during raids against various airfields inside the cauldron. The weather deteriorated further on the following day, with snowfall, thick fog, and temperatures around zero degrees Celsius, which created thick icing on the aircraft. A few courageous KGrzbV 700 crews still attempted to make the hazardous flight to Stalingrad but two of them were shot down. Not a single transport landed inside the cauldron on 3 December.[233]

In this increasingly desperate situation, between 60 and 70 transport crews made it through the fog to Stalingrad on 4 December.

By this time, the air transport fleet available to VIII. *Fliegerkorps* had grown to muster eleven Ju 52 *Gruppen* with a total of around 200 aircraft, four He 111 *Gruppen* with 65 aircraft, and two new *Kampfgruppen zu besonderen Verwendung* with 20 Ju 86s[234]. In addition, Italian 71 *Gruppo O.A.* and Rumanian *Escadrila* 105 *Transport Greu* participated in the transport flights. Fiat BR. 20Ms from this Italian group and three Rumanian Ju 52s took part in the transport flights on 4 December. A total of 141 tons of

## Novikov's Blockade Zones

On 4 December 1942 *General-Polkovnik* Aleksandr Novikov ordered 8 VA and 16 VA to focus their forces primarily on the suppression of the German air bridge into Stalingrad. Novikov also drew up the tactical outlines for the air blockade of Stalingrad. Four circular air blockade zones were formed around the cauldron.

The First, outer, zone was divided between 8 VA in the southern and 17 VA in the northern sectors. The Second zone was divided into five sectors, of which 16 VA was responsible for the two in the north, and 8 VA for the three in the south. The Third zone constituted a five mile-wide anti-aircraft "belt" around the cauldron. The Fourth, inner, zone constituted the airspace above the cauldron itself and, here, the responsibility for suppressing the transport flights fell mainly

upon the shoulders of 16 VA, supported by 8 VA's 214 ShAD. To accomplish its new task, a considerably reinforced 8 VA could muster a total of 761 aircraft, including 441 serviceable – 190 fighters, 143 Il-2s, and 108 bombers (including 53 U-2 biplanes) – on 1 December.[1] On the same date, 16 VA reported a strength of 258 aircraft, including 174 serviceable – 54 Yak fighters, and two LaGG-3s, 39 Il-2s, 75 U-2s, and two Bostons and two Pe-2s used as reconnaissance aircraft.[2] Later in December, 16 VA was reinforced through the arrival of *General-Major* Ivan Turkel's 2 BAK, mustering 122 serviceable Pe-2s.

1. TsAMO, f. 8 VA
2. TsAMO, f. 16 VA.

*This aircraft was engaged in the supply of Stalingrad in late December 1942, when it was attacked by three Soviet fighters. The co-pilot was wounded in the attack and the machine was damaged to the extent that its starboard undercarriage collapsed on landing. It is believed that the machine belonged to KGzbV 102.*

were lost on 6 December. These aircraft losses should be compared with the total number of transport aircraft that landed inside the cauldron that day – forty-four. This figure increased to 199, delivering a total of 350 tons of supplies, on 7 December. By that time, *Generaloberst* Friedrich von Paulus had been forced to reduce his mens' rations by one-third or half.

Meanwhile, *General-Polkovnik* Novikov's new air blockade zones were also functioning. In the Second and Third air blockade zones – south and west of Stalingrad – 8 VA had already installed one fighter command and control centre and fighter aircraft were constantly on patrol. Throughout 7 December, Soviet fighters fell on Axis transport aircraft that tried to take advantage of the clouds to sneak into Stalingrad without fighter escort. 201 IAD's *Kapitan* Petr Naumov became the most successful pilot of the day, bringing home two individual and two shared victories. *Mayor* Nikolay Gorev, 181 IAP's leader, and 13 IAP's *Lt.* Mikhail Ignatyev also scored doubles, while 622 ShAP's *St.Lt.* Vladimir Dogayev shot down a Ju 52 for his first victory at the controls of his Il-2. In total, 8 VA submitted 27 victory claims on 7 December. According to Axis statistics, 15 transports were lost on that day – eight German Ju 52s, six He 111s, [240] and a Rumanian Ju 52.[241]

supplies – a new record – were delivered, and 710 injured men were flown out.[235] The Soviet counter-activity was notably hampered by the bad weather. Bätcher did not encounter any enemy opposition on either of his two supply flights on 4 December.[236] The transport losses that day were limited to three aircraft – two German aircraft and an Italian Fiat BR. 20M.[237]

A thaw with thick fog, low cloud ceiling and snowfall intermingled with rain showers continued to hamper fighter activity on 5 December, when a KGrzbV 50 Ju 52 which fell to 3 GIAP's *Lt.* Petr Bazanov was the only success attained by Soviet fighters against the air bridge. On the following day, the new emphasis in the battle against the transport flights – which had been ordered by *General-Polkovnik* Novikov – began to show results. Five Ju 52s, five He 111 transports[238] and a 71 *Gruppo* Fiat BR. 20M[239]

Soviet fighter interception of the transport aircraft that day was facilitated by the attack which 1st Tank Corps of South-western Front's 5th Tank Army launched in the Chir region, 55 miles south-west of Stalingrad. This operation not only ruined *Generalfeldmarschall* von Manstein's plans to launch a relief offensive to Stalingrad from that area; it also forced VIII. *Fliegerkorps* to dispatch all available aircraft against 1st Tank Corps. The Bf 109s of JG 3 were tasked with supporting SchG 1 in low-level attacks at Chir, an effort which cost six Bf 109s.[242]

On 8 December the focus of the ground battle shifted eastwards when *General-Leytenant* Rokossovskiy moved elements of his Don Front to attack the Stalingrad cauldron's north-western corner. This diverted the *Luftwaffe's* attention from the Chir area, and brought considerable relief to the troops

*Troops working dangerously close to the revolving propellers of a Ju 52/3m while busily engaged in clearing a path for the machine to taxi.*

## 9 GIAP - The Ace Unit

In order to balance the inequality in terms of experience between VVS and *Luftwaffe* fighter units, 8 VA's commander, *General-Mayor* Khryukin, decided to form a special "ace unit" composed entirely of aces. In October 1942, *Podpolkovnik* Lev Shestakov was informed that his 9 GIAP had been selected for this purpose. This was not by accident. Shestakov had led the unit successfully during the defensive battle for Odessa in 1941 and it had already become known as "the regiment of the Heroes of the Soviet Union". No less than twelve of 69 IAP's pilots were appointed Heroes of the Soviet Union after the battle of Odessa. The unit was pulled out of combat and had its LaGG-3s exchanged for better Yak-1s.

In various other fighter units, successful pilots received orders to transfer to 9 GIAP. Notable among these were *Kapitan* Arkadiy Kovachevich from 27 IAP, *Kapitan* Mikhail Baranov from 183 IAP, *St.Lt.* Sultan Amet-Khan and *Lt.* Pavel Golovachyob from 168 IAP, and *M.Lt.* Ivan Borisov and *Starshina* Vladimir Lavrinenkov from 4 IAP.

The period October to early November 1942 was used for intense training. 9 GIAP copied the methods of the *Jagdwaffe* straight off – free hunting missions and operations in the tactical formations of two and four – *Para* and *Zveno*. All the fighter planes in 9 GIAP also were equipped with the best radio transmitters and receivers available.

In mid-November 1942, the unit was brought forward to an airfield near Zety, not far from the front line. But 9 GIAP continued to be held back for several weeks. It was not until 10 December that it was ordered to commence operations.

The next day, 11 December, the new ace unit performed its first combat mission. Its Yak-1s were instructed to cooperate with La-5-equipped 3 GIAP – which also was one of the best Soviet fighter units at the time. The two fighter units intercepted a formation of eighteen Ju 52s with fighter escort in clear weather in the Third air blockade zone outside Stalingrad. Although this was the anti-aircraft artillery's "free fire" area, the Soviet pilots pressed home their attacks with vigour. Eight Ju 52s broke off and turned for home, and ten were claimed shot down – four by 9 GIAP[1] and six by 3 GIAP, including three by *Lt.* Petr Bazanov. In addition, 9 GIAP's *M.Lt.* Ivan Serzhov bagged one of the escorting Bf 109s.

[1.] TsAMO, f. 9 GIAP.

---

of 1st Tank Corps. Two-thirds of *Luftflotte* 4 – including the He 111s which had been tasked with flying in supplies – were brought in to support VI. *Armee* against Rokossovskiy's attack. It was a day with clear skies and bombers and Stukas, together with ground troops, claimed around 60 Soviet tanks destroyed.[243] The Don Front's incursions were sealed off shortly after noon.

With the Bf 109s dispersed between a multitude of tasks, and often unable to escort the transports all the way into Stalingrad, Bf 110s of ZG 1 flew in from the Caucasus to Tatsinskaya in order to reinforce the fighter escort. But not even the presence of Bf 110 escort fighters with their considerably greater endurance managed to stave off heavy losses among the Ju 52s. It was on this date, 8 December, that "the Soviet fighter groups managed to tear up the Ju 52 formations during repeated attacks."[244] According to *Luftwaffe* records, 20 transports – twelve Ju 52s and eight He 111s – were lost at Stalingrad that day.[245] Only around 30 Ju 52s and 70 He 111s were able to break through and land at Stalingrad. *Luftwaffe Oberst* Hermann Plocher observed the fact that "*Luftwaffe* airmen attempted to counter Soviet anti-aircraft defences by constantly changing their flight routes," while "Soviet interceptor attacks became a more serious problem for the *Luftwaffe*, especially for the Ju 52 and Ju 86 transports."[246]

The clear weather also allowed the Soviets to carry out numerous airbase raids on 8 December. Four Ju 52s were destroyed on the ground inside the cauldron. Morozovsk and Tatsinskaya were subjected to attacks throughout the day, resulting in six aircraft destroyed and fifteen casualties on the ground.[247] ZG 1 and II./JG 52 were among the units hit.

These strikes against Tatsinskaya were part of the preparation for the next major Soviet offensive. Assigned the code-name "Saturn," the plan aimed at the total destruction of *Heeresgruppen* B and *Don*, plus the surrounding of *Heeresgruppe* A in the Caucasus. Operation "*Saturn*" would open with South-western Front attacking the Italian 8th Army's positions along the middle Don. Air support would be provided by 17 VA – which was reinforced by *General* Vladimir Aladinskiy's 3 SAK from the *Stavka* reserve – and parts of 2 VA. In preparation for the offensive, *Polkovnik* Ivan Antoshkin's Boston-equipped 221 BAD launched strikes against the airfields at Tatsinskaya, Millerovo, and Glubokaya by day. At night, 262 NBAD targeted the airfields at Starobelsk, Kamensk, and Chernyshkovskiy.[248] These operations had taken place since 3 December, but due to weather conditions, they could not be carried out with any significant result until 8 December.

Renewed heavy snowfalls on 9 December again closed down the air bridge completely. Two KGrzbV 5 He 111s which tried to make it into Stalingrad were intercepted and shot down by Soviet fighters. Two attacks by single Soviet bombers against Tatsinskaya aerodrome destroyed four Ju 52s, set an army fuel depot ablaze, and exploded an ammunition dump.[249]

With slightly improved weather conditions on 10 December, 64 transports struggled into Stalingrad. 16 VA replied by sending in 74 aircraft in a total of 116 sorties to attack various targets inside the cauldron.

Pouncing on German troops in the sector Zapadnovka - Bolshaya Rossoshka, the Soviet airmen reported the destruction of 75 motor vehicles, five railway cars, and two artillery pieces.[250] The airfield at Bolshaya Rossoshka also was attacked, with 31 German aircraft claimed destroyed on the ground.[251] But at the same time, the JG 3 detachment at Pitomnik gave proof of its ability to deal the VVS attackers a bloody nose. Of seven Il-2s dispatched by 622 ShAP against Pitomnik on 10 December, four were shot down and two of the remainder returned with battle damage.[252] The *Platzschutz Staffel's Oblt.* Franz Beyer and *Lt.* Georg Schentke raised spirits among the men on the ground at Pitomnik by downing three of these Il-2s and three of their escorting fighters during a twenty-minute dogfight – their victories Nos. 67-69 and 75-77 respectively. *Uffz.* Fritz Linke, gunner in a 5./KG 55 He 111, wrote:

"Today we made two flights into the cauldron. We are faced with the usual opposition: anti-aircraft fire, bomb-dropping *Shturmoviks*, et cetera. During our second flight – the sky was almost cloudless over Pitomnik – two Me 109s swept the skies and found a rich harvest. While our aircraft was hastily unloaded, between landing and take-off, we saw three Russian aircraft plunge earthwards."[253]

The Soviet fighter pilots fared better on free hunt sorties. On 10 December, the female pilot *St.Lt.* Yekaterina Budanova of 437 IAP claimed two Bf 110s shot down during one of these missions. In total, 16 VA reported ten victories against nine aircraft lost on operations, all but one in air combat – a loss rate of almost 8 per cent.[254] The fighters of VIII. *Fliegerkorps* meanwhile claimed 14 victories above Stalingrad for no loss. This reflects the fact that the *Luftwaffe* still enjoyed a qualitative superiority against the VVS, although the gap had narrowed since the September battles.

The VVS still suffered from the extreme losses which it had sustained during the first 15 months of the war and, in order to build up the new air forces which supported the offensive at the Don, the practice of shortened pilot training schemes had to be maintained. In the meantime, the *Luftwaffe* pilots still received first class training. Added to that came the fact that the core of veterans in the *Luftwaffe* by this time had amassed experience which was absolutely unparalleled.

When II./JG 52's *Hptm.* Johannes Steinhoff shot down a LaGG-3 on 10 December – recorded as his 126th victory – he also logged his 728th combat mission.[255] Virtually no Soviet pilot could compete with such a depth of experience. The next day Steinhoff again engaged Soviet fighters – near Oblivskaya – and submitted two claims for Yak-1s shot down for his 127th and 128th victories. Steinhoff on this occasion was brought down himself – falling to anti-aircraft fire. The German ace escaped with no more than a few bruises.[256]

But there also was a core of very skilful aces in service on the Soviet side. Undoubtedly the best VVS unit in action in the Stalingrad area in the winter of 1942/1943 was *Podpolkovnik* Lev Shestakov's 9 GIAP. This had been an "ordinary" unit previously – although always more successful than the average because of Shestakov's able command – but in the autumn of

# RUNNING THE GAUNTLET
## The Stalingrad Airlift

Pitomnik airfield
Lost to Soviet forces on
16 January

The slow transports
proved an easy
target for both
fighters and flak

Having survived the outward
mission, the crews then had
to turn and face the Soviet
defences to return to safety

Appalling flying
conditions further
added to the losses

With the airfields lost, the
transports resort to air-
dropping supplies.

Many
supplies
fail to
reach the
trapped
6th Army

Stalingrad

Final 6th Army perimeter,
surrendered by Field Marshall
von Paulus on 31 January

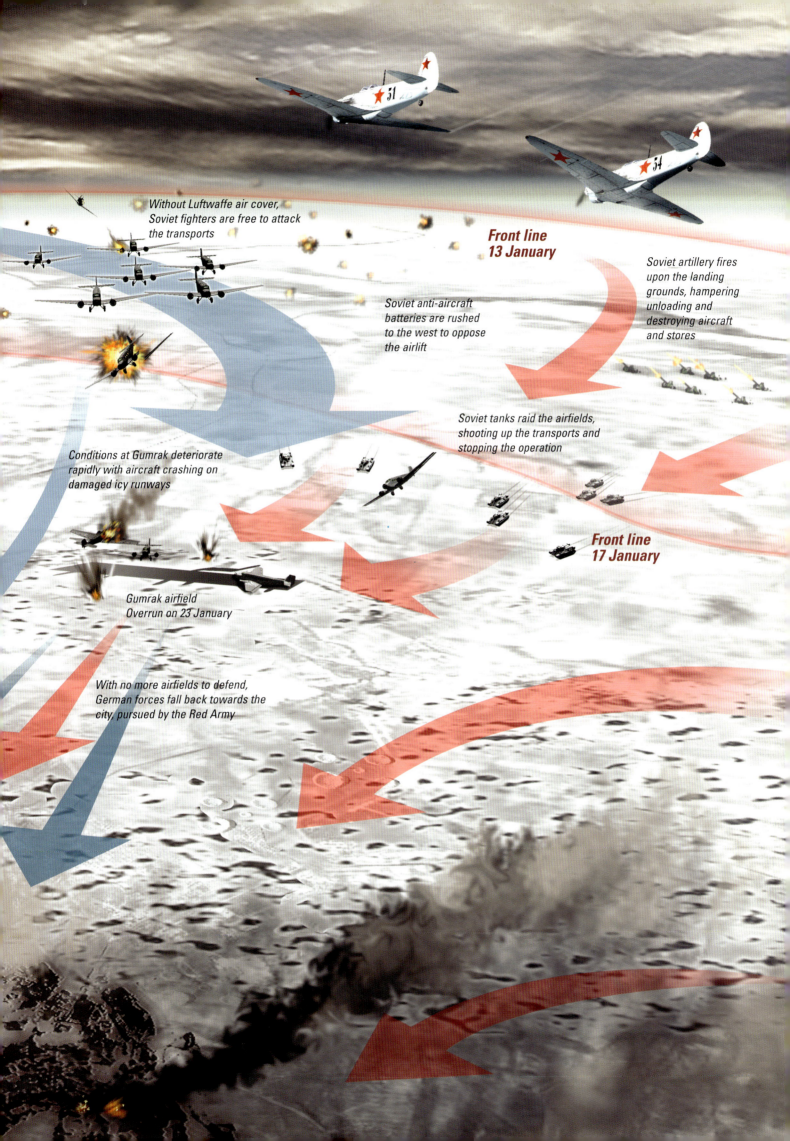

Without Luftwaffe air cover, Soviet fighters are free to attack the transports

**Front line 13 January**

Soviet artillery fires upon the landing grounds, hampering unloading and destroying aircraft and stores

Soviet anti-aircraft batteries are rushed to the west to oppose the airlift

Soviet tanks raid the airfields, shooting up the transports and stopping the operation

Conditions at Gumrak deteriorate rapidly with aircraft crashing on damaged icy runways

**Front line 17 January**

Gumrak airfield
Overrun on 23 January

With no more airfields to defend, German forces fall back towards the city, pursued by the Red Army

*Ju 52s and an He 111 at an airfield in the Don Bend area in late 1942. Since the Ju 52 could carry a load of two tons and the He 111 a total of 1.2 tons, Göring was not entirely wrong to assume that the Sixth Army could be supplied from the air. However, there were other factors which tipped the scales to the Germans' disadvantage. (Mombeeck)*

This was just the latest of several measures aimed at meeting the targets for the airlift – to bring in 500 tons of supplies per day. By this time, the *Luftwaffe* had made every effort to reach this requirement. As in the case of the Demyansk operation, flight schools had to give up aircraft and experienced crews for the Stalingrad airlift. New transport units were formed and sent directly to VIII. *Fliegerkorps*. Two of the latter were KGrzbV 21 and KGrzbV 22, both of which were equipped with the venerable twin-engined Ju 86. They were subordinated to *Oberst* Hans Förster, who commanded the Ju 52s at Tatsinskaya. The fighter force of VIII. *Fliegerkorps* was likewise reinforced to stand at the level it had stood at when the main offensive against the city had been launched three months earlier. When II./JG 3 arrived, four *Jagdgruppen* – plus the *Stab.*/JG 3 – were concentrated in the Stalingrad area, yet the daily average of delivered supplies to Stalingrad during the first eleven days of December was no more than 97.3 tons.

The prime factor in the German failure was

1942 it was transformed into a formal "ace unit". In this form, it commenced operations on 10 December 1942. Among the Axis aircraft losses on 11 December, several were due to 9 GIAP.

In total, VIII. *Fliegerkorps* lost at least 20 aircraft on 11 December – 14 transport aircraft, four Bf 109s, a Ju 87, and a C.202 Folgore. The latter belonged to Italian 21 *Gruppo Autonomo*, which had a total of 17 Macchi C.202 Folgores on strength – the most modern Italian fighter plane, definitely comparable to a Yak-1. However, 21 *Gruppo* was economic in the deployment of these aircraft. Only a total of 17 missions were flown with Folgores on the Eastern Front during a four-month period. One of these operations was as escort to Ju 52s flying to Stalingrad on 11 December, which resulted in *Tenente Pilota* Gino Lionello baling out when his Folgore was shot down.[257]

In spite of the accomplishments of individual German aces, it was painfully clear that the German fighters were unable to provide the transports with sufficient protection. In consequence, it was decided to cancel all transport flights in clear weather in daytime and instead try to avoid detection by the Soviet fighters by flying under cover of darkness or cloudy weather.

the VVS – perhaps not the improved standards of the Soviet pilots so much as better fighter tactics and, above all, *General-Polkovnik* Aleksandr Novikov's air blockade method. This was a development that had not been encountered at Demyansk – and which the Germans could not have anticipated when the airlift operation commenced. VIII. *Fliegerkorps* statistics show that on average, out of ten transports dispatched, only six managed to reach Stalingrad – and no more than three or four of them ever returned to base. KGrzbV 20 alone, which had arrived to participate in the airlift operation in early December, recorded 18 He 111s lost to hostile action between 6 and 12 December.[258] Such disastrous losses could not be tolerated. Added to this were the results of the incessant Soviet air attacks against the transports on the airfields inside the cauldron. Pitomnik was subjected to 42 air raids between 10 and 12 December. All of this inevitably had a negative impact on the combat morale of the flight crews. "The mood is one of complete dismay and shock", wrote *Hptm.* Hans Grah in his diary, having arrived with I./KG 55 in Morozovsk a few days later.[259]

By this time, it was already clear that the VVS had won the air battle. The only hope for VI. *Armee* was a ground offensive.

*Heinkel He 111s played an important role during the Stalingrad airlift. Individual aircrews pushed themselves to the limit to deliver supplies to the beleaguered troops inside the cauldron. 1./KG 100's Staffelkapitän, Hptm. Hansgeorg Bätcher landed his He 111 at Morozovsk after his first supply flight to Stalingrad at 11.22 hrs on 4 December. Twenty-two minutes later he took off again, in another He 111, loaded with provisions for an army that was starting to suffer from hunger. By this time Bätcher had carried out over 400 combat missions. A total of seven He 111 Gruppen were assigned to transport and supply duties during the Stalingrad operation and, with its superior speed, the He 111 was well-suited to the task of air supply, especially when Soviet fighter opposition increased. In most He 111 supply operations, the supplies were dropped by parachute in special containers.*

The Ju 52 crews often preferred flying in adverse weather rather than relying on fighter escort. Hans Ellendt, who flew a Bf 109 as an Unteroffizier with II./JG 52 during that time recalled in an interview with the author: 'As far as I can judge, the Ju 52 pilots didn't want to have anything to do with us as far as fighter escort was concerned. The Ju 52 was very slow and the guys who flew them at Stalingrad really knew how to fly. They could use the aircraft's slow speed to carry out evasive turns. But in the main, they relied on their relative invisibility. They flew so low that they almost crept close above the ground. Only in the vicinity of the front line did they climb to around 1000 metres in order to avoid small-arms fire from below. Moreover, they never used the same flight routes. In this way, they hoped to reach Stalingrad without drawing the attention of the Russian fighters. I feel that the Ju 52 crews really did not trust the efficiency of our fighter escort."

*This Il-2 was fitted with skis to facilitate landings on snow-covered ground. (Viktor Kulikov Photograph Collection)*

## Chapter Fifteen

# Winter Storm and Little Saturn

During the close cooperation between the *Luftwaffe* and the Army in the final battles of the Kerch Peninsula and Sevastopol in the spring and summer of 1942, Wolfram *Freiherr* von Richthofen and Erich von Manstein had proved to be a successful team. So when *Generalfeldmarschall* von Manstein's new *Heeresgruppe Don* launched its counter-attack towards Stalingrad from Kotelnikovo in the south-west, supported by *Generaloberst* von Richthofen's *Luftflotte 4*, the Germans had good reason to be optimistic. The operation, dubbed "*Wintergewitter*" ("Winter Storm"), commenced early on 12 December in "nice, cold weather."[260] LVII. *Panzerkorps* of *Generaloberst* Hermann Hoth's re-built IV. *Panzerarmee*, mustering 230 tanks – many of which were of the latest models, such as the Tiger – was massed against positions held by a numerically and technically much weaker Soviet 51st Army. In one blow, this destroyed the Soviet plan for Operation "Saturn" – which would have been a combined offensive aimed at the complete destruction of *Heeresgruppen B* and *Don*.

Von Richthofen assigned *General* Kurt Pflugbeil's IV. *Fliegerkorps* to provide "Winter Storm" with air support. In *Blitzkrieg* fashion, the attack was opened by the Bf 110s of ZG 1 which hit Abganerovo – the main Soviet airbase in the sector – early on 12 December. Eight Soviet aircraft – including four of 811 ShAP's Il-2s – were knocked out on the ground.[261] The next phase saw aircraft of St.G 2, St.G 77 and ZG 1 up on close-support missions, breaking up Soviet defence positions. I.A.R. 81 dive-bombers from Rumanian *Grupul 6 Bombardament in Picaj* also took part in these operations. Meanwhile, Ju 88 bombers and He 111s – the latter temporarily relieved from their task of flying in supplies to the besieged army in Stalingrad – created havoc among the Soviet lines of communications, troop quarters and supply bases in the rear area. *General Armii* Zhukov laid the emphasis on the intense German air attacks as a major reason for Soviet 51st Army's failure to hold its positions.[262]

*Hptm.* Johannes Steinhoff of II./JG 52 recalled: "An aviator sees the ground below like a miniature landscape. Each day, as he flies over the terrain, he notices the changes in the front line, and he is able to judge what the troops on the ground will be able to accomplish. The scenes of advance on the ground below in the Kotelnikovo sector looked promising, and I expected that Stalingrad would soon be relieved. I was filled with optimism, and flew my missions with great determination."[263]

Steinhoff's II./JG 52 was responsible for the task of clearing the skies above the advancing *Panzer* troops of Soviet aircraft. This could be accomplished without any difficulty on 12 December because Soviet aviation reacted only slowly to the German offensive. 8 VA and 16 VA remained focused on the task of isolating the Stalingrad cauldron and so 51st Army was left with little air support. Flying a new Bf 109 G-2, 'White 4' – after his regular "double chevron" had been shot down the previous day – *Hptm.* Steinhoff spotted and shot down a single Pe-2 reconnaissance aircraft on 12 December. This was the only Soviet aircraft downed in the Kotelnikovo sector on the first day of Operation "Winter Storm".

Nevertheless, in order to thwart any possible attempt by VI. *Armee* to make a breakout attempt towards the west – 16 VA's bombers and *Shturmoviks* made heavy and repeated attacks against German troop positions in and around the Karpovka River valley, west of the city of Stalingrad, on 12 December. Other Soviet aircraft continued their raids against the aerodromes inside the cauldron. Pilots of 520 IAP claimed four Ju 52s and three Bf 109s in one combat in the vicinity of Bolshaya Rossoshka - Krivomusginskaya, for the loss of a single Yak-1.[264] This appears to be the combat in which 9./JG 3 lost *Uffz.* Hermann Boll, who was shot down and baled out in a combat with "around a dozen LaGG-3s."[265] In the same engagement, the Germans claimed to have shot down four "LaGG-3s," including two by *Lt.* Wilhelm Lemke. The Germans admitted the loss of ten Ju 52s in the Stalingrad area on 12 December,[266] although the loss files of the *Generalquartiermeister der Luftwaffe* only listed four of these.[267]

*Lt.* Georg Schentke – undoubtedly the most energetic pilot in JG 3's Stalingrad detachment – was in action over Stalingrad from dawn to dusk on 12 December, reportedly shooting down six Soviet aircraft in five different missions. His *Geschwaderkommodore*, *Major* Wolf-Dietrich Wilcke, meanwhile claimed a La-5 and three Yak-1s during an escort mission to Stalingrad. In total, the Germans claimed 22 aerial victories in the Stalingrad – Don Bend sector on 12 December. Yet only 55 Axis transport planes managed to land inside the cauldron that day.[268] Apart from the ten Ju 52s mentioned above, eight aircraft from He 111-equipped KGrzbV 5 and KGrzbV 20 were lost, plus a Fiat BR20M from Italian 71 *Gruppo*, and the Ju 86 "RB+NI" piloted by KGrzbV 22's *Uffz.* Erlbeck. The latter became the first Ju 86 to be lost in the Stalingrad area. It was shot down *en route* from

Tatsinskaya to Pitomnik by 9 GIAP's *St. Lt.* Arkadiy Kovachevich, who filed this "rare bird" as a "Do 215".[269]

8 VA and 16 VA remained concentrated on the Stalingrad blockade on 13 December – a day which saw heavy rain and fog. Despite this adverse weather, 16 VA made repeated small-scale attacks against the airfields inside the Stalingrad cauldron, with 220 IAD claiming ten enemy aircraft destroyed on the ground. The same weather caused *Luftwaffe* unit commanders to hesitate about deploying their airmen. *Generaloberst* von Richthofen was furious. "In Zimovniki, a *Jagdgruppe* [II./JG 52] and *Stukageschwader* 77 were kicked out of their sleep. They spoke about bad weather!" he wrote angrily.[270] After von Richthofen's harsh intervention, an officer from LVII. *Panzerkorps'* 6th *Panzerdivision* would witness the following:

"The effect of the Stuka bombing was devastating. The [Soviet] tanks wildly drove into each other and tried to seek cover in the Yablokhnaya Ravine. The Stukas renewed their attack in the afternoon, and continued until darkness fell. Scout troops from the 2nd Battalion of the 4th Armoured Infantry Regiment were able to establish that half of the [Soviet] tanks were destroyed or damaged and that the Russian equipment and dead had to be abandoned. On the whole, it appeared that the Russians were interrupted in their construction of a continuous defensive line on the Aksay and that the division could now continue its preparations."[271]

With their ranks badly depleted through these aerial onslaughts, the troops of Soviet 51st Army asked themseleves where their own air force had gone. They had no chance of preventing Hoth's troops from crossing the frozen Aksay River, about 18 miles north of Kotelnikovo. Meanwhile, on the German side, von Richthofen vented his anger at Hoth's troops, accusing them of "fumbling around" while the *Luftwaffe* struck heavily against "a weak enemy." When Soviet 5th Tank Army later on 13 December renewed its attack in the River Chir sector farther to the north, the German aircraft had to abandon the Aksay sector and instead concentrate on fending off the Soviet offensive against the Chir bridges. In fact it was mainly due to *Luftwaffe* attacks that the Soviets failed to seize these key bridges. But at the same time, relieved from air attacks, Soviet 51st Army was able to halt German LVII *Panzerkorps* at Verkhne Kumskiy, halfway between the Aksay and Myshkova Rivers.

The weather continued to deteriorate, and on 14 December the fog was so thick that both sides had to refrain from air operations – apart from those carried out by crews trained on instruments. Sixty-nine transport aircraft landed in Stalingrad and no more than two were lost.

From the German point of view, the greatest achievement of Operation "Winter Storm" was the thwarting of Stalin's Operation "*Saturn*" before it could even be launched. *General* Rodion Malinovskiy's 2nd Guards Army, which originally was supposed to carry out a large-scale pincer movement in cooperation with the South-western Front farther north, had to leave its positions at the Chir River and transfer down to the Myshkova River in order to prevent Hoth's *Panzer* troops from reaching the Stalingrad cauldron, 35 miles farther to the north. Meanwhile, Hoth's *Panzer* troops remained bogged down. The momentum thus gained was used by *General Armii* Georgiy Zhukov and *Marshal* Aleksandr Vasilyevskiy to modify the offensive plan. Operation "*Saturn*" became Operation "*Malyy Saturn*" (Little Saturn) – a strike by the Voronezh and South-western Fronts against the Don River sector immediately to the (north-) west of the area where Operation "*Uranus*" had been launched in November.

*Johannes Steinhoff led II./JG 52 with great success during the Battle of Stalingrad. Although known as a harsh commander, Steinhoff undoubtedly was one of the most successful German fighter pilots on the Eastern Front during the winter of 1942/43. On 2 February 1943, the very same day as the last resistance in Stalingrad was broken, Steinhoff attained his 150th aerial victory. This photograph, taken during that winter shows Steinhoff bearing clear signs of the severity of combat. Johannes Steinhoff passed away in 1994.*
*(Wägenbaur – TG JG 52)*

The Axis forces had noted signs of an impending attack against this sector, which was held by the Italian 8th Army, during the first week of December. I./JG 52 – the only *Jagdgruppe* available against the Voronezh Front's 2 VA – had been shifted southwards, from Staryy Oskol between Voronezh and Kursk, to Rossosh on 7 December. But by that time, only 2. *Staffel* was available for front line duty since the bulk of the *Jagdgruppe* was in the rear, in Nikolayev, for rest and recuperation.[272] Over the following days, German and Italian reconnaissance aircraft observed heavy military movements in front of the Italian lines. "Softening-up raids" by 17 VA's bombers against airfields in the rear area, south of Italian 8th Army, failed to produce any significant material damage but served to reinforce the suspicion of a forthcoming Soviet offensive in this sector. Farther to the north, 2 VA launched twenty-eight air raids against Hungarian 2nd Army's positions on 12 December,[273] but it was a futile attempt to divert the attention from the preparations that were being made against Italian 8th Army. Thus, when "Little Saturn" was launched by Soviet 6th and 1st Guards Armies on 16 December, the Italians and their Allies were prepared.

The Soviets were of the opinion that their aviation would be their trump card for "Little Saturn"; on the eve of the offensive, 17 VA could muster 632 aircraft. The weak Italian air corps was hampered by a chronic lack of fuel and spare parts, and comprised no more than 32 MC. 200 fighters, 11 MC. 202s, 17 Fiat BR20s, 15 Ca 311s, and 12 SM. 81s. The only real threat against 17 VA's operations came from I./JG 52. Nevertheless, due to prevailing bad weather conditions, 17 VA was unable to provide the initial attack with any significant air support.

2./JG 52's *Hptm.* Johannes Wiese was out on a routine patrol over the front line when he came across a concentration of Soviet tanks and troops moving against the Italian positions.[274] He immediately flew back to base to make his report. *Luftflotte* 4's headquarters was alerted. II./ZG 1, III./St.G 77, KG 27 and KG 51 were released from other operations and instructed to direct all available forces to support Italian 8th Army. More

*One of the Bf 109 G-2s which Johannes Steinhoff flew during the winter battle of late 1942. It is seen here having its radio equipment checked. (Wägenbaur – TG JG 52)*

At least one pilot, (third from left) and members of the ground crew of the all-ace unit 9 GIAP in front of one of the Regiment's Yak-1s during the battle of Stalingrad. (Karlenko)

*Luftwaffe* reinforcements were also called in. The elements of I./JG 52 which had been resting in Nikolayev hastily made it back to the combat zone. Even KG 3 *Blitz* (excluding II. *Gruppe*, which was rested in Germany) was removed from its commitment in the Velikiye Luki area in the north – where a powerful Soviet offensive had surrounded a force from *Heeresgruppe Mitte* – and ordered to join the fight against South-western Front's offensive.

When the weather conditions improved in the afternoon of 16 December, the Soviet attack waves were mowed down by concentrated air attacks. The operations on 16 December cost II./ZG 1 five Bf 110s. In 8./St.G 77, the *Staffelkapitän* Oblt. Theodor Langhart force-landed in Soviet-controlled territory after his Ju 87 had been hit by ground fire. But before Red Army soldiers had reached the crash site, another 8./St.G 77 pilot – *Fw.* Herbert Dawedeit – landed and picked up the distressed Stuka crew.

As a result of Stalin's impatience, Operation "Little Saturn" was badly affected in its opening stage by a lack of fighter aircraft on the Soviet side. The offensive was launched before the complete 207 IAD – with 5 GIAP, 814 IAP, 867 IAP and 897 IAP – had arrived in the combat zone.[275] The La-5s of 5 GIAP – another Soviet elite unit – landed at Morshansk airfield on 14 December,[276] and on 16 December St.Lt. Igor Shardakov achieved the unit's first victory in this area by claiming a Bf 109. But apart from 5 GIAP's aircraft, there were hardly any other Soviet fighters in the air over South-western Front's breakthrough area on 16 December. In consequence, I./JG 52 – to which the new 1. *Ungarische JaboStaffel* with eight Hungarian Bf 109s was attached – was able to take a terrible toll among 267 ShAD's *Shturmovik* formations which were harassing the Italian troops.

On 16 December, 2./JG 52's *Fw.* Wilhelm Freuwörth claimed six Il-2s shot down, and his *Staffelkapitän*, Hptm. Johannes Wiese, bagged another five in only eight minutes.[277] The 1. *Ungarische JaboStaffel* brought home its first victories by claiming four Il-2s, including two by *Hadnagy* (Lieutenant) Imre Pánczél.[278] In consequence, the 200 sorties performed by 17 VA on 16 December were met with only limited success – contrary to those of their opponent. 4./SchG 1's six Hs 129s, armed with MK 101 anti-tank cannon, succeeded in knocking out ten Soviet tanks without loss to themselves on 16 and 17 December.[279] The German airmen who supported the Italian Army

claimed to have destroyed 14 Soviet tanks and shot down 28 aircraft on 17 December.[280] Six of the latter were chalked up by another of 2./JG 52's aces, *Fw.* Rudolf Trenkel. Thanks to this air support, the Italian Army managed to hold the Soviets at bay.

This was not what the Soviet planners had anticipated. It was obvious that the lack of air support was a key factor in the recent failures on both flanks of the Stalingrad combat zone. 3 SAK's 207 IAD was hurriedly shifted forward to take part in 17 VA's operations and, in order to improve the situation in the south, the *Stavka* released 8 VA from the Stalingrad air blockade and directed it to support the hard-pressed Stalingrad Front against *Generaloberst* Hoth's Operation "Winter Storm".

The aircraft of 8 VA arrived over the battlefield just in time. German 17th *Panzerdivision* arrived to bolster LVII. *Panzerkorps* at Verkhne Kumskiy. This, and the increased *Luftwaffe* activity in the good flying conditions, enabled Hoth to break through Soviet 51st Army's lines on 17 December. German air attacks also delayed *General* Malinovskiy's Soviet 2nd Guards Army in its march to join the 51st Army. But by now Soviet aircraft were a strong presence in this sector. By carrying out 499 combat sorties against the German *Panzer* columns on 17 and 18 December, the airmen of 8 VA contributed to slowing down the German advance – albeit at a high price to themselves.

The elite 9 GIAP managed well in the air fighting on 17 December, claiming two Bf 109s, two Bf 110s, an He 111 and an Fw 189 shot down[281] – of which all but a Bf 109 can be confirmed through *Luftwaffe* loss files.[282] But less experienced Soviet air units fared worse. JG 3, which through the arrival of its II. *Gruppe* was united for the first time in several months, claimed 27 Soviet aircraft shot down on 17 December. Five of these were filed by *Hptm.* Kurt Brändle, II./JG 3's *Gruppenkommandeur*, and the *Geschwaderkommodore*, *Major* Wolf-Dietrich Wilcke, surpassed his 150-victory mark by bagging three. In II./JG 52, *Hptm.* Johannes Steinhoff shot down a P-40 and a Yak-1 for his 132nd and 133rd kills, and Oblt. Gerhard Barkhorn achieved his 95th through 97th.

On 18 December, an entire *Zveno* of four Il-2s led by 686 ShAP's *Kapitan* M. N. Slobodnichenko was annihilated by four Bf 109s at

Gromoslavka near the Myshkova River. 2./JG 3's *Uffz.* Kurt Hofrath and *Lt.* Fritz-Hermann Hellfritzsch shot down the first two Il-2s at 09.35 hrs while *Major* Wolf-Dietrich Wilcke bagged the last two at 09.35 and 09.38 hrs – all at Gromoslavka.[283] The Il-2s' fighter escort seems to have been taken care of by II./JG 52's *Oblt.* Barkhorn, who claimed a Yak-1 at Gromoslavka at 09.45 hrs. About an hour later, II./JG 52 attacked eight Yak-1s in the same area and claimed to have shot down all but one.[284]

In the north, the deployment of another Soviet Army, the 3rd Guards, and strengthened air support from 17 VA, settled the fate of the Italian 8th Army. The increased presence of Soviet fighters over the battlefield in this sector was painfully experienced by 8./St.G 77's *Fw.* Herbert Dawedeit, who was shot down by a 5 GIAP La-5 on 18 December. This time, the roles were changed, as Dawedeit's *Staffelkapitän Oblt.* Langhart landed and rescued him. Also on 18 December, 897 IAP achieved its first victory with 207 IAD – against a Ju 88 south of Nikolayenkov.[285] This is probably the same aircraft which, piloted by 3./KG 3's *Staffelkapitän*, *Hptm.* Gustav Quass, was posted as missing after being shot down by Soviet fighters.[286]

Although 16 VA was assigned the task of sealing off Stalingrad from the air when 8 VA was deployed on tactical operations south of the city, the German transport pilots did not note any immediate reduction in the Soviet air blockade. In the clear skies which followed as a result of a high pressure zone and a cold spell on 17 December, "the air above the cauldron was littered with enemy fighters."[287] In consequence, the German airlift operation to Stalingrad almost came to a complete standstill once again. A mere ten tons of supplies were flown into the cauldron on 18 December.

While some of its fighters turned away the German transports which were trying to reach Stalingrad, 16 VA's main force was concentrated against German troop positions near the Yablonevaya Ravine inside the Stalingrad cauldron. In excellent flying weather on 18 December, a total of 112 aircraft took part in the opening onslaught – 74 Pe-2s from 2 BAK, ten Il-2s from 228 ShAD and 28 Yak-1s led by 512 IAP's *Mayor* Vasiliy Shishkin. The same area was then repeatedly attacked by groups of seven to nine Soviet aircraft during the remainder of the day. In total, 16 VA carried out 459 combat sorties on 18 December.

That evening, an upset *Generalmajor* Arthur Schmidt – von Paulus' Chief-of-Staff – contacted *Generalleutnant* Martin Fiebig, the *Luftversorgungsführer Stalingrad,* to demand an immediate explanation for the meagre air lift performance of the past two days. Fiebig excused the inadequate performance by pointing to the risk of ice formation on the He 111s at Morozovsk, fog at the Ju 52 base Tatsinskaya, "and the engines of the Ju 86s that failed to come afloat."[288]

To make up for the failure by day, the transport units flew throughout the following night and delivered 70 tons of supplies.

The next day, 19 December, *Generalmajor* Schmidt and his commander could see some light at the end of the tunnel. In the south, *Generaloberst* Hoth's reinforced LVII. *Panzerkorps* finally reached the Myshkova River, the last natural barrier on its route towards Stalingrad. This compelled the *Stavka* also to release 16 VA from the air blockade mission and dispatch its units against Hoth's troops in the south. This was badly needed, since 8 VA was suffering at the hands of II./JG 52 and JG 3 over the Myshkova sector. On 19 December, this air army performed 523 combat sorties and lost 12 aircraft.[289] 16 VA was instructed to employ its forces against the Myshkova sector during the next two days.

The Germans immediately took advantage of the absence of Soviet fighters over Stalingrad to intensify their supply flights. Seventy-three He 111s, fifty Ju 52s and thirteen Ju 86s flew in 270 tons of supplies on 19 December – this included 220 tons of rations that were delivered to the starving army. On 20 December, the figures were 100 He 111s, plus 80 Ju 52s and Ju 86s, which delivered a total of 291 tons of supplies. These achievements and the limited losses during those two days – two damaged Ju 86s, a Ju 52, and two He 111s – demonstrate the important role played by Soviet fighters in isolating Stalingrad from the air. Among individual performances it should be noted that 1./KG 100's *Staffelkapitän*, *Hptm.* Hansgeorg Bätcher, flew six supply flights to Pitomnik on 20 December, without encountering more than weak anti-aircraft fire on two occasions.[290] With this, Bätcher had completed 442 combat sorties and on the following day – after flying two more supply sorties – he was awarded the Knight's Cross.

But the Soviet tactic of concentrating its aviation to halt LVII. *Panzerkorps* proved to be the right one. At the Myshkova River, Hoth's troops could see the columns of smoke from the fighting around Stalingrad 35 miles farther to the north, but there they were halted by Soviet troops

who were provided with overwhelming air support. 16 VA's official chronicle states: "As a result of intense aerial combats near Myshkova, the German fighters were dislodged from the battlefield, which allowed our bombers and *Shturmoviks* to operate freely."[291] This is hardly surprising in light of the fact that II./JG 52 was down to just twelve serviceable Bf 109s on 20 December.

The situation in II./JG 52 was no exception. In II./SchG 1, all Bf 109s had been lost[292] and in I./JG 52 – assigned the task of combatting the combined forces of 2 VA and 17 VA – only eleven serviceable Bf 109s remained by 20 December.

The effect of combat losses was exacerbated by the parlous state of the German supply system in the East. The five *Jagdgruppen* serving in the Don Bend and the Caucasus – JG 3 *Udet*, and II. and III./JG 52 – recorded 91 Bf 109s lost through December 1942. During the same period, these units received no more than 34 Bf 109s as replacements.[293] Meanwhile, the German aircraft industry produced 488 fighter planes in November and 554 in December 1942.[294] Reflecting the desperate situation on the German side, 4./JG 54 was released from *Luftflotte* 1's II./JG 54 in the northern combat zone and sent south to reinforce I./JG 52.

By that stage, the Italian front lines in the north had totally collapsed and Soviet tank columns penetrated deep into the rear area, threatening the Stalingrad airlift's main bases. Early on 20 December, Soviet 18th Tank Corps reached within striking distance of the *Luftwaffe* base at Millerovo, which was hastily abandoned by KG 3, KG 27 and II./SchG 1. Morozovsk – the He 111 transport base – was repeatedly targeted by the Boston bombers of *Polkovnik* Ivan Antoshkin's 221 BAD.

On 21 December, the Bostons of 221 BAD's 57 BAP attacked both the airfield at Morozovsk and supply trains on the Likhaya-Morozovsk railway. The bomber crews reported seventeen Ju 88s destroyed or damaged and three major conflagrations were observed in the railway station area following their attack.[295] German sources show that three of KGrzbV 22's Ju 86s were put out of commission through a Soviet bombing raid against Tatsinskaya.[296] Four II./JG 3 Bf 109s engaged the bombers, but only managed to shoot down one Boston[297] – although three were claimed – while the German formation leader, 67-victory ace *Oblt.* Werner Lucas, had to take to his parachute after his Bf 109 was set ablaze by the Boston gunners, Melnikov and Yegorov.

Of course, individual German veteran pilots could still produce remarkable accomplishments, such as 2./JG 52's *Fw.* Rudolf Trenkel's interception of four Il-2s on 21 December. He immediately shot down two of the *Shturmoviks*. What happened next was described by Trenkel himself; "Following my second victory, I dived out of the haze and spotted another Il-2 which tried to dive away on my right hand side. I immediately attacked the enemy aircraft from behind, and at 50 metres altitude I opened fire from a very short distance. Pieces flew off its fuselage and wings, and bright flames became visible. The aircraft crashed into the ground, exploding on impact. I saw the 'White 10' of my *Rottenflieger Lt.* Meier pursuing the fourth Il-2 at low level, and opening fire from astern. I witnessed how the enemy aircraft took hits in the wings and fuselage and the undercarriage let down. But in spite of this the Il-2 held its course towards the north-east. My *Rottenflieger* broke off, so I attacked the enemy aircraft from behind. I hit it and forced it down onto the village road through Shelyayevka. It smashed into a house."[298]

In fact, such individual achievements were *Luftflotte* 4's only chance of compensating for its numerical weakness, but they were no longer enough to alter the situation. Apart from the four Il-2s claimed by Trenkel, two fighters shot down by *Hptm.* Johannes Wiese were I./JG 52's only accomplishment against the forces of 2 VA and 17 VA, which tore German *Heeresgruppe Don's* northern flank apart.

One month of severe fighting had weakened the Axis air forces in the area to a point where they were no longer able to intervene with any notable effect. The upsurge in combat activity in support of Operation "Winter Storm" had been *Luftflotte* 4's last show of strength in the Stalingrad - Don Bend region, and it also consumed the air fleet's last offensive resources.

Only slightly more than 200 German Stukas, *Zerstörer*, ground-attack planes, fighters, and bombers were now available for a range of tasks – defensive operations against South-western Front's wide offensive, supporting the thin defence lines along the Chir River, providing the troops in Stalingrad with air support, and providing support for Hoth's relief offensive which had now stalled. As an example, 8./St.G 77 flew dive-bombing missions against one sector after another with a shrinking number

*In early December 1942, the Bf 110-equipped ZG 1 was transferred from the Caucasus to Tatsinskaya to reinforce the fighter escort force. Soon, however, the Zerstörer pilots found that they were being used as a 'fire brigade', shifted from one mission to another. In mid-December 1942 the Zerstörer supported Hoth's relief offensive, Operation 'Winter Storm.' Only a few days later they were rushed northwards to support the defensive fight against the new Soviet offensive against Italian 8th Army, Operation 'Little Saturn.' The latter missions were particularly costly. Over the three days 16-18 December alone, ZG 1 lost eleven Bf 110s to Soviet action. (Mombeeck)*

of Ju 87s, losing six Ju 87s between 16 and 19 December. By 20 December, III./St.G 77 reported no more than seven serviceable Ju 87s, and on 22 December, 8./St.G 77's *Staffelkapitän*, *Oblt.* Theodor Langhart, was shot down and killed. Thus *Luftflotte* 4 lost another of its veterans; Langhart had carried out 342 Stuka missions and was posthumously awarded with the Knight's Cross on 22 January 1943.

Supported by *Shturmoviks* that flew close above their heads, Soviet 24th and 25th Tank Corps and 1st Guards Mechanised Corps advanced deep behind what had formerly been the Italian - German lines along the central Don. On 23 December, *General-Mayor* Vasiliy Badanov's 24th Tank Corps seized Skasyrskaya, where the staff of *Fliegerkorps* VIII under the command of *Obstlt.* Lothar von Heinemann was based, and continued southward towards Tatsinskaya – the main base of all Ju 52s and Ju 86s in the Stalingrad airlift under *Oberst* Hans Förster's centralised command. Meanwhile, the 25th Tank Corps and 1st Guards Mechanised Corps approached Morozovsk, where *Oberst* Ernst Kühl's He 111 units were based together with elements of St.G 2 and St.G 77.

Since 21 December, *Generalleutnant* Fiebig, commander of VIII. *Fliegerkorps* and *Luftversorgungsführer Stalingrad*, had been desperately requesting permission to evacuate Morozovsk and Tatsinskaya. His nearest superior, *Generaloberst* von Richthofen, noted that Fiebig was "really nervous." But the *Luftversorgungsführer* received a negative response. Morozovsk and Tatsinskaya must be held, *Reichsmarschall* Göring ordered from East Prussia – and at the same time, Hitler awarded Fiebig the Oak Leaves to the Knight's Cross.

Having advanced 150 miles in five days of continuous battle – during which 6,700 Italian and German troops were reportedly killed,[299] while the Soviet tank corps was reduced to less than 40 per cent of its initial strength[300] – *General-Mayor* Badanov's 24th Tank Corps reached and penetrated the village of Tatsinskaya from various directions in the early morning hours of 24 December. One troop detachment seized and destroyed a train on the Likhaya - Stalingrad railway, which was found to be loaded with dismantled aircraft.[301] The attack against the airfield itself was preceded by an artillery barrage which was begun at around 03.30 hrs. This severed the German telephone communications from Tatsinskaya. Ninety minutes later, a tank detachment commanded by *Kapitan* Nechayev launched the attack, which immediately created panic on the airfield. There were 170 Ju 52s and Ju 86s at Tatsinskaya and all were threatened with being wiped out in a single Soviet strike. *Generalleutnant* Fiebig ordered *Oberst* Förster, the Ju 52 commander, to order all crews to take off without delay and to fly to Novocherkassk, 80 miles further to the south-west.

For one month, engine troubles, low serviceability due to a lack of spare parts, the risk of ice formation, and other reasons had been reported to explain to *Reichsmarschall* Göring and *Generaloberst* von Paulus why 200 Ju 52s could make no more than a couple of dozen sorties a day into Stalingrad. Now – "in thick ground fog and absolutely impossible flying weather"[302] – all aircraft that could be saved from the disaster were airborne

within twenty minutes. A total of 124 transport planes – 108 Ju 52s and 16 Ju 86s – made it through the clouds and fog to safe landings at Novocherkassk, Salsk, and a variety of other airfields. In the words of historian Franz Kurowski, "this mass take-off at Tatsinskaya was the most splendid effort carried out by the *Luftwaffe*."[303]

Through this "aerial Dunkirk," the Junkers transport force was saved from Badanov's intended death-strike. But the German materiel losses at Tatsinskaya were severe enough to constitute a major blow against *Luftflotte* 4. At least 50 aircraft were overrun by Badanov's tank troops at Tatsinskaya – 24 Ju 86s, 22 Ju 52s, two I./KG 51 Ju 88s, and two 3.(F)/10 aircraft. The Soviets also captured hundreds of tons of supplies – including 300 tons of gasoline and oil, and five complete ammunition stores, according to Soviet accounts[304] – and valuable equipment such as engine-warming wagons and fuel trucks.[305]

The operation by the 25th Tank Corps and 1st Guards Mechanised Corps against Morozovsk was less successful, although it affected the He 111s' ability to fly in supplies to Stalingrad. When the Soviet troops had reached to within ten miles of Morozovsk, the air transport commander, *Oberst* Ernst Kühl, acted on his own authority and ordered all He 111s and Ju 87s to evacuate to Novocherkassk.

"The cloud ceiling was low and an icy wind blew, billowing clouds of snow through the air," recalls 1./KG 100's *Hptm.* Hansgeorg Bätcher, "but we divided the ground personnel between our operational aircraft, and took off despite the mist. In my aircraft, the artificial horizon failed during the take-off, and it heeled over strongly as we came out of the clouds. The time it took us to pass through the clouds felt like an eternity, but apart from my observer, no one else had noticed this misfortune. Thank God there was a gap in the clouds above our flight destination."[306]

When the skies cleared on 25 December – bringing temperatures down to around minus 20 degrees Celsius – the bombers and Stukas could be brought in against the motorised columns which threatened Morozovsk. "We found the roads on which the Russians advanced to be filled with tanks and other vehicles," remembered Hansgeorg Bätcher. "The visibility was unusually good and the Russians had no chance against the concentrated attacks from our bombers and Ju 87s. I made two sorties against the same target that day, and only on the second occasion was there any noteworthy opposition – in the shape of two fighters whose attacks were warded off by my gunners."[307] In I./St.G 2, which could field only around a dozen operational Ju 87s, *Fw.* Hans Ludwig destroyed six trucks and three sledge-mounted guns. *Uffz.* Heinrich Meyering flew nine sorties on 25 December. The impact of these aerial onslaughts against unprotected Soviet troops who were caught on the open, snow-white steppe, could be seen even from the ground at Morozovsk. "The sky in the north-west, north, and north-east is red from burning villages," wrote KG 55's chief meteorologist, Friedrich Wobst.[308] That same day, the He 111s started returning to Morozovsk.

At Tatsinskaya, *General-Mayor* Badanov's weakened 24th Tank Corps was left beyond the range of any supply column, and also lost radio contact with South-western Front headquarters. The German 11th *Panzerdivision* was rapidly deployed to the area and succeeded in surrounding Badanov's troops. Two attempts were made to restore communication with the surrounded troops by sending U-2 liaison aircraft to the airfield, but on both occasions the aircraft were destroyed by German anti-aircraft fire.

Although 11th *Panzerdivision* could block the Soviet advance toward Rostov and save Morozovsk, it had become clear to everyone from Christmas 1942 that Stalingrad was doomed. By now, the fighter pilots of 16 VA had suppressed the resistance put up by JG 3's fighters based at Pitomnik.[309] On 25 December, *Lt.* Georg Schentke – the brightest star among the German fighter pilots inside Stalingrad – was shot down in aerial combat and landed in his parachute on the Soviet side of the front line. The loss of this 90-victory ace was a great blow to the rapidly sinking fighting spirit of the remaining men of the *Platzschutzstaffel Pitomnik*. I./JG 3's *Uffz.* Walther Hagenah recalled:

"The troops lost their confidence when it became obvious that the Stalingrad cauldron could not be relieved. Despair became widespread, some

The Soviet fighter ace Mayor Boris Yeryomin, the Commanding Officer of 273 IAP, seen in his Yak-1 at Solodovka airfield on 20 December 1942. Yeryomin was among the most successful Soviet aces in 1942. When the all-ace unit, 9 GIAP, was formed in October of that year, Yeryomin was transferred to it from 296 IAP. However, after just a few weeks he was ordered to assume command of 31 GIAP (formerly 273 IAP) of the same Diviziya as 9 GIAP (268 IAD) in 8 VA. A short while later, he was presented with a brand new Yak-1 which was the result of a financial donation from Ferapont Golovatyy, a worker at the 'Stakhanovets' collective farm. The inscription on the aircraft reads: 'To the pilot of the

Stalingrad Front, Comrade Guards Major Yeryomin, from the collective farmer of the 'kolkhoz' 'Stakhanovets,' Comrade Golovatov.' By that time, Yeryomin had attained a total of seven aerial victories. He flew the donated aircraft in combat for almost 18 months, scoring eight victories. On 29 May 1944, when he was ordered to fly to Saratov airfield in order to pick up a new fighter, he was surprised to find that this too was the result of a donation from Ferapont Golovatyy. This time it was a Yak-3. Yeryomin attained another six victories with this aircraft – the last one being against an Fw 190 on 10 May 1945 during the 'overtime war' in Czechoslovakia. (Drabkin)

talked about committing suicide, many cursed the superior command. We pilots were looked upon with envy. After each combat flight, or when we returned from an escort mission, we were met with the same questions: What does the situation look like? Exactly where is the enemy? Do we have any chance at all?"[310]

When Ju 52 transports – now using Salsk in the northern Caucasus as their main base – again landed inside the cauldron in the afternoon of 25 December, VI. *Armee* had been without any airlifted supplies for almost 48 hours.[311] Forty transport aircraft brought 78 tons of supplies to Stalingrad on 26 December. Five were shot down, according to German sources, and another eight were reported destroyed on the ground by pilots of Soviet 520 IAP.

At a time when German resources were rapidly declining, the need for airlifted supplies increased. By now, not only VI. *Armee*, but also the German 298th Infantry Division and scattered remnants of the Italian 8th Army who were surrounded at Kantemirovka, were depending on airlifted supplies, as were parts of XXIX. *Armeekorps* north of the Gnilaya River. The 298th Infantry Division was in a particularly grave situation. It had been cut to pieces by Soviet 18th Tank Corps, and its dispersed fragments "stumbled westward, dodging Russian tank columns, harassed by the Soviet aircraft."[312]

The few remaining fighters of I./JG 52 flew as much as possible to provide the 298th with air cover. 2./JG 52's *Uffz*. Werner Peltz succeeded in bringing down two Il-2s at dawn on 26 December. Shortly afterward, *Fw.* Georg Schwientek of the same *Staffel* intercepted five Il-2s, two of which he destroyed.[313] On *Uffz*. Peltz's next mission that day, he flew with I./JG 52's *Gruppenkommandeur*, *Hptm*. Helmut Bennemann in the Novaya Kalitva area. The two German pilots spotted two La-5s below, and what followed is also described in Soviet 207 IAD's files. One of these La-5s was

flown by *St.Lt*. Ibraghim Bikmukhametov, deputy *Eskadrilya* commander and one of the best pilots in 5 GIAP. The two Bf 109s carried out two diving attacks from the sun and shot down first Bikmukhametov's La-5, followed by the fighter piloted by *Lt*. Zhdanov, his wingman. Zhdanov survived by baling out and was able to return to his unit, but Bikmukhametov was killed.[314] The loss of such an outstanding airman, credited with at least 11 victories, was a hard blow for 5 GIAP. A third La-5 lost by 5 GIAP later that day was claimed by *Fw*. Schwientek.

Aircraft of KG 3 and ZG 1 which were dispatched against the Soviet advance in the area, were met by aggressive Soviet fighters. 814 IAP, another regiment in 17 VA's 207 IAD, reported five German aircraft shot down on 26 December – two Ju 88s, two Hs 126s, one Bf 109 and a Bf 110 – against the loss of only one Yak-1 in two different engagements at Boguchar and Millerovo.[315] *St.Lt*. Kirill Lebedev and *St.Serzh*. Vladimir Ivanov claimed two victories each. Moreover, teaming with Il-2s of 290 ShAD, the same fighter unit claimed to have destroyed more than ten other enemy aircraft on the ground at an airfield north-east of Millerovo.

Farther south, other Soviet fighters came close to shooting down *Luftflotte* 4's commander himself, *Generalfeldmarschall* von Richthofen, who had a very narrow escape in his Fi 156 Storch on 26 December.[316]

The troops of VI. *Armee* saw their hopes literally disappear on the horizon as *General* Rodion Malinovskiy's Soviet 2nd Guards Army forced LVII. *Panzerkorps* to abandon its positions on the Myshkova, 35 miles south of Stalingrad, and continued to push the Germans backwards. On 26 December, much of Hoth's supplies were destroyed when *Mayor* Dmitriy Valentik, 284 BAP's commander, blew up a train at Kotelnikovo's railroad station through a dive-bombing attack with his Pe-2. When Soviet 51st Army on 27 December shattered Rumanian VII Army

*Pe-2 bombers at a snow-covered airfield. One of the most successful Soviet bomber units during the Battle of Stalingrad was the Pe-2 equipped 284 BAP, commanded by Mayor Dmitriy Valentik. Born on 23 February 1907, Valentik had served with the Red Army since 1929. He graduated from flight school in 1931 and served in the Winter War against Finland in 1939-1940, for which he was appointed a Hero of the Soviet Union on 7 May 1940. When the war with Germany broke out in 1941, Valentik was one of the* most experienced Soviet airmen. One of the most successful individual Soviet air attacks during the Battle of Stalingrad was attained on 26 December 1942 when Valentik destroyed a whole ammunition train at Kotelnikovo rail station by dive-bombing the target with his Pe-2. Thus the Germans lost a large part of the fuel needed for Operation 'Winter Storm'. Valentik flew a total of 115 bombing missions during the war. He passed away on 30 March 1969. (Karlenko)*

Corps, on the right flank of LVII. *Panzerkorps*, Hoth had to abandon the plan to rebuild his lines at the Aksay River. To evade encirclement, Hoth's battered troops were pulled back towards Kotelnikovo, eighteen miles farther to the south. The airfield at this place was evacuated by *Hptm.* Steinhoff's II./JG 52.[317] Steinhoff remembers that this transfer was carried out at night time, precipitately, and several unserviceable aircraft were left behind.[318] What remained of II./JG 52 was shifted to Zimovniki, some twenty miles farther to the south-west.

To the north-west, parts of Soviet 24th Tank Corps that had broken through the German encirclement at Tatsinskaya launched another raid against Morozovsk aerodrome on 27 December. *Major* Ernst *Freiherr* von Bibra's III./KG 51 – which recently had returned to first-line service after a period of badly needed rest – was dealt a severe blow by Soviet bombers at Rostov's airbase on this 27 December, losing six Ju 88s with many more damaged.[319] *Hptm.* Klaus Häberlen – a KG 51 veteran who had flown 114 combat missions between July 1941 and June 1942 before he served a period as flight instructor – was back in first-line service and took command of 2./KG 51. He flew his first operation during his second tour against Soviet troops near Morozovsk on 27 December.[320] In the same area, Bf 109s of 9./JG 3 clashed with seven LaGG-3s led by *St.Lt.* Bardin, whereby 87-victory ace *Lt.* Wilhelm Lemke survived colliding with one of the Soviet fighters, and *Uffz.* Franz Thümer was shot down and killed. The Soviet pilots filed five claims against Bf 109s, including two through *tarans*.

Although the tank raid against Morozovsk was repulsed, and Tatsinskaya was retaken by the Germans on 28 December, the South-western Front's deep intrusion made it impossible to continue flying supplies to Stalingrad from these two bases. It was decided to evacuate the He 111s from Morozovsk to Novocherkassk, north-east of Rostov, and keep the Junkers transporters stationed at Salsk.

With rations at Stalingrad down to a daily 50 grams of bread per soldier[321] and *Generaloberst* Hoth's relief offensive stalled, the supply flights became more important than ever. Eighty-six transport planes struggled into Stalingrad on 29 December, bringing in a far from sufficient 124 tons of supplies. At least ten of the transport planes were lost or severely damaged. With one of them, *General* Enrico Pezzi, the commander of the Italian

expeditionary Air Force, went missing. He took off from Pitomnik in an S.M. 81 from 246 *Squadriglia*, with as many wounded soldiers as possible on board, and was never seen again.

"On 29 December, I landed my Heinkel 111 at Pitomnik at 10.10 hrs, carrying butter, salt, mail, and 600 litres of fuel in my 'supply bombs,'" recalled *Hptm.* Bätcher. "Wounded were loaded and an hour later we took off for the flight back to Morozovsk. We had barely left the ground before we came under attack from a string of fighters. My skilful gunners were able to ward off most of their attacks, but the Russians did not relent. They were very aggressive and each of them made eight to ten individual attacks. Time and again, my plane was hit by their fire – and this included five cannon shells. Several of the wounded soldiers on board received additional injuries and I wanted to land as quickly as possible in order to have their wounds seen to. But when the soldiers heard of my intentions, they pleaded with me to fly on to the main base. They wanted to get as far away from Stalingrad as possible!"[322]

The sufferings at Stalingrad spurred the transport pilots to overcome their difficulties. Aided by adverse weather conditions which hampered VVS activity, 118 sorties brought in 180 tons on 30 December, and 152 planes delivered 320 tons on the last day of the year. I./KG 100's *Fw.* Erich Jeckstat contributed to the latter figure with three flights, and *Hptm.* Bätcher also landed in Pitomnik three times that day. On their way back from the cauldron, the transports flew out 4,120 men – mainly wounded – during the last week of 1942. This gave a small ray of hope to the men in Stalingrad, but the price paid by the transport units was indeed disastrous.

The actual number of transport aircraft lost during the Stalingrad airlift operation will never be known. The monthly reports on aircraft strength and losses – *Flugzeugbestand und Bewegungsmeldungen* – for December 1942 are missing for most of the transport units which operated at Stalingrad. The *Generalquartiermeister der Luftwaffe* files record a total of 278 aircraft of units involved in the Stalingrad airlift as lost or severely damaged between 20 November and 31 December 1942. Of this total, 216 were lost in the air – including 101 totally destroyed and 35 severely damaged to hostile action or for unknown reasons – but the daily loss returns to the *Generalquartiermeister der Luftwaffe* appear to be far from complete for the

*US-designed Bell P-39 Airacobra fighters in Soviet use, lined up on a snow covered airfield, prior to another combat operation. (Viktor Kulikov Photograph Collection)*

same period. According to figures available to historian Franz Kurowski, "in December alone, 246 aircraft were lost to enemy fire and crashes during supply flights to Stalingrad and subsequent return flights. To this figure should be added losses due to technical malfunctions."[323]

Soviet sources show that the majority of the transports were lost on the southern route to and from Stalingrad, which was covered by 8 VA. This air army claimed to have shot down 112 Ju 52s – including 96 through 2 SAK – between 20 November and 20 December 1942.[324] Meanwhile, 16 VA – covering the air above and immediately to the north of the cauldron – reported a mere 16 Ju 52s shot down between 19 November and 31 December 1942.[325] For other transport aircraft, 8 VA claimed 20 He 111s between 20 November and 20 December 1942[326] and 16 VA claimed ten He 111s between 19 November and 31 December 1942.[327] None of these air armies claimed any Ju 86s or other Axis transport aircraft. Only one of the Ju 86s lost to Soviet fire can be traced – a "Do 215" claimed by 9 GIAP's *St.Lt.* Arkadiy Kovachevich.

In total, 8 VA reportedly shot down 236 enemy aircraft against 133 own aircraft losses (69 fighters, 57 Il-2s, five Pe-2s, and one each R-5 and U-2) between 20 November and 20 December 1942.[328] 8 VA's 2 SAK (201 IAD, 235 IAD, and 214 ShAD) claimed 172 victories (including 38 Bf 109s) for the loss of 82 own aircraft (36 La-5s, 30 Il-2s, and 16 Yak-1s).[329] The élite 9 GIAP contributed with 27 German aircraft shot down (eight Ju 52s, seven He 111s, five Bf 109s, three Bf 110s, three Ju 88s, and a Ju 87) during 349 combat sorties in December 1942.[330] The files for 16 VA show 75 aerial victories (including 44 Bf 109s) between 19 November and 31 December 1942,[331] and 64 own aircraft (24 of them fighters) shot down in December 1942.[332] The most successful unit in 16 VA through December 1942 was 220 IAD, which chalked up 41 enemy aircraft shot down (21 Bf 109s, ten Ju 52s, nine He 111s, and one "Focke-Wulf") against 16 own aircraft and nine pilots lost in combat during that month.[333] 17 VA claimed to have destroyed around 300 German aircraft in the air and on the ground through December 1942.[334]

The ADD also made a significant contribution: it flew 962 sorties, both in night attacks against the German rear area in the Don Bend sector and in flying supplies to Soviet troops, between 19 November and 31 December 1942. Overall, the reformation of the Soviet bomber arm into the ADD proved to be very successful. Between March and December 1942, the ADD performed 38,154 combat sorties and lost 477 aircraft with 320 crews. This amounts to a loss rate of merely 1.25 per cent – less than one-third of the loss rate sustained by RAF Bomber Command in the same period. By the end of the year, the ADD numbered 564 aircraft and 699 crews.[335]

One of the most experienced ADD pilots was *Kapitan* Aleksandr Molodichiy of 3 AD's 2 GAP. He had been appointed Hero of the Soviet Union for 390 bombing missions in October 1941. On 31 December 1942 Molodichiy became the sixth Soviet combat aviator to be appointed a Hero of the Soviet Union for a second time. The navigator in his Il-4 crew, *Mayor* Sergey Kulikov, also received the title and, on the same day, seventeen other airmen of the ADD were also appointed Heroes of the Soviet Union.

With regard to individual performances, the claims made by the German fighters at Stalingrad surpassed anything else. JG 52 had reported its 4,000th victory on 7 December 1942. JG 3's *Geschwaderkommodore, Major* Wolf-Dietrich Wilcke, surpassed the 150-victory mark ten days later, and III./JG 3 attained its 1,500th victory on 28 December. But even if JG 3's and JG 52's victory-for-loss results were quite impressive, the events from the onset of Operation "*Uranus*" show that they failed in their general task, namely to take control of the air and provide the transport flights with sufficient air cover. This is a clear indication of the substantial improvement in the VVS since the first round of the Battle of Stalingrad. Moreover, the disparity between VIII. *Fliegerkorps* victory claims and VVS loss figures in Soviet unit archives for the period in question is greater than for most previous campaigns. Between 19 November and 31 December 1942, JG 3 claimed around 275 victories in the Stalingrad - Don Bend area against 28 Bf 109s destroyed or severely damaged due to hostile activity or for unknown reasons. Meanwhile, I. and II./JG 52 reported 219 victories for 13 of its Bf 109s destroyed or severely damaged due to hostile activity or for unknown reasons. The sum of around 500 *Jagdwaffe* claims in the Stalingrad - Don Bend area between 19 November and 31 December 1942 amounts to probably a two-fold exaggeration.

# Chapter Sixteen

# Air operations during the Caucasus retreat

While the German Front in the Stalingrad - Don Bend area collapsed, the situation in the Caucasus to the south was characterised by stalemate throughout November and most of December 1942. Powerful Soviet forces had not only blocked German *Heeresgruppe A's* possibility of advancing in any direction, but had also seized the initiative. To the south of the Soviet Stalingrad Front, Southern Front with its single 28th Army covered the lower Volga, east of the mighty Kalmyk Steppe, down to Astrakhan north of the Caspian Sea. The Caucasian region between the Caspian Sea in the east and the Black Sea in the west was defended by the Transcaucasus Front, which was divided into two first-line groupments: the Northern Groupment (9th, 34th, 44th, and 58th Armies, plus 4th and 5th Guards Cavalry Corps, all supported by *General-Mayor* Nikolay Naumenko's 4 VA), and the Black Sea Groupment (15th, 46th, 47th and 56th armies, supported by *General-Mayor* Sergey Goryunov's 5 VA and *General-Mayor* Vasiliy Yermachenkov's VVS ChF) in the west and south-west. In addition, the ADD's 50 AD acted in cooperation with 5 VA. Mention must be made of *Lt.* Erich Hartmann's first kill in this sector on 5 November.

By late November 1942, 4 VA could muster around 400 aircraft, 5 VA around 135, and VVS ChF 289.

Most of the *Luftwaffe's* offensive components in the Caucasus were transferred to either the Mediterranean area during the latter half of November 1942 – to help fight the Allied landings in Algeria and Morocco – or northwards, to participate in the defensive fight at the Don Bend. Up to that point, *General* Kurt Pflugbeil's IV. *Fliegerkorps* had been responsible for German air operations in the Caucasus. But now IV. *Fliegerkorps* transferred its headquarters to Salsk, and the new *Luftwaffengruppe Kaukasus* was provided with an entirely defensive task. By 20 November 1942, it was composed of NAGr 1, NAGr 3, and NAGr 9 (with altogether around 30 serviceable aircraft); II./St.G 77 (19 serviceable Ju 87s), and the *Ergänzungsstaffel* of St.G 77; *Stab* and III./JG 52 (31 serviceable Bf 109 G-2s); and 13./JG 52 (six serviceable Bf 109 Es). In addition, a few *Fernaufklärungsstaffeln* operated regularly over the Caucasus, as did KG 51's Ju 88 bombers occasionally. Not surprisingly, German air activity in the Caucasus tailed off considerably and the Soviets gained air supremacy.

On the western flank, the bulk of Soviet 5 VA's missions were sorties to fly in supplies to the troops of Black Sea Groupment in the mountainous areas. It was here that their opponents activated the Bf 109 E-equipped Slovakian 13./JG 52. The Slovakian Bf 109-pilots *Porucik* Vladimir Krisko and *Catnik* Jozef Jancovic attained the unit's first success by claiming three I-153s shot down – of which at least one was confirmed destroyed – near Tuapse on 28 November 1942.[336] But as an indication of the low combat activity in the air over western Caucasus during this period, 13./JG 52 would add no more than three victories prior to the end of the year, for no losses. As for their opponents, *Podpolkovnik* Vasiliy Kudryashov's 236 IAD/5 VA filed nine aerial victories against three combat losses through December 1942.[337] During November and December 1942, the units of 5 VA made only 1,177 offensive sorties.[338]

In the south-east, the situation was more tense. Here the Soviets made a strong attempt to push back the 1st *Panzerdivision* from its positions near the Grozny oil fields south of the Terek River in late November. On the first day of the attack, 27 November, 4 VA dispatched a total of 120 aircraft (including 53 Il-2s) in three waves against targets near Ardon in a raid lasting over three hours. 230 ShAD performed 97 sorties and claimed to have destroyed four tanks and 40 other motor vehicles, but suffered dearly at the hands of III./JG 52. This *Diviziya* alone lost five Il-2s and three LaGG-3s to III./JG 52's Bf 109 pilots.[339] Two of the former were recorded as Knight's Cross holder *Ofw.* Alfred Grislawski's 69th and 70th victories. These massive air attacks were repeated during the next two days, and on 29 November, 7./JG 52's *Fw.* Hans Dammers shot five of the attackers out of the sky – attaining his victories Nos. 85 through to 89. The Soviet ground attack was bogged down on 30 November.

7./JG 52, led by *Ofw.* Grislawski in the air, was a particularly dangerous opponent for the units of 4 VA. This was again painfully demonstrated to 230 ShAD's 7 GShAP on 10 December, when Grislawski intercepted four of its Il-2s and shot down three in a matter of four minutes. In this combat, 7 GShAP lost one of its best pilots, *Lt.* Petr Rudenko. He had been appointed a Hero of the Soviet Union on 16 November 1942, for 96 combat sorties, and had been credited with the destruction of 40 tanks and 30 aircraft on the ground.

To strike back, 4 VA flew against the German airfields at Soldatskaya, Krasnogvardeyskaya, and Zolotaryov at dawn on 12 December. But their claims for 33 planes destroyed on the ground, plus another ten damaged,[340] are refuted by both *Luftwaffe* files and the recollections of German pilots who were present. In fact it appears that the Soviets failed to destroy even a single German aircraft. Instead, Grislawski shot down four of 4 VA's fighters.

In all, *Stab* and III./JG 52 submitted 46 victories claims – including 13 by *Ofw.* Grislawski – through December 1942.[341] The unit's only combat loss that month was 7. *Staffel's Uffz.* Friedrich Heeg, who on 14 December was killed when, blinded by the sun during a dogfight, he collided with the I-153 piloted by 84 IAP's *Lt.* Viktor Makutin (who was also killed). 4 VA filed a total of 50 own aircraft shot down or missing in December 1942 – compared to 86 in November 1942.[342] 5 VA filed eight combat losses (two LaGG-3s, two Il-4s, and one each Yak-1, Il-2, Boston, and U-2) in December 1942.[343] VVS ChF completed 2,000 combat sorties in the period 26 November through 20 December 1942.[344]

The situation in the Caucasus changed when the Stalingrad Front's 51st and 2nd Guards Armies in late December 1942 halted Operation "Winter Storm" in the north and began throwing back the badly mauled LVII. *Panzerkorps* of *Generaloberst* Hoth's IV. *Panzerarmee* south of Stalingrad. The German attempt to relieve Stalingrad thus abruptly evolved into a scenario threatening *Heeresgruppe A* in the far south of the Caucasus with the risk that the Army Group would become sealed off. On 29 December 1942 the OKH authorized the evacuation of I. *Panzerarmee* of *Heeresgruppe A* from its positions south of the Terek River. The *Panzer* Army was allowed to pull back to the River Kuma, around 60 miles north-west of the Terek.[345] It was intended to use the latter sector as a springboard for a renewed offensive against the Caucasus in the spring of 1943.

The Germans had little choice. In the north on 29 December, Stalingrad Front's 51st Army seized Kotelnikovo – the point of departure for *Generaloberst* Hoth's offensive a fortnight earlier – and continued toward Zimovniki. On 51st Army's northern flank, the 2nd Guards Army swept past scattered German and Rumanian troops and reached the area south of Tsimlyansk on the Don, halfway between Stalingrad and Rostov. Zimovniki had been abandoned by Hoth's troops on that same day. Remnants of the Rumanian 4th Army "without weapons, without officers, and without order were fleeing."[346] Soviet optimism soared at the prospect of creating "a second Tatsinskaya" at the new Junkers transport airfield at Salsk. In something of a possible foretaste of such an event, II./JG 52 hurriedly evacuated its airfield at Zimovniki and withdrew to Gigant, some 90 miles farther south-west.

Unable to establish any solid defence position against the advancing Soviet forces, the Germans called in the *Luftwaffe* to save the situation. "There was only one assignment during my next nine missions in the period 30 December to 2 January – low-level attacks," wrote II./JG 52's *Lt.* Helmut Lipfert.[347] II./St.G 77, plus *Stabsstaffel*/JG 52, and a III./JG 52 detachment led by *Oblt.* Günther Rall which comprised of 8. and 9. *Staffeln*, from the southern Caucasus.

8 VA was assigned to provide the offensive in the Kotelnikovo - Zimovniki area with air cover, but by that time only 220 of its 640 aircraft were serviceable.[348] In two days of action (29 and 30 December), Stukas – most notably those of *Oblt.* Alexander Gläser's 4./St.G 77 – claimed 51 Soviet tanks destroyed on the battlefield at Zimovniki. For this feat, *Oblt.* Gläser was later awarded the Knight's Cross. The Stukas suffered no losses on 29 December, but then Soviet fighters were called in. On the 30th, two of II./St.G 77's aircraft were shot down. On 2 January 1943, seven Ju 87s of Gläser's 4./St.G 77 were intercepted by three 236 IAP Yak-1s, led by the *Polk* commander *Kapitan* Sergey Petukhov. In the ensuing combat, the Soviets claimed three Ju 87s shot down and chased away the remainder. Two losses were filed by 4./St.G 77 on 3 January 1943 and so the exact date cannot be established.[349] In the meantime, a contingent of brand new German Tiger tanks had arrived at the sector, and Soviet 51st Army had to discontinue its offensive and regroup.

Again, the *Luftwaffe* had given proof of its ability to intervene decisively in the ground battle by concentrating its forces. And again this had been achieved at the cost of other sectors. Far down south, a handful of Bf 109s from 7./JG 52 was all the *Luftwaffe* could offer against the forces of 4 VA after the departure of *Stabsstaffel*/JG 52 and *Oblt.* Rall's III./JG 52 detachment to Gigant in the north on 30 December. 5 VA and VVS ChF had no opponents other than the Bf 109s of 13./JG 52.

When the Transcaucasus Front's Northern Groupment initiated its offensive in the Grozny sector on New Year's Day, German I. *Panzerarmee*

was forced to speed up its retreat. The Germans were instructed to destroy "all vehicles in tow that cannot be repaired as soon as possible with the means at hand."[350] In consequence, 3.(H)/11 had to destroy all of its seven aircraft, and on 2 January 1943, nine of 7./JG 52's Bf 109s were blown up by their own personnel.[351] That same day the German troops withdrew across the Terek River at Mozdok. By this time, their retreat columns towards Mineralnyye Vody, 80 miles north-west of Mozdok, were covered from the air by nothing more than *Ofw.* Alfred Grislawski's 7./JG 52 *Schwarm*. Mozdok was seized by the Soviet 58th Army on 3 January and the next day 4 VA's 217 IAD started operating from JG 52's old airbase at Soldatskaya.[352]

Meanwhile, in the north-west, the forward elements of German XVII. *Armee* started to abandon their positions north-east of the Black Sea port of Tuapse. In order to cover this retreat, I./KG 51 was instructed to carry out two bombings of Tuapse on 4 January.[353] Soviet 5 VA's 236 IAD scrambled against these attacks, but achieved little. 975 IAP's *Serzh.* Shcherbina claimed a Ju 88 (which actually force-landed in friendly territory with 20 per cent damage) while the LaGG-3 piloted by 269 IAP's *Serzh.* Ivchenko was shot down.[354]

In the north-eastern Caucasus, Soviet Stalingrad Front merged with the Southern Front – the designation Stalingrad Front being abandoned – and continued to push LVII. *Panzerkorps* westwards, against Rostov. On 7 January, LVII. *Panzerkorps* was ousted from Zimovniki. A temporary and local German superiority in the air was secured when II./JG 52 clashed with the elite 3 GIAP that day – with the latter losing five La-5s, plus two pilots killed and two wounded, against only one Bf 109 shot down. With one of the destroyed La-5s, *Lt.* Heinz Schmidt of 5./JG 52 attained his 125th victory. Mostly without interference from Soviet fighters over the following days, KG 51's Ju 88s were in constant action against the advancing Soviet troops. The Ju 88 crews were instructed to carry out individual free hunts against enemy march columns in the Zimovniki area. But this did not prevent mobile elements of Southern Front from advancing rapidly westwards, along the Sal River, farther to the north-west. After crossing the Sal, the 2nd Guards Army crossed the Manych River south of the Don and seized Vesyolyy on 8 January, and the 3rd Guards Tank Corps of 51st Army halted its advance only at Manychskaya on the Don – less than 20 miles from Rostov.

The latter advance, which was carried out swiftly across the steppe while skilfully avoiding contact with enemy troops, caught the Germans by surprise. Quite unexpectedly the crews of KG 51 found themselves coming under anti-aircraft fire from an area they had believed was in friendly hands. On 8 January, KG 51's *Geschwaderkommodore*, *Oberst* Heinrich Conrady, was killed when his Ju 88 sustained a direct flak hit over the Manychskaya bridgehead. This aircraft was one out of three lost by KG 51 to enemy activity on this day.[355] "From this day on, [KG 51] was pursued by bad luck," wrote historian Wolfgang Dierich in KG 51's chronicle. "In only three days, I. *Gruppe* lost thirteen crews!"[356]

Meanwhile, 8 VA made an effort to neutralise the large Ju 52 airfield at Salsk from the air. 2 SAK was assigned the task, and on 5 and 6 January its fighters carried out several reconnaissance flights over the Salsk airbase in order to map the exact locations of the parking grounds and the flak nests. The attack was scheduled to take place on 7 January, but adverse weather conditions compelled the Soviet commanders to postpone the attacks for two days.

Two attempts by 214 ShAD/2 SAK were repulsed by German fighters,[357] while the third, on 9 January, was more successful – with 72

---

## Soviet aviation available to support the Transcaucasus Front on 1 January 1943

4 VA: 216 SAD, 217 IAD, 229 IAD, 218 NBAD, 219 BAD, 230 ShAD, 288 BAP, 446 SAP, 750 SAP.

5 VA: 236 IAD, 295 IAD, 132 BAD, 763 LBAP, 718 SAP, 742 RAP.

Army aviation: 974 BAP.

Also available for operations in the Caucasus were:

VVS ChF: 62 IAB (6 GIAP, 7 IAP, 25 IAP, 32 IAP, 62 IAP), 63 BAB (5 GMTAP, 40 BAP), 18 ShAP, 23 ShAP, 46 ShAP 47 ShAP, 36 BAP, 119 MRAP, plus four reconnaissance *Eskadrilyas*.

ADD: 50 AD.

PVO: 105 IAD (with 182 IAP, 234 IAP, 738 IAP, and 822 IAP).

---

*Ofw. Alfred Grislawski enjoys a break between combat missions to read a letter from his fiancée in Germany, Ilse Hartmeyer. Grislawski served with III./JG 52 from the autumn of 1940, and attained his first victory in September 1941. He survived 800 combat missions,* *was credited with 132 aerial victories and awarded with the Knight's Cross with Oak Leaves. Alfred Grislawski passed away on 19 September 2003. (Grislawski)*

Ju 52s knocked out, according to Soviet sources. This operation has acquired a certain notoriety in Soviet and Russian accounts, contrary to accounts based on German sources, and thus is regarded as one of the curiosities of the air war in the East. Even if other Soviet sources date this incident on 2 January 1943 (erroneously), nothing on the German side even remotely supports the Soviet claims of success. The loss statistics recorded by the *Generalquartiermeister der Luftwaffe* register just one Ju 52 – of KGrzbV 50 – destroyed at Salsk on 9 January 1943 (and none on 2 January 1943). These statistics indeed may be wrong for this date, but historian Joel S. A. Hayward made an important point when he remarked that "had Soviet squadrons destroyed any aircraft at Salsk that day, all three German commanders [Pickert, Fiebig, and von Richthofen] would have recorded that fact in their diaries"[358] – which none of them did.

The attackers' own report of this raid, located in the TsAMO archives in Podolsk, however, sheds some new light on the circumstances:

"On 9 January 1943, the commander of 622 ShAP, *Mayor* Yemelyanov, and 236 IAP's commander, *Kapitan* Petukhov, assigned the combat task to the *Shturmovik* task force's leader, *Eskadrilya* commander *Kapitan* Bakhtin, and the leader of the escort fighter group, *Eskadrilya* commander *St. Lt.* Belousov. (. . .)

At 10.30 hrs, the group of seven 622 ShAP Il-2s escorted by seven 236 IAP Yak-1s took off to carry out the strafing attack against the [Salsk] airfield. While assembling their formation, a radio link between the two airborne groups and the ground control was established. During the approach flight, our airmen took advantage of the low cloud ceiling to escape detection. The strafing run was performed from the south, with our aircraft diving out of the clouds. The enemy was apparently caught by surprise. Our airmen remained over the target between 11.08 and 11.23 hrs, i.e. 15 minutes, during which time six strafing runs were carried out. During the first two runs the crews selected their targets individually and dropped their bombs from 400m altitude. During the following runs the crews attacked their targets with RS projectiles, cannon and machine gun fire. FAB-100 bombs were used. A total of twenty-six FAB-100s, fifty RS-82s, 1,386 VYa cannon shells, 300 ShVAK cannon shells, 120 BS rounds, and 3,830 ShKAS rounds was expended. A total of seventy-two Ju 52 aircraft

were damaged and destroyed as a result of the raid *according to an official account from workers on the airfield that day*. [author's italics.] Another two Ju 52s were shot down over the airfield. Il-2 pilot *M.Lt.* Mordovtsev shot down one Ju 52 that attempted to land, and one Me 109 which tried to attack the *Shturmoviks*. During the withdrawal from the target area, the air gunner *Serzh*. Svetlishnev shot down one Me 109 that tried to take off. The escort fighters carried out an air combat with four Me 109s during the strafing raid. As a result, *St. Lt.* Lipin shot down one Me 109.

After the first strafing run the enemy's anti-aircraft artillery opened up with heavy fire against the *Shturmoviks*. Up to seven anti-aircraft batteries were observed. Losses: two Il-2s were hit by anti-aircraft fire and belly-landed in enemy-held territory. Two Yak-1s failed to return from the mission."[359]

Thus it is clear that the disputed claims for 72 destroyed or damaged Ju 52s originated from apparently less than reliable *Hiwis* at Salsk. In conclusion, this air operation – which in Soviet literature, even military lectures, has been portrayed as a model example of a successful airbase attack – was in fact a failure.

To 236 IAP, the operations on 9 January were quite costly. *St.Serzh.* Kubanov and *Serzh*. Kochetov were posted as missing from the mission against Salsk – with the latter returning to base on foot.[360] The pilots of 236 IAP had barely landed after the Salsk mission before they were ordered to escort Il-2s which were to attack a German vehicle column at Zimovniki. Led by *Kapitan* Aleksandr Shvaryov, five 236 IAP Yak-1s took off.[361] In the target area, 236 and 296 IAP's Yak-1s and the Il-2s of 206 ShAD were attacked by *Hptm.* Johannes Steinhoff and *Oblt.* Gerhard Barkhorn with their respective wingmen. The two German aces each claimed two Yak-1s shot down and withdrew without loss. Back at the airfield at Gigant, Steinhoff filed his 140th and 141st, and Barkhorn his 103rd and 104th victories. 236 IAP recorded that initially in that particular combat, one Yak-1 was shot down and another force-landed with severe battle damage. The pilot of the latter, *M.Lt.* Vasiliyev, managed to escape from his downed aircraft before a Bf 109 – most definitely piloted by Barkhorn – swept down to set it ablaze in a strafing run. *Kapitan* Shvaryov and *St. Serzh.* N. V. Davydov failed to return, although Shvaryov survived and later returned to his unit.[362] Steinhoff's two claims probably were against 296 IAP, which reported two Yak-1s lost to Bf 109s in this combat.[363]

The Ju 88s of KG 51 continued to bomb the Soviet Manychskaya bridgehead east of Rostov. *Hptm.* Klaus Häberlen carried out four sorties here on 10 January.[364] That day, eight Yak-1s of the crack 9 GIAP were dispatched to provide the Soviet troops at Manychskaya with air support. The Yaks were divided into two groups – one led by *St.Lt.* Aleksey Alelyukhin and one led by the regimental commander, Hero of the Soviet Union *Podpolkovnik* Lev Shestakov. *St.Lt.* Arkadiy Kovachevich, Shestakov's wingman on that mission, recalled: "There were thick clouds and we failed to spot any German aircraft, so Shestakov instructed us to go down below the clouds to see if we could find any enemy planes there. Meanwhile he remained above the clouds. Then we lost him, and suddenly we heard his voice on the radio reporting air combat."[365]

Meantime, *Oblt.* Gerhard Barkhorn's 4./JG 52 *Schwarm* spotted and attacked a group of eight Il-2s which were strafing German ground troops in the River Sal area. Flying alone, Shestakov arrived just in time to see a Bf 109 latch on to the tail of an Il-2 and close to within firing position. It was *Uffz.* Hans Ellendt's 'White 2.' Lev Shestakov opened the throttles wide and was behind the '109, but not before it had dealt the Il-2 a decisive burst of fire. The Il-2 plunged into the ground.[366] Hans Ellendt recalled: "I shot down an Il-2 but at that moment I became aware of a dark shadow behind me. I radioed my wingman to ask if it was him, but in the next second I discovered that it was a Yak-1. Then there was a loud bang and my tailfin had gone. I pulled the stick as hard as possible and in doing so, I was able to prevent my '109 from going down steeply. I descended slowly and made a crash landing in no-man's land. I was lucky that my fighter did not explode on impact."[367]

*Podpolkovnik* Shestakov was unable to see that he had actually shot down his oppenent (Shestakov only claimed a damaged Bf 109), since he was immediately embroiled with *Oblt.* Barkhorn. "Over the radio our commander reported that his aircraft had been hit in the tail. We tried to find him, but in vain. Next he reported that he was going to make a forced landing," said Arkadiy Kovachevich.[368] Hemmed in by Barkhorn and his wingman, Shestakov's Yak-1 was severely hit. The Soviet ace put down his Yak-1 on its belly, but that was not the end of the story. Barkhorn came diving down to finish off the aircraft, strafing the crash-landed Soviet fighter. Shestakov was lucky to survive with injuries.[369] His

completely destroyed aircraft was filed by Gerhard Barkhorn as his 105th victory.

Meanwhile, farther south, 8 VA's other elite unit, 3 GIAP, was also dealt a severe loss at the hands of another II./JG 52 veteran, *Hptm.* Rudolf Resch. Flying as *Lt.* Helmut Lipfert's wingman, Resch attacked a pair of La-5s over the Manych, and shot down both within less than two minutes. Little did Resch know that his victims were the commander of 3 GIAP, *Polkovnik* Daniil Shpak, and the *Eskadrilya* commander *Kapitan* Stepan Shtanukhin.[370] For 3 GIAP, 10 January 1943 was indeed a gloomy day. No less than ten of that unit's La-5 pilots failed to return from reconnaissance missions over the Manych. However, after several days missing, eight pilots were safe and sound – they had lost their orientation due to poor visibility and made landings on the steppe. However, Shpak and Shtanukhin never returned. *Polkovnik* Shpak was a veteran who had been credited with six individual and five shared victories. Only forty years later were their fates elucidated when a group of schoolchildren by chance happened upon their remains.

In the south, it was German I. *Panzerarmee's* sheer luck that adverse weather conditions and an increased distance from the Soviet airfields to the combat zone limited 4 VA's ability to intervene in full force against the supply line from Mineralnyye Vody to Rostov. But Hitler's hope of holding the River Kuma sector as a springboard for a renewed offensive in the spring of 1943 was frustrated when tanks of Transcaucasus Front's Northern Groupment crossed the Kuma and entered Mineralnyye Vody on 10 January. Here they wrought havoc among German military equipment waiting to be evacuated – including much of III./JG 52's technical equipment. German trains loaded with tanks and ammunition were destroyed.

In the north-western Caucasus, the offensive which should have been initiated by Soviet Transcaucasus Front's Black Sea Groupment had been delayed due to an adverse logistical situation. But on 11 January they finally launched Operation "*Gory*" (Mountain). The 18th, 46th, and 56th Armies attacked to the north from the sector between Tuapse and Novorossiysk, with the aim of seizing Krasnodar and blocking *Heeresgruppe A's* retreat from the south. 5 VA was instructed to support this offensive with the new air offensive doctrine, comprising three stages – preparatory air attacks, air support for the troops, and air cover for the troops, all according to the new Field Manual PU-43. For this purpose, 5 VA had been reinforced and could field 270 aircraft, including 90 I-16s and I-153s, and 60 bombers (Bostons,

*Three of the most successful pilots of 7./JG 52 during the Battle of the Caucasus. From the left: Hans Dammers (113 victories, KIA 17 March 1944), Alfred Grislawski (132 victories); and Edmund Rossmann (93 victories, POW 9 July 1943). Edmund Rossmann passed away on 4 April 2005. (Grislawski)*

*A victorious Soviet fighter pilot proudly poses next to the wreck of a Ju 87 which he has shot down.*

Il-4s, SBs and U-2s).[371] But the realities of combat would put many obstacles in the path of the new Soviet air doctrine.

5 VA opened the offensive by launching a "preparatory attack" against the German airfield at Krasnodar on 11 January. The attack nevertheless failed – leading only to three I-16 pilots from 975 IAP being lost to Krasnodar's AAA.[372] 611 and 975 IAP continued to raid the airfield at Krasnodar for two days and claimed to have destroyed nine German aircraft on the ground. Meanwhile, the mountainous and forested terrain rendered any air support for the ground troops difficult. On 12 January, on the Black Sea Groupment's western flank, in the Novorossiysk region, the 47th Army launched Operation "More" (Sea). This offensive aimed at seizing Novorossiysk and the Taman Peninsula, thus depriving *Heeresgruppe A* of the possibility of evacuating through this area.

Operation "*More*" was supported by *General-Mayor* Pavel Kvade's MAG NOR – the Soviet Black Sea Fleet Air Force's special Naval Aviation Group of the Novorossiysk Defence Region. With its main base at Gelendzhik, MAG NOR numbered 90 aircraft, divided between VVS ChF's 18 ShAP, 47 ShAP, 6 GIAP, 62 IAP, and 119 MRAP. Support for "*More*" was also temporarily furnished by *Polkovnik* Nikolay Tokarev's 63 BAB/VVS ChF, which comprised 40 BAP/VVS ChF (Pe-2s) and 5 GMTAP/VVS ChF (Il-4s).

A handful of Ju 87 crews from St.G 77's *Ergänzungsstaffel* did whatever they could to intervene in the ground fighting, but they were hopelessly outnumbered and lost their *Staffelkapitän*, Knight's Cross holder *Oblt*. Hans-Karl Sattler, on 13 January. Instead, Soviet aircraft constantly attacked the German and Rumanian troop positions and march columns in this area. These air operations were carried out only with small formations, but still had an important psychological impact on the harassed ground troops – who saw no intervention from Axis fighters. This was pointed out in a report to the German Army High Command.[373] Thus, on 13 January, three Il-2 groups from 47 ShAP/VVS ChF attacked the Germans in Akhtyrskaya and Abinskaya and five other Il-2s dropped 16 bombs against troops in Mingrelskaya village. At noon that day, 63 BAB/VVS ChF dispatched two 40 BAP Pe-2s and four 5 GMTAP Il-4s to bomb Abinskaya's railway station.

The fighter pilots of 5 VA's 236 IAD logged a total of 190 combat sorties between 9 and 13 January,[374] without encountering much opposition in the air. During these missions, only one victory was claimed by 236 IAD (in a scrap with 13./JG 52 over Krasnodar on 11 January), while five of its own fighters were lost to ground fire.[375] Indeed, ground fire was the main danger to the Soviet airmen who operated in this sector, and on 14 January, *St.Lt.* A. A. Kuksin of 5 VA's 611 IAP landed his aircraft in German-held territory south of Abinskaya and picked up

*St. Serzh.* N. F. Yevseyev, whose I-153 had been shot down by anti-aircraft guns.[376]

On 15 January, Abinskaya was raided again by Pe-2s and Il-4s from 40 BAP and 5 GMTAP of VVS ChF's 63 BAB. On 16 January, VVS ChF's 47 ShAP (Il-2s) and 62 IAP (I-15s and I-153s), escorted by I-16s from 5 VA, carried out 167 offensive sorties against railways, march columns, and troop positions in the Azovskaya - Severskaya - Ilinskiy - Yerivanskaya area in support of Operation "More." The Soviet airmen claimed to have destroyed 27 trucks, ten railway cars, and nine anti-aircraft guns, losing only one Il-2 to enemy fighter interception during these attacks.

*Polkovnik* Tokarev directed the Pe-2s and Il-4s of his 63 BAB/VVS ChF against German supply shipping across the Straits of Kerch. But by that time, 5 VA started to experience a serious shortage of bombs due to supply problems.[377] On 16 and 17 January, 63 BAB/VVS ChF could cary out only 35 sorties against the ports of Taman and Kerch. On 17 January, eight crews from 5 GMTAP and two from 40 BAP claimed to have sunk the tow *Daniel* and damaged a barge in the port of Kerch.[378]

Just like the Stuka airmen of Erg/St.G 77, 13./JG 52's Slovakian airmen experienced great difficulties in this area. Early on 17 January, two 13./JG 52 pilots clashed with six I-16s from 975 IAP/236 IAD. The latter pilots shot down *Catnik* Jozef Vincúr's Bf 109 (*Starshina* Shadrin and *Serzh.* Lebedev filed claims) without loss to themselves.[379] A few hours later, the Slovak *Catnik* Ján Reznák avenged this loss by downing the I-153 piloted by 975 IAP's *Kapitan* Filatov, but on the next mission that day Reznák's Bf 109 E-4 was badly shot up by *Mayor* Shirov from 236 IAD's staff unit (flying a LaGG-3).[380]

The Slovakian fighter pilots received welcome reinforcements when *Ofw.* Grislawski's 7./JG 52 was shifted from Armavir to Krasnodar. Grislawski opened up by shooting down two Il-2s in the morning of 18 January.[381] These marked Grislawski's personal 90th and 91st victories, and 7./JG 52's 600th and 601st victories. However, when Grislawski and his wingman, *Lt.* Erich Hartmann, bounced a formation of I-16s on the next mission that day, they were charged from behind by 611 IAP's *Kapitan* Shitikov, who raked Grislawski's Bf 109 and set it ablaze. The German pilot was able to nurse his burning '109 back over the German lines, where he baled out. Later he was picked up by Hartmann in a Fi 156 Storch.[382]

Soviet Black Sea Groupment failed to achieve any decisive breakthrough, due in part to the problems of supply. After seven days of fighting, the battle between the Black Sea Groupment and German XVII. *Armee* south of Krasnodar calmed down. A short while later, MAG NOR's commander, *General-Mayor* Kvade, was replaced by *Podpolkovnik* Rozhdestvenskiy.

In the north-east, Soviet Southern Front and 8 VA met with increasing difficulties, particularly regarding the supply situation, during the offensive against Rostov and Salsk. On 16 January, the entire 268 IAD (9 GIAP, 31 GIAP, 296 IAP) was grounded due to a complete lack of fuel and pressurised oxygen at the forward airfield at Kotelnikovo. 268 IAD's various logbooks repeatedly make reference to the severe fuel crisis through the remainder of January and most of February 1943.[383]

Airborne supplies by the Li-2s – licence-built, American-designed DC-3s, previously designated PS-84s by the Soviets – of 1 AD/ADD could only barely make up for the logistical problems created by strung-out supply lines. The 51st Army advanced slowly westwards from Zimovniki and reached Proletarskaya on 16 January. With the enemy now only 15 miles north-east of the Junkers transporters' main base at Salsk, the Germans were forced to abandon the airfield. Nevertheless, SS-Panzerdivision Wiking's Tiger tanks and Luftwaffe attacks managed to hold the Soviets at bay near Proletarskaya for four days. The low-level strafings in this area on 16 January cost the life of II./JG 52's twenty-three victory ace Ofw. Franz Gilhaus, whose Bf 109 was hit and brought down by ground fire.

When Polkovnik Ivan Georgiyev's 53 AD arrived (from 15 January onward) to join the supply flights to Southern Front, the situation improved somewhat. This unit was equipped with old four-engine TB-3s, capable of carrying a cargo of over five tons. On 20 January, assault troops of Soviet 51st Army broke through at Proletarskaya and shortly afterwards reached the airfield at Salsk. Here, however, they found only one abandoned transport, a Ju 86. Four days previously, the Junkers transporters had been pulled out of the endangered northern Caucasus and transferred to Zverevo, 70 miles north-east of Rostov.

But the increased pace of Southern Front's offensive placed the forward elements of Stab, II., and III./JG 52 in a difficult situation. As Soviet troops rolled into Salsk, two II./JG 52 pilots managed to take off from this airfield in their Bf 109s at the last moment and flew to Gigant. But this location was also under threat. The 28th Army of the original Southern Front – which was advancing from the Kalmyk Steppe in the south-east – outflanked SS-Panzerdivision Wiking and approached Gigant, which also had to be abandoned by the German fighters. With only seven serviceable Bf 109s remaining, Oblt. Günther Rall's III./JG 52 Gigant detachment received instructions to hand over its aircraft to II./JG 52 and withdraw to Taganrog for rest and refit. During its eleven days of operations from Gigant, Rall's detachment had carried out mainly strafing attacks in support of their own troops, claiming the destruction of 140 trucks and only two aerial victories.[384] II./JG 52 meanwhile was shifted back to Sernovoyy, and then from there to Rostov-North.

In capturing Gigant on 23 January, the forward troops of 28th Army linked up with forward elements of 4th and 5th Guards Cavalry Corps who had advanced from the south, far ahead of the main body of Transcaucasus Front's Northern Groupment. These forces now made a united thrust toward Rostov from the south-east, pushing the SS Panzer troops towards Yegorlykskaya, about 60 miles from Rostov. Thus the Southern Front was able to threaten the German bottleneck at Rostov from two directions – from the left bank of the River Manych in the south-east, and from Manychskaya at the mouth of the Manych in the east.

The most immediate threat still came from the 3rd Guards Tank Corps at Manychskaya, less than 20 miles to the east of Rostov, and Generalfeldmarschall von Manstein, commander of Heeresgruppe Don, concentrated his counter-attack against this bridgehead. On 23 January von Manstein attacked Manychskaya from two directions – using the 11th Panzerdivision from the north, and 16th Infantry Division (which had retreated from Elista in the Kalmyk Steppe) from the south. Again, the team of von Manstein and von Richthofen cooperated splendidly. Generaloberst von Richthofen ordered IV. Fliegerkorps to focus on attacks against Manychskaya, and instructed his airmen: "The main task is to carry out relentless rolling attacks in order to pave the way forward for the three ground divisions."[385] The combined effect of this onslaught forced the 3rd Guards Tank Corps out of Manychskaya on 25 January.

While this battle raged, Soviet Transcaucasus Front's Northern Groupment was reformed into the independent North-Caucasian Front. Its 4th and 5th Guards Cavalry corps – followed by the 44th and 58th Armies – joined forces with Southern Front's 28th Army to reach Rostov from the south-east. They seized Yegorlykskaya on 26 January and assaulted Mechetinskaya, ten miles farther north-west. This threatened to completely outflank German LII. Armeekorps – the retrograde force of I. Panzerarmee, which was withdrawing from Armavir to Tikhoretsk, 60 miles south-west of

Lt. Vladimir Levitan (right) of 166 IAP/4 VA next to his LaGG-3 in the Caucasus in early 1943. Levitan earned fame for his many daring low-level attacks during the first years of the war. In just two months of combat over the so-called Kuban area in the north-western Caucasus in early 1943, he was reported to have destroyed 25 motor vehicles, one locomotive and an anti-aircraft battery. The fact that Levitan was shot down three times in 1941 and 1942 testifies to the hazardous nature of his missions. He nevertheless survived the war, attaining 23 aerial victories and becoming a Hero of the Soviet Union. (Karlenko)

Mechetinskaya. The I. Panzerarmee's XXXX. Panzerkorps had taken up positions around Tikhoretsk, but in the steppe between this location and the River Manych at Salsk in the north-east there was a 50 mile-wide gap in the German lines through which Soviet 4th and 5th Guards Cavalry Corps could infiltrate.

Even if 4 VA and 8 VA were negatively affected by increasing distances between their airfields and the front lines, some of the missions carried out against the German withdrawal routes were met with considerable success. On 26 January, the 7 GShAP Shturmovik pilots, Lt. S. I. Smirnov and M.Lt. S. A. Slepnov, hit four trains loaded with ammunition and fuel at Malorossiyskiy's railway station – on the railroad from Tikhoretsk to Rostov – with the result that the entire railway station burned down. The blazing inferno from the exploding ammunition trains could be seen from a distance of 20 miles and was visible during the rest of the day. With the station infrastructure destroyed, the railway was paralysed for four days.

But Fliegerkorps IV's intervention ensured that 1. Panzerarmee's escape route north to Rostov remained open and, on 26 January, LII. Armeekorps managed to complete its withdrawal across the Kuban River at Kropotkin, 40 miles south-east of Tikhoretsk. The German retreat could continue, albeit at the price of much of their equipment. "Blown vehicles and destroyed equipment, burned-out ration stores and euthanised horses littered the routes," wrote German historian Wilhelm Tieke. "By the time they reached Rostov the 3rd Panzerdivision had lost half of its trucks and tanks."[386]

Von Richthofen's orders for 26 January read: "Fliegerkorps IV, reinforced through ZG 1, shall concentrate on supporting 4. Panzerarmee's retrograde battles on the Manych rivermouth."[387] Even the last remnants of the Rumanian Eastern Front aviation (which had been re-designated *Corpul Aerian*) – since 21 January subordinated to KG 51 as its *NachtStaffel* [388] – regularly flew against Soviet troop concentrations at the Manych.[389]

2./KG 51's *Hptm.* Klaus Häberlen, who on 27 January carried out three sorties, all low-level attacks against Soviet troops on the Yegorlykskaya - Mechetinskaya battlefield, recalled: "Our attacks were met with great success, and we destroyed large quantities of Russian war equipment."[390] This is confirmed by Soviet reports. By this time, Soviet 2nd Guards Army had only 29 tanks left. The Army's 5th Mechanised Guards Corps was down to a strength of 2,200 men and seven tanks.

Southern Front's Headquarters reported: "The forces of the Front continued its offensive operations toward the Bataysk - Rostov sector on 27 January. But due to stubborn resistance and enemy counter-attacks along the entire advance front, no real progress could be made. Our troops were even pushed back 3 - 5 kilometres near Bolshaya Talovaya and Donskoy. Enemy aviation bombed the combat formations of the advancing 51st and 28th armies throughout the day."[391]

Most of KG 51's missions escaped the attention of Soviet fighters, but on 27 January, 8 VA's 31 GIAP (formerly 273 IAP) intervened with four Yak-1s against one of KG 51's operations. The aces *St.Lt.* Aleksey Reshetov and *Lt.* Fotiy Morozov worked in tandem to set one Ju 88 ablaze. Reshetov then made a firing pass against the two German crew as they hung in their parachute straps.[392] In return, both Reshetov's and Morozov's Yak-1s were hit by the gunners of other Ju 88s. *Lt.* Nikolay Glazov meanwhile bagged a second Ju 88. KG 51 actually lost two aircraft.[393] *Oblt.* Alfons "Ali" Berger – one of I./KG 51's most experienced pilots, who had completed more than 300 combat sorties – was killed when his Ju 88 exploded only a few feet above the ground. Miraculously, two men from his crew survived, albeit with wounds. "This was observed by *Lt.* Karl-Heinz Geruschke, who immediately landed in front of the Russians and picked up the two injured comrades," recalled *Hptm.* Häberlen.[394] Although Klaus Häberlen recalled Berger's Ju 88 as being shot down by anti-aircraft fire, the official loss report registered it as having been downed by Soviet fighters.[395]

Häberlen made another four missions against the Mechetinskaya battlefield on 28 January[396] and the next day *Generaloberst* von Richthofen noted: "All available aviation forces are concentrated against the Russians south of Rostov. The Russians are making deep penetrations in large numbers – but without armour, only with infantry and cavalry. Our bombs inflict terrible losses among the masses of enemy troops."[397]

Although rarely evoked in accounts, IV. *Fliegerkorps'* intense air attacks against the Southern Front's troops on both sides of the River Manych during these days – which in combination with von Manstein's counter-attack prevented Soviet Southern Front from closing the escape route through Rostov – represented some of the most significant air operations of the Second World War. Had Rostov been seized before the fourth week in January 1943 and I. *Panzerarmee* been trapped in the Caucasus and unable to join IV. *Panzerarmee* north of Rostov, the consequences would have been incalculable.

Meanwhile, II./JG 52 had regained its previous fighting strength after some chaotic days of airfield changes. Reinforced by the Bf 109s that III./JG 52 had left behind, this *Jagdgruppe* was now well-accommodated at the large aerodrome Rostov-North. In incessant action over the battlefields on both sides of the River Manych, its pilots managed to suppress much of 8 VA's air activity. "The Messerschmitts offered a very tough resistance," 437 IAP's *Lt.* Pavel Boykov expressed it.[398] On 30 January, sixteen 190 ShAP Il-2s escorted by eighteen La-5s from 437 IAP managed to attack a German tank column on the road from Manych to Rostov . But on the return flight, the Soviet airmen came under attack from *Hptm.* Steinhoff's fighters. In the ensuing combat, the La-5 pilots managed to save the Il-2s – but in doing so lost two pilots, including Sergey Filippov, an ace with eight victories, with another two pilots being seriously injured. II./JG 52's *Hptm.* Rudolf Resch and *Lt.* Helmut Lipfert each claimed one La-5. (Earlier that day, *Hptm.* Resch had claimed two other La-5s.) Although 437 IAP filed hollow victory claims – nine Bf 109s! – no losses can be found in II./JG 52's registers.[399]

On 30 January, *Hptm.* Klaus Häberlen conducted no less than eight combat missions, including his 200th.[400] On 31 January, KG 51 managed to destroy the 51st Army's headquarters south-east of Salsk – as reported by 8 VA: "It is clear that the enemy knew the exact location of the 51st Army's Headquarters in the Politodelskoye settlement. 10 Ju 88s and He 111s took part in the raid. The enemy aircraft had dived out of the clouds and dropped

thirty 100 - 250 kg bombs from an altitude of 600 - 500 metres. As a result, the communications centre, the working offices of the chief-of-staff, of the commander of the Headquarter's operational department, and of the operational duty officer, were completely destroyed. Up to twenty buildings – Headquarters personnel billets – were also destroyed. A large number of men and horses were killed."[401]

Meanwhile, I. *Panzerarmee's* XXXX. *Panzerkorps* established contact with elements of IV. *Panzerarmee's* LVII. *Panzerkorps* in the area between Tikhoretsk and Mechetinskaya, while a detachment from the 3rd *Panzerdivision* blocked Soviet thrusts at Novo Aleksandrovka, around 30 miles east of Kropotkin. Manstein's army group now held a fragile bridgehead in a half circle around 40 to 50 miles east and south-east of Rostov and connecting with XXXX. *Panzerkorps* at Tikhoretsk, 100 miles south of Rostov.

In about a month, the Soviets had swept away the threat against their oil fields in the Caucasus. This of course was of incredible value, but the task of eliminating *Heeresgruppe A* had yet to be completed. Heavy preparations were made in order to wipe out German XVII. *Armee* and parts of 1. *Panzerarmee*, which were gathering in what would become the so-called "Kuban Bridgehead," based on Novorossiysk and Krasnodar in the north-western Caucasus. Thus, 5 VA was reinforced with sixty LaGG-3s and twenty Il-2s and Soviet air superiority in this region became further bolstered. This made it practically impossible for German aerial reconnaissance to carry out any missions here. Three German reconnaissance aircraft were lost in this area on 27 January. 164 IAP's *St.Serzh.* Lev Shimanchik survived ramming an Fw 189 – piloted by 7.(H)/32's *Fw.* Friedrich Nitsche, who also survived, albeit with injuries, while his two crew members were killed. Within a short while, the skies above the Kuban bridgehead would be the scene of the heaviest air fighting to date on the Eastern Front.

In analysing the Soviet offensive across the Caucasus in January 1943, it is obvious that although operating with very limited forces, the *Luftwaffe* gave a most valuable contribution to the German withdrawal. By pulling together most of what was available, *Luftwaffe* forces were able to intervene forcefully at the most critical points. In doing so, they were able to benefit from the fact that Soviet 4 VA and 8 VA were hampered by several factors.

Due to the vast no-man's land from Armavir to the region north of Salsk – an area where advancing Soviet cavalry forces and retreating German columns were virtually intermingled – the distance from 4 VA's airfields to the battlefield (up to 200 miles) allowed no swift intervention from 4 VA fighters and limited the number of sorties that could be made each day. Even if 4 VA carried out a total of 2,091 combat sorties through January 1943, it claimed only 12 enemy aircraft shot down in the course of these operations (four Ju 88s, three Bf 110s, two Bf 109s, two Fw 189s, and a Ju 52). Combat losses were 21 (eight Il-2s, four Bostons, four LaGG-3s, four I-16s, and a Pe-2).[402]

8 VA, with the bulk of its fighters tied up in the air blockade of Stalingrad, could only allocate limited forces to provide Southern Front's troops with air cover. Only in the west was the Soviet aviation, 5 VA and VVS ChF, able to achieve full air superiority, but here shortages of supplies held back Soviet efforts. (5 VA's shortage of bombs was overcome temporarily only when Soviet troops seized St.G 77's old bomb storage at Belorechenskaya aerodrome on 28 January.) 5 VA filed a total of 20 combat losses and ten aerial victories through January 1943[403] – an indication of the weak resistance that met the air army.

Due to incomplete German files from this period, the exact number of *Luftwaffe* aircraft shot down during the Battle of the Caucasus in January 1943 will never be known. For instance, historian Milan Krajci has identified at least four 13./JG 52 Bf 109s shot down or severely damaged in combat in January 1943,[404] but only one of them – a damaged fighter able to return to base – can be found in the *Luftwaffe Generalquartiermeister* list. Similarly, the loss of *Ofw.* Alfred Grislawski's 7./JG 52 Bf 109 does not appear in the latter files as shot down on 18 January 1943 (which is confirmed by both Grislawski's logbook and his own memory); instead it can be found registered as "destroyed by own troops" on 2 January 1943.[405] It may be assumed that the numbers of *Luftwaffe* and Soviet aircraft shot down during the Battle of the Caucasus in January 1943 were about equal.

# Chapter Seventeen

# Soviet victory in the air over Stalingrad

On 30 December 1942, the *Stavka* ordered *General-Leytenant* Konstantin Rokossovskiy's Don Front to eliminate the encircled German VI. *Armee* in the Stalingrad cauldron. For this purpose, the Don Front was assigned with the 57th, 62nd and 64th Armies from the Stalingrad Front, which meant that Rokossovskiy could muster 212,000 soldiers, 6,500 artillery pieces and 250 tanks. Although *Generaloberst* von Paulus' surrounded troops enjoyed a slight numerical superiority over the Don Front,[406] the situation was utterly desperate for the Germans. In early January 1943, the Red Army's iron ring around Stalingrad had been strengthened after *Generaloberst* Hoth's attempt to break the encirclement from the south had failed. The VVS had effectively turned *Reichsmarschall* Hermann Göring's air bridge to Stalingrad into mere illusion. Instead of the daily 500 tons of supplies that Göring had promised von Paulus, in December 1942 the *Luftwaffe* could not even manage a daily average of 120 tons. With rations in VI. *Armee* reduced to 50 grams of bread per soldier each day,[407] morale was breaking down. From early January 1943, an increasing number of German soldiers began to desert to the Red Army troops who surrounded Stalingrad.[408]

The air blockade, meanwhile, was upheld by *General* Sergey Rudenko's 16 VA – which numbered around 300 aircraft in early January 1943 – with support from ADD forces. 17 and 50 AD had been the main elements of the ADD since the Battle of Stalingrad commenced, but from late 1942, 1 AD, 3 AD, 24 AD, 53 AD and 62 AD also took part in the battle. 8 VA and 17 VA, the two other VVS KA air armies which initially had been engaged in the air blockade, were engaged in tactical support of the Soviet ground troops. 8 VA covered the Stalingrad Front's (later re-designated Southern Front) offensive south of the lower Don, and 17 VA covered South-western Front's southern-bound advance from the upper Don. Both these Fronts aimed at reaching Rostov and the Don's outflow into the Sea of Azov and, should this be achieved, the entire German *Heeresgruppe A* would be sealed off in the Caucasus.

Meanwhile the Germans were confronted with four major problems – holding out at Stalingrad; increasing the air supply to Stalingrad; evacuating *Heeresgruppe A* from its positions down south in the Caucasus; and holding the vital bottleneck at Rostov. For the latter task, *Generalfeldmarschall* von Manstein – commanding *Heeresgruppe Don* – had divided his forces into three *ad hoc* formations: Army Detachment Hoth south of the lower Don;

Army Detachment Hollidt at Morozovsk and Tatsinskaya immediately to the north of the lower Don; and Army Detachment Fretter-Pico with a stronghold at Millerovo farther to the north-east.

*General-Leytenant* Vatutin's South-western Front had managed to rout the Italian 8th Army at the Don north-east of Millerovo during the latter half of December. More than 50,000 Italian soldiers ended up in Soviet confinement, and South-western Front's troops came close to crushing German *Heeresgruppe Don's* entire northern flank. VIII. *Fliegerkorps'* intense air attacks against the Soviet columns out on the open steppe was the decisive factor that prevented Vatutin from achieving a swift and total victory over von Manstein. The key to this German success was the rapid creation of a new *Schwerpunkt* – the concentration of forces of *Luftflotte* 4 in general and VIII. *Fliegerkorps* in particular. Thus, the temporary weakening of *Luftflotte* 4 in December 1942 was overcome. Out of 1,715 German combat aircraft deployed on the Eastern Front on 15 January 1943, no less than 1,140 were assigned to *Luftflotte* 4.

---

## *Luftflotte* 4 in January 1943

In January 1943, the strength of *Luftflotte* 4 was rapidly revitalized through the arrival of units from other combat zones.

By early January 1943, I./KG 1, *Stab*/KG 3, I./KG 3, III./KG 3, II./KG 4, III./KG 4, II./KG 53, III./St.G 2, III./St.G 77, II./JG 3, 4./JG 54 had arrived to bolster *Luftflotte* 4 since the opening of Operation "Uranus". They were divided between *Luftwaffenkommando Don* (*Generalleutnant* Günther Korten) for the support of *Heeresgruppe B*, grouped between *Heeresgruppen Don* and *Mitte*; VIII. *Fliegerkorps* (*Generalleutnant* Martin Fiebig) for combat and supply missions in support of the 6th Army; IV. *Fliegerkorps* (*General* Kurt Pflugbeil), engaged in combat against the Soviet Southern Front; and *Luftwaffengruppe Kaukasus* (*General* Otto Dessloch), supporting the withdrawal of *Heeresgruppe A* in the Caucasus. The most powerful of these commands undoubtedly was VIII. *Fliegerkorps*.

---

*An He 111 of an unidentified unit on its way to attack a target over the Eastern Front. It carries a single SC 1000 bomb on its fuselage rack. On the Heinkel, all bombs of larger calibre than an SC 250 had to be mounted externally.*

During the battles of Tatsinskaya and Morozovsk – the two main airfields for VIII. *Fliegerkorps'* airlift operation to Stalingrad – the South-western Front sustained bloody losses. At the turn of the year, the main battle was in fact a clash fought out between German aviation – *Fliegerkorps* VIII – and the ground troops of South-western Front's 1st Guards Army at Millerovo and 3rd Guards Army at Morozovsk.

The Hs 129s from 13.(Pz)/JG 51 and II./SchG 1, and Bf 110s from I. and II./ZG 1 constituted the backbone in the defensive fight upheld by Army detachments Hollidt and Fretter-Pico. Thus, for instance, a Soviet tank attack at Antonovka near Millerovo broke down largely due to the intervention of an Hs 129 *Schwarm* from II./SchG 1 on 2 January 1943.[409]

But the German aircraft were unable to prevent the Soviets from surrounding elements of German 3rd Mountain Division north of Millerovo. The battles around Millerovo cost KG 3 two Ju 88s on 3 January, and with one of them, the *Geschwaderkommodore* – *Major* Jobst-Hinrich von Heydebreck – was posted as missing.

Soviet 3rd Guards Army pushed forward towards Morozovsk. Leaving a large quantity of supplies and equipment behind – including several Bf 109s from JG 3, Ju 87s from St.G 2, He 111s from KGrzbV 20 and KG 55, Ju 86s from KGrzbV 21, and Hs 123s from 7./SchG 1[410] – the *Luftwaffe* evacuated Morozovsk on 2 and 3 January. VIII. *Fliegerkorps'* close support units were shifted from Morozovsk to Tatsinskaya. There they were brought together into the new *Fliegerdivision Donets* (*Generalleutnant* Alfred Mahnke) – an *ad hoc* formation of VIII. *Fliegerkorps* units primarily engaged in operations to support Army Detachment Hollidt.

Air fighting during this period was restricted by adverse weather conditions. Added to I./JG 3's losses on the ground at Morozovsk were two Bf 109s with their pilots who were reported missing after a transfer flight from Pitomnik to Morozovsk on 3 January. In return, *Hptm.* Kurt Brändle, II./JG 3's *Gruppenkommandeur*, shot down one of 17 VA's Il-2s. This was JG 3's only victory on 3 January 1943 – and it was filed as Brändle's 120th, and JG 3's 4,000th victory. But eventually, the rebuilt strength of *Luftflotte* 4 melted away at a fearsome pace.

On 3 January the Soviet fighter pilots *Serzh.* Guskov and *St.Serzh.* Zhuravel of 520 IAP engaged an He 111 east of Kalach, which they shot down. The Heinkel belly-landed on Soviet territory and a total of eleven German officers, passengers in the He 111, were captured.[411] This aircraft was probably the same aircraft, commanded by 3./KG 27's *Hptm.* Werner von Hasselbach, which was reported missing after being shot down by fighters on a mission to Stalingrad.

Taking advantage of thick clouds where they could hide from 16 VA's fighters, the German transports brought in 250 tons of supplies and flew out 1,220 wounded and sick men from Stalingrad on 4 January. But the tactic of utilising bad visibility to escape fighter interception also led to high losses. *Generalleutnant* Martin Fiebig, in charge of the entire airlift operation, noted that 62 Ju 52s were lost or damaged so badly that they had to be taken out of service between 28 December 1942 and 4 January 1943. (The *Generalquartiermeister der Luftwaffe* files only list 49 for the same period.) Of this total, half were due to weather-related accidents.[412] In addition to these, 25 He 111s and four Ju 86s participating in the Stalingrad airlift are listed by *Generalquartiermeister der Luftwaffe* as destroyed or severely damaged from 28 December 1942 through 4 January 1943.

When the skies cleared temporarily on 5 January, bringing down temperatures to minus 30 degrees Celsuis, both sides upped the tempo of their combat operations in the air. North of Millerovo, 17 VA dispatched Il-2s with fighter cover and *Polkovnik* Ivan Antoshkin's Boston-equipped 221 BAD against Army Detachment Fretter-Pico's counter-attack against South-western Front's Soviet 6th Army. Operating in this sector since Christmas was *Hptm.* Heinrich Jung's 4./JG 54. Jung's *Staffel* engaged 17 VA's formations and claimed five victories. *Uffz.* Friedrich Lüer contributed with three – against two 221 BAD Bostons, and the La-5 flown by 5 GIAP's *Lt.* Petr Barsuk, who was shot down and killed whilst landing at Radchenskoye's airfield.[413] In return, 4./JG 54 lost three Bf 109s with two pilots wounded. In the area between Morozovsk and Tatsinskaya farther south, the ground-attack aircraft of SchG 1 were in action against the 3rd Guards Army. This cost the Germans two Hs 129s and a Bf 109 E-7 fighter-bomber, but resulted in much higher Soviet losses on the ground.

JG 3, relocated farther to the west at Shakhty, attained eight victories for no losses on 5 January. But the distance from Shakhty to Stalingrad was 250 miles, and this was well beyond the Bf 109's combat range. Thus, all transport flights to Stalingrad had to be carried out without any fighter escort. 16 VA's fighter pilots waited in vain for the Ju 52s to turn up in the clear blue skies over Stalingrad on 5 January. Not a single Ju 52 took off that day. "Due to icing in the air and on the ground they were not serviceable."[414] Instead the He 111s, now based at Novocherkassk, slightly north-east of Rostov, took off. Altogether 21 He 111s landed in Stalingrad, unloading 40 tons of ammunition, fuel and medical supplies. None of them was shot down by Soviet defences.

With the onset of a new low pressure system the next day, the Germans began to reconsider their initial view on the "blessings" of bad weather. After it had become impossible for them to operate from the relatively forward airbases at Morozovsk and Tatsinskaya, the long flights to Stalingrad involved great risks. *Generalleutnant* Fiebig railed at "bad visibility, icing up both at ground level and at higher altitudes, snow flurries, and very changeable conditions between take-off and landing at our destinations." Only 40 transport flights were made on 6 January and seven of the few Ju 52s that did take off were lost – at least five of them due to bad visibility or icing.[415]

That day, Soviet aircraft dropped thousands of leaflets over Stalingrad, offering the Germans surrender terms. But the Germans refused to give in. The fighting and suffering continued. A mere 160 tons of supplies were flown in to Stalingrad on 6 and 7 January. Forty-four flights were made on 8 January – at a cost of nine lost Ju 52s.[416] There was no reply from *Generaloberst* von Paulus to Rokossovskiy's message.

Early on 9 January, a huge, four-engined aircraft landed at Stalingrad's main airfield, Pitomnik. It was an Fw 200 piloted by *Ofw.* Karl Wittmann. In reply to the increased demands for long-range supply flights to Stalingrad, 1. and 3./KG 40 with Fw 200s had been shifted to the Eastern Front and re-designated KGrzbV 200, commanded by *Major* Hans-Jürgen Willers. Designed as an airliner, the Fw 200 was capable of carrying heavy cargoes over large distances. The new KGrzbV 200 was stationed at Stalino, more than 300 miles from Stalingrad, but close to the rail routes where large stocks of supplies could be brought forward. A total of seven Fw 200s landed in Pitomnik on 9 January, bringing in five tons of fuel, nine tons of ammunition and 22.5 tons of rations. On the return flight they brought 156 wounded men all the way back to Stalino.

With no positive reply from von Paulus on the offer to surrender, Rokossovskiy initiated Operation "Koltso" ("Ring") on 10 January – the attack aimed at the complete elimination of the Stalingrad *Kessel*. By that time, 16 VA had been reinforced and numbered 525 aircraft – including 215 fighters, 103 *Shturmoviks*, 105 day bombers, 87 night bombers, 15 reconnaissance aircraft, and 75 liaison and transport planes.[417]

At 08.05 hrs on 10 January, the positions of VI. *Armee* were subjected to a 55-minute aerial bombardment and artillery barrage prior to a charge mounted by troops of the Don Front. On this day, 16 VA carried out 676 sorties, including 198 by the Pe-2s of 2 BAK. In total, the pilots of 16 VA claimed the destruction of 17 tanks and 145 trucks during the course of its bombing attacks. In addition, 14 German aircraft were claimed shot down during 25 air combats.

KGrzbV 200's *Ofw.* Werner Bune crashed his Fw 200 at Pitomnik; *Ofw.* Hartig's Fw 200 came down in Pitomnik with several hits in its engines and tail; while the two Fw 200s piloted by *Ofw.* Karl Gruner and *Ofw.* Eugen Reck were shot down by the Soviets (the latter aircraft carrying 21 wounded men from Stalingrad). *Lt.* Stoye's Fw 200 was abandoned in

*A Ju 290 A-1 photographed in late 1942 during the Stalingrad airlift. Together with a Staffel of Ju 90s and the Fw 200s of I./KG 40, some of which may also be seen in this photograph, the Ju 290s were amalgamated throughout the airlift into a single, mixed Gruppe known as KGrzbV 200.*

Pitomnik. In addition, at least three Ju 52s and an He 111 from *Stab*/KG 55 were lost.

The few remaining Bf 109s in JG 3's *Platzschutz Staffel Pitomnik* plus the three last Ju 87s of St.G 2's *Stuka-Sonderstaffel*, commanded by *Lt.* Heinz Jungclausen were nonetheless in action. The *Platzschutz Staffel's Lt.* Franz Daspelgruber claimed five Soviet aircraft and *Fw.* Kurt Ebener claimed three shot down on 10 January. But this had little impact on the overall situation.

In the midst of the Soviet offensive, another new very large German transport aircraft appeared in the sky. Bringing in 10 tons of supplies, a four-engined Ju 290 piloted by *Flugkapitän* Walter Hänig landed in Pitomnik, and flew out with 78 injured men on board.

16 VA's units kept up their bombing and strafing attacks on VI. *Armee* troops in formations of six to nine aircraft, and conducted 900 combat sorties on 11 and 12 January. Without being able to achieve any success, *Platzschutzstaffel Pitomnik* lost one pilot to Soviet fighter interception on 11 January. In view of the almost total Soviet air superiority above the cauldron, it was decided to dispatch ADD bomber units by day. On 12 January the skies were almost completely clear, and between 09.45 and 22.30 hrs, the bombers of the ADD's 3 AD, 17 AD, 53 AD and 62 AD subjected the German positions at Stalingrad to constant bombardment. Heavy bombs such as FAB-500 and FAB-250 were used. *Platzschutzstaffel Pitomnik's* pilots intercepted but only managed to damage three ADD bombers; all ADD crews returned to base.[418] Instead, *Platzschutzstaffel Pitomnik* was more successful against 16 VA's units – claiming four LaGG-3s, two Il-2s and a Pe-2 for no own losses on 12 January. The aces *Lt.* Daspelgruber and *Fw.* Ebener claimed three aircraft shot down each. With one of the claimed "LaGG-3s" – in reality a Yak-1 – 512 IAP's *Lt.* Igor Ilchenko was killed.[419] Meanwhile, four Yak-1 pilots led by *St.Lt.* Mikhail Makarevich of 176 IAP/283 IAD/16 VA claimed to have shot down three

German aircraft near Bolshaya Rossoshka. The ADD's and 16 VA's air support greatly aided the troops of the Don Front in their difficult task of penetrating the well fortified lines of the defenders of VI. *Armee.*

The German crisis was further deepened when on 12-13 January the Voronezh Front – positioned along the River Don to the north of the South-western Front – launched a major offensive against the Hungarian 2nd Army near Liski, 50 miles south of Voronezh, and around 80 miles farther south against the remnants of Italian 8th Army at Novaya Kalitva. *General-Mayor* Konstantin Smirnov's 2 VA was tasked to support this offensive.

Numbering over 500 aircraft, including around 200 Il-2s and over 200 fighters, 2 VA possessed significant numerical superiority over the Axis aviation in the area – *Generalleutnant* Korten's *Luftwaffenkommando Don.* Apart from reconnaissance units – NAGr 10 (three *Staffeln*) plus 2.(F)/22 and 3.(F)/100 – and quite weak Hungarian and Italian aviation groups, Korten could muster three *Kampfgruppen* (I. and III./KG 3, and I./KG 1) and III./St.G 2 for offensive operations, plus I./JG 52. Adverse weather nevertheless kept the majority of the aircraft grounded during the first days of the Voronezh Front's offensive. 2 VA carried out 84 combat sorties on 12 January – including 39 at night-time – and claimed to have destroyed ten trucks.[420] *Luftwaffenkommando Don's* response was weak. One of 1./KG 1's Ju 88s was shot down by Soviet fighters during an attack against troops near Davydovka, 20 miles north-west of Liski, on 12 January. Although the enemy had known of the attack plan in advance, the Voronezh Front's 3rd Tank Army and 40th Army rapidly smashed *Colonel-General* Gusztav Jany's 194,000-man strong 2nd Hungarian Army into pieces and drove back what was left of Italian 8th Army.

While these dramatic events unfolded, Soviet pressure against *Fliegerkorps* VIII's transport airfields further south increased, both from the air and on the ground. On 13 January, 16 VA claimed the destruction of

*Ju 52 transports attempted to avoid detection by Soviet fighters by flying at extremely low altitude. In weather with bad visibility, this proved quite an effective method.*

29 Ju 52s and He 111s on the airfields inside the Stalingrad cauldron. Among the German losses on this day was the Ju 290 "BJ+OV," piloted by *Flugkapitän* Hänig, which crashed with 80 injured men on board shortly after take-off from Pitomnik. A second Ju 290, flown by *Major* Wiskrand, was badly shot-up by intercepting LaGG-3s and only barely made it to a protecting layer of clouds.

By this time, Soviet troops closed in on Pitomnik from three directions. On 13 January, all available Ju 88s from KG 51 were temporarily deployed to Stalingrad to support the German ground troops.[421] During the night of 13-14 January, fifty-five Ju 52s and forty-one He 111s flew in 160 tons of supplies. The next night, 14-15 January, the ADD's 17 AD claimed to have destroyed six Ju 52s on the ground during raids against Pitomnik.[422] II./KG 53, which had arrived from Germany to reinforce the air supply force on the previous day, lost at least one He 111 through Soviet bombings against Pitomnik on 14 January. Another two He 111s from 5./KG 53 crashed at Pitomnik on 14 and 15 January.

The *Platzschutzstaffel Pitomnik* made a final stand in the air over Stalingrad on 15 January. It started shortly after dawn when *Fw.* Kurt Ebener and *Uffz.* Theodor Kaiser attacked a formation of Il-4s and claimed five shot down, three of those by Kaiser. Next, they covered German transport planes by fighting formations of Soviet fighters, resulting in claims for three LaGG-3s, two of which were filed by Ebener. One of these was probably piloted by the commander of 176 IAP's 3rd *Eskadrilya*, *Lt.* Mikhailenok, who was killed in the combat with German fighters in the vicinity of Bolshaya Rossoshka that day.[423] In total, Ebener was credited with the destruction of 32 Soviet aircraft in the air fighting over the surrounded Stalingrad since mid-December 1942.

In order to reinforce the *Platzschutzstaffel Pitomnik*, II./JG 3's 69-victory ace *Oblt.* Werner Lucas and his wingman, *Fw.* Hans Frese, set out on a one-way escort mission for Ju 52s to Pitomnik during the day on 15 January. Arriving over their destination, Lucas and Frese spotted a formation of ADD Li-2s from 1 AD which were dropping bombs over the airfield at Pitomnik. The subsequent encounter cost the unfortunate 1 AD five Li-2s. Lucas shot down three of these, and Frese the other two. In total, the German fighter pilots reported 17 Soviet aircraft shot down over Stalingrad during that last day of air fighting over the city. But that was the end of it.

After landing at Pitomnik, Lucas found the situation absolutely appalling. The place was littered with corpses, horse carcasses, destroyed equipment of all kinds, and dozens of wrecked aircraft. Two dressing stations were packed with injured men. Everything seemed to be in disorder.

During the following night, Pitomnik was subjected to both intense aerial bombardment and artillery shelling.

Outside the ring surrounding Stalingrad, 3 SAK/17 VA carried out a successful air raid against Starobelsk's airfield with fifteen Pe-2s escorted by eleven 814 IAP Yak-1s on 15 January. Here, *Luftwaffenkommando Don's Transportstaffel* – assigned to fly in supplies to the scattered remnants of the Hungarian and Italian troops still fighting the Voronezh Front – was badly hit. All participating Soviet aircraft returned to base, despite interception efforts by III./JG 3.

When *Generalfeldmarschall* Erhard Milch, the *Luftwaffe's* deputy commander, arrived on 16 January at von Richthofen's headquarters to supervise the air supply as Hitler's political commissar, the air bridge was breaking down. Milch was informed that only forty-one He 111s, fifteen Ju 52s and a single Fw 200 were operational – figures that the *Generalfeldmarschall* found reason to doubt. Inside the cauldron, the airfield at Pitomnik had been evacuated in the face of advancing Soviet troops early that morning. Historian Gerhard Bracke describes the chaotic circumstances during which the fighters, Stukas and reconnaissance planes were shifted from Pitomnik to Gumrak, six miles closer to the city of Stalingrad:

"The engine in *Oblt.* Lucas' Messerschmitt is started. The pilot taxies out on the runway, gives more throttle, and immediately after heaving from the ground carries out a low-level attack against Russian infantry which is advancing towards the outskirts of the airfield. He makes a turn, rocks the wings of his aircraft to his comrades, and then flies off towards the west. (...)

*Hptm.* Germeroth gives the order: 'Everything to Gumrak!' The instruction 'officers remain here' is supported by a drawn pistol. While he points his gun at [*Oblt.* Gustav] Frielinghaus, who also wanted to leave for Gumrak, the others set in motion without any delay."[424]

Leaving behind twelve Bf 109s at Pitomnik, five pilots of the *Platzschutzstaffel* flew five Bf 109s to Gumrak. "The Bf 109s took off in the midst of heavy artillery fire and flew towards Gumrak. Upon their arrival there, they found that the runway had not been ploughed. The first aircraft which landed skid into a snow wall and turned over. The third, fourth and fifth Bf 109s also crashed during their landings."[425]

Both Pitomnik's and Basargino's airfields inside the cauldron were seized on 16 January by the Don Front's troops advancing towards the city of Stalingrad from the west. Soviet pilots who defied the snowfalls found rich hunting grounds on the roads leading eastwards from Pitomnik and Basargino, which were crammed with fleeing German soldiers. The ADD carried out intense bombardment of the Stalingrad suburbs of Gumrak,

Gorodishche, Aleksandrovka, Kamenyy Buyerak, and Uvarovka. A dejected *Generaloberst* von Paulus reported: "Our troops are in a temperature of 30 degrees below zero, without any bunkers, throughout the day defencelessly subjected to Russian dive-bomber wings with bombs of heaviest calibre. Our Stukas, fighters and reconnaissance planes either shot down or have left."

The arrival of 20 new four-engined He 177s from *Major* Kurt Schede's I./KG 50 to bolster the air supply strength is another measurement of German desperation. Each of these aircraft was unable to fly in more than around 1.1 tons of supplies – while at the same time consuming 4,000 litres of fuel. Only seven of the He 177s were serviceable when the unit entered service at Stalingrad. *Major* Schede was shot down during I./KG 50's first mission to Gumrak, also on 16 January. A total of thirteen missions to Stalingrad cost a loss of seven He 177s.

To make things even worse, Salsk in the northern Caucasus, the main base for the Ju 52 transport fleet, had to be evacuated in the face of the advancing troops of Soviet Southern Front. This also happened on 16 January. The Ju 52s were shifted to Zverevo, some 60 miles south-west of the contested Millerovo, where they immediately became the subject of Soviet air raids. KGrzbV 500 reported two Ju 52s totally destroyed during an air raid against Zverevo on 16 January.[426] Meanwhile eight 5 GIAP La-5 pilots commanded by *Mayor* Vasiliy Zaytsev strafed the airfield at Garmashevka, 10 miles west of Millerovo, reportedly knocking out ten *Luftwaffe* aircraft on the ground, while *St.Lt.* Dmitriy Shtokolov and *M.Lt.* Vitaliy Popkov claimed to have shot down both aircraft in the Bf 109 alert *Rotte* which scrambled.

On 17 January, the situation deteriorated further, from the German point of view. In the north, Soviet Voronezh Front's two pincers met and encircled both the Italian Alpine Corps and German XXVI. *Panzerkorps* in the region north of Rossosh. By that time, the Hungarian 2nd Army had been almost completely obliterated. Farther south, South-western Front's 1st Guards Army finally managed to break into Millerovo. A last effort by 25 Macchi 200s and 202s of the Italian 21 *Gruppo* carrying out strafing attacks against the Soviet troops and tanks, could not alter the situation. This would be the final Italian air mission in the East.

From within Stalingrad, declared a "Fortress" by Hitler, von Paulus reported on 17 January: "Since midnight there are relentless enemy air attacks against the Fortress. We have no more fighter protection and almost no anti-aircraft artillery." 17 VA ensured that there would be almost no Ju 52 flights to Gumrak that day. Eight waves each of five to seven Soviet aircraft attacked the airbase at Zverevo on 17 January. The airfield had been created by ploughing a relatively narrow runway through a corn field. Because of the limited time to prepare this, the Ju 52s stood parked tightly on the runway and offered easy targets to the attacking aircraft. *Oberst* Fritz Morzik, the air transport expert who had been assigned to lead the Ju 52 missions from Zverevo, was terrified to see large numbers of aircraft and supply stocks go up in flames. Fifty-four Ju 52s were hit, of which twelve were irrevocably lost. Morzik wrote: "The Rumanian AA gunners ran under cover during the attack, while the German 2-cm AA position shot down an Ilyushin."[427]

With the Ju 52s at Zverevo neutralized, only about 45 transport planes made it to Gumrak aerodrome, where they unloaded 82 tons of supplies – including 28 tons of ammunition and 48 tons of medical equipment. *Hptm.* Karl Mayer, 9./KG 27's *Staffelkapitän*, reported the situation at Gumrak, where he landed at noon on 17 January:

"As soon as we had landed, about 80 to 100 injured men stormed the aircraft. They not only made the unloading of the aircraft very difficult, but also pushed themselves into the aircraft in a state of total panic. There were no personnel available to handle the unloading of the aircraft, and no one there to bring order to the mass of injured men who stormed the aircraft, so this had to be executed by the crew of the aircraft. (…)

Shortly before take-off, a *Luftwaffe Ofw.* appeared with a sub-machine gun, which he used to turn away wounded men from the by now crammed aircraft. Finally, eleven wounded men were on board. (…) The crew of the aircraft had no possibility of judging which of the wounded men should be allowed to enter the aircraft. Due to their better physical condition, the less injured were able to gain a place in the aircraft at the expense of those who were more seriously injured, and thus also more exhausted. The behaviour by panicking, injured men who had failed to gain a place in the aircraft, made it difficult even to start the engines. Some of them tried to prevent the aircraft's take-off by throwing themselves in front of the landing gear."[428]

Such impressions inevitably had a strong negative effect on the combat spirits of the German airmen. Moreover, Major Mayer's conclusions were that any further daylight supply missions were made almost impossible from

*Despite their obsolescence, U-2 biplanes played an important role during the Battle of Stalingrad. At 19.30 hrs on 6 January 1943, a lone U-2 piloted by 970 NBAP's Serzh. Oleg Petrov and with Serzh. Vitaliy Skachkov as navigator, droned in over the airfield at Bolshaya Rossoshka inside the cauldron. Defying intense ground fire, it dropped leaflets with an offer from Rokossovskiy to Generaloberst von Paulus to surrender. Next, the unfortunate U-2 crew crashed their badly shot up U-2, whereby the pilot was injured. The two men managed to reach their own base where their regimental commander accused them of not having completed their mission. Petrov and Skachkov were saved from being court-martialled only when German PoWs confirmed that the leaflets actually had been dropped over the airfield. (Karlenko)*

"hostile action through artillery fire and air attacks, some of which were carried out in skilful low-level flight."[429]

That evening, a desperate *Generaloberst* von Paulus radioed Hitler: "My *Führer*! Your orders in respect of the supply of the Army have not been obeyed. Since early on 16 January, it has been possible to land at Gumrak's airfield." Early next morning, the message from the 6th Army read: "Night of 17-18 January (…) Numerous bomb attacks. No supply aircraft have landed, in spite of the fact that all ground installations are in good order, and in similar conditions as previously at Pitomnik. When pilots report the opposite, it is not true and only a proof of their lacking serviceability (*Einsatzbereitschaft*)."

On 18 January, the previous day's successful air attack against Zverevo was followed by two raids against Gartmashevka airfield. The first started at 11.50 hrs, when Il-2s of 290 ShAD and four La-5 of 5 GIAP made strafing passes. *Podpolkovnik* Vasiliy Zaytsev and *Lt.* Kildushev of the latter unit reportedly destroyed two Ju 52s on the ground, while the other pair of Lavochkins claimed to have shot down a Bf 109 which attempted to take off. Later that day, four Yak-1s of 867 IAP attacked Gartmashevka airfield again. They opened up by firing against the AAA positions, claiming to have neutralized two AA guns and three AA machine guns. They also conducted several firing passes against parked planes but saw no damage inflicted as a result.[430]

The Soviet pressure from the air against the surrounded Stalingrad increased, but at the price of losses for the attackers. Also on 18 January, 285 ShAP's *Lt.* Ivan Bibishev's Il-2 was severely hit by anti-aircraft fire during a raid against Gumrak's airbase. Bibishev was a veteran who had conducted 140 combat sorties since May 1942 and was credited with the destruction of 20 tanks and around 50 other motor vehicles. On this, his 141st combat mission, he reportedly crashed his doomed Il-2 into the dispersal area on the German airfield. For this feat he was postumously awarded the title of Hero of the Soviet Union. One of 176 IAP's *Eskadrilya* commanders, *Kapitan* Zhilo, was shot down and wounded by a Ju 88's rear gunners.[431] 512 IAP's C.O., *Mayor* Lev Binov, was killed when his Yak-1 was shot down by ground fire during a strafing mission. Both these fighter pilots succumbed on 18 January. Meanwhile, four Yak-1s led by 520 IAP's *Starshina* V. F. Vinogradov claimed to have shot down two He 111s over Gumrak.

That day, only eight aircraft from the Ju 52 armada took off on supply flights to Stalingrad. Five aborted due to technical faults and the other three never returned. "Even flying at all is a heroic achievement," Fiebig tried to explain to *Generalfeldmarschall* Milch. But Hitler's minister came to the conclusion that much of the failure to supply Stalingrad from the air could be attributed to lacking spirits among the *Luftwaffe's* men. On 18 January, Milch relieved *Generalmajor* Viktor Carganico from his position as *Luftversorgungsführer* Stalingrad. Next he threatened to court-martial those who failed. But Milch could not halt the Red Army. On 18 January, Millerovo was seized by the Soviets and at Kantemirovka, VVS aircraft put four Ju 52s of *Transportstaffel Luftwaffenkommando Don* out of commission. This was also the day when the aviation of the Italian ARMIR abandoned the Germans in the East. The remaining 30 MC200s and nine MC202s started their flight back to Italy, leaving fifteen unserviceable Italian aircraft behind at Voroshilovgrad.[432]

During the night of 18-19 January, six He 111s and one of KGrzbV 200's Fw 200s landed in Gumrak. Another forty-five transport planes – forty-one He 111s, three Ju 52s, and one Fw 200 – air-dropped supplies. On its return flight, the Fw 200 which had landed in Gumrak brought out *General* Hans Hubem, who was there at the special request of Hitler who had demanded to hear the truth "from an Army officer." Hube reported to Milch a few hours later and disclosed several deficiencies – including the fact that several transport planes had landed in Pitomnik with only half the cargo they were capable of carrying.

Milch found more to express criticism about, which was more or less justified. The organisation of the *Wehrmacht's* entire supply system had left much to be desired for quite some time. Milch discovered that new aircraft, aircrew, and other materiel were "stuck" somewhere between Germany and the Stalingrad area. The central supply store at Krakow, where large stocks of spare parts, aircraft, etc. arrived in order to be distributed eastwards, proved to be a crucial bottleneck. Milch immediately sent a harsh message to the commander in charge at *Luftpark Krakav*, threatening all who were found guilty of delaying distribution of goods to the Front with death sentences. This had an immediate effect and, in a matter of days, the air transport force increased to number 668 transport aircraft – 355 He 111s, 308 Ju 52s and five Fw 200s. Milch also addressed the *Luftwaffe* unit commanders: "I will have every *Kommandeur* who fails to comply with my commands shot!"

Despite a raging blizzard, 40 transport aircraft flew 62 tons of supplies on 19 January. Four Ju 52s and three He 111s were lost. To the north, the advanced columns of the Voronezh Front who had reached the Oskol River were attacked by small groups of III./St.G 2 *Immelmann's* Stukas. On his 434th combat sortie, *Ofw.* Siegfried Huber – one of the *Immelmanngeschwader's* veterans – crashed his Ju 87 in the bad visibility and was killed. That same day it was announced that Huber had been awarded with the *Luftwaffe's* 800th Knight's Cross.

Milch's harsh methods clearly bore fruit when on 21 January around 200 tons of supplies were landed at Gumrak. But that evening, Gumrak was captured by troops of the Don Front. The last remaining airstrip in German hands inside the cauldron was Stalingradskiy. Eighty-one transport planes set off for here on 22 January. Twenty-six attempted to land, but most of them crashed as they taxied into snow-covered bomb craters.

Meanwhile, German Army detachments Fretter-Pico and Hollidt managed to fend off Soviet attempts to capture the air transport bases Novocherkassk and Zverevo, thereby holding open the passage from the Caucasus through the bottleneck at Rostov. This was much due to the

Mayor Vasiliy Shishkin, who commanded 581 IAP during the final stage of the Battle of Stalingrad, poses beside his Yak-1 fighter in January 1943. Shishkin served with 43 IAP at the outbreak of the war with Germany in 1941, and by February 1942 had performed 126 combat missions, including 65 ground-attack sorties. For this he was appointed a Hero of the Soviet Union. In December 1942 he was posted to 581 IAP at Stalingrad, where he assumed command of the unit. 581 IAP was part of 220 IAD, which was 16 VA's most successful fighter unit during the Battle of Stalingrad. In total, this Diviziya was credited with 334 aerial victories during the Battle of Stalingrad. Shishkin's Yak-1, seen in this picture, was Serial No. 34104 and had been donated by workers at the 'Signal Revolutsiy' Collective Farm. The inscription on the aircraft reads 'To the Hero of the Soviet Union Mayor Shishkin from the Collective farmers of Kolkhoz 'Signal of the Revolution' in the Voroshilovsk area in the Saratov Region.' Shishkin ended the war with a total of 30 victories. (Karlenko)

efforts by *Fliegerkorps* VIII. The German air operations inflicted severe losses on South-western Front's ground troops, but occasionally also led to heavy *Luftwaffe* losses. I. and II./ZG 1's operations on 21 January came at a loss of six Bf 110s.[433]

By holding the gate over Rostov open, *Generalfeldmarschall* von Manstein succeeded in saving *Heeresgruppe A* in the Caucasus from being surrounded. Without doubt, the largest contribution to this was provided by the 6th Army, which tied down the entire Don Front for two months. On 22 January, *Generaloberst* von Paulus turned down a new Soviet invitation to surrender. As a consequence, the Don Front began its final offensive against Stalingrad. With the fighters of 16 VA in complete control of the Stalingrad skies, the Soviet aviation could act absolutely freely. The bombers of both 16 VA and ADD began to operate in formations of 40 aircraft. On 23 January, the last German aircraft took off from Stalingradskiy, the last operational airfield inside the cauldron. It was an He 111, carrying 19 injured soldiers and seven mail bags. Then the Soviet troops also reached Stalingradskiy. Supported by air attacks in rolling waves, they managed to cut through the cauldron, splitting it into two halves. In the evening of 23 January, VVS aircraft caught the retreat column of German 3rd, 29th, and 276th Infantry divisions on an open road leading eastwards to the city of Stalingrad. During the next four hours these German troops, unable to leave the road due to high walls of snow, were subjected to complete carnage from the air.

"Terrible conditions (...) At least 20,000 wounded men are left without any provisions at all, and at least as many soldiers suffer from frostbite and starvation," was reported from the 6th Army in the evening of 24 January. And yet, on 25 January, only seven transport planes made it to Stalingrad, dropping a mere 13 tons of supplies. The next night, only eleven out of sixty-two serviceable Ju 52s took off. Again, Milch expressed his strong doubts regarding the *Luftwaffe* airmen's true commitment and made new threats of court-martials. The result was that during the night of 26-27 January, the fifty serviceable He 111s carried out 104 sorties while the fifty-six serviceable Ju 52s made sixty flights to Stalingrad. A total of 100 tons of provisions, plus ammunition, were air-dropped to the starving and doomed army.

But by this time there was nothing which could be done to prevent the 6th Army from disintegrating rapidly. According to Soviet figures, 40,000 of the 6th Army's troops were killed and 28,000 captured between 10 and 26 January. Another 18,000 ended up in Soviet confinement between 27 and 30 January. What remained of the 6th Army – once the mightiest single army in the world – was 91,000 starving men, one-third of them injured. In vain, VIII. *Fliegerkorps* performed another 196 transport flights between 27 and 29 January, air-dropping around 200 tons of provisions.

30 January was the tenth anniversary of Hitler's seizure of power. It was a day of great symbolic value. *Generalfeldmarschall* Milch had finally received the drop tanks for long-distance fighter missions to Stalingrad which he required. At 10.45 hrs on 30 January, six Bf 109 G-2s from *Stab*/JG 3 and five Bf 110 G-2s from I./ZG 1 took off for the first long-range fighter mission to Stalingrad. They returned with two victory claims, while their own formation leader, Knight's Cross holder *Oblt.* Eduard Tratt, barely survived a crash at Rovenki. The skies over Stalingrad undoubtedly

belonged to the VVS. A formation of one hundred Soviet aircraft appeared over the city. The red-starred planes swept past the beleaguered troops at an altitude of 1,500 feet, in a perfect parade formation, without firing a single bullet, without dropping a single bomb.

II./KG 53's *Oblt.* Gilbert Geisendorfer had quite a different impression of 30 January 1943: "On 30 January, I took off in adverse weather for my last flight to Stalingrad, together with the crew of *Uffz.* Staib. Shortly after take-off we were attacked by eight Russian fighters. Staib's crew was shot down, but managed a forced landing in enemy-held territory and made it back to our unit on foot on 4 February."[434]

New air supply flights sufficed as little as the effort to dispatch two drop-tank equipped Bf 109s to Stalingrad on 31 January. That day Friedrich von Paulus – promoted to *Generalfeldmarschall* – surrendered. On 2 February the troops of the Don Front broke the last resistance in Stalingrad. The 91,000 survivors, many of whom were in very bad physical condition, were marched into Soviet confinement. An estimated 130,000 - 140,000 German and Rumanian soldiers had become prisoners of war during the Battle of

*A Soviet Yak-7B fighter taking off from a snow-covered airfield. In January 1943, the VVS had achieved an unbreakable air supremacy over Stalingrad and this settled the fate of the Stalingrad airlift. (Rybalko via Drabkin)*

Stalingrad since Operation "*Uranus*" had been launched. According to a Soviet "body count" – completed in November 1943 – 146,300 German soldiers were killed during the battle.

But the Axis defeat was much greater than this. According to official figures, the Rumanian Army suffered 158,854 casualties (killed, missing, and wounded) between 19 November 1942 and 7 January 1943. The Italian losses were similarly heavy. Out of 220,000 men in Italian 8th Army, about 25,000 were killed and 70,000 captured in December 1942 and January 1943. The 2nd Hungarian Army lost 68,000 men killed or missing in action

in a period of less than three weeks in January 1943.[435] In total, the Soviet offensive in the Don area in the winter of 1942-1943 cost the Axis the loss of almost half a million troops. Five whole Axis armies were completely annihilated. The Red Army's Voronezh, South-western, Don, and Southern Fronts lost approximately 175,000 men killed or missing between November 1942 and early February 1943.

In the air, the *Luftwaffe* had sustained its greatest defeat since the Battle of Britain.

*A crashed Focke-Wulf Fw 200 B-2. Between 10 and 31 January 1943, the Stalingrad airlift operation cost KGrzbV 200 the loss of eight Fw 200s. Of those, only three could be repaired and five were total losses. (Mombeeck)*

# Chapter Eighteen

# The Air Battle over Stalingrad – a critical review

Prior to the Battle of Stalingrad, the Soviet aviation had attained several important successes in the war against Germany. But the Battle of Stalingrad was the *Luftwaffe's* first great defeat in the war on the Eastern Front.

The rather incomplete loss files of the *Generalquartiermeister der Luftwaffe* register over 900 German aircraft destroyed or badly damaged from all causes on the Eastern Front between 19 November 1942 and 31 January 1943.

*Generaloberst* von Richthofen's *Luftflotte* 4 – which in the summer and autumn of 1942 had been the mightiest single air command in the world – suffered a bloodletting comparable to the disastrous losses suffered by the Axis ground troops. By the end of January 1943, *Luftflotte* 4 was in shambles. The air fleet had received numerous reinforcements since November 1942 – more than six whole *Kampfgruppen*, two *Stukagruppen*, and more than a whole *Jagdgruppe*, plus hundreds of transport planes. Yet still, by 1 February 1943, *Luftflotte* 4 had shrunk to 240 serviceable and 384 unserviceable aircraft, transport planes excluded.

The hardest blows had been dealt against the Air Forces of Germany's allies operating within *Luftflotte* 4. The aviation of Italian ARMIR was withdrawn from the Eastern Front on 18 January, bringing 30 Macchi C.200 and nine Macchi C.202 fighters back to Italy and leaving 15 unserviceable aircraft behind. A total of 66 Italian aircraft had been lost on the Eastern Front – against, according to official figures, 88 victories claimed during seventeen months of action in that theatre. The Italian Air Force would never return to fight the VVS. The Hungarian and Rumanian aviation detachments in the East also became more or less obliterated during the Soviet winter offensive of 1942/1943. The Rumanian Eastern Front aviation (re-designated into *Corpul Aerian* on 1 January 1943) lost 91 out of approximately 100 aircraft during the winter battle and diminished to a strength of exactly three Bf 109s and one He 111. Both the Hungarian and Rumanian aviation detachments on the Eastern Front virtually disappeared as a result of their losses that winter.

Several of *Luftflotte* 4's German units met with the same fate during the winter battle. Four of the transport units which had been involved in the Stalingrad operation – KGrzbV 700, KGrzbV 900, I./KGzbV 1, and II./KGzbV 1 – were formally dissolved.[436]

*Aufklärungsgruppe Fleischmann*, which united the *Luftwaffe's* tactical reconnaissance units inside the Stalingrad cauldron, was completely annihilated. As a result of their losses at Stalingrad, no fewer than ten *Heeresaufklärungsstaffeln* ceased to exist – 1. (H)/10, and 4.(H)/10; 1.(H)/12, and 3.(H)/12; 3.(H)/13, and 6.(H)/13; 2.(H)/31, plus 3.(H)/31, and 6.(H)/31; and 7.(H)/LG 2. These units had a combined strength of 83 aircraft by the time Stalingrad was surrounded in November 1942. *Stab*/NAGr 7 – formerly commanding the 6th Army's own *Heeresaufklärungsstaffeln* – also perished, with 91 men disappearing to an uncertain fate when Stalingrad surrendered. NAGr 12 lost a total of 385 of its ground personnel when Stalingrad fell.[437]

St.G 2 *Immelmann* also had an establishment which had operated from within the surrounded Stalingrad. Hans-Ulrich Rudel, *Oblt.* and *Staffelkapitän* of 1./St.G 2, described the situation after the Battle of Stalingrad: "Through relentless combat missions and the bitterness of the battle, the number of aircraft which we are able to bring into the air each day became quite limited. At one stage, the whole *Gruppe* had a strength equivalent to only a *Staffel.*"[438] II./St.G 2's *Assistenzarzt* Dr. Hermann Roer noted in his diary: "During its operations to ward off attacks against the German lines of defence, 4. *Staffel* [of St.G 2] became almost obliterated."[439]

In the bomber aviation, KG 27 was down to no more than 18 serviceable He 111s (out of a total of 66) on 1 February 1943. KG 55 *Greif*, which completed 2,260 sorties during the Battle of Stalingrad, lost 59 He 111s between 29 November 1942 and 3 February 1943.[440] On the latter date, the whole *Kampfgeschwader Greif* had twelve air worthy He 111s (with another 40 unserviceable). II./KG 53 had freshly returned from one month's rest and recuperation in Germany when it joined the Stalingrad air supply force on 12 January 1943. Three weeks later, 15 of its He 111s had been lost, together with 24 flying personnel, and the *Gruppe* was in desperate need of another period of rest. Gilbert Geisendorfer, who served as an *Oblt.* with II./KG 53, recalls: "After the fall of Stalingrad, our II./KG 53 was badly depleted. Only 10 crews remained for further operations."[441]

In KG 51 *Edelweiss*, II. *Gruppe* was pulled out of combat for rest and recuperation after the Battle of Stalingrad. The same had to be done with II./KG 27, *Stab*/KG 55, II./KG 55 and III./St.G 77.

*The sad remnants of Macchi C.200 Saetta fighters of Italian 21 Gruppo Autonomo in the Don Bend area in early 1943. (Karlenko)*

*Luftflotte* 4 had two famous *Jagdgeschwader*, JG 3 *Udet* and JG 52, which had produced impressive victory scores for the period 19 November 1942 through 31 January 1943 – around 350 by JG 3 and 320 by JG 52. But in doing so, these two *Jagdgeschwader* had been largely less wing-clipped. In early February 1943, III./JG 52 – the *Jagdgruppe* where *Major* Hermann Graf, the first pilot to surpass the 200-victory mark, had served – was "licking its wounds" at Nikolayev in the rear. After the Battle of Stalingrad, JG 3 *Udet* – which had earned fame and respect among the Soviet airmen in the autumn of 1942 – had only one *Gruppe*, II./JG 3, remaining in first-line service. I./JG 3 had been found completely demoralised and was withdrawn from the Eastern Front before the Battle of Stalingrad was over. "In view of the *Gruppe's* completely 'war-weary' state, further operations were absolutely out of the question," wrote historians Jochen Prien and Gerhard Stemmer in the unit's chronicle.[442] (I./JG 3's last experience on the Eastern Front was a Soviet bomber attack against the railway station at Rostov on 1 February 1943, when eleven of the *Gruppe's* personnel were killed.) III./JG 3 was unable to conduct any more sorties after 17 January 1943 and a week later it was pulled back to Gorlovka in the rear.

Overall, these *Jagdgeschwader* had failed in their task of clearing the skies of marauding VVS fighters. According to statistics worked out by *Generalfeldmarschall* Milch's headquarters, the Stalingrad supply operation from 24 November 1942 to 2 February 1943 cost 488 transport aircraft – 274 destroyed or missing and 214 damaged beyond repair. Among these losses were 266 Ju 52s – one-third of all Ju 52s on strength in the *Luftwaffe* – and 165 He 111s which had been lost on transport missions. Other losses reported in Milch's statistics included 42 Ju 86s from KGrzbV 21 and KGrzbV 22, nine Fw 200s (from KGrzbV 200), five He 177s (from I./KG 50), and a Ju 290 of the *Lufthansa*. With approximately 4,000 transport sorties carried out (*Oberst* Hans-Detlef Herhudt von Rohden, von Richthofen's chief-of-staff, gave the figure 3,400 transport sorties for the period 22 November 1942 through 16 January 1943[443]), this means an average loss rate of over 10 per cent.

It is interesting to note that the VVS claims are well in line with these figures. 16 VA submitted claims for 164 enemy aircraft shot down between 1 December 1942 and 31 January 1943,[444] including approximately 100 transport planes. During its participation in the air blockade, 8 VA claimed 132 transport planes shot down.[445]

The *Luftwaffe's* failure to provide the encircled 6th Army with an adequate amount of supplies has been widely discussed. During the 70 days from 25 November 1942 to 2 February 1943, the *Luftwaffe* delivered a total of 6,591 metric tons of supplies to Stalingrad – a daily average of 94 tons. In addition to this, the transport planes on their return flights brought 24,760 wounded and 5,150 "key personnel" or "experts" to safety outside the cauldron.

Comparison with previous accomplishments by the German air transport fleet on the Eastern Front highlights the failure at Stalingrad. At Demyansk, a smaller air fleet had managed to fly in 24,303 tons between 19 February and 18 May 1942 – i.e. a daily average of 273 tons.[446]

During the period 10 August through mid-November 1942, *Luftflotte* 4's air transport fleet flew in 42,000 tons of supplies to the Don Front area, i.e. a daily average of 442 tons! In addition to these cargoes, the same transport aircraft also brought forward 27,044 fresh troops and evacuated 51,018 wounded men during the same period.[447] The latter figures were accomplished by the same force which in November 1942 became responsible for the airlift to the surrounded Stalingrad: KGrzbV 5, KGrzbV 9, KGrzbV 50 and KGrzbV 900 were the same since early August 1942; by November 1942, III./KGzbV 1, KGrzbV 4 and KGrzbV 102 had been exchanged for I./KGzbV 172, KGrzbV 500 and KGrzbV 700. The total number of serviceable aircraft in the transport units of *Luftflotte* 4 was 156 on 27 July and 146 on 20 November 1942. This is more or less equal to the number of serviceable transport aircraft available to the Demyansk airlift when this formally commenced on 19 February 1942.[448]

As we have seen, several new air transport units arrived to reinforce the Stalingrad airlift once the cauldron had been established through the Soviet offensive, as was the case regarding the Demyansk airlift, while *Luftflotte* 4's air transport services had to manage without any reinforcements prior to late November 1942.

*General-Mayor Timofey Khryukin.*

Although these comparisons are not entirely fair, they are not altogether irrelevant. Several attempts have been made to describe the Stalingrad airlift as doomed beforehand due to meteorological conditions alone. "That the Sixth Army could not be adequately supplied under these conditions should have been obvious", writes Hermann Plocher, and he points out that "Russian winter conditions and their impact were well known since the critical winter of 1941-42, which should have suggested the strong possibility that weather conditions would eventually make airlift operations impossible because of rising clouds, icy rains, and snowstorms."[449] But as we have seen, these conditions were present to at least the same extent during the Demyansk airlift operation, while other "objective conditions" were more favourable at Stalingrad – ie. airfields inside the surrounded territory and the use of *X-Gerät* and *Y-Gerät* landing radio beacons.

It should also be taken into account that the transport pilots were trained and often very skilful on instruments and they often chose to fly in "bad flying weather" in order to escape detection by VVS fighters.

The major factor which decided the outcome of the Stalingrad airlift operation was the greatly improved VVS opposition which countered the transports on their way to and from Stalingrad in the winter of 1942/1943.

Without doubt, the Soviet Air Force achieved its greatest victory at Stalingrad in the winter of 1942/1943. The VVS not only prevented German attempts to establish a successful air bridge to Stalingrad, but also provided the Red Army with important and often decisive support. *General* Batov, the commander of the Don Front's 65th Army, acknowledged the contribution by the Soviet aviation to the ground battle in his day order of 29 January 1943:

One new Soviet fighter, the Yak-9, was introduced at the end of the Battle of Stalingrad. This boded ill for the Luftwaffe. The aircraft in the photograph were among the first batch to be delivered to 168 IAP. The inscription reads 'Small theatre to the front'. (Drabkin)

"Our airmen's courageous attacks against ground targets have given a vital contribution to our aim – the final destruction of the surrounded armies."[450]

It should be kept in mind that this was achieved only a few months after the huge air battles in the summer and autumn of 1942, when 8 VA and 16 VA were beaten into chaos by *Luftflotte* 4 and the Germans attained complete air superiority over Stalingrad. The Soviet aviation had indeed made a remarkable recovery.

Indeed, large numerical reinforcements were sent to the VVS in the Stalingrad - Don area, but the Soviet victory in the air over Stalingrad could not have been achieved without improvements in the quality of the VVS – mainly in the areas of technology and tactics.

The method of guiding air units via radio from the ground was established at Stalingrad and it became one of the key factors in the successful operations against the German transport aircraft. The more flexible use of Soviet air units – contrary to the rigid tying of air units to individual ground armies in 1941 – was also of great importance, as were *General-Leytenant* Novikov's Blockade Zones. Inside these Zones, Soviet fighter pilots operated offensively – now using the German *Rotte - Schwarm* fighter tactic, or *Para - Zveno* as it was called in the VVS; this was in stark contrast to the defensive doctrine which had hampered Soviet fighter operations during the first fifteen months of the war.

Barely any new Soviet aircraft were introduced during the Battle of Stalingrad; the latest, "lightened" versions of the Yak-1 and Yak-7B with more powerful engines had been introduced in the spring and early summer of 1942. Indeed, the La-5 made its combat debut in August 1942, but it is doubtful whether this aircraft can be regarded as a leap forward compared with the latest Yak-1 version. The new Yak-9 was introduced towards the end of the Battle of Stalingrad, but production of this aircraft commenced only in October 1942 and, during the next four months, no more than 195 Yak-9s were produced.

However, the Battle of Stalingrad saw several important advances regarding the Il-2 *Shturmovik*. Firstly, the Il-2 appeared over Stalingrad in decisively large numbers. The sheer volume of 575 Il-2 ground-attack aircraft massed for Operation "*Uranus*" was without precedent. The increasing importance of the Il-2 to VVS operations is obvious from the fact that the Il-2's share of all combat sorties made by the VVS increased from 8.6 per cent in the period 12 July - 18 November 1942 (6,673 sorties with Il-2s) to 15.2 per cent in the period 19 November 1942 - 2 February 1943. Of 5,463 sorties with Il-2s during the latter period, 82 per cent were conducted in direct cooperation with the ground armies.

The Il-2 pilots also learned to modify their tactics, performing their attacks in a shallow dive and increasing strike precision. In addition to this, the Il-2s improved their defensive capacity against enemy fighters. Starting

with improvised improvements installed at unit level in the autumn of 1942, more and more Il-2s were modified into two-seaters and equipped with a rear gun. Experience also taught Il-2 pilots that they had better chances of survival by countering the Bf 109 in combat rather than acting passively. A number of Bf 109s fell to Il-2 pilots from the autumn of 1942 onwards – much to the surprise of the German pilots who survived.[451]

In the VVS bomber units, the Pe-2 crews also learned how to perform dive-bombings, thus attaining greater accuracy. The dive-bombing tactics were pioneered by 150 SBAP's *Podpolkovnik* Ivan Polbin, who was appointed a Hero of the Soviet Union on 23 November 1942. Under Polbin's supervision, the Pe-2 fliers developed the so-called *vertushka* ("carousel"), where the bombers circled above the target, with one aircraft after another diving against the target and then climbing back into position in the circle.

As we have seen on repeated occasions, the Soviet airmen gave ample proof of self-denying acts of courage in the air fighting over Stalingrad. This was particularly evident during the desperate defensive stage of the battle – in September 1942 – when on average one *taran* was recorded almost every second day in the air over Stalingrad alone. The fact that this number dropped to three in November and zero in December 1942 is mainly a reflection of the fact that by that time the Soviet airmen had gained control of the situation and thus did not have to resort to such desperate measures.

*Podpolkovnik* Lev Shestakov' ace unit 9 GIAP was in the lead as far as Soviet fighter successes were concerned. During the Battle of Stalingrad, 9 GIAP's *Lt.* Pavel Golovachyov performed 150 combat missions and was credited with eight victories, while *Kapitan* Arkadiy Kovachevich of the same unit attained the same number. Other fighter units with a large number of very experienced pilots in the Stalingrad - Don area were 3 GIAP and 5 GIAP. *Lt.* Petr Bazanov of the former unit earned fame when on 11 December he shot down three Ju 52s in a row. 5 GIAP, which operated in 17 VA from mid-December 1942, recorded 45 victories during the battle of the Don Bend – six of these by the unit commander, Hero of the Soviet Union, *Major* Vasiliy Zaytsev.

In 16 VA, *Kapitan* Ivan Motornyy of 512 IAP was reported to have shot down eight enemy aircraft during the Stalingrad battle. He was appointed a Hero of the Soviet Union on 28 January 1943, simultaneously with two other fighter aces of 16 VA: *Kapitan* Valentin Makarov (also of 512 IAP), who had reached a total score of 15 personal and four shared victories, and *Kapitan* Zakhar Semenyuk, who had reached a total score of 14 personal and four shared victories.

In 8 VA, twelve men became Heroes of the Soviet Union during the Battle of Stalingrad, while nineteen others were recommended for this award and received it later. More than one thousand servicemen and women in 8 VA were awarded with various medals during the Battle of Stalingrad. After the battle, all servicemen and women who had participated received the special award "For the Defence of Stalingrad".

A considerable number of VVS units were elevated to Guards units for their performances in the Battle of Stalingrad.

In 8 VA, *Podpolkovnik* Fyodor Boldyrikhin's 226 ShAD became the first Guards *Shturmovik Diviziya* of VVS KA, 1 GShAD. During the Battle of Stalingrad, the airmen of 226 ShAD performed 1,458 combat sorties during which they claimed to have destroyed 211 enemy aircraft (198 on the ground and 13 in the air), and either destroyed or damaged 633 tanks, 41 artillery pieces, 53 AA guns and 2,569 motor vehicles.[452] With the elevation of 226 ShAD into 1 GShAD, its regiment 504 ShAP became 74 GShAP, 505 ShAP became 75 GShAP, and 225 ShAP became 76 GShAP. Among several airmen in the new 1 GShAD who were appointed Heroes of the Soviet Union during the Battle of Stalingrad, 504 ShAP's *Lt.* Ivan Dokukin deserves to be mentioned. During the Battle of Stalingrad, he conducted 70 combat missions and was credited

Soviet II-4 bombers in the air over the Eastern Front. The II-4 – designated DB-3F prior to March 1942 was, in fact, a superior modern bomber in 1941 and 1942. It constituted the backbone of the Soviet strategic air force, the DBA (later reformed into the ADD). Nevertheless, a lack of fighter escort forced the Soviets to restrict II-4 operations to the hours of darkness. (Karlenko)

The Ju 88-equipped KG 51 played an important role during attacks against the port which were used by the Soviet Black Sea Fleet. KG 51 damaged the tanker 'Kuybyshev' in the Caucasian port of Novorossiysk on 17 March, and the transport ship 'Georgiy Dimitrov' (3689 GRT) in Sevastopol three days later. On 23-25 March, KG 51 made repeated attacks against the port of Tuapse, sinking the transport ship 'Yalta' and the depot ship 'Neva', plus two minelayers and one motor torpedo boat, as well as damaging two submarines, the tanker 'Sovneft' and the tug 'SP-44'.

General-Leytenant Aleksandr Novikov, the new C-in-C of VVS KA.

with the destruction of 20 tanks, 32 motor vehicles and six anti-aircraft batteries.

In 16 VA, *Polkovnik* Vasiliy Stepichev's 228 ShAD was transformed into 2 GShAD. During the Battle of Stalingrad, this *Diviziya* recorded 2,927 combat sorties and reportedly destroyed 332 enemy aircraft on the ground and in the air, plus 674 tanks and 3,062 motor vehicles. Its subordinated 285 ShAP, 688 ShAP, 243 ShAP and 313 ShAP were elevated into 58 GShAP, 59 GShAP, 78 GShAP and 79 GShAP.

Also in 16 VA, the fighter *Diviziya* 220 IAD was appointed the first Guards fighter *Diviziya*, 1 GIAD. By submitting a total of 334 aerial victories, 220 IAD was one of the most successful fighter units during the Battle of Stalingrad. The *Diviziya's* three regiments – 512 IAP, 237 IAP, and 581 IAP – were re-designated 53 GIAP, 54 GIAP and 55 GIAP respectively. 512 IAP recorded 22 combat losses during its tour of operations over Stalingrad from 9 October 1942 to 31 January 1943.[453]

Other VVS units rewarded with a Guards title for their accomplishments during the Battle of Stalingrad included *Mayor* Ivan Kleshchyov's 434 IAP, which became 32 GIAP; 520 IAP, which was credited with 95 victories during the Battle of Stalingrad and was elevated into 56 GIAP; and 150 SBAP which became 35 GBAP.

The ADD played an important role during the whole Battle of Stalingrad. During the defensive stage - from 17 July to 19 November 1942 - it conducted 11 317 sorties in the Stalingrad area, which amounts to 49 percent of all ADD sorties during this period. 454[454]

The ADD also made an important contribution to the Soviet victory at Stalingrad. During the offensive stage of the Battle of Stalingrad, it conducted 3,334 sorties – including 1,138 against railway sites and 846 against German airfields[455].

The ADD made another vital contribution to the Soviet offensive by flying in supplies to the spearheads of the ground troops which had advanced far from their supply bases, or by bringing wounded men to hospitals. For example, Soviet 51st Army was able to break through at Proletarskaya on 20 January 1943 largely due to supplies brought in by Li-2s and TB-3s of the ADD's 1 AD and 53 AD. On the same day, the ADD flew 507 critically wounded soldiers of the Don Front to hospitals in the rear.

*General-Mayor* Aleksandr Golovanov, ADD's C-in-C who had supervised ADD operations at Stalingrad since August 1942, was awarded with the new Suvorov Order of the First Grade (*Orden Suvorova 1-y (Pervoy) stepeny*) on 23 January 1943.

Supplementing the ADD's nocturnal attacks, the light night bombers of the Soviet air armies had been in relentless action every night during the whole battle, adding to the exhaustion suffered by the German troops. Numerous letter and diary entries by German soldiers in Stalingrad testify to the nerve-racking effect of these harassment raids. The first of the VVS regiments elevated to Guards unit during the Battle of Stalingrad in fact was *Mayor* Mikhail Khoroshikh's U-2-equipped 709 NBAP which, on 22 November 1942, became 25 GNBAP.

However, the accomplishments by the VVS during the Battle of Stalingrad should not obscure the fact that the Soviet air forces still had a

## Combat Sorties carried out by 8 VA, 16 VA and 17 VA in December 1942 and January 1943

| Type of mission | Number of combat Sorties | Number of combat Sorties | Total number of combat Sorties |
|---|---|---|---|
| Attacks against troop encampments and marching columns | 1838 | 4483 | 6321 |
| Attacks against aircraft | 4147 | 2389 | 6536 |
| *Of the above were:* | | | |
| Attacks against airfields | 2856 | 638 | 3494 |
| Patrol missions | 273 | 359 | 632 |
| Interception of aircraft | 468 | 111 | 579 |
| Fighter sweeps | 550 | 338 | 888 |
| Airfield blockade missions | 933 | 933 | |
| Covering troops | 252 | 252 | |
| *Tactical support:* | | | |
| Close support | 1757 | 661 | 2418 |
| Reconnaissance | 1505 | 373 | 1878 |
| Missions against railways | 204 | 204 | |
| Other missions | 756 | 494 | 1250 |
| **Total** | **10459** | **8400** | **18859** |

One of the first Douglas Bostons – or 'B-3' as it became known among the Soviets – to see Soviet service. Due to the employment of better combat tactics, 8 VA's Boston-equipped 221 BAD was more successful in operations and sustained lower losses than the similarly-equipped 244 BAD of 2 VA. In June and July 1942, 221 BAD lost 22 Bostons while 244 BAD lost 62. (Karlenko)

Kapitan Mikhail Avdeyev waves signals to ground crew from the cockpit of his Yak-1 at Stalingrad in the early summer of 1942.

long way to go before they could overcome the qualitative deficiencies which had their roots in the curtailed training schemes of the early 1940s and which had been deepened as a result of the enormous losses in 1941 and 1942. By the end of the Battle of Stalingrad, the Soviet Air Forces had narrowed the gap with the *Luftwaffe* in terms of equipment and methods, but its airmen still received an inadequately short training.

One effect of this was the frequent cases of Soviet air attacks against their own troops, due to navigation difficulties. "Due to an absolute absence of cooperation between the armies and 1 SAK, our aviation is bombing our own troops very frequently,"[456] *General-Leytenant* Nikolay Vatutin, South-western Front's commander, complained on 22 January 1943. The situation was so serious that Vatutin even threatened to have 1 SAK's commander, *General-Mayor* Vladimir Shevchenko, arrested and the guilty airmen executed if such an incident was to be repeated again.[457]

The qualities lacking in the VVS also resulted in continued heavy losses. In 945 ShAP, one Il-2 was lost for every 11 sorties in December 1942. Soviet aircraft losses during the Stalingrad offensive 19 November 1942 – 2 February 1943 totalled 706, with another 236 aircraft lost by 4 VA, 5 VA

and 8 VA during the Caucasus offensive from 1 January – 4 February 1943. In total, 942.[458]

As we have seen, while the *Luftwaffe* failed to save VI. *Armee* or to prevent the major Soviet breakthroughs in November – December 1942, it contributed decisively to holding open the bottleneck at Rostov, thus enabling *Heeresgruppe A* to escape the trap in the Caucasus. In this situation, the VVS failed utterly. The *Luftwaffe* also demonstrated a rare ability to recover quickly from December 1942 to January 1943, owing both to the method of creating *Schwerpunkte* and to improved logistics. As the VVS learned much from its opponent, the men of the *Luftwaffe* learned from the Soviets in many respects. After Stalingrad, the German airmen showed a determination and stamina which clearly owed much to the impact of such qualities perceived in their enemy.

Indeed, following the Battle of Stalingrad, the strategic initiative passed to the Soviet side, but many hard battles remained to be fought before Germany was conclusively defeated. The phase which immediately followed the Battle of Stalingrad would result in two of the greatest air battles ever to be fought – at the Kuban bridgehead in the north-western Caucasus and at the new bulge around Kursk.

| Unit | Aircraft type | Number of aircraft available | Number of serviceable aircraft |
|---|---|---|---|
| 3.(H)/11 | Bf 110 | 7 | 7 |
| 1.(H)/21 | Fw 189 | 8 | 5 |
| 6.(H)/13 | Fw 189 | 7 | 7 |
| 2.(H)/41 | Fw 189 | 2 | 2 |
| 1.(H)/10 | Fw 189 | 7 | 0 |
| 4(H)/10 | Fw 189 | 8 | 0 |
| 6.(H)/41 | Fw 189 | 9 | 3 |
| 7.(H)/LG2 | Bf 110 | 7 | 4 |
| 2.(H)/10 | Fw 189 | 7 | 4 |
| 7.(H)/32 | Fw 189 | 12 | 4 |
| 5.(H)/11 | Fw 189 | 9 | 2 |
| 2.(H)/32 | Fw 189 | 5 | 3 |
| 5.(H)/41 | Fw 189 | 5 | 3 |
| 3.(H)/12 | Fw 189 | 5 | 3 |
| 5.(H)/12 | Fw 189 | 7 | 2 |
| 3.(H)/31 | Bf 110 | 5 | 1 |
| 2.(F)/ObdL | Ju 88 | 9 | 4 |
| 3.(F)/10 | Ju 88 | 8 | 2 |
| Nachtaufklärungsstaffel 1 | Do 17 and He 111 | 9 | 4 |
| 3(F)/121 | Ju 88 | 10 | 6 |
| 4.(F)/122 | Ju 88 | 9 | 6 |
| Stab/JG 3 | Bf 109 | 7 | 4 |
| I./JG 3 | Bf 109 | 39 | 18 |
| III./JG 3 | Bf 109 | 23 | 18 |
| Stab/JG 52 | Bf 109 | 6 | 4 |
| 2./JG 52 | Bf 109 | 22 | 13 |
| II./JG 52 | Bf 109 | 43 | 27 |
| III./JG 52 | Bf 109 | 40 | 27 |
| 13. (Slow.)/JG 52 | Bf 109 | 8 | 6 |
| Stab/ZG 1 | Bf 110 | 2 | 2 |
| I./ZG 1 | Bf 110 | 32 | 18 |
| II./ZG 1 | Bf 110 | 23 | 13 |
| Stab/SchG 1 | Bf 109 | 6 | 5 |
| 3. and 8./SchG 1 | Bf 109 | 12 | 4 |
| 6. and 7./SchG 1 | Hs 123 and Hs 129 | 25 | 11 |
| Stab/KG 1 | Ju 88 | 3 | 2 |
| I./KG 1 | Ju 88 | 27 | 16 |
| II./KG 1 | Ju 88 | 36 | 22 |
| Stab/KG 27 | He 111 | 1 | 1 |
| II./KG 27 | He 111 | 31 | 15 |
| III./KG 27 | He 111 | 29 | 11 |
| Stab/KG 51 | Ju 88 | 1 | 0 |
| I./KG 51 | Ju 88 | 34 | 16 |
| 4. and 5./KG 51 | Ju 88 | 32 | 19 |
| Stab/KG 55 | He 111 | 3 | 2 |
| I./KG 55 | He 111 | 25 | 11 |
| II./KG 55 | He 111 | 17 | 6 |
| Elements of II./KG 76 | Ju 88 | 7 | 3 |
| Elements of III./KG 76 | Ju 88 | 7 | 3 |
| I./KG 100 | He 111 | 13 | 4 |
| 4./St.G 1 | Ju 87 | 13 | 5 |
| I./St.G 2 | Ju 87 | 29 | 24 |
| II./St.G 2 | Ju 87 | 26 | 18 |
| Stab/St.G 77 | Ju 87 and Bf 110 | 11 | 4 |
| I./St.G 77 | Ju 87 | 26 | 13 |
| II./St.G 77 | Ju 87 | 25 | 19 |
| 3./SAGr 125 | BV 138 | 9 | 5 |

## Appendix 2 VVS KA and PVO aviation in the Stalingrad - Don Bend area, November - December 1942

### 8 VA, Strength Report on 10 November 1942

| Korpus | Subordinate Diviziya | Subordinate Polks | Base | Aircraft type | Number of serviceable aircraft | Number of unserviceable aircraft |
|---|---|---|---|---|---|---|
| 2 SAK | 214 ShAD | 190 ShAP | Bolshevik | Il-2 | 29 | 3 |
| | | 618 ShAP | Vishnevka | Il-2 | 25 | 0 |
| | | 622 ShAP | Vishnevka | Il-2 | 32 | 0 |
| | 201 IAD | 13 IAP | Leninsk | La-5 | 31 | 0 |
| | | 236 IAP | Bolshevik | Yak-1 | 22 | 0 |
| | | | | Yak-7B | 10 | 0 |
| | | 437 IAP | Zhitkur | La-5 | - | - |
| | 235 IAD | 181 IAP | Yelton | Data unavailable | | |
| | | 239 IAP | Zhitkur | Data unavailable | | |
| | | 326 IAP | Zhitkur | Data unavailable | | |
| 268 IAD | | 9 GIAP | Zhitkur | LaGG-3 | 4 | 1 |
| | | | | La-5 | 0 | 1 |
| | | | | Yak-1 | 11 | 0 |
| | | 11 IAP | Kapustin Yar | Yak-1 | 4 | 9 |
| | | 273 IAP | Solodovka | Yak-1 | 7 | 12 |
| | | 274 IAP | Vladimirovka | Yak-1 | 7 | 3 |
| | | 296 IAP | Solodovka | Yak-1 | 4 | 6 |
| | | | | Yak-7B | 0 | 1 |
| | | Disciplinary Eskadrilya | - | - | - | - |
| 287 IAD | | 27 IAP | Srednaya Akhtuba | La-5 | 5 | 10 |
| | | 293 IAP | Srednaya Akhtuba | Yak-1 | 5 | |
| 226 SAD | | 2 IAP | Demidov | Yak-1 | 3 | 2 |
| | | 4 IAP | Demidov | Yak-1 | 2 | 4 |
| | | | | Yak-7B | 4 | 3 |
| | | 15 IAP | Stolyarovo | LaGG-3 | 2 | 9 |
| | | 225 ShAP | Katrichev | Il-2 | 3 | 8 |
| | | 504 ShAP | Demidov | Il-2 | 14 | 9 |
| | | 505 ShAP | Stolyarovo | Il-2 | 8 | 3 |
| | | 944 ShAP | Demidov | Il-2 | 3 | 12 |
| 206 ShAD | | 503 ShAP | Solodovka | Il-2 | 9 | 10 |
| | | 686 ShAP | Kapustin Yar | Il-2 | 2 | 6 |
| | | 807 ShAP | Kapustin Yar | Il-2 | 11 | 7 |
| | | 811 ShAP | Kapustin Yar | Il-2 | 6 | 10 |
| | | 945 ShAP | Karakul | Il-2 | 6 | 8 |
| 289 SAD | | 148 IAP | Nachalova | LaGG-3 | 4 | 0 |
| | | | | Yak-1 | 3 | 3 |
| | | 232 ShAP | Nachalova | Il-2 | 10 | 10 |
| | | 806 ShAP | Ivanovskiy | Il-2 | 13 | 4 |
| 270 BAD | | 10 GBAP | Yelton | SB | 6 | 4 |
| | | | | Il-4 | 0 | 4 |
| | | 30 BAP | Yelton | Pe-2 | 3 | 8 |
| | | 52 BAP | Yelton | Su-2 | 7 | 8 |
| | | 86 BAP | Vishnevka | Pe-2 | 2 | 11 |
| | | 284 BAP | Vishnevka | Pe-2 | 4 | 6 |
| | | 623 NLBAP | Yelton | R-5 | 2 | 7 |
| 272 NBAD | | 596 NLBAP | Novo Nikolskoye | U-2 | 16 | 1 |
| | | 621 NLBAP | Lugo-Vodyanoe | U-2 | 11 | 3 |
| | | 633 NLBAP | Novo Nikolskoye | U-2 | 10 | 3 |
| | | 709 NLBAP | Novo Nikolskoye | U-2 | 16 | 2 |
| | | 765 NLBAP | Lugo-Vodyanoe | U-2 | 13 | 1 |
| | | 969 NLBAP | Lugo-Vodyanoye | U-2 | 13 | 3 |
| | | Disciplinary Eskadrilya | Novo Nikolskoye | U-2 | 1 | 1 |
| 8 RAP | | | Karakul | Pe-2 | 1 | 6 |
| | | | | Pe-3 | 0 | 1 |
| 40 OAES | | | Kalinin state farm | U-2 | 13 | 2 |

## 16 VA, Strength Report on 19 November 1942

| Diviziya | Aircraft type | Number of serviceable aircraft | Number of unserviceable aircraft |
|---|---|---|---|
| 220 IAD | Yak-1 | 28 | 7 |
| 283 IAD | Yak-1 | 28 | 16 |
| 228 ShAD | Il-2 | 24 | 16 |
| 291 ShAD | Il-2 | 40 | 17 |
| 271 NBAD | U-2 | 83 | 10 |
| Totals | | 203 | 66 |

## 17 VA, Order of Battle on 19 November 1942

| Unit | Commander |
|---|---|
| 1 SAK | General-Mayor Shevchenko |
|     - 288 IAD | Podpolkovnik Konovalov |
|     - 267 ShAD | Podpolkovnik Kolomeytsev |
| 282 IAD | Podpolkovnik Ryazanov |
| 221 BAD | Polkovnik Antoshkin |
| 262 NBAD | Polkovnik Belitskiy |
| 208 ShAP | |
| 637 ShAP | |

## 17 VA, Strength Report on 19 November 1942

| Aircraft type | Number of serviceable aircraft | Number of unserviceable aircraft |
|---|---|---|
| Bombers | 118 | 14 |
| Shturmoviks | 133 | 15 |
| Fighters | 166 | 22 |
| Reconnaissance aircraft | 6 | - |
| Totals | 423 | 51 |

## 102 IAD PVO, Order of Battle on 10 December 1942

| Unit | Base | Aircraft type | Number of serviceable aircraft | Number of unserviceable aircraft | Number of pilots |
|---|---|---|---|---|---|
| 572 IAP | Verkhniy Baskunchak | LaGG-3 | 5 | 3 | 22 |
| | | I-16 | 2 | 1 | |
| | | I-15bis | 1 | 1 | |
| | | P-40 Kittyhawk | - | 2 | |
| 629 IAP | Ventilevka | Hurricane | 6 | 2 | 34 |
| | | I-16 | 1 | - | |
| | | I-153 | - | 1 | |
| | | I-15bis | 1 | - | |
| | Saykhin | Hurricane | 5 | 1 | |
| | | I-153 | 1 | 1 | |
| | Pallasovka | I-16 | 2 | - | |
| 652 IAP | Astrakhan | I-15bis | 2 | 1 | 20 |
| | | Yak-1 | 10 | 1 | |
| | | Hurricane | 1 | 4 | |
| | Guryev | I-15bis | 4 | - | |
| 788 IAP | Vladimirovka | Yak-1 | 6 | 1 | 14 |
| | | Yak-7B | 1 | - | |

## Appendix 3  The Soviet Air Blockade Zones at Stalingrad in December 1942

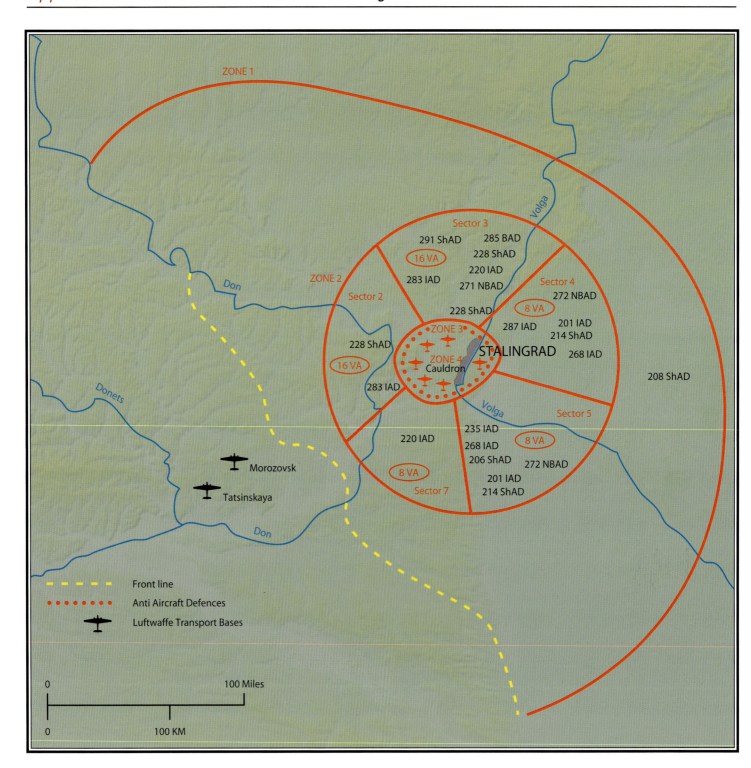

ZONE 1

ZONE 2

Sector 3

291 ShAD    285 BAD
16 VA    228 ShAD
220 IAD
283 IAD    271 NBAD

Don

Sector 2

Sector 4
272 NBAD
228 ShAD    8 VA
287 IAD    201 IAD
214 ShAD

ZONE 3
228 ShAD
16 VA    ZONE 4    268 IAD
Cauldron
Donets    283 IAD    208 ShAD

Volga

Sector 5
235 IAD
220 IAD    268 IAD    8 VA
206 ShAD    272 NBAD
8 VA    201 IAD
Morozovsk    Sector 7    214 ShAD

Tatsinskaya

Don

STALINGRAD

Volga

— — — —    Front line
• • • • • • •    Anti Aircraft Defences
✈    Luftwaffe Transport Bases

0        100 Miles

0    100 KM

## The Structure of the Luftwaffe

The basic tactical unit of the *Luftwaffe* normally was the *Geschwader*. Each *Geschwader* was identified by a number and had a prefix according to its branch of service:

*Jagdgeschwader* (JG) = fighter.
*Nachtjagdgeschwader* (NJG) = night fighter.
*Zerstörergeschwader* (ZG) = heavy fighter.
*Schlachtgeschwader* (Sch.G., later SG) = ground-attack.
*Sturzkampfgeschwader* (St.G.) = dive-bomber.
*Schnellkampfgeschwader* (SKG) = high-speed bomber.
*Kampfgeschwader* (KG) = bomber.
*Kampfgeschwader zu besonderen Verwendung* (KG.z.b.V.) = transport (later *Transportgeschwader*, TG).
*Lehrgeschwader* (LG) = operational training unit (originally formed for the purpose of training unit leaders).

Several *Geschwader* were given traditional or honorary titles, such as ZG 26 *Horst Wessel* (a Nazi streetfighter 'Hero' of the 1930s).

Each *Geschwader* normally comprised three or four *Gruppen*, numbered with Roman characters:

III./JG 52 = third *Gruppe* of *Jagdgeschwader* 52.

The *Gruppe* comprised three (occasionally four) *Staffeln*, numbered with Arabic numerals:

9./JG 52 = ninth *Staffel* of *Jagdgeschwader* 52.

The exception was the Reconnaissance Wing (*Aufklärungsgruppe*), which was simply abbreviated due to its strategical (*Fernaufklärungsgruppe*) or tactical (*Heeresaufklärungsgruppe*) role. Such as: 4.(F)/122 = 4th *Staffel* of *Fernaufklärungsgruppe* 121, or 1.(H)/32 = 1st *Staffel* of *Heeresaufklärungsgruppe* 32. A particular Reconnaissance Wing was *Aufklärungsgruppe Oberbefehlshaber der Luftwaffe* (AufklObdL), which was directly subordinate to the commander of the German Air Force, *Reichsmarschall* Hermann Göring.

The fighter-*Staffel* was made up of three tactical formations, the so-called *Schwarm*.
Each *Schwarm* was made up of two basic tactical formations, the so-called *Rotte*, two aircraft.
The bomber- and dive-bomber-*Staffel* was made up of four tactical formations, the so-called *Kette*, three aircraft.
Thus, the intended outfit of a *Staffel* normally was twelve aircraft.

Apart from the three *Staffeln*, the *Gruppenstab* (Staff) also had a *Stabsschwarm*.
Apart from the three or four *Gruppen*, the *Geschwaderstab* also had a *Stabsstaffel*.

The normal structure of a *Geschwader* was the following:

### *Stabsstaffel* **of the** *Geschwader*

### **I. *Gruppe*:**
*Stabsschwarm*
*1. Staffel*
*2. Staffel*
*3. Staffel*

### **II. *Gruppe*:**
*Stabsschwarm*
*4. Staffel*
*5. Staffel*
*6. Staffel*

### **III. *Gruppe*:**
*Stabsschwarm*
*7. Staffel*
*8. Staffel*
*9. Staffel*

### **(IV. *Gruppe*:**
*Stabsschwarm*
*10. Staffel*
*11. Staffel*
*12. Staffel)*

The commander of a *Geschwader* was the *Geschwaderkommodore* or *Kommodore*, which was not a rank in itself. His rank would be *Major*, *Oberstleutnant* or *Oberst*.
The commander of a *Gruppe* was the *Gruppenkommandeur* or *Kommandeur*. His rank would be *Major* or *Hauptmann*.
The commander of a *Staffel* was the *Staffelkapitän*. His rank would be *Hauptmann*, *Oberleutnant* or *Leutnant*.

Several *Geschwader* were organized into a *Fliegerkorps* (Air Corps, numbered with Roman numerals), or a *Fliegerdivision* (Air Division, numbered with Arabic numerals), or a *Fliegerführer*.
The largest tactical organisation within the German Air Force of World War II was the *Luftflotte* or *Luftwaffenkommando*, which normally comprised two *Fliegerkorps* or *Fliegerdivisionen* or *Fliegerführer*. The Luftflotte roughly corresponds to a numbered U.S. Army Air Force.

## Appendix 5 *The Structure of the Soviet Air Forces in 1942*

### Organisation

During the latter half of 1942, the Soviet air forces were organizationally divided between:

VVS KA (the Air Forces of Red Army). Commander: *General-Leytenant* Aleksandr Novikov.

ADD (the Long-Range Aviation). Commander: *General-Mayor* Aleksandr Golovanov.

IA PVO (Fighter Aviation of Home Air Defence). Commander: *General-Mayor* Aleksandr Osipenko.

VVS VMF (the Naval Air Forces ). Commander: *General-Leytenant* Semyon Zhavoronkov.

GVF (Civil Aviation). Chief of the Main Directorate of the GVF: *General-Leytenant* Fyodor Astakhov.

### Air Armies

From May 1942, the aviation of the Red Army Fronts (the equivalent of Army groups) were reorganized into air armies – *Vozdushnaya Armiya, VA*.

Until November 1942, seventeen air armies were formed, thirteen of these on the Soviet-German Front. Four other air armies were formed in the eastern part of the Soviet Union (Far East and Trans-Baykal). In 1942, an air army consisted of five to thirteen *Diviziya*, plus a few independent *Polks* and *Eskadrilyas*.

### The Supreme High Command (RVGK) Reserve Aviation

The Supreme High Command (RVGK) Reserve aviation was formed to meet the needs in the war in the late summer of 1941. In August - October 1941, six reserve aviation groups (RAG) - each consisting of four to eight aviation regiments (80-100 aircraft) - were formed as a rapid deployment reserve force.

Between March and May 1942, two so-called Manoeuvre Aviation Groups (*Manevrennaya Aviagruppa*, MAG) and ten so-called Strike Aviation Groups (*Udarnaya Aviagruppa*, UAG) were formed, each comprising two to eight regiments (40-160 aircraft). These groups were allocated to certain strategic directions (North-western, Western, South-western) and were frequently shifted between the air forces of various armies and fronts within these directions. In the summer of 1942, these aviation groups were disbanded.

Instead, on 1 July 1942, a new reserve aviation force was formed in the shape of specialised air armies – fighter air armies and a bomber air army. Two fighter air armies (1 IA and 2 IA) and one bomber aviation army (1 BA) were formed. Among these, only 1 IA saw combat action in full force. The two others were disbanded before completion of their formation. 1 IA's initial operations showed that the aviation army was too large and cumbersome, and it was decided to create smaller and more flexible reserve forces, which easily could be included into the structure of an air army after their arrival to the front - and likewise easily excluded from it after completing their combat tasks.

From the autumn of 1942, the main form of aviation reserves of the Stavka VGK were the aviation corps and independent aviation divisions of the RVGK. From 10 September 1942, the RVGK's aviation corps - each comprising two or three aviation divisions and between 120 and 270 aircraft - were formed. These were composite – *Smeshannyy Aviatsionnyy Korpus*, SAK – and thus comprised various types of aviation.

The first of these were 1 SAK, 2 SAK and 3 SAK, which all went into first-line service in November 1942.

### IA PVO (Fighter Aviation of the Home Air Defence)

From January 1942, all fighter aviation corps, divisions, and regiments of the Home Air Defence were subordinated to the independent Troops of the Home Air Defence, *Voyska PVO Strany*. The *Voyska Strany* was composed of anti-aircraft artillery, searchlight units, the Troops of the VNOS (Aerial Observation, Information, and Communication), and the fighter aviation—the IA PVO. In May 1942, the IA PVO was organized into three fighter aviation *Korpus*, thirteen fighter aviation *Diviziyas*, and nine independent fighter *Polks*.

### VVS-VMF (the Naval Air Forces)

The Soviet Navy had its independent air arm. The four Soviet fleets and a number of flotillas were assigned their own air forces.

VVS ChF was the air force of the Black Sea Fleet.

### GVF (Civil Aviation)

The Soviet Civil Aviation was operatively subordinated to the Peoples' Commissariat of the Defence from the outbreak of the war in June 1941. While a part of the GVF carried out civil transport flights in the rear areas, another part was mobilized for combat service. Already in July 1941, six special aviation groups of the GVF had been formed on the basis of the territorial detachments of the GVF, and the personnel of these aviation groups were conscripted into the Red Army. The main tasks of these groups were divided between transportation of military supplies and evacuation of injured soldiers, supplying partisan detachments in the enemy's rear area, and liaison flights. By the autumn of 1942, fifteen different GVF units had been brought into first-line service, all subordinated to the military councils of the fronts and armies.

From 26 April 1942, the Chief Administration of the GVF was subordinated to the C-in-C of VVS KA, while the Chief of the Main Directorate of the GVF was appointed Deputy C-in-C of VVS KA.

### Tactical Formations

The basic tactical unit of the Soviet aviation was the regiment, the *Polk*. In early 1942, the nominal strength of a *Polk* normally was two nine-aircraft squadrons (*Eskadrilya*) plus a staff *Zveno* (flight) of three to four aircraft. With an increasing number of aircraft arriving from production lines, many regiments were expanded to include three *Eskadrilyas* from mid-1942.

Each *Polk* consisted of a number of *Zveno* - normally three aircraft each, piloted by the *Zveno* leader and his two wingmen.

The fighter aviation's three-plane *Zveno* formation was successively replaced by the four-aircraft *Zveno* from mid-1942. The fighter aviation's new four-aircraft *Zveno* was divided into two *Para* (Pair), each consisting of two aircraft - piloted by the *Para* leader and his wingman.

Between two to five *Polks* formed a *Diviziya*, with all *Polks* subordinated to a certain *Diviziya* operating in a certain territorial sector.

There were also independent reconnaissance *Eskadrilyas*.

The largest Soviet aviation unit was the *Korpus* (aviation corps). The *Korpus* were the basis of the PVO and the Supreme High Command (RVGK) Reserve Aviation. A total of thirteen aviation corps of the RVGK (four IAKs, three ShAKs, three BAKs, and three SAKs) were formed from September 1942 until the end of 1942. Each Reserve Aviation *Korpus* comprised two or three aviation divisions with between 120 and 270 aircraft altogether.

Each *Korpus, Diviziya* and *Polk* had a unique number – like the *Korpus* 1 SAK, the *Diviziya* 220 IAD and the *Polk* 27 IAP. This is similar to the number system of *Wings, Groups* and *Squadrons* in the RAF or the USAAF. The *Eskadrilyas* which were subordinated to a *Polk* did not have a unique number. This is similar to the number system of *Staffeln* in the *Luftwaffe*.

Particularly distinguished Soviet military units were awarded with the honorary title *Gvardeyskiy* (Guards) units. Such a unit received a special Guards banner at a Guards Award ceremony, each of the soldiers serving in such a unit were awarded with the Guards Emblem, and its officers' ranks were prefixed 'Guards' (*Guards Kapitan*, etc). The unit was also renumbered into a new Guards unit, according to the order in which it had been appointed a Guards unit. Thus, 434 IAP became 32 GIAP, and 288 ShAP became 33 GShAP.

## The Iron Cross awards of the Wehrmacht in 1941

**Das Eiserne Kreuz 2. Klasse.**
The Iron Cross of Second Grade.

**Das Eiserne Kreuz 1. Klasse.**
The Iron Cross of First Grade.

**Das Ritterkreuz des Eisernen Kreuzes.**
The Knight's Cross of the Iron Cross. About 7,500 awards during World War II, including about 1,730 to servicemen of the *Luftwaffe*.

**Das Ritterkreuz des Eisernen Kreuzes mit Eichenlaub.**
The Knight's Cross with Oak Leaves. A total of 860 awards during World War II, including 192 to servicemen of the *Luftwaffe*.

**Das Ritterkreuz des Eisernen Kreuzes mit dem Eichenlaub mit Schwertern.**
The Knight's Cross with Oak Leaves and Swords. A total of 154 awards during World War II, including 41 to servicemen of the *Luftwaffe*.

**Das Ritterkreuz des Eisernen Kreuzes mit dem Eichenlaub mit Schwertern und Brillanten.**
The Knight's Cross with Oak Leaves, Swords and Diamonds. A total of 27 awards during World War II, including 12 to servicemen of the *Luftwaffe*.

**Das Grosskreuz des Eisernes Kreuzes.**
The Great Cross. Only awarded once, to *Reichsmarschall* Hermann Göring, the C-in-C of the *Luftwaffe*.

Each of the above orders could be awarded to the same individual only once.

During Operation *Barbarossa*, eight German fighter pilots and three dive-bomber pilots and one bomber aviator on the Eastern Front were awarded with the Knight's Cross with Oak Leaves, three fighter pilots were awarded with the 'Swords' and one fighter pilot – *Oberstleutnant* Werner Mölders – with the 'Diamonds'.

## The highest military awards and recognitions of the Soviet Union in 1941

**Orden Krasnoy Zvezdy.** The Red Star Order. More than 2,860,000 awards during the wars against Germany and Japan from 1941 to 1945.

**Orden Krasnogo Znameni.** The Red Banner Order. More than 580,000 awards during the war.

**Orden Lenina.** The Lenin Order. More than 41,000 awards during the war.

**Geroy Sovetskogo Soyuza.** Hero of the Soviet Union. More than 11,000 men and women—2,420 in the VVS—were appointed Heroes of the Soviet Union during the war. Of these, 104—including 65 serving in the VVS—were appointed twice, and three—including two serving in the VVS—were appointed triple Heroes of the Soviet Union.

The appointment as a Hero of the Soviet Union was the highest recognition for courage or remarkable feats. It was no military 'award'; it was an honorary title. The men and women who were appointed Heroes of the Soviet Union were simultaneously awarded with the Lenin Order and the Golden Star Medal. The Golden Star Medal was the token of a special distinction, not an award in itself. In the few cases where individuals were appointed Heroes of the Soviet Union a second or a third time, they also were awarded with a second and a third Golden Star Medal, respectively.

Each of the above orders could be awarded to the same individual several times.

## Appendix 7 *Aircraft combat losses in the air in the Stalingrad area in September 1942*

| Date | Luftwaffe combat losses by aircraft type | Total Luftwaffe combat losses | Combat losses by 8 VA | Combat losses by 16 VA | Total combat losses by 8 VA and 16 VA |
|---|---|---|---|---|---|
| 1 September | 1 Fw 189 | 1 | 4 Il-2<br>3 Yak-1<br>1 Yak-7B<br>1 Pe-2 | - | 9 |
| 2 September | 1 He 111<br>3 Ju 87<br>3 Bf 110 | 7 | 2 Il-2<br>8 Pe-2<br>9 Yak-1<br>3 Yak-7B<br>2 La-5<br>2 Kittyhawk | - | 26 |
| 3 September | 2 Ju 88<br>1 Bf 109 | 3 | 3 Il-2<br>3 Pe-2<br>4 Yak-1<br>3 Yak-7B<br>3 La-5 | - | 16 |
| 4 September | 1 Ju 87<br>1 Fw 189<br>2 Bf 109 | 4 | 1 Yak-1<br>1 LaGG-3<br>1 La-5 | 3 Il-2<br>17 Yak-1 | 23 |
| 5 September | 2 Ju 87<br>1 Fw 189<br>3 Bf 109 | 6 | 2 Pe-2<br>4 Yak-1<br>3 LaGG-3<br>2 La-5<br>3 Kittyhawk | 2 Il-2<br>1 Yak-1 | 17 |
| 6 September | 1 Ju 87<br>1 Fi 156<br>1 Bf 109 | 3 | 6 Il-2<br>3 LaGG-3<br>2 La-5 | 10 Il-2<br>3 Yak-1 | 24 |
| 7 September | 2 Ju 88<br>1 Fw 189<br>1 Bf 109 | 4 | 2 Il-2<br>1 Pe-2<br>2 Yak-7B<br>2 La-5 | 10 Il-2<br>5 Yak-1 | 22 |
| 8 September | 2 Ju 88<br>1 He 111<br>3 Bf 109 | 6 | 12 Il-2<br>1 Pe-2<br>4 Yak-1<br>2 Yak-7B<br>4 La-5 | 7 Il-2<br>20 Yak-1 | 50 |
| 9 September | 1 Ju 88<br>1 He 111<br>1 Bf 109 | 3 | 10 Il-2<br>1 Pe-2<br>1 Yak-7B | 2 Il-2<br>13 Yak-1 | 27 |
| 10 September | 1 Ju 88<br>2 Ju 87<br>4 Bf 109 | 7 | 8 Il-2<br>5 Pe-2<br>1 Yak-1<br>1 Yak-7B<br>1 LaGG-3<br>1 La-5 | 2 Il-2<br>7 Yak-1 | 26 |
| 11 September | 1 Ju 88<br>2 Ju 87 | 3 | 4 Pe-2<br>1 Yak-1<br>4 La-5<br>3 Yak-7 | 7 Yak-1 | 19 |
| 12 September | 1 Ju 88<br>1 Ju 87<br>2 Bf 109<br>1 Bf 110 | 5 | 1 Pe-2<br>1 Yak-1<br>1 Yak-7B<br>3 La-5 | 1 Il-2<br>6 Yak-1 | 13 |
| 13 September | 1 Bf 109 | 1 | 4 Il-2<br>2 Yak-1<br>7 Yak-7B<br>2 La-5 | 4 Yak-1 | 19 |
| 14 September | 1 Ju 88<br>1 Fw 189<br>1 Bf 110 | 3 | 4 Il-2<br>2 Pe-2<br>4 Yak-1 | 1 Yak-1 | 11 |
| 15 September | 1 Ju 88<br>1 Bf 110<br>1 Bf 109 | 3 | 7 Il-2<br>2 Yak-1<br>1 Yak-7B<br>2 La-5 | 1 Yak-1<br>2 U-2 | 15 |
| 16 September | 1 Bf 109<br>1 Bf 110 | 2 | 4 Il-2<br>2 Pe-2<br>2 Yak-7<br>1 La-5 | 2 Il-2<br>6 Yak-1<br>1 Yak-7B | 18 |
| 17 September | 1 He 111<br>2 Ju 88<br>1 Bf 109 | 4 | 2 Il-2<br>2 Yak-1<br>1 Yak-7B | 6 Yak-1<br>1 Yak-7B | 12 |
| 18 September | 1 Ju 87<br>1 Fw 189<br>1 Ju 88 | 3 | 2 Il-2<br>3 Pe-2 | 12 Il-2<br>18 Yak-1<br>2 Yak-7B | 37 |
| 19 September | 1 Ju 88<br>1 Fw 189<br>2 Bf 110<br>2 Bf 109 | 6 | 1 Il-2<br>1 Yak-7B | 2 Il-2<br>6 Yak-1<br>1 Yak-7B<br>10 LaGG-3 | 21 |
| 20 September | 2 Ju 87<br>1 Fw 189<br>1 Bf 110<br>2 Bf 109 | 6 | 2 Il-2<br>2 Yak-1<br>3 Yak-7B | 6 Yak-1<br>5 Yak-7B | 18 |
| 21 September | 2 He 111<br>2 Ju 88<br>1 Bf 109 | 5 | 2 Il-2<br>2 Yak-7B | 3 Yak-1<br>1 Yak-7B | 8 |
| 22 September | 1 He 111<br>1 Ju 87<br>1 Hs 129 | 3 | 4 Yak-1 | 10 Yak-1<br>3 Yak-7B | 17 |
| 23 September | 1 He 111<br>1 Bf 109 | 2 | 1 Il-2<br>1 Yak-1 | 4 Yak-1<br>7 Yak-7B | 13 |
| 24 September | 1 Ju 88<br>1 Hs 123 | 2 | - | 8 Yak-1 | 8 |
| 25 September | 2 Ju 87 | 2 | 4 Yak-1<br>1 LaGG-3<br>1 La-5 | 10 Yak-1 | 16 |
| 26 September | 4 Ju 87<br>1 Bf 109 | 5 | - | 1 Il-2<br>1 Yak-7B | 2 |
| 27 September | 1 Ju 88 | 1 | Il-2<br>1 Yak-1<br>4 Yak-7B | 1 Yak-1 | 7 |
| 28 September | - | - | 3 Il-2<br>1 Yak-7B | 6 Il-2<br>6 Yak-1 | 16 |
| 29 September | 1 Ju 87<br>1 Fw 189<br>1 Bf 109 | 3 | 4 Il-2<br>1 Yak-1<br>2 Yak-7B | - | 7 |
| 30 September | - | - | - | 1 Il-2<br>4 Yak-1 | 3 |
| Totals | | 103 | | | 520 |

### Total aircraft losses sustained by 102 IAD PVO at Stalingrad in September 1942

| Regiment | Pilot losses | | Aircraft losses |
|---|---|---|---|
| | Killed | Missing | |
| 572 IAP | 2 | - | 4 |
| 629 IAP | 4 | 1 | 8 |
| 652 IAP | - | - | - |
| 731 IAP | 2 | 7 | 16 |
| 788 IAP | 1 | 4 | 8 |
| Totals | 9 | 12 | 36 |

# Chapter Notes

**CHAPTER 1**

1. Morzik, *Die deutschen Transportflieger im Zweiten Weltkrieg*, p. 131 – 132.
2. Ibid., p. 145

**CHAPTER 2**

3. Interrogation with *Ofw.* Alexander Mudin, TsAMO.
4. *Kriegstagebuch des LIV. Armeekorps*, 26.12.1941. Bundesarchiv/Militärarchiv.
5. Erickson, *The Road to Stalingrad*, p. 290.
6. Soviet Documents on the Use of War Experience, vol. 3, 1942. Quoted in Hayward, *Stopped at Stalingrad*, p. 35.
7. Tieke, *Kampf um die Krim*, p. 111.
8. Falaleyev, *V stroyo krylatykh: Iz vozpomikakiy*, p. 85.
9. Erickson, *The Road to Stalingrad*, p. 329.
10. TsAMO, f. 319, op. 4789, d. 22.
11. Kiehl, *Kampfgeschwader Legion Condor 53*, p. 185.
12. *Traditionsgeschichte der I. /Jagdgeschwader 52.*
13. TsAMO, f. 208, op. 2511, l. 89-96.
14. *Flugzeugunfälle und Verluste bei den Verbänden (täglich)*, Ob.d.L. Gen.Qu. Gen. 6. Abt. Bundesarchiv/Militärarchiv RL 2 III/1179.
15. TsAMO, f. 208, op. 2589, d. 150, l. 7-14.
16. *Flugzeugunfälle und Verluste bei den Verbänden (täglich)*, Ob.d.L. Gen.Qu. Gen. 6. Abt. Bundesarchiv/Militärarchiv RL 2 III/1179.
17. Plocher, *The German Air Force Versus Russia, 1942*, p. 104.
18. TsAMO, f. 6 VA.
19. *Flugzeugunfälle und Verluste bei den Verbänden (täglich)*, Ob.d.L. Gen.Qu. Gen. 6. Abt. Bundesarchiv/Militärarchiv RL 2 III/1180.
20. *Flugzeugunfälle und Verluste bei den Verbänden (täglich)*, Ob.d.L. Gen.Qu. Gen. 6. Abt. Bundesarchiv/Militärarchiv RL 2 III/1180.
21. TsAMO, f. 6 VA.
22. *Flugzeugunfälle und Verluste bei den Verbänden (täglich)*, Ob.d.L. Gen.Qu. Gen. 6. Abt. Bundesarchiv/Militärarchiv RL 2 III/1179-1181.
23. TsAMO, f. 6 VA.

**CHAPTER 3**

24. *Kriegstagebuch des Oberkommandos der Wehrmacht*, vol. III, p. 5.
25. Hayward, p. 67.
26. *Kriegstagebuch des Oberkommandos der Wehrmacht*, vol. III, p. 322. 16 April 1942.
27. *Kriegstagebuch des Oberkommandos der Wehrmacht*, vol. III, p. 318. 9 April 1942.
28. *Kriegstagebuch des Oberkommandos der Wehrmacht*, vol. III, p. 324. 20 April 1942.
29. Hayward, p. 70.
30. Ibid., p. 69.

**CHAPTER 4**

31. Skripko, *Po tselyam blizhnim i dal'nim*, p. 152.
32. TsAMO, f.743 IAP op.530424 d.1.
33. Shevchuk, *Komandir atakuyet pervym*, p. 10-11.
34. TsAMO, f. 215, op. 1196, d. 1.
35. *Flugzeugunfälle und Verluste bei den Verbänden (täglich)*, Ob.d.L. Gen.Qu. Gen. 6. Abt. Bundesarchiv/Militärarchiv RL 2 III/1180
36. TsAMO, f.743 IAP op.530424 d.1.
37. *Hptm.* Alfred Grislawski, logbook.
38. TsAMO, f. 57 GIAP.
39. Polyam, *Moy Voyna*, p. 73.
40. TsAMO, f. 215, op. 1196, d. 1.
41. Skripko, *Po tselyam blizhnim i dal'nim*, p. 152.
42. Skripko, Ibid., p. 172.
43. Ivanov, *Skorost', manyovr, ogon'*, p. 83.
44. Skripko, *Po tselyam blizhnim i dal'nim*, p. 169.
45. *Istoriya Vyelikoy Otyechyestvyennoy Voyny Sovyetskogo.*
46. Erickson, *The Road to Stalingrad*, p. 349.
47. *Fw.* Alfred Grislawski, 9./JG 52. *Gefechtsbericht* of 9 May 1942.
48. Ivanov, *Skorost', manyovr, ogon'*, p. 83.
49. Prien, *Geschichte des Jagdgeschwaders 77*, p. 997.
50. Ivanov, *Skorost', manyovr, ogon'*, p. 83.
51. Pegg, *Hs 129 Panzerjäger*, pp. 70-71.
52. Skripko, *Po tselyam blizhnim i dal'nim*, p. 169.
53. Polyam, *Moy Voyna*, p. 78.
54. *Voyenno-Istoricheskiy Zhurnal*, 2/1999, p. 5.
55. Krivosheyev, *Grif sekretnosti snyat. Poteri vooruzhyonnykh sil SSSR v voynakh, boyevykh deystviyakh i voyennykh konfliktakh*, p. 212.
56. TsAMO, f. 215, op. 1196, d. 1.

**CHAPTER 5**

57. Falaleyev, Fedor Yakovlevich, *Vstroyokrylatykh: Iz vozpomikakiy*, Izhevsk: Udmyrtiya, 1978, p. 85.
58. Karlenko and Antipov, Kharkov, May 1942: *Khronika Sobyytiy, in Mir Aviatsii*, No 1/2003.
59. TsAMO, f. 282 IAP.
60. Schwabedissen, *The Russian Air Force in the Eyes of German Commanders*, p. 222.
61. TsAMO, f. 53 GIAP.
62. TsAMO, f. 53 GIAP.
63. *Lt.* Hermann Wolf, Flugbuch.
64. TsAMO, f. 13 GBAP.
65. TsAMO, f. 6 IAP.
66. Prien et al, *Die Jagdfliegerverbände der Deutschen Luftwaffe 1934 bis 1945, Teil 9/II*, p. 546.
67. TsAMO, f. 4 RAG.
68. Karlenko and Antipov, Kharkov, May 1942: Khronika Sobyytiy, in Mir Aviatsii, No 1/2003.
69. Dickfeld, *Footsteps of the Hunter*, p. 104.
70. *Zeugenbericht von Lt. Graf, 14.5.1942.* Via *Hptm.* Alfred Grislawski.
71. Via *Hptm.* Alfred Grislawski.
72. TsAMO, f. 4 RAG.
73. Halder, *Kriegstagebuch*, Vol. III, p. 442.
74. *Flugzeugunfälle und Verluste bei den Verbänden (täglich)*, Ob.d.L. Gen.Qu. Gen. 6. Abt. Bundesarchiv/Militärarchiv RL 2 III/1181.
75. Bundesarchiv/Militärarchiv, RL 10/120.
76. Karlenko and Antipov, *Kharkov, May 1942: Khronika Sobyytiy, in Mir Aviatsii*, No 1/2003.
77. Pokryschkin, *Himmel des Krieges*, pp. 152-153.
78. Johannes Steinhoff, Flugbuch; TsAMO, f. 53 GIAP.
79. Johannes Steinhoff's logbook.
80. Johannes Steinhoff's logbook
81. TsAMO, f. 230 ShAD.
82. TsAMO, f. 319, op. 4799, d. 22.
83. Pegg, *Hs 129 Panzerjäger*, p. 72.
84. TsAMO, f. 1579, op. 52681, d. 2, l. 1-2.
85. *Flugzeugunfälle und Verluste bei den Verbänden (täglich)*, Ob.d.L. Gen.Qu. Gen. 6. Abt. Bundesarchiv/Militärarchiv RL 2 III/1181.
86. Pegg, *Hs 129 Panzerjäger*, p. 71.
87. *Traditionsgeschichte der I. /Jagdgeschwader 52.*
88. *Abschuss einer P-2, W. Sawinzy, 26.5.42, 1609 Uhr, Höhe: 500 m.* Via Alfred Grislawski.
89. Prien and Stemmer, *Messerschmitt Bf 109 in Einsatz bei der Stab und I. /Jagdgeschwader 3*, p. 221.
90. TsAMO, f. 4 RAG.
91. *Hptm.* Helmut Bennemann, I./JG 52. *Gefechtsbericht* of 27 May 1942.
92. *Lt.* Friedrich-Karl Bachmann, I./JG 52. *Gefechtsbericht* of 27 May 1942.
93. Polynin, *Boyevyye marshruty*, pp. 141-142.
94. Polynin, *Boyevyye marshruty*, pp. 142.
95. Plocher, p. 174.

**CHAPTER 6**

96. Bätcher, logbook.
97. Bätcher, logbook.
98. Hayward, *Stopped at Stalingrad*, p. 97.
99. Karpov, *The Commander*, p. 86. Quoted in Hayward, *Stopped at Stalingrad*, p. 97.
100. Manstein, p. 277.
101. Dierich, *Kampfgeschwader 51 "Edelweiss,"* pp. 185-186.
102. Manstein, p. 274.
103. Hayward, p. 110.
104. Kusnezow, *Gefechtsalarm in den Flotten*, p. 171.
105. Bätcher, logbook.
106. Manstein, p. 281.
107. Balke, *Kampfgeschwader 100 "Wiking,"* p. 116.
108. *Flugzeugunfälle und Verluste bei den Verbänden (täglich)*, Ob.d.L. Gen.Qu. Gen. 6. Abt. Bundesarchiv/Militärarchiv RL 2 III/1181-1182.

**CHAPTER 7**

109. TsAMO, f. 146 GIAP; *Generalquartiermeister der Luftwaffe.*

110. *Flugzeugunfälle und Verluste bei den Verbänden (täglich), Ob.d.L. Gen.Qu. Gen. 6.Abt.* Bundesarchiv/Militärarchiv RL 2 III/1181.
111. TsAMO, f.346, op. 5760, d., l.70.
112. Hermann Graf in letter to Frau Steinbatz, quoted in Fast: *Das Jagdgeschwader 52,* Part 3, n. 107.
113. Bergström and Pegg, *Jagdwaffe: Barbarossa, The Invasion of Russia June-December 1941,* p. 155.
114. KTB OKW, Vol. III, p. 440.

CHAPTER 8
115. *Kriegstagebuch des Oberkommandos der Wehrmacht,* Vol. III, p. 455.
116. Dierich: *Kampfgeschwader 55 "Greif "* D. 244.
117. Rossmann, logbook.
118. Waiss, *Chronik Kampfgeschwader Nr. 27 Boelcke,* Band IV, p.81.
119. *Flugzeugunfälle und Verluste bei den Verbänden (täglich), Ob.d.L. Gen.Qu. Gen. 6.Abt.* Bundesarchiv/Militärarchiv RL 2 III/1181.
120. TsAMO, f. 2 VA and f. 8 VA.
121. TsAMO, f. 8 VA.
122. Polynin, *Boyevyyemarshruty.* 2nd ed, p. 42.
123. *Lagebericht OKH, 2. Juli 1942.* KTB OKW, vol. III, p. 468.
124. *Lagebericht OKH, 3. Juli 1942.* KTB OKW, vol. III, p. 472.
125. Gubin and Kiselyov, p. 18.
126. *Flugzeugunfälle und Verluste bei den Verbänden (täglich), Ob.d.L. Gen.Qu. Gen. 6.Abt.* Bundesarchiv/Militärarchiv RL 2 III/1182.
127. TsAMO, f. 8 VA.
128. TsAMO, f. 8 VA.
129. Tieke, *The Caucasus and the Oil,* p.14.

CHAPTER 9
130. *Flugzeugunfälle und Verluste bei den Verbänden (täglich), Ob.d.L. Gen.Qu. Gen. 6.Abt.* Bundesarchiv/Militärarchiv RL 2 III/1182.
131. Waiss, *Chronik Kampfgeschwader Nr. 27 Boelcke,* Band IV, p. 97.
132. TsAMO, f. 2 VA.
133. *Flugzeugunfälle und Verluste bei den Verbänden (täglich), Ob.d.L. Gen.Qu. Gen. 6.Abt.* Bundesarchiv/Militärarchiv RL 2 III/1182.
134. TsAMO, f. 2 VA.
135. *Lagebericht OKH, 30. Juli 1942. Kriegstagebuch des Oberkommandos der Wehrmacht,* vol.III, p. 538.
136. TsAMO, f. 8 VA.
137. TsAMO, f. 270 BAD, d. 69, l. 60.
138. Waiss, *Chronik Kampfgeschwader Nr. 27 Boelcke,* Band IV, p. 106.
139. TsAMO, f. 8 VA:
140. *Flugzeugunfälle und Verluste bei den Verbänden (täglich), Ob.d.L. Gen.Qu. Gen. 6.Abt.* Bundesarchiv/Militärarchiv RL 2 III/1182.
141. Prien, *Jagdgeschwader 53: A History of the Pik As Geschwader Volume 2: May 1942 – January 1944.* pp. 419-420.

CHAPTER 10
142. *Eingegengene Meldungen Generalstab Luftwaffe während des 29.7.42. Kriegstagebuch des Oberkommandos der Wehrmacht,* vol. III, p. 537.
143. TsAMO, f. 319, op. 4798, d. 55, l. 48-49.

CHAPTER 11
144. Bundesarchiv/Militärarchiv, N 671/9.
145. Bätcher, logbook.
146. *Aufzeichnungen des Generalmajor Pickert.* Bundesarchiv/Militärarchiv.
147. TsAMO, f. 270 BAD.
148. Beevor, Stalingrad, p. 93
149. TsAMO, f. 8 VA.
150. *Lagevortrag beim Fü.Hq. 2. September 1942. Kriegstagebuch des Oberkommandos der Wehrmacht,* vol. III, p. 669.
151. ZG 1 Documents. Via Jan Bobek.
152. TsAMO, f. 270 BAD.
153. TsAMO, f. 270 BAD.
154. TsAMO, f. 8 VA.
155. *Flugzeugunfälle und Verluste bei den Verbänden (täglich), Ob.d.L. Gen.Qu. Gen. 6.Abt.* Bundesarchiv/Militärarchiv RL 2 III/1182.
156. TsAMO, f. 135 GBAP.
157. *Lagebericht OKH, 3. September 1942. Kriegstagebuch des Oberkommandos der Wehrmacht,* vol. III, p. 675.
158. *Lagebericht OKH, 4. September 1942. Kriegstagebuch des Oberkommandos der Wehrmacht,* vol. III, p. 680.
159. *16-ya vozdushnaya,* p. 23.
160. TsAMO, f. 16 VA.
161. TsAMO, f. 8 VA, 16 VA, 102 IAD; *Flugzeugunfälle und Verluste bei den Verbänden (täglich), Ob.d.L. Gen.Qu. Gen. 6.Abt.*

162. Bundesarchiv/Militärarchiv RL 2 III/1182.
162. *Lagebericht OKH, 5. September 1942. Kriegstagebuch des Oberkommandos der Wehrmacht,* vol. III, p. 685.
163. Waiss, *Chronik Kampfgeschwader Nr. 27 Boelcke,* Band IV, p. 120.
164. *Flugzeugunfälle und Verluste bei den Verbänden (täglich), Ob.d.L. Gen.Qu. Gen. 6.Abt.* Bundesarchiv/Militärarchiv RL 2 III/1183.
165. TsAMO, f. 22 GIAD.
166. Bätcher, Flugbuch.
167. TsAMO, f. 129 GIAP.
168. TsAMO, f. 16 VA, op. 6476, d. 48.
169. *Flugzeugunfälle und Verluste bei den Verbänden (täglich), Ob.d.L. Gen.Qu. Gen. 6.Abt.* Bundesarchiv/Militärarchiv RL 2 III/1183.
170. *16-ya Vozdushnaya,* pp. 18-19.
171. TsAMO, f. 129 GIAP.
172. TsAMO, f. 16 VA.
173. TsAMO, f. 135 GBAP.

CHAPTER 12
174. Bundesarchiv/Militärarchiv, N 671/9.
175. *Hermann Wolf, Flugbuch.*
176. TsAMO, f. 16 VA.
177. TsAMO, f. 8 VA.
178. TsAMO, f. 8 VA; TsAMO, f. 16 VA.
179. TsAMO, f. 16 VA, op. 6479, d. 48.
180. TsAMO, f. 16 VA, op. 6479, d. 48.
181. *Flugzeugunfälle und Verluste bei den Verbänden (täglich), Ob.d.L. Gen.Qu. Gen. 6.Abt.* Bundesarchiv/Militärarchiv RL 2 III/1183.
182. Bundesarchiv/Militärarchiv, N 671/9.
183. Golovanov, *Dalnyaya bombardirovochnaya,* p. 265.
184. TsAMO, f. 629 IAP; Bergström and Antipov with Grislawski, *Graf & Grislawski: A Pair of Aces,* p. 132.
185. Bundesarchiv/Militärarchiv, N 671/9.
186. *Kriegstagebuch Nr. 9 Sturzkampfgeschwader "Immelmann" Nr. 2.* Bundesarchiv/Militärarchiv, RL 10/484.
187. Bundesarchiv/Militärarchiv, N 671/9.
188. *Kriegstagebuch Nr. 9 Sturzkampfgeschwader "Immelmann" Nr. 2.* Bundesarchiv/Militärarchiv, RL 10/484.
189. *Kriegstagebuch Nr. 9 Sturzkampfgeschwader "Immelmann" Nr. 2.* Bundesarchiv/Militärarchiv, RL 10/484.
190. Beevor, *Stalingrad,* p. 195.
191. Erickson, *The Road to Stalingrad,* p. 461.
192. Bundesarchiv/Militärarchiv, N 671/9.
193. *Operationsbefehl Nr. 1 vom 14. Oktober 1942 betr. weitere Kampfführungen im Osten; Kriegstagebuch des Oberkommandos der Wehrmacht,* vol. IV, p. 1301.

CHAPTER 13
194. *Românii la Stalingrad,* pp. 229-230.
195. Ibid., p. 506.
196. Rudel, *Stuka Pilot,* p. 57.
197. Beevor, *Stalingrad,* p. 245.
198. *17-ya Vozdushnaya Armiya v boyakh ot Stalingrada do Veny,* p. 13.
199. *Românii la Stalingrad,* pp. 229-230.
200. Dierich, *Kamfgeschwader 55 "Greif",* p, 268.
201. Via Hansgeorg Bätcher.
202. *SturzKampfgeschwader "Immelmann" Nr. 2, Kriegstagebuch Nr. 9.* 21 November 1942. Bundesarchiv/Militärarchiv, RL 10/484.
203. *Flugzeugunfälle und Verluste bei den Verbänden (täglich), Ob.d.L. Gen.Qu. Gen. 6.Abt.* Bundesarchiv/Militärarchiv RL 2 III/1184.
204. *SturzKampfgeschwader "Immelmann" Nr. 2, Kriegstagebuch Nr. 9.* 21 November 1942. Bundesarchiv/Militärarchiv, RL 10/484.
205. Via Dénes Bernád.
206. War Diary *Luftflotte* 4, 21 November 1942. Bundesarchiv/Militärarchiv, RL 7/482.
207. Nauroth, p. 213.
208. *Flugzeugbestand und Bewegungsmeldungen Stab, I. und II./St.G 2.* Bundesarchiv/Militärarchiv RL 2 III/875.
209. *Flugzeugunfälle und Verluste bei den Verbänden (täglich), Ob.d.L. Gen.Qu. Gen. 6.Abt.* Bundesarchiv/Militärarchiv RL 2 III/1184.
210. *SturzKampfgeschwader "Immelmann" Nr. 2, Kriegstagebuch Nr. 9.* 23 November 1942. Bundesarchiv/Militärarchiv, RL 10/484.
211. *SturzKampfgeschwader "Immelmann" Nr. 2, Kriegstagebuch Nr. 9.* November 24 1942. Bundesarchiv/Militärarchiv, RL 10/484.

CHAPTER 14
212. *Kriegstagebuch des Generalmajors Wolfgang Pickert, Befehlshaber der 9.*

*Flakdivision.*

213. *Kriegstagebuch des Oberkommandos der Wehrmacht,* vol. IV, p. 1031. 27 November 1942.

214. KTB OKW, Vol. IV, p. 1031. 27 November 1942.

215. Nowarra, *Über Europas Fronten,* p. 40.

216. *Flugzeugbestand und Bewegungsmeldungen 30.11 1942.* Bundesarchiv/Militärarchiv, RL 2 III/875.

217. Plocher 1942, p. 281.

218. *Lagebericht OKH, 25 November 1942. Kriegstagebuch des Oberkommandos der Wehrmacht,* vol. IV, p. 1022.

219. *Kriegstagebuch des Generalleutnants Fiebig, Kommandierende General VIII. Fliegerkorps.* Bundesarchiv/Militärarchiv, RL 8/56.

220. Rudel, *Trotzdem,* p. 68.

221. Rudel, *Trotzdem,* p. 68.

222. Obermaier, *Die Ritterkreuzträger der Luftwaffe 1939 – 1945: Band II, Stuka- und Schlachtflieger,* p.23.

223. Beevor, p. 279.

224. War Diary *Luftflotte 4,* 26 November 1942. Bundesarchiv/Militärarchiv, RL 7/482.

225. Johannes Steinhoff, Logbook.

226. Gerhard Barkhorn, Logbook.

227. *Flugzeugunfälle und Verluste bei den Verbänden (täglich), Ob.d.L. Gen.Qu. Gen. 6. Abt.* Bundesarchiv/Militärarchiv RL 2 III/1184.

228. *Flugzeugunfälle und Verluste bei den Verbänden (täglich), Ob.d.L. Gen.Qu. Gen. 6. Abt.* Bundesarchiv/Militärarchiv RL 2 III/1184.

229. Bernád, *Rumanian Air Force,* p. 53.

230. War Diary *Luftflotte 4,* 1 December 1942. Bundesarchiv/Militärarchiv, RL 7/482.

231. *Flugzeugunfälle und Verluste bei den Verbänden (täglich), Ob.d.L. Gen.Qu. Gen. 6. Abt.* Bundesarchiv/Militärarchiv RL 2 III/1184.

232. *Kriegstagebuch des Oberkommandos der Wehrmacht,* vol. IV, p. 1072.

233. *Kriegstagebuch des Oberkommandos der Wehrmacht,* vol. IV, p. 1076.

234. War Diary *Luftflotte 4,* 5 December 1942. Bundesarchiv/Militärarchiv, RL 7/482.

235. *Kriegstagebuch des Generalleutnants Fiebig, Kommandierende General VIII. Fliegerkorps.* Bundesarchiv/Militärarchiv, RL 8/56.

236. Hansgeorg Bätcher. Logbook.

237. Via Chris Dunning.

238. *Flugzeugunfälle und Verluste bei den Verbänden (täglich), Ob.d.L. Gen.Qu. Gen. 6. Abt.* Bundesarchiv/Militärarchiv RL 2 III/1184.

239. Via Chris Dunning.

240. *Flugzeugunfälle und Verluste bei den Verbänden (täglich), Ob.d.L. Gen.Qu. Gen. 6. Abt.* Bundesarchiv/Militärarchiv RL 2 III/1184.

241. Bernád, p. 72.

242. *Flugzeugunfälle und Verluste bei den Verbänden (täglich), Ob.d.L. Gen.Qu. Gen. 6. Abt.* Bundesarchiv/Militärarchiv RL 2 III/1184.

243. War Diary *Luftflotte 4,* 9 December 1942. Bundesarchiv/Militärarchiv, RL 7/482.

244. Kurowski, *Luftbrücke Stalingrad,* p. 52.

245. *Flugzeugunfälle und Verluste bei den Verbänden (täglich), Ob.d.L. Gen.Qu. Gen. 6. Abt.* Bundesarchiv/Militärarchiv RL 2 III/1184.

246. Plocher, *The German Air Force Versus Russia,* 1942, p. 292.

247. Kurowski, *Luftbrücke Stalingrad,* p. 52.

248. *17-ya Vozdushnaya Armiya v boyakh ot Stalingrada do Veny,* p. 21.

249. War Diary *Luftflotte 4,* 9 December 1942. Bundesarchiv/Militärarchiv, RL 7/482.

250. TsAMO, f. 16 VA.

251. TsAMO, f. 16 VA.

252. *Aviatsiya i Kosmonavtika,* May – June 2001.

253. Dierich, *Kampfgeschwader 55 "Greif",* pp. 274 – 275.

254. TsAMO, f. 16 VA.

255. Johannes Steinhoff, Logbook.

256. Interview with Johannes Steinhoff.

257. Via Chris Dunning.

258. *Flugzeugunfälle und Verluste bei den Verbänden (täglich), Ob.d.L. Gen.Qu. Gen. 6. Abt.* Bundesarchiv/Militärarchiv RL 2 III/1184.

259. Dierich, *Kampfgeschwader 55 "Greif",* p. 278.

## CHAPTER 15

260. War Diary *Luftflotte 4,* 12 December 1942. Bundesarchiv/Militärarchiv, RL 7/482.

261. *Aviatsiya i Kosmonavtika,* May – June 2001.

262. Zjukov, *Minnen och reflexioner,* p. 119.

263. Interview with Johannes Steinhoff.

264. TsAMO, f. 283 IAD.

265. Prien and Stemmer, *Messerschmitt Bf 109 im Einsatz bei der III./Jagdgeschwader 3,* p. 198.

266. *Eingegangene Meldungen Generalstab Luftwaffe während des 14. 12. 42.. Kriegstagebuch des Oberkommandos der Wehrmacht,* vol. IV, p. 1138.

267. *Flugzeugunfälle und Verluste bei den Verbänden (täglich), Ob.d.L. Gen.Qu. Gen. 6. Abt.* Bundesarchiv/Militärarchiv RL 2 III/1184.

268. *Kriegstagebuch des Generalmajors Wolfgang Pickert, Befehlshaber der 9. Flakdivision.*

269. Via Arkadiy Kovachevich.

270. War Diary *Luftflotte 4,* 13 December 1942. Bundesarchiv/Militärarchiv, RL 7/482.

271. Quoted in Haupt, *Army Group South,* p. 216.

272. Via Bernd Barbas.

273. Punka, *Messer,* p. 20.

274. Via Bernd Barbas.

275. TsAMO, f. 11 GIAD.

276. TsAMO, f. 5 GIAP.

277. Bundesarchiv/Militärarchiv, RL 10/437.

278. Via Csaba Becze.

279. Pegg, *Hs 129 Panzerjäger,* p. 94.

280. *Lagebericht OKH, 17 December 1942. Kriegstagebuch des Oberkommandos der Wehrmacht,* vol. IV, p. 1148.

282. *Flugzeugunfälle und Verluste bei den Verbänden (täglich), Ob.d.L. Gen.Qu. Gen. 6. Abt.* Bundesarchiv/Militärarchiv RL 2 III/1184.

283. Via Donald Pearson.

284. Via Donald Pearson.

285. TsAMO, f. 11 GIAD.

286. *Flugzeugunfälle und Verluste bei den Verbänden (täglich), Ob.d.L. Gen.Qu. Gen. 6. Abt.* Bundesarchiv/Militärarchiv RL 2 III/1184..

287. *Kurowski, Luftbrücke Stalingrad,* p. 75.

288. *Kurowski, Luftbrücke Stalingrad,* p. 75.

289. TsAMO, f. 8 VA.

290. Hansgeorg Bätcher, Logbook.

291. *16-ya Vozdushnaya,* p. 56.

292. Pegg, *Hs 129 Panzerjäger,* p. 95.

293. *Flugzeugbestand und Bewegungsmeldungen.* Bundesarchiv/Militärarchiv RL 2 III/875.

294. Vajda/Dancey, *German Aircraft Industry and Production 1933 – 1945,* p. 138.

295. TsAMO, f. 57 BAP, op. 201865, d. 114-115.

296. *Flugzeugunfälle und Verluste bei den Verbänden (täglich), Ob.d.L. Gen.Qu. Gen. 6. Abt.* Bundesarchiv/Militärarchiv RL 2 III/1184.

297. TsAMO, f. 57 BAP, op. 201865, d. 114-115.

298. Fw. Rudolf Trenkel, *Abschussbericht 21.12. 1942.* Bundesarchiv/Militärarchiv, RL 10/437.

299. Zjukov, p. 120

300. Glantz and House, *When Titans Clashed,* p. 140

301. Zjukov, p. 120

302. War Diary *Luftflotte 4,* 24 December 1942. Bundesarchiv/Militärarchiv, RL 7/482.

303. Kurowski, *Luftbrücke Stalingrad,* p. 85.

304. *17-ya Vozdushnaya Armiya v boyakh ot Stalingrada do Veny,* p. 25.

305. Plocher, *The German Air Force Versus Russia,* 1942, p. 295.

306. Interview with Hansgeorg Bätcher.

307. Interview with Hansgeorg Bätcher.

308. Dierich, *Kampfgeschwader 55 "Greif",* p. 284.

309. *16-ya Vozdushnaya,* p. 57.

310. Quoted in Prien, *Messerschmitt Bf 109 im Einsatz bei Stab und 1./Jagdgeschwader 3,* p.253.

311. *Lagebericht OKH, 26 December 1942. Kriegstagebuch des Oberkommandos der Wehrmacht,* vol. IV, p. 1188.

312. Nipe, *Last Victory in Russia,* p. 23.

313. *Fw. Georg Schwientek, Abschussmeldung 26. 12. 1942.* Bundesarchiv/Militärarchiv, RL 10/437.

314. TsAMO, f. 11 GIAP.

315. Ibid.

316. War Diary *Luftflotte 4,* 26 December 1942. Bundesarchiv/Militärarchiv, RL 7/482.

317. Hans Waldmann, Logbook; Johannes Steinhoff, Logbook.

318. Interview with Johannes Steinhoff.

319. Interview with Klaus Häberlen.

320. Klaus Häberlen, Logbook.

321. Kurowski, p. 91.

322. Interview with Hansgeorg Bätcher.

323. Kurowski, *Luftbrücke Stalingrad,* p. 94.

324. TsAMO, f. 8 VA.

325. TsAMO, f. 16 VA.

326. TsAMO, f. 8 VA.

327. TsAMO, f. 16 VA.

328. TsAMO, f. 8 VA.
329. Ibid.
330. TsAMO, f. 9 GIAP.
331. TsAMO, f. 16 VA.
332. Ibid.
333. TsAMO, f. 1 GIAD.
334. *17-ya Vozdushnaya Armiya v boyakh ot Stalingrada do Veny*, p. 29.
335. Golovanov, *Dalnyaya bombardirovochnaya*, p. 265.

CHAPTER 16
336. 13./JG 52 Victory List. Boris Sudnik via Peter Kassak.
337. TsAMO, f. 5 VA.
338. Davtyan, *Pyataya Vozdushnaya*.
339. TsAMO, f. 230 ShAD.
340. Vershinin, *Chertvyortaya Vozdushnaya*, p. 195.
341. *III. Jagdgeschwader 52 Traditionsgeschichte*. Via Alfons Altmeier; Major Alfred Grislawski, Logbook.
342. TsAMO, f. 4 VA.
343. TsAMO, f. 5 VA.
344. *Boyevaya Letopis' Voyenno-Morskogo Flota 1941–1942*.
345. Manstein, p. 393.
346. Tieke, *The Caucasus and the Oil*, p. 275.
347. Lipfert, *The War Diary of Hptm. Helmut Lipfert*, p. 20.
348. Gubin and Kiselyov, p. 113.
349. *Flugzeugunfälle und Verluste bei den Verbänden (täglich), Ob.d.L. Gen.Qu. Gen. 6.Abt.* Bundesarchiv/Militärarchiv RL 2 III/1185.
350. Tieke, *The Caucasus and the Oil*, p. 261.
351. *Flugzeugunfälle und Verluste bei den Verbänden (täglich), Ob.d.L. Gen.Qu. Gen. 6.Abt.* Bundesarchiv/Militärarchiv RL 2 III/1185.
352. TsAMO, f. 101 GIAP.
353. War Diary *Luftflotte* 4, 4 January, 1943. Bundesarchiv/Militärarchiv, RL 7/482.
354. TsAMO, f. 236 IAD.
355. *Flugzeugunfälle und Verluste bei den Verbänden (täglich), Ob.d.L. Gen.Qu. Gen. 6.Abt.* Bundesarchiv/Militärarchiv RL 2 III/1185.
356. Dierich, *Kampfgeschwader 51 "Edelweiss"*, p. 192.
357. *Aviatsiya i Kosmonavtika*, May – June 2001.
358. Hayward, p. 284.
359. TsAMO, f. 346, op. 5755, d. 121.
360. TsAMO, f. 10 GIAD, op. 1, d. 12.
361. Drabkin, *Ya dralsya istrebitelye: Prinyavshiye pervyy udar 1941-1942*, p. 88.
362. TsAMO, f. 10 GIAD, op. 1, d. 12.
363. TsAMO, f. 6 GIAD.
364. Klaus Häberlen, Logbook.
365. Interview with Arkadiy Kovachevich.
366. Hans Ellendt, Logbook.
367. Interview with Hans Ellendt.
368. Interview with Arkadiy Kovachevich.
369. TsAMO, f. 6 GIAD.
370. TsAMO, f. 3 GIAP.
371. Davtyan, *Pyataya Vozdushnaya*, p. 36.
372. TsAMO, f. 5 VA.
373. *Kriegstagebuch des Oberkommandos der Wehrmacht*, Vol. V, p. 47. 17 January, 1943.
374. Davtyan, *Pyataya Vozdushnaya*, p. 38.
375. TsAMO, f. 236 IAD.
376. TsAMO, f. 5 VA.
377. Davtyan, *Pyataya Vozdushnaya*, p. 39.
378. *Boyevaya Letopis' Voyenno-Morskogo Flota 1941 – 1942*.
379. TsAMO, f. 236 IAD.; Milan Krajci in *Luftwaffe Verband Journal*, 11/1997.
380. TsAMO, f. 236 IAD.; Milan Krajci in *Luftwaffe Verband Journal*, 11/1997.
381. Hptm. Alfred Grislawski, Logbook.
382. Bergström and Antipov with Grislawski, pp. 150-152.
383. TsAMO, f. 6 GIAD.
384. *III. Jagdgeschwader 52 Traditionsgeschichte vom 1.12.42 – 4.1.43*. Via Alfons Altmeier.
385. *Luftflottenkommando 4, Führungsabt. Ia, op Nr. 576/43 g.Kdos. Befehl für die Kampfführung an 25.1.43.*
386. Tieke, p. 269.
387. *Luftflottenkommando 4, Führungsabt. Ia, op Nr. 538/43 g.Kdos. Befehl für die Kampfführung an 26.1.43*
388. War Diary *Luftflotte* 4, 21 January, 1943. Bundesarchiv/Militärarchiv, RL 7/482.
389. *Luftflottenkommando 4, Führungsabt. Ia, op Nr. 538/43 g.Kdos. Befehl für die Kampfführung an 26.1.43.*

390. Klaus Häberlen. Logbook
391. Southern Front, Combat report 0028 to the Supreme Commander, 27 January, 1943, 2400 hours. *Russkiy arkhiv: Velikaya Otechestvennaya. Prelyudiya Kurskoybitvy*. Vol. 15 (4 - 3).
392. 6 GIAP Documents. TsAMO.
393. *Flugzeugunfälle und Verluste bei den Verbänden (täglich), Ob.d.L. Gen.Qu. Gen. 6.Abt.* Bundesarchiv/Militärarchiv RL 2 III/1185.
394. Interview with Klaus Häberlen.
395. *Flugzeugunfälle und Verluste bei den Verbänden (täglich), Ob.d.L. Gen.Qu. Gen. 6.Abt.* Bundesarchiv/Militärarchiv RL 2 III/1185.
396. Klaus Häberlen. Logbook.
397. War Diary *Luftflotte* 4, 29 January, 1943. Bundesarchiv/Militärarchiv, RL 7/482.
398. Boykov, *Na glavnykh napravleniyakh*, Moscow: Voyenizdat, 1984, p. 59.
399. *Flugzeugunfälle und Verluste bei den Verbänden (täglich), Ob.d.L. Gen.Qu. Gen. 6.Abt.* Bundesarchiv/Militärarchiv RL 2 III/1185.
400. Klaus Häberlen. Logbook.
401. TsAMO, f. 346, op. 5755, d. 121.
402. TsAMO, f. 4 VA.
403. TsAMO, f. 5 VA.
404. Milan Krajci in *Luftwaffe Verband*, 11/1997.
405. *Flugzeugunfälle und Verluste bei den Verbänden (täglich), Ob.d.L. Gen.Qu. Gen. 6.Abt.* Bundesarchiv/Militärarchiv RL 2 III/1185.

CHAPTER 17
406. Kurowski, *Luftbrücke Stalingrad*, p. 198.
407. Kurowski, p. 91.
408. Beevor, p.339.
409. Pegg, *Hs 129 Panzerjäger*, pp. 137 – 138.
410. *Flugzeugunfälle und Verluste bei den Verbänden (täglich), Ob.d.L. Gen.Qu. Gen. 6.Abt.* Bundesarchiv/Militärarchiv RL 2 III/1185.
411. TsAMO, f. 283 IAD.
412. Kurowski, p. 88.
413. TsAMO, f. 11 GIAP.
414. Kurowski, p. 107.
415. *Flugzeugunfälle und Verluste bei den Verbänden (täglich), Ob.d.L. Gen.Qu. Gen. 6.Abt.* Bundesarchiv/Militärarchiv RL 2 III/1185.
416. *Flugzeugunfälle und Verluste bei den Verbänden (täglich), Ob.d.L. Gen.Qu. Gen. 6.Abt.* Bundesarchiv/Militärarchiv RL 2 III/1185.
417. *16-ya Vozdushnaya*, p. 58.
418. Skripko, p. 253.
419. TsAMO, f. 53 GIAP.
420. Voronezh Front, Combat Report No. 0012, 12 January 1943, 24.00 hours. *Russkiy arkhiv: Velikaya Otechestvennaya. Prelyudiya Kurskoy bitvy.* Vol. 15 (4 - 3). Vol.15 (4 - 3), Moscow: TERRA, 1997.
421. War Diary *Luftflotte* 4, 13 January 1943. Bundesarchiv/Militärarchiv, RL 7/482.
422. Skripko, p. 253.
423. TsAMO, f. 283 IAD.
424. Bracke, *Gegen vielfache Übermacht*, p. 64.
425. Kurowski, p. 118.
426. *Flugzeugunfälle und Verluste bei den Verbänden (täglich), Ob.d.L. Gen.Qu. Gen. 6.Abt.* Bundesarchiv/Militärarchiv RL 2 III/1185.
427. Morzik, *Die deutschen Transportflieger im Zweiten Weltkrieg*, p.159.
428. *Kriegstagebuch Sonderstab Gen.Feldm. Milch 15.1. – 3.2. 1943, Anlageband 2, Befehle und Meldungen.* NARA, T-321/R18.
429. *Kriegstagebuch Sonderstab Gen.Feldm. Milch 15.1. – 3.2. 1943, Anlageband 2, Befehle und Meldungen.* NARA, T-321/R18.
430. TsAMO, f. 11 GIAP.
431. TsAMO, f. 283 IAD.
432. Via Chris Dunning.
433. *Flugzeugunfälle und Verluste bei den Verbänden (täglich), Ob.d.L. Gen.Qu. Gen. 6.Abt.* Bundesarchiv/Militärarchiv RL 2 III/1185.
434. Kiehl, *Kampfgeschwader "Legion Condor"* 53, p. 241.
435. Via Csaba Becze.

CHAPTER 18
436. Morzik, *Die deutschen Transportflieger im Zweiten Weltkrieg*, p. 172.
437. *Flugzeugunfälle und Verluste bei den Verbänden (täglich), Ob.d.L. Gen.Qu. Gen. 6.Abt.* Bundesarchiv/Militärarchiv RL 2 III/1185.
438. Rudel, *Trotzdem*, p. 71.
439. Nauroth, *Stukageschwader 2*, p. 216.
440. Dierich, *Kamfgeschwader 55 "Greif"*, p. 296.
441. Kiehl, *Kampfgeschwader "Legion Condor"* 53, p. 216.
442. Prien & Stemmer, *Jagdgeschwader 3 Udet in World War II*, Vol.I : Stab and I./JG 3 in action with the Messerschmitt Bf 109, p. 202

443. Plocher, *The German Air Force Versus Russia 1942*, p. 353.
444. TsAMO, f. 16 VA.
445. TsAMO, f. 8 VA.
446. Morzik, *Die deutschen Transportflieger im Zweiten Weltkrieg*, p. 145.
447. Plocher, *The German Air Force Versus Russia 1942*, p. 233.
448. Morzik, p. 138.
449. Plocher, *The German Air Force Versus Russia 1942*, pp. 344-345.
450. TsAMO, f. 368, op. 6476, d. 93, l. 16.
451. Compare with Bergström and Antipov with Grislawski, Graf & Grislawski: *A Pair of Aces*, pp. 146-147.
452. TSAMO, f. 20002, op. 1, d. 1, l. 5.
453. TsAMO, f. 53 GIAP.
454. Golovanov, *Dalnyaya bombardirovochnaya*, p. 266.
455. Ibid., p. 259.
456. Order No. 0067 from Southwestern Front's C.O. *Russkiy arkhiv: Velikaya Otechestvennaya. Prelyudiya Kurskoy bitvy.* Vol. 15 (4 - 3).
457. Ibid.
458. *Krivosheyev, Grif sekretnosti snyat: Poteri Vooruzhyonnykh Sil SSSR v voynakh, boyevykh deystviyakh i voyennykh konfliktakh*, p. 370.

## Sources and Bibliography

### ARCHIVES
4 GIAP/VVS-KBF Museum and Archive.
108 Rava-Russkiy GShAP Museum and Archive.
146 GvIAP/PVO Private Museum.
Bundesarchiv-Militärarchiv, Freiburg.
Bundesarchiv, Koblenz.
Imperial War Museum, London.
Jagdgeschwader 52 Traditionsgemeinschaft & Luftwaffen Museum, Singen.
Krigsarkivet, Stockholm.
Luftfahrtmuseum Hannover-Laatzen.
Monino Air Force Museum, Moscow.
National Archive, Kew.
National Archives and Records Administration, Washington, D.C.
Radomsko Museum, Radomsko.
Rosvoyentsentr, Moscow.
Russian Aviation Research Trust.
Russian Central Military Archive TsAMO, Podolsk.
Russian State Military Archive RGVA, Moscow.
Suchgruppe 45 "Günther Rosipal," Salzwedel.
WASt Deutsche Dienststelle, Berlin.

### UNPUBLISHED SOURCES
*Abschussmeldungen JG 52.* Via Alfons Altmeier.
Antipov Vlad, *Patriots or Red Kamikaze?* 1999.
Bätcher, *Major* Hansgeorg, Logbook.
Bob, *Major* Hans-Ekkehard, Logbook.
Budke, *Oberfeldwebel* Wilhelm, various documents, Via Rolf Zydek.
*Chronik der I./JG 54.* Via Hans-Ekkehard Bob.
15./JG 52 War Diary. Via Tomislav Haramincic.
Flores, S. A. *The "Escuadrillas Azul" of the Spanish Air Force in World War II. Russia 1941 – 1944.*
----- *Pilotos ex-fuerza Aerea Republicana Española en servicio de la Fuerza Aerea Rusa en la Segunda Guerra Mundial 1933-1945.*
Gollob, Gordon. Personal diary.
Graf, *Oberst* Hermann, various interrogation protocols with, and other POW documents related to. RGVA (Rossiyskiy Gosudarstvennyy Voennyy Arkhiv - Russian State Military Archive), Moscow.
Graf, *Oberst* Hermann, various personal correspondence. Courtesy of Manfred Wägenbaur/ Traditionsgemeinschaft JG 52, Jagdgeschwader 52 Museum.
Graf, *Oberst* Hermann, Personal Diary excerpts. Courtesy of Manfred Wägenbaur/ Traditionsgemeinschaft JG 52, Jagdgeschwader 52 Museum.
Graf, *Oberst* Hermann, Personal-Nachweis. Courtesy of Manfred Wägenbaur/ Traditionsgemeinschaft JG 52, Jagdgeschwader 52 Museum.
Graf, *Oberst* Hermann, Soldbuch. RGVA (Rossiyskiy Gosudarstvennyy Voennyy Arkhiv – Russian State Military Archive), Moscow.
Graf, *Oberst* Hermann, Wehrpass. RGVA (Rossiyskiy Gosudarstvennyy Voennyy Arkhiv – Russian State Military Archive), Moscow.
Grislawski, *Hauptmann* Alfred, *Abschussberichte.*

Grislawski, *Hauptmann* Alfred, private archive.
Grislawski, *Hauptmann* Alfred, Logbook.
Grubich, *Kapitan* Viktor, Logbook.
Häberlen, *Major* Klaus, Logbook.
Hrabak, *Oberst* Dietrich, Logbook.
*JG 52 Archiv.* Courtesy of Alfons Altmeier.
*JG 54 "Grünherz" Archiv.* Courtesy of Günther Rosipal.
*Kampfgeschwader 1 "Hindenburg": Geschwadergeschichte in Kurzfassung.* Av Oberst a.D. Gerhard Baeker.
*Kratkaya istoricheskaya spravka boyevogo puti 108 Gvardeyskogo Shturmovogo Aviatsionnogo Rava-Russkogo Ordena Suvorova Polka.* [History of 108 Rava-Russkiy GShAP.] Sovet veteranov 108 Gv.ShAP, 1992. Via Aleksandr Pavlichenko.
*Kriegstagebuch I./SKG 210.* Via Jan Bobek.
Kurayev, *Starshina* Vasiliy, Logbook.
Luftwaffe aircraft loss list. Courtesy of Matti Salonen.
*Meldungen über Flugzeugunfälle und Verluste bei den fl. Verbänden (täglich), Ob.d.L. Gen.Qu. Gen. 6. Abt.* Bundesarchiv/Militärarchiv. Cited as *Generalquartiermeister der Luftwaffe.*
Meroño Pellicer, Francisco, *Biografia de José María PASCUAL Santamaría.* Unpublished manuscript.
Pavlichenko, Guards *Polkovnik* Aleksandr, Logbook.
Rall, *Generalleutnant* Günther, Logbook.
Rossmann, *Leutnant* Edmund, Logbook.
Schack, *Hauptmann* Günther, *Leistungsbuch.*
Schack, *Hauptmann* Günther, Logbook.
*Staffel-Chronik der III. Jagdgeschwader 54, 9. Staffel.*
Steinhoff, *General* Johannes, Logbook.
Trautloft, *General* Hannes, Personal Diary.
*Tageseinsatz-Meldung Fliegerführer Süd.*
*Tageseinsatz-Meldung Fliegerführer Süd.*
*Traditionsgeschichte der I./Jagdgeschwader 52.* Via Alfons Altmeier.
*Traditionsgeschichte III. Jagdgeschwader 52.* Via Alfons Altmeier.
Waldmann, *Oberleutnant* Hans, *Leistungsbuch.*
Waldmann, *Oberleutnant* Hans, Logbook.
Wolf, *Leutnant* Hermann, Logbook.

### BOOKS
*17-ya Vozdushnaya Armiya v boyakh ot Stalingrada do Veny.* Moscow: Voyenizdat, 1977.
Abramov, A.S. *Dvyenadtsat' taranov.* Sverdlovsk: Sredne-Ural'skoe knizhnoe izdatel'stvo, 1970.
Anfinogenov, A.Z. *Mgnoveniye – vechnost.* Moscow: Moskovskiy rabochniy, 1994.
Anishchenkov, P.S., and V. Shurinov. *Tret'ya Vozdushnaya.* Moscow: Voyenizdat, 1984.
Arias, A. *"Arde el cielo": Memorias de un piloto de caza participante en la guerra de España (1936 - 1939) y en la Gran Guerra Patria de la U.R.S.S. (1941 - 1945).* Silla (Valencia): A. Delgado Romero, 1995.
Arkhipenko, F.F. *Zapiski lyotchika-istrebitelya.* Moscow: NPP Delta, 1999.
Avdeyev, M.V. *U samogo Chyornogo morya.* Moscow: DOSAAF, 1968.
Babak, I. I., *Zvyozdy na kryl'yakh.* Moscow: DOSAAF, 1981.
Balke, U. *Kampfgeschwader 100 "Wiking."* Stuttgart: Motorbuch Verlag, 1981.
Bayevskiy, G.A. *S aviatsiyey cherez XX vek.* Moscow: Delta-NB, 2001.
Becze, C. *Elefeljetett Hosök.* Puedlo Kiadó, 2007.
Beevor, A. *Stalingrad: The Fateful Siege: 1942 - 1943.* New York: Penguin Books, 1998.
Bekker, C. *The Luftwaffe War Diaries.* New York: Ballantine Books, 1969.
----- *Angriffshöhe 4000.* Oldenburg: Gerhard Stalling Verlag, 1964.
Bergström, C., and A. Mikhailov. *Black Cross/Red Star: The Air War Over the Eastern Front.* Vol. 1, *Operation Barbarossa, 1941.* Pacifica: Pacifica Military History, 2000.
----- *Black Cross/Red Star: The Air War Over the Eastern Front.* Vol. 2, *Resurgence, January – June 1942.* Pacifica: Pacifica Military History, 2001, and Burgess Hill: Classic Publications, 2001.
Bergström, C., and V. Antipov, with A. Grislawski, and C. Sundin. *Graf & Grislawski: A Pair of Aces.* Hamilton: Eagle Editions, 2003.
Bergström, C., and E. Mombeek, with M. Pegg. *Jagdwaffe: The War in Russia January – October 1942.* Ian Allan Publishing Ltd. 2003.
Bergström, C., with M. Pegg. *Jagdwaffe: The War in Russia November 1942 – December 1943.* Ian Allan Publishing Ltd. 2004.
Bergström C., A. Dikov, and V. Antipov. *Black Cross/Red Star: The Air War*

*Over the Eastern Front*. Vol. 3, *Everything for Stalingrad*. Hamilton: Eagle Editions, 2006.

Bergström, C. *Barbarossa: The Air Battle*. Surrey: Midland, 2007.

Bernád, D. *Rumanian Air Force: The Prime Decade, 1938 - 1947*. Carrollton: Squadron/Signal Publications, 1999.

----- *Henschel Hs 129 in Action*. Carrollton: Squadron/Signal Publications, 2001.

----- *Rumanian Aces of World War 2*. Oxford: Osprey Publishing, 2003.

Beskorovaynyy, A.I. *Geroi ryadom*. Moscow: DOSAAF, 1979.

*Bessmerten podvig ikh vysokiy*. Tula: Priokskoe knizhnoe izdatel'stvo, 1983.

Bodrikhin, N. *Stalinskiye Sokoly*. Moscow: NPP *Delta*, 1997.

----- *Sovyetskiye Asy*. Moscow: ZAO KFK "TAMP," 1998.

Bogatyryov, S.V., R.I. Larintsev, and A.V. Ovcharenko *Morskaya voyna na Baltike. Spravochnik-khronika. Part I. Poteri flota protivnika na Baltiyskom more v 1941-1943*, Arkhangelsk, 1997.

Bogdanov, N.G. *V nebe Gvardeyskiy Gatchinskiy*. Leningrad: Lenizdat, 1980.

*Boyevaya deyatel'nost' aviatsii VMF v Velikoy Otechestvennoy voune Sovetskogo Soyuza 1941-1945*, Part II, *Voyenno-vozdushnyye sily Krasnoznamyonnogo Baltiyskogo flota v Velikoy Otechestvennoy voyne*, Voyenizdat: Moscow, 1963.

*Boyevaya Letopis' Voyenno-Morskogo Flota 1941 – 1942*. Moscow: Voyenizdat, 1983.

*Boyevoy put' Sovetskogo Voyenno-Morskogo Flota*. 4th ed. Moscow: Voyenizdat, 1988.

Boykov, P. M. *Na glavnykh napravleniyakh*. Moscow: Voyenizdat, 1984.

Bracke, G. *Gegen vielfache Übermacht*. Stuttgart: Motorbuch Verlag, 1977.

Brown, J. *Ryssland kämpar*. Stockholm: Steinsviks bokförlag, 1943.

Brütting, G. *Das waren die deutschen Kampffliegerasse 1939 - 1945*. Stuttgart: Motorbuch Verlag, 1975.

----- *Das waren die deutschen Stuka-Asse 1939 - 1945*. 3rd ed. Stuttgart: Motorbuch Verlag, 1979.

Buchner, H. *Stormbird: Flying Through Fire as a Luftwaffe Ground Attack Pilot and Me 262 Ace*. Aldershot: Hikoki Publications, 2000.

Bucurescu, I., et al. *Aviatia Romana-Pe frontul de est si in apararea teritotiului*. Romania: Tehnoprod, 1993.

Burov, A.V. *Tvoi Geroi Leningrad*. Leningrad: Lenizdat, 1970.

----- *Ognennoye Nebo*. Leningrad: Lenizdat, 1974.

Butayev, B. *Amet-Khan Sultan*. Moscow: Politizdat, 1990.

Carell, P. *Unternehmen Barbarossa: der Marsch nach Russland*. Frankfurt-am-Main: Verlag Ullstein, 1963.

Chazanov (Khazanov), D. *Nad Stalingradem*. Warsaw: Wydawnictwo Altair, 1995.

Chechelnitskiy, G.A. *Lyotchiki na voyne*. Moscow: Voyenizdat, 1974.

Churchill, W. *The Second World War*, vol. IV *The Hinge of Fate*. Hougton Mifflin Company, 1950.

Chuykov, V.I. *Ot Stalingrada do Berlina*. Moscow: Sovetskaya Rossiya, 1985.

Davtyan, S.M. *Pyataya Vozdushnaya*. Moscow: Voyenizdat, 1990.

Denisov, K.D. *Pod nami — Chernoye more*. Moscow: Voyennoye izdatel'stvo, 1989.

Dickfeld, A. *Footsteps of the Hunter*. Winnipeg: J. J. Fedorowicz Publishing, 1993.

Dierich, W. *Kampfgeschwader 51 "Edelweiss."* Stuttgart: Motorbuch Verlag, 1975.

----- *Kampfgeschwader 55 "Greif."* Stuttgart: Motorbuch Verlag, 1975.

*Die Wehrmachtberichte 1939 – 1945*, vol. II: *1. Januar 1942 bis 31. Dezember 1943*. Köln: Gesellschaft für Literatur und Bildung, 1989.

Dolgov, I.A. *Zolotye Zvezdy Kalinintsev*. 2nd ed. Moskovskiy rabochiy, Moscow 1983.

Dorokhov, A.P. *Geroi chernomorskogo neba*. Moscow: Voyenizdat, 1972.

Drabkin, A. *Ya dralsya istrebitelye: Prinyavshiye pervyy udar 1941-1942*. Moscow: Yauza, 2006.

Dubrovin, L.A. *Pikirovshchiki*. Moscow: Voyenizdat, 1986.

Dvoryanskiy, Ye.M., and A.A. Yaroshenko. *V ognennom kol'tse*. Tallinn: Eesti Raamat, 1977.

Dyachenko, G.Kh. *Nasledniki Nesterova*. Moscow: Voyenizdat, 1963.

Dzhurayev, T.D. *Vernye syny Rodiny*. Tashkent: Uzbekistan, 1964.

Einsiedel, H. *I Joined the Russians*. New Haven: Yale, 1958.

Erickson, J. *The Road to Stalingrad: Stalin's War with Germany*, vol. I. New York: Harper & Row, 1979.

Falaleyev, F. Ya. *V stroyu krylatykh: Iz vozpomikakiy*. Izhevsk: Udmyrtiya, 1978.

Fast, N. *Das Jagdgeschwader 52*. Bergisch Gladbach: Bensberger Buch Verlag, 1988 - 1992.

Fuglewicz, W. *Skrzydla niosa odwet*. Warsaw: Wydawnictwo MON, 1975.

----- *Minuta nad twierdza*. Warsaw: Wydawnictwo MON, 1977.

----- *Rakietowym w czolgi*. Warsaw: Ministerstwo Obrony Narodowej, 1979.

----- *Stalinowskie sokoly*. Gdynia: AJ Press, 1995.

Fyodorov, A.G. *V nebe Petlaykovy*. Moscow: DOSAAF, 1976.

----- *Zvyozdy nemerknushchey slavy*. 3rd ed. Simferopol: Tavriya, 1984.

----- *V nebe – pikirovshchiki*. Moscow: DOSAAF, 1986.

Gaczowski, B. *Atakuje taranem*. Rzeszow: Krajowa Agencja Wydawnicza, 1985.

*Geroi ognennykh let*. 3rd ed. Yaroslavl: Verkhne-Volzhskoye knizhnoye izdatel'stvo, 1985.

*Geroi Sovetskogo Soyuza*. Moscow: Voyenizdat, 1987.

*Geroi Sovetskogo Soyuza Mogilyovchane*. Minsk: Polyma, 1965.

*Geroi - Volgogradtsy*. Volgograd: Nizhne-Volzhskoye knizhnoye izdatel'stvo, 1967.

*Geroyam Rodiny - slava!* Petrozavodsk: Kareliya, 1985.

Geust, C.-F., K. Keskinen, and K. Stenman. *Soviet Air Force in World War Two: Red Stars*. Kangasala: Ar-Kustannus Oy, 1993.

Gilyarevskiy, V.P. *Voyna: Morskiye lyotchiki o boyevom puti 47-go Shturmovogo Aviapolka VVS VMF*. Vol.1, *Chyornoye more*. Moscow:- NIISU, 1992.

Girbig, W. *Mit Kurs auf Leuna: Die Luftoffensive gegen die Triebstoffindustrie und der deutsche Abwehreinsatz 1944 - 1945*. Stuttgart: Motorbuch Verlag, 1980.

Glantz, D.M., and J. House. *When Titans Clashed: How the Red Army Stopped Hitler*. Lawrence: University Press of Kansas, 1995.

Golovanov, A. Ye. *Dalnyaya bombardirovochnaya*. O.O.O. Delta NB, Moscow 2004.

Golubev, V. F. *Kryl'ya krepnut v boyu*. 2nd ed. Leningrad: Lenizdat, 1984.

Gordon, Ye., and D. Khazanov. *Soviet Combat Aircraft of the Second World War. Volume One: Single-Engined Fighters*, Midland Publishing Ltd., Earl Shilton 1998.

----- *Soviet Combat Aircraft of the Second World War. Volume Two: Twin-Engined Fighters, Attack Aircraft and Bombers*, Midland Publishing Ltd., Earl Shilton 1999.

Grechko, S.N. *Resheniya prinimalis' na zemle*. Moscow: Voyenizdat, 1984.

Grichenko, I. T., and N. M. Golovin. *Podvig*. 3rd ed. Kharkov: Prapor, 1983.

Groehler, O. *Geschichte des Luftkriegs*. Berlin (GDR): Militärverlag, 1981.

Gubin, B.A., and V.A. Kiselyov. *Vos'maya vozdushnaya*. Moscow: Voyenizdat 1986.

Gundelach, K. *Kampfgeschwader "General Wever" 4*. Stuttgart: Motorbuch Verlag, 1978.

Halder, F. *Kriegstagebuch*. Edited by Hans-Arnold Jacobsen. Stuttgart: W. Kohlhammer Verlag, 1964.

Hardesty, V. *Red Phoenix: The Rise of the Soviet Air Power 1941 - 1945*. Washington, D.C.: Smithsonian Institution Press, 1982.

Haupt, W. *Army Group Center: The Wehrmacht in Russia 1941 - 1945*. Atglen: Schiffer, 1997.

----- *Army Group North: The Wehrmacht in Russia 1941 - 1945*. Atglen: Schiffer, 1997.

-----*Army Group South: The Wehrmacht in Russia 1941 - 1945*. Atglen: Schiffer, 1998.

Hayward, J. *Stopped at Stalingrad: The Luftwaffe and Hitler's Defeat in the East*. Lawrence: University Press of Kansas, 1998.

Hooton, E.R. *Eagle in Flames: The Fall of the Luftwaffe*. London: Arms and Armous Press, 1999.

Il'in, N. *V boyakh za chistoye nebo*. Moscow: Izdatelstvo "Patriot", 2002.

*Istoriya Velikoy Otechestvennoy voyny Sovetskogo Soyuza 1941 - 1945*. Moscow: Voyenizdat, 1960.

Ivanov, A. L. *Skorost', manyovr, ogon'*. Moscow: DOSAAF, 1974.

Ivanov, P. N. *Kryl'ya nad morem*, Moscow: VIMO, 1973.

*I vozvrashchalis' s pobedoy*. Leningrad: Lenizdat, 1986.

Jacobsen, H.-A., and J. Rohwer. *Entscheidungsschlachten des zweiten Weltkrieges*. Munich: Bernard & Graefe Verlag, 1960.

Jochim, B.K. *Oberst Hermann Graf: 200 Luftsiege in 13 Monaten*. Rastatt: Erich Pabel Verlag, 1970.

Jokipii, M. *Panttipataljoona. Suomalaisen SS-pataljoonan historia*. 4th edition. Veljesapu ry, Helsinki. Jyväskylä: Gummerus Kirjapaino Oy. 2000.

Jukes, G. *Stalingrad - vändpunkten*. Stockholm: Aldus, 1972.

Kalinin, V.V., and D.G. Makarenko. *Geroi podvigov na Khar'kovshchine*. Kharkov: Prapor, 1970.

Kaufmann, J. *Sotilaslentäjänä 1935-1945. 1. painos*. Helsinki: Koala-

Kustannus, Karisto Oyn kirjapaino, Hämeenlinna, 2002.

Kaufov, Kh. Kh. *Oryol umirayet v polyote*. Nalchik: Elbrus, 1970.

*Kavalery Zolotoy Zvezdy*. Donetsk: Donbas, 1976.

Khanin, L. *Geroi Sovetskogo Soyuza—syny Tatarii*. Kazan: Tatknigozdat, 1963.

Kiehl, H. *Kampfgeschwader "Legion Condor" 53*. Stuttgart: Motorbuch Verlag, 1996.

Kislitsyn, A. S. *Oveyannyye slavoy*. Chelyabinsk: Yuzhno-Ural'skoe knizhnoe izdatel'stvo, 1965.

Korolyov, V.O. *Gvardeytsy Pervoy Shturmovoy*. Moscow: Voyenizdat, 1980.

Kozhevnikov, A.L. *Startuyet muzhestvo*. Moscow: Voyenizdat, 1975.

Kozhevnikov, M.N. *Komandovaniye i shtab VVS Sovyetskoy Armii v Velikoy Otyechestvyennoy Voyny 1941 - 1945*. Moscow: Nauka, 1977.

Kozlov, N.A. *V ogne srazheniy*. Grozny: Checheno-Ingushskoye knizhnoye izdatelstvo, 1968.

Krasovskiy, S.A. *Zhizn' v aviatsii*. Moscow: Voyenizdat, 1968.

Krepak, B.A., and L.A. Krushinskaya. *V poyedinkakh na vsyote*. Minsk: Belarus, 1989.

*Kriegstagebuch des Oberkommandos der Wehrmacht 1939 - 1945*. Edited by Percy E. Schramm. Munich: Bernard & Graefe Verlag, 1982.

Krivosheyev, G. *Grif sekretnosti snyat: Poteri Vooruzhyonnykh Sil SSSR v voynakh, boyevykh deystviyakh i voyennykh konfliktakh*. Moscow: Voyenizdat, 1993.

Kurowski, F. *Luftbrücke Stalingrad*. Herrsching: Manfred Pawlak Verlagsgesellschaft, 1988.

Kusnezow, N. G. *Gefechtsalarm in den Flotten*. 3rd ed. Berlin (GDR): Militärverlag, 1984.

Kuzovkin, A. I., and A. T. Belyayev. *Orlinoye plemya Kolomentsev*. Moscow: DOSAAF, 1985.

Lavrinenkov, V. *Vozvrashcheniye v nebo*. Moscow: Voyenizdat, 1974.

Liddell-Hart, B. H. *The Other Side of the Hill*. vol. III, *Through German Eyes*. 1st ed. London: Cassell and Company Ltd., London, 1948.

Lipfert, H., and W. Girbig. *The War Diary of Hauptmann Helmut Lipfert*. Atglen: Schiffer Publishing, 1993.

Luganskiy, S. *Nebo ostayotsya chistym: Zapiski voyennogo lyotchika*. Alma-Ata: Izdatelstvo *Zhazushi*, 1970.

Lyadskiy, T., *Zapiski iz lyotnogo plansheta: Voyennyye dnevniki*. Minsk: Asobny Dakh, 2001.

*Lyudi geroicheskoy professii*. Moscow: DOSAAF, 1976.

*Lyudin bessmertnogo podviga*. Moscow: Voyennaya Liyteratura, 1992.

von Manstein, E. *Verlorene Siege*. Bonn: Athenäum Verlag, 1955.

Maslennikov, Yu. I. *Taktika v boyevykh primerakh*. Moscow: Voyenizdat, 1985.

Maslov, M. *Istrebiteli I-16*. Moscow: Armada, 1997.

Meroño, F. *Aviadores Españoles en la Gran Guerra Patria*. Moscow: Editorial Progreso, 1986.

Michulec, R. *Stalinowskie sokoly*. Gdynia: AJ Press, 1995.

Mikoyan, S. A. *Stepan Anastasovich Mikoyan: An Autobiography*. Shrewsbury: Airlife, 1999.

Morozov, M. E. *Morskaya aviatsiya Germanii 1939 - 1945. Chast' 1. Torpedonostsy,* Moscow: Armada, 1996.

Morzik, F. *Die deutschen Transportflieger im Zweiten Weltkrieg*. Frankfurt am Main: Bernard & Graefe Verlag, 1966.

Moskalenko, K. S. *Na Yugo-Zapadnom napravlenii*. Vol. I. Moscow: Voyenizdat, 1979.

Murray, W. *Luftwaffe: Strategy for Defeat 1933 - 45*. London: Grafton Books, 1985.

Myles, B. *Night Witches: The Amazing Story of Russia's Women Pilots in World War II*. Chicago: Academy Chicago Publishers, 1990.

*Na pole ratnom*. Moscow: Moskovskiy rabochiy, 1977.

*Nashi Zemlyaki—Geroi Sovetskogo Soyuza*. 3rd ed. Cheboksary: Chuvashskoye knizhnoye izdatel'stvo, 1980.

Nauroth, H. *Stukageschwader 2 Immelmann*. Preussisch Oldendorf: Verlag K. W. Schütz, 1988.

Neulen, H.W. *Am Himmel Europas: Luftstreitkräfte an deutscher Seite 1939 - 1945*. Munich: Universitas Verlag, 1998.

Nipe, G.M. *Last Victory in Russia*. Atglen: Schiffer Publishing, 2000.

Noggle, A. *A Dance with Death: Soviet Airwomen of World War II*. College Station: Texas A & M University Press, 1994.

Nowarra, H. J. *Über Europas Fronten: Das technisch-historische Porträt der Ju 52*. Rastatt: Erich Pabel Verlag, 1978.

Obermaier, E. *Die Ritterkreuzträger der Luftwaffe: Band 1—Jagdflieger 1939 - 1945*. Mainz: Verlag Dieter Hoffmann, 1966 and 1989.

----- *Die Ritterkreuzträger der Luftwaffe 1939 - 1945: Band II—Stuka/ und Schlachtflieger*. Mainz: Verlag Dieter Hoffmann, 1976.

Osipov, G.A. *V nebe bombardirovshchiki,* series Biblioteka zhurnala Shchelkovo, Shchelkovo 2003.

Pavlov, G. R. *Odnopolchane*. Moscow: DOSAAF, 1985.

----- *Kryl'ya muzhestva*. Kazan: Tatarskoye knizhnoye izdatel'stvo, 1988.

Perov, V., and O. Rastrenin. *Shturmovik Il-2*. Special Issue of *Aviatsiya I Kosmonavtika,* May-June 2001.

Plocher, H. *The German Air Force Versus Russia, 1942*. USAF Historical Division, Air University. New York: Arno Press, 1966.

----- *The German Air Force Versus Russia, 1943*. USAF Historical Division, Air University. New York: Arno Press, 1966.

*Pobratimy Nikolaya Gastello*. Moscow: MOF "Pobyeda-1945 GOD," 1995.

*Podvigi vo imya Otchizny*. 2nd ed. Kharkov: Prapor, 1985.

*Podvigom slavny tvoi zemlyaki*. Zaporozh'ye: Zaporozhskoye knigo-gazetnoy izdatel'stvo, 1962.

Pokryschkin [Pokryshkin], A. I. *Himmel des Krieges*. Berlin (GDR): Deutscher Militärverlag, 1970.

----- *Na istrebitele*. Novosibirsk: Novosibgiz, 1948.

----- *Kryl'ya istrebitelya*. Moscow: Voyenizdat, 1948.

----- *Nebo voyny*. Moscow: Voyenizdat, 1980.

----- *Poznat' sebya v boyu*. Moscow: DOSAAF, 1986.

Polak, T., and C. Shores. *Stalin's Falcons: The Aces of the Red Star: A tribute to the Notable Fighter Pilots of the Soviet Air Forces, 1918 - 1953*. London: Grub Street, 1999.

Polyam, P.M. *Moy Voyna,* Irkutsk, 1998.

Polyanskiy, V.V. *10 lyet s Vasiliyem Stalinym*. Tver: Vikant, 1995.

Polynin, F.P. *Boyevyye marshruty*. 2nd ed. Moscow: Voyenizdat, 1981.

Prien, J. *"Pik-As:" Geschichte des Jagdgeschwaders 53*. Eutin: Struve-Druck, 1990, 1991.

----- *Geschichte des Jagdgeschwaders 77*. Eutin: Struve-Druck, 1992 - 1994.

Prien, J., and G. Stemmer. *Messerschmitt Bf 109 im Einsatz bei der III./Jagdgeschwader 3*. Eutin: Struve Druck, n.d.

----- *Messerschmitt Bf 109 im Einsatz bei der II./Jagdgeschwader 3*. Eutin: Struve-Druck, n.d.

----- *Messerschmitt Bf 109 im Einsatz bei Stab und I./Jagdgeschwader 3*. Eutin: Struve-Druck, 1997.

Prien, J. *Jagdgeschwader 53: A History of the "Pik As" Geschwader Volume 2: May 1942 – January 1944*. Atglen: Schiffer Military History, 1998.

Prien, J., G. Stemmer, P. Rodeike, and W. Bock. *Die Jagdfliegerverbände der Deutschen Luftwaffe 1934 bis 1945, Teil 9/I-III,* Struve Druck, Eutin 2005 - 2006.

Prussakov, G. K. *16-ya vozdushnaya: Voyenno-istoricheskiy ocherk o boyevom puti 16-y vozdushnoy armii 1942 - 1945*. Moscow: Voyenizdat, 1973.

----- *Doletim do Odera*. Moscow: Voyenizdat, 1985.

Pstygo, I. I. *Na boyevom kurse*. Moscow: Voenizdat, 1989.

Punka, G. *Hungarian Air Force*. Carrollton: Squadron/Signal Publications, 1994.

*Messer: The Messerschmitt 109 in the Royal Hungarian "Honvéd" Air Force"*. Budapest: OMIKK, 1995.

Pustovalov, B.M. *Tè trista rassvetov*. Moscow: Voyenizdat, 1990.

Radtke, S. *Kampfgeschwader 54*. Munich: Schild Verlag, 1990.

Rajlích, J., and J. Sehnal. *Slovensti Letci 1939 - 1945*. Kolín: Vydavatelství Kolinske noviny, 1991.

Rajlich, J., Z. Stojczew, and Z. Lalak. *Sojusznicy Luftwaffe, czesc* 1. Warsaw: Books International, 1997.

Rall, G. *mein Flugbuch: Erinnerungen 1938 – 2004*. Moosburg: Neunundzwanzigsechs Verlag, 2004.

Rechkalov, G.A. *Dymnoye nebo voyny*. Sverdlovsk: Sredne-Ural'skoye knizhnoye izdatel'stvo, 1968.

Röhricht, E. *Probleme der Kesselschlacht, dargestellt an Einkreisungs-Operationen im Zweiten Weltkrieg*. Karlsruhe: Condor-Verlag, 1958.

Roman, V. *Aerokobra vstupayet v boy*. Kiev: Aerokhobbi, 1993.

*Românii la Stalingrad*. Bucharest: Ed. Militar?, 1992.

Rudel, H.-U. *Trotzdem*. Göttingen: Verlag K. W. Schütz, 1970.

Rudel, H.-U. *Stuka Pilot*. Costa Mesa: Noontide Press, 1990.

Rudenko, S.I. *Kryl'ya Pobedy*. Moscow: Mezhdunarodnyye otnosheniya, 1985.

Rumyantsev, N.M. *Lyudi legendarnogo podviga*. Saratov: Privolzhskoye knizhnoye izdatel'stvo, 1968.

*Russkiy arkhiv: Velikaya Otechestvennaya: Stavka VGK: Dokumenty i materialy: 1942 god. T 16 (5 - 2)*. Moscow: TERRA, 1996.

Salisbury, H.E. *The Unknown War*. New York: Bantam Books, 1978.

Samsonov, A. M. *Stalingradskaya bitva*. Moscow: Nauka, 1988.

Schmidt, R. *Achtung – Torpedos los! Die strategiche und operative Einsatz des*

*Kampfgeschwaders 26 Löwengeschwader.* Bonn: Bernard & Greafe Verlag, n.d.

Schreier, H. *JG 52: Das erfolgreichste Jagdgeschwader des II. Weltkrieges.* Berg am See: Kurt Vowinckel Verlag, n.d.

Schwabedissen, W. *The Russian Air Force in the Eyes of German Commanders.* USAF Historical Division, Air University. New York: Arno Press, 1960.

Seaton, A. *The Russo-German War 1941 - 1945.* New York: Praeger Publishers, 1970.

Seidl, H. *Stalin's Eagles: An Illustrated Study of the Soviet Aces of World War II and Korea.* Atglen: Schiffer, 1998.

Semyonov, A.F. *Na vzlyote.* Moscow: Voyenizdat, 1969.

Shevchuk, V.M. *Komandir atakuyet pervym.* Moscow: Voyenizdat, 1980.

Shirer, W. *Det tredje rikets uppgång och fall.* Stockholm: Forum, 1989.

Shmelyov, A.N. *Nebo dobroye i zloye.* Moscow: DOSAAF, 1979.

Skripko, N.S. *Po tselyam blizhnim i dal'nim.* Moscow: Voyenizdat, 1981.

Skulski, P., J. Bargiel, and G. Cisek. *Asy frontu wschodniego.* Wroclaw: Ace Publication, 1994.

*Sovetskiye VVS v Velikoy Otechestvennoy voyne 1941 - 1945.* Moscow: Voyenizdat, 1968.

Stepanenko, I. N. *Plamennoye nebo.* Kiev: Politizdat Ukrainy, 1983.

Starck, M. *Allmän sjökrigshistoria, del 2 1942 - 1945.* Stockholm: Bonnier/Marinlitteraturföreningen, 1972.

Steinhoff, J. *Kampen om Messinasundet.* Malmö: Berghs förlag, 1973.

----- *In letzter Stunde: Verschwörung der Jagdflieger.* Munich: Paul List Verlag, 1974.

*Sto Stalinskikh sokolov v boyakh za rodinu.* Moscow: Voyenizdat, 1949.

*The Soviet Air Force in World War Two.* New York: Doubleday & Co., 1973.

Tieke, W. *Kampf um die Krim,* Private edition, Erbland, n.d. Gesellschaft für Literatur und Bildung, 1989.

----- *The Caucasus and the Oil.* Winnipeg: Fedorowicz Publishing, 1995.

Timofeyev, A. *Pokryshkin.* Moscow: Molodaya Gvardiya, 2003.

Toliver, R.F., and T.J. Constable. *Das waren die deutschen Jagdfliegerasse 1939 -1945.* Stuttgart: Motorbuch Verlag, 1973.

*Uchebnik boytsa i mladshego komandira podrazdeleniy mestnoy PVO.* Moscow: Upravleniye protivovozdushnoy oborony RKKA, Voyenizdat, 1939.

Vajda, F., and P. Dancey, *German Aircraft Industry and Production 1933–1945.* Shrewsbury: Airlife, 1998.

*Velikaya Otechestvennaya voyna. Tsyfry i fakty.* Moscow: Prosveshcheniye, 1995.

Vershinin, K. A. *Chetvyortaya vozdushnaya.* Moscow: Voyenizdat, 1975.

*V nebe frontovom.* Moscow: Molodaya Gvardia, 1971.

*Vo imya Rodiny.* Moscow: Politizdat, 1982.

*Voyska Protivovozdushnoy Oborony Strany.* Moscow: Voyenizdat, 1968.

*V sozvezdii slavy.* 2nd ed. Volgograd: Nizhne-Volzhskoye knizhnoye izdatel'stvo, 1976.

Waiss, W. *Chronik Kampfgeschwader Nr. 27 Boelcke, Band IV.* Aachen: Helios Verlag, 2005.

*Die Wehrmachtsberichte 1939-1945. Band 2 – 1. Januar 1942 bis 31. Dezember 1943,* Köln: Gesellschaft für Literatur und Bildung, 1989.

Werth, A. *Russia at War 1941 - 1945.* New York: Dutton, 1964.

Yakimenko, A. *V atake - mech.* Moscow: DOSAAF, 1973.

Yakimov, G. *Pike v byessmyertiye.* Alma-Ata: Kazakhstan, 1973.

Yemel'yanenko, V.B. *V voyennom vozdukhe surovom.* Moscow: Sovetskaya Rossiya, 1985.

Yeryomin, B.N. *Vozdushnyye boytsy.* Moscow: Voyenizdat, 1987.

Zholudev, L.V. *Stal'naya eskadril'ya.* Moscow: Voyenizdat, 1972.

Zhukov, Yu. *Odin "MiG" iz tysyachi.* Moscow: Molodaya Gvardiya, 1963.

Zimin, G.V. *Taktika v boyevykh primerakh.* Moscow: Istrebitel'naya aviatsionnaya diviziya, Voyenizdat, 1982.

----- *Istrebiteli.* Moscow: Voyenizdat, 1988.

Zjukov, G. *Minnen och reflexioner.* Moscow: Progress, 1988.

*Zolotyye zvyozdy.* Dnepropetrovsk: Promin', 1967.

*Zvyozdy doblesti ratnoy.* 2nd ed. Novosibirsk: Zapadno-Sibirskoye knizhnoye izdatel'stvo, 1986.

*Zvyozdy nemerknushchey slavy.* 3rd ed. Simferopol: Tavriya, 1984.

## PERIODICALS

*52er Nachrichtenblatt (Traditionsgemeinschaft JG 52).*
*Aeroplano.*
*Der Adler.*
*Air Combat.*
*Airfoil.*
*AviaMaster.*
*Aviatsiya i Kosmonavtika.*
*Aviatsiya i Vremya.*
*Classic Wings Downunder.*
*The Dispatch Magazine.*
*Fly Past.*
*Jägerblatt.*
*Jet und Prop.*
*Krasnaya Zvezda.*
*Luftwaffe Verband Journal.*
*Militaria.*
*Mir Aviatsii.*
*Morskoy Sbornik.*
*Pravda.*
*Revi.*
*Skrzydlata Polska.*
*Vestnik Vozdushnogo Flota.*
*Voyenno-Istoricheskiy Zhurnal.*
*VVS i PVO.*

## PHOTO CREDITS

4 GIAP/VVS VMF Museum and Archive, *Adler,* Ferdinando D'Amico, Aleksey V. Andreev, Vlad Antipov, *Oberst* Gerhard Baeker, Michael Balss, Bernd Barbas, *Oberstleutnant* Hansgeorg Bätcher, Csaba Becze, Dénes Bernád, *Major* Hans-Ekkehard Bob, Jan Bobek, *Oberleutnant* Johannes Broschwitz, Eddie Creek, *Hauptmann* Hugo Dahmer, Andrey Dikov, Chris Dunning, Artem Drabkin, Santiago A. Flores, Robert Forsyth, *Generalleutnant* Adolf Galland, *Hauptmann* Alfred Grislawski, Jürgen Grislawski, *Kapitan* Viktor Alekseyevich Grubich, *Major* Klaus Häberlen, Damian Hallor, Peter Hallor, Bert Hartmann, *Oberfeldwebel* Karl-Heinz Höfer, Ivanova Maya Ivanovna, Dmitriy Karlenko, Peter Kassak, *General-Leytenant* Arkadiy Fyodorovich Kovachevich, Krigsarkivet/Stockholm, Viktor Kulikov, *Starshina* Vasiliy Vasilyevich Kurayev, *Oberleutnant* Erwin Leykauf, Andrey Mikhailov, Eric Mombeek, *Leutnant* Hermann Neuhoff, *Polkovnik* Aleksandr Aleksandrovich Pavlichenko, *General* Günther Rall, Rune Rautio, Günther Rosipal, *Leutnant* Edmund Rossmann, Yuriy Rybin, Pär Salomonson, *Signal, General* Johannes Steinhoff, Peter Taghon, *Traditionsgemeinschaft JG 52, Generalleutnant* Hannes Trautloft, John Vasco, Peter Vollmer, Manfred Wägenbaur, Walter Waiss and Director Lyudmila P. Zapryagayeva.

# Index